FROM THE MOTOR CITY TO THE MEDITERRANEAN

FROM THE MOTOR CITY TO THE MEDITERRANEAN

Travels of a Truck, a Sedan, and an Inquisitive Photographer
1924–1926

Lauren E. Talalay

Kelsey Museum Publication 18
Ann Arbor, Michigan, 2024

Cover Image
The Dodge sedan on a ferry, just before landing at Djerba, Tunisia, April 10, 1925 (Kelsey Museum neg. no. 7.1916).

ISBN: 978-1-7330504-5-6
Library of Congress Control Number: 2024941297

Published by
Kelsey Museum of Archaeology
434 South State Street
Ann Arbor, Michigan 48109-1390

Edited by Emily Allison-Siep
Cover design by Eric Campbell

Distributed by
ISD
70 Enterprise Drive, Suite 2
Bristol, Connecticut 06010
Email: orders@isdistribution.com
Web: isdistribution.com

This book is available for free download at lsa.umich.edu/kelsey/publications

Printed by Foresight Group in Lansing, Michigan

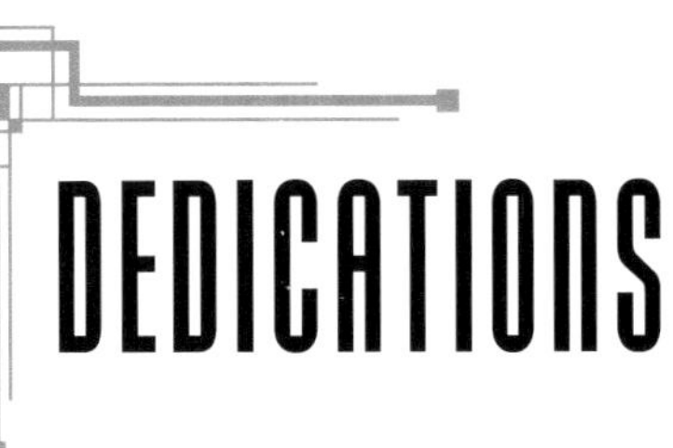

DEDICATIONS

In memory of my extraordinary and loving parents: my father, an inventor and a talented photographer, who had his first "one-man" photography exhibition at the young age of 80, and my mother, cofounder of the Museum of Contemporary Art Cleveland (moCa), who taught me how to look at art and to celebrate the creative process.

And to my "other mother," Nan, a treasured traveling companion. What wonderful memories we share. Nan still travels the world at the age of 97.

Finally, to Steve, my exceptional, creative, and quirky husband, who makes me laugh every day.

CONTENTS

Preface ix
1. Introduction 1

Part I: The Age of Automobiles

2. Horseless Carriages and the Michigan Cars 13
3. The Pioneering Brothers 19

Part II: George R. Swain: The Man Behind the Lens (1866–1947)

4. George R. Swain: A Brief Biography 29
5. Swain and His Cameras 39

Part III: Back Roads, Lotus Eaters, and Monastic Life: The 1924–1926 Expeditions

6. Life on the Road: Overview of the 1924–1926 Expeditions 49
7. Travels of 1924 53
8. Travels of 1925 79
9. Travels of 1926 103

Part IV: Observations a Century Later

10. Refocusing the Lens 121

Acknowledgments 131
Endnotes 135
References 145
Index 151
About the Author 155

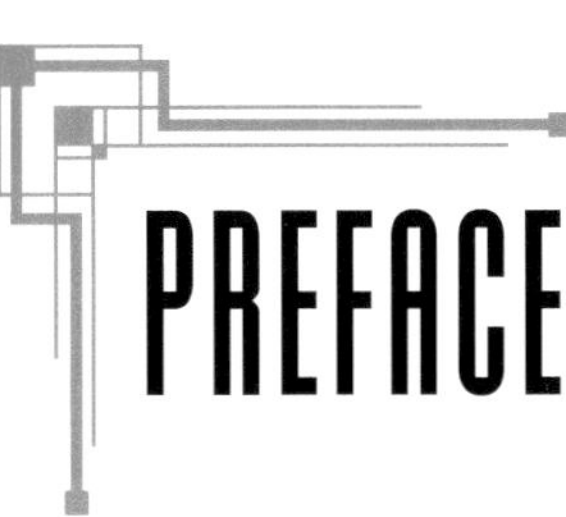

PREFACE

Most of the time, my head is buried in the past, exploring the prehistory of the Mediterranean. My research focuses on the Neolithic period, ancient figurines, and gender, with occasional forays into the use of classical images in modern advertising and political cartoons. When not contemplating the multiple meanings of ancient imagery, I worked as associate director and curator at the University of Michigan's Kelsey Museum of Archaeology. The museum houses over 100,000 artifacts from ancient Greece, Rome, Egypt, and the Near East, as well as countless photographs—many of them from the early decades of the 20th century.

Over the years, I would periodically disappear into the museum's archives, ferreting through photographs from the 1920s. Although I was usually searching for information on ancient sites and finds, I was increasingly drawn to a different collection of images—photographs of villages and people that have long since vanished and landscapes now radically altered. As I sorted through the stacks, I noted a series of pictures that featured two automobiles: a truck and a sedan—carefully staged, caught in precarious circumstances, or sometimes hidden in the background. At some point, I realized that these dig cars had a story to tell about their far-flung adventures.

Gradually, this book emerged, shaped not only by the photographs but also by a felicitous discovery at the University of Michigan's Bentley Historical Library: a trove of letters chronicling the vehicles' trips to Europe and the greater Mediterranean.

I am the last person one would suspect might write a book involving cars. I drive fewer than 3,000 miles a year, only notice the colors and shapes of automobiles, and don't have a clue how a piston works. Even though I have owned a variety of cars over the last five decades—and live an hour from the "Motor City"—I am woefully ignorant about the mechanics, models, and history of automobiles. I do believe, however, that I have a talent for naming my cars and am decidedly more informed than my twin sister who, upon buying her first new car in the late 1970s, asked the dealer, "Does the car come with tires, or do I have to pay extra?"

Writing this book has prompted me to reflect on my own history with cars, from my first automobile (inherited from my grandmother) to my last two Hondas, both of which I kept for over 20 years, neither breaking the 100,000-mile mark. What I discovered is that I have had a long and storied attachment to my cars. Talking one day to my husband,

Steve, a forensic psychologist, I asked if he would mind adding a short "analysis" of my relationship with the cars I (and we) have owned. So here is his backseat-driver contribution, recounting the lighter side of my life with cars during the past 50 years.

I first sensed Laurie's lack of familiarity with car culture when she asked why I was reading about chauffeur services. The magazine in my hands was Car & Driver.

Laurie's relationship with cars began when she and "Sophie"—her grandmother's 1954 blue-and-white Olds—drove to high school together. For whatever reasons—perhaps because cars represent first independence for teenagers—Laurie bonded with her Detroit Steel. And became an uninformed car enthusiast.

Years later, when Laurie and I were in graduate school, we drove a 1968 Olds F-85, which was stolen by youths who took it for a joyride and burned it in a field. Only one thing survived the fire: the basketball (after all, we were in Indiana). Our second Bloomington set of wheels was a 1970 brown Ford Pinto—a model best known for bursting into flames if you tapped its rear bumper. So it wouldn't be a total loss if we were incinerated, Laurie and I put an uncooked chicken and a bottle of barbecue sauce in the trunk of "Brownie" (Laurie's aforementioned belief aside, she is not known for groundbreaking car nicknames).

During the mid-1970s, when I was interning in Boston, our blue three-speed Camaro 327 was sideswiped on Storrow Drive by what turned out to be a stolen vehicle. After "Cammie" stopped skidding, Laurie—clearly frightened—told me she couldn't move. I suggested she release the seat belt.

In 1978, we moved to Ann Arbor, where Laurie bought a very used VW. She had never driven a stick shift. And didn't know how to get the car home. After I gave her a brief phone lesson on clutching and shifting, Laurie bravely drove her bright-yellow Bug, lurching all the way.

Laurie's come-to-NASCAR moment occurred on a desolate country road when—driving alone—she gunned her silver Mustang's V8 to the century mark. The only other time I've known my wife to move that fast is when she's heading to a taverna after a long day of digging.

Your author will tell you that she likes driving cars. She just doesn't like driving at night. Or on the highway. Or during snow, rain, wind, or high humidity. From a psychologist's perspective, Laurie's writing about cars in dangerous predicaments smacks of counterphobia. From an archaeological viewpoint, dig cars deserve recognition. As does Laurie's love of "carchaeology." Reflecting on the University of Michigan's overseas expeditions, I now realize how much easier their travels could have been if they had only used Car & Driver*'s chauffeur service.*

—Steve Bank, Ann Arbor, Michigan

After writing this book, I can proudly say that I now understand how a piston works and the enormous social importance of the first combustion engine. I also have a renewed admiration for the wheeled members of early archaeological projects. What follows in the ensuing pages, however, is more than a story of two intrepid vehicles. It is the story of how the truck and sedan—two of the ostensible protagonists of this book—transported a team of archaeologists, specialists, and a photographer (George R. Swain) to often far-off parts of the world in the 1920s, allowing them not only to excavate the distant past but also to observe life as it was lived during a pivotal time in recent history. These were daunting trips, not guided by accurate maps or GPS, with every day an adventure of frustration, endurance, and discovery. By digging into the crevices of several archives and piecing together photographs and associated letters, I was able to retrieve a singular narrative of lives and times—mostly in small, remote villages—that might otherwise have remained forever buried.

Chapter 1
INTRODUCTION

> [One] of my pet recollections is that of a gander who started to waddle hurriedly across the road in front of the sedan; six feet away he evidently decided he'd be darned if he, an African gander, would hurry out of the way of any car made in Detroit, so he turned and came directly at us hissing like a small steam boiler. Three seconds later he was staggering out of a nimbus of flying feathers, wondering if [the devil had got him] and metaphorically feeling . . . his neck with both hands to see if it still functioned—someway it had made no impression on our front axle.[1]
>
> —*George R. Swain, Tunisia, 1925*

As any archaeologist will tell you, "dig cars" are the unsung heroes of most expeditions. They transport teams from their home base to scattered sites and isolated locations, haul essential and often cumbersome equipment into the field, scale seemingly impassable gradients on back-mountain passes, and ferry the team's weekend revelers to their well-deserved breaks at nearby towns, taverns, and beaches. The indispensable dig car may even be christened with a name. I have fond memories of a vintage French Peugeot station wagon, probably built in the 1970s, that served our crew for many years in the town of Karystos, Greece. Dubbed the "YAK-Mobile" (based on the first three letters of its license plate, not our constant chattering), our car soldiered on bravely for multiple seasons. It was a quirky, battered vehicle, and the director of the project confessed that when the YAK would stall on steep inclines—a not infrequent occurrence—he pulled up the emergency brake and resorted to a few prayers.[2]

Despite their importance (and personalities), dig cars—perhaps not surprisingly—are rarely mentioned in archaeological notes or reports. The University of Michigan archives, however, proved an exception. As noted in the "Preface," while gathering information on the university's early excavations in the Mediterranean and Near East, I unexpectedly encountered numerous photographs of two vehicles—a Dodge Brothers sedan (fig. 1) and a Graham Brothers closed-body truck (fig. 2), both manufactured in the early 1920s. Often captured in cinematic poses, they are shown artfully positioned alongside bridges in the French countryside (see fig. 65, p. 57), straddling gullied roads (fig. 3), raised

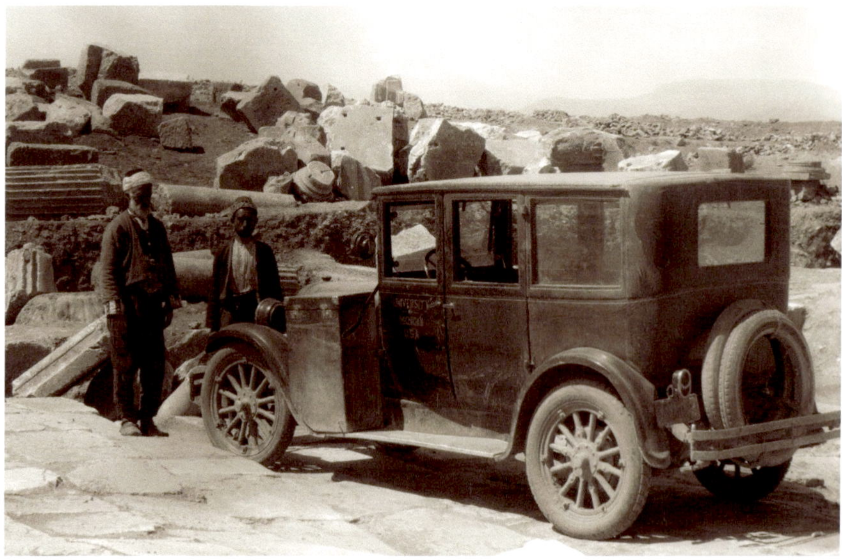

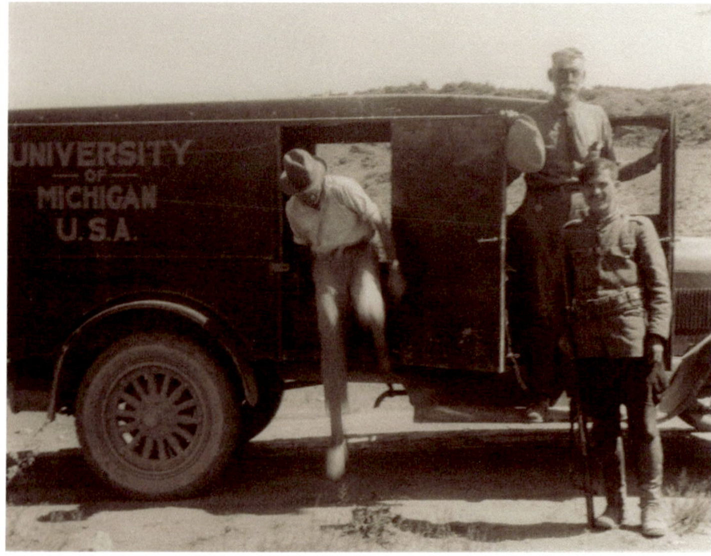

Fig. 1. The Dodge sedan at the site of Antioch, Turkey, August 1924 (Kelsey Museum neg. no. 7.1627).

Fig. 2. The Graham Brothers truck with Easton Kelsey, George R. Swain, and a guard near Ak-Shehir, Turkey, September 2, 1924 (Kelsey Museum neg. no. KR 098.06).

warily by hoists onto steamers (see fig. 66, p. 57), and unhappily stranded in the proverbial middle of nowhere (fig. 4).

My curiosity was further piqued after I discovered a wealth of other images, often ethnographic in nature, that were clearly connected to the vehicles' travels during the 1920s. The photos were taken primarily by George R. Swain (fig. 5), the official photographer for many of the university's expeditions. While his principal remit was documenting Michigan's excavations and finds (fig. 6)—as well as photographing various biblical and ancient manuscripts (fig. 7)[3]—Swain was often "distracted by modernity," turning his camera toward the world around him. Ranging from small-size Kodak prints to large-format photos and specially designed panoramas, his images illustrate the minutiae of daily life, including local customs, dress, and practices once common throughout the Mediterranean and beyond (figs. 8–9).

As I dug deeper into various university records, I uncovered an extensive collection of Swain's letters,[4] cables, and reports that not only detail the journeys and travails of the sedan and truck but also provide firsthand accounts of local culture in remote locations.[5] By following the often hazardous and occasionally humorous journeys of the two vehicles, I was able to gaze into aspects of life and behavior not typically seen by the outside world, selectively captured by an American photographer. What began as a possible chronicle about the expeditions' two dig cars slowly developed into a more layered enterprise.

Swain's overseas work on behalf of the university included trips to Europe, the Near East, and North Africa. Ultimately, he produced more than 20,000 photographs from these expeditions. Of those 20,000 images, approximately 14,000 survive as prints or negatives; the remaining 6,000 were either destroyed or are missing.[6]

In addition to his work as the expeditions' photographer, Swain was the "concierge" of both vehicles, keeping track of spare parts, charting all land and sea routes, maintaining the automobiles' upkeep, and occasionally rescuing the sedan and truck from impending disasters. He was a vital member of a select team of international scholars and specialists

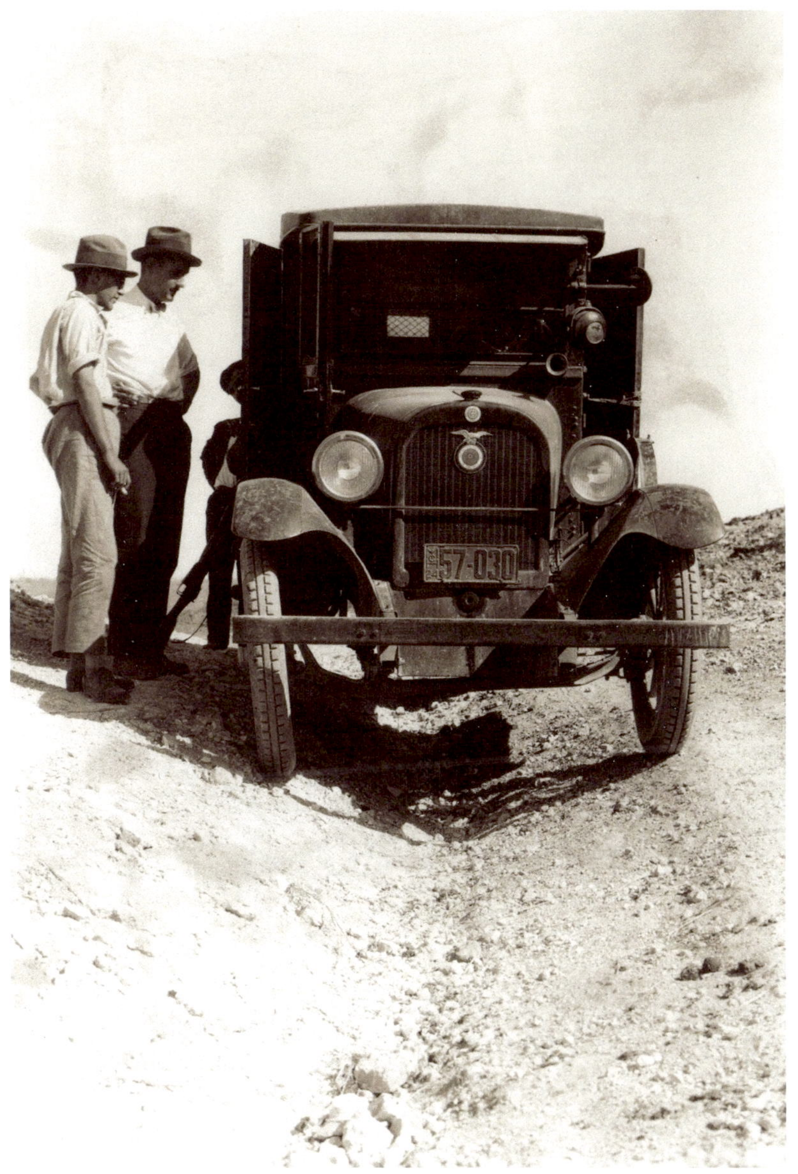

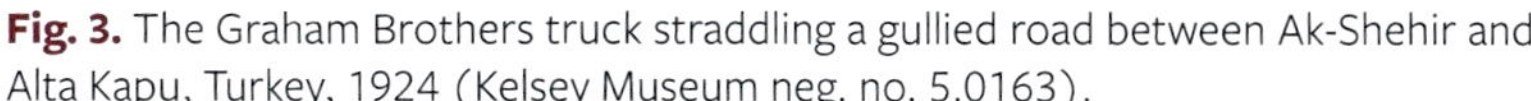

Fig. 3. The Graham Brothers truck straddling a gullied road between Ak-Shehir and Alta Kapu, Turkey, 1924 (Kelsey Museum neg. no. 5.0163).

Fig. 4. A "mishap" with the Graham Brothers truck on the road to Yalivadj, Turkey, June 29, 1924 (Kelsey Museum neg. no. KS 276.08).

Fig. 5. George R. Swain and his camera at the Giza pyramids, Egypt, March 26, 1920 (detail) (Kelsey Museum neg. no. KK 090).

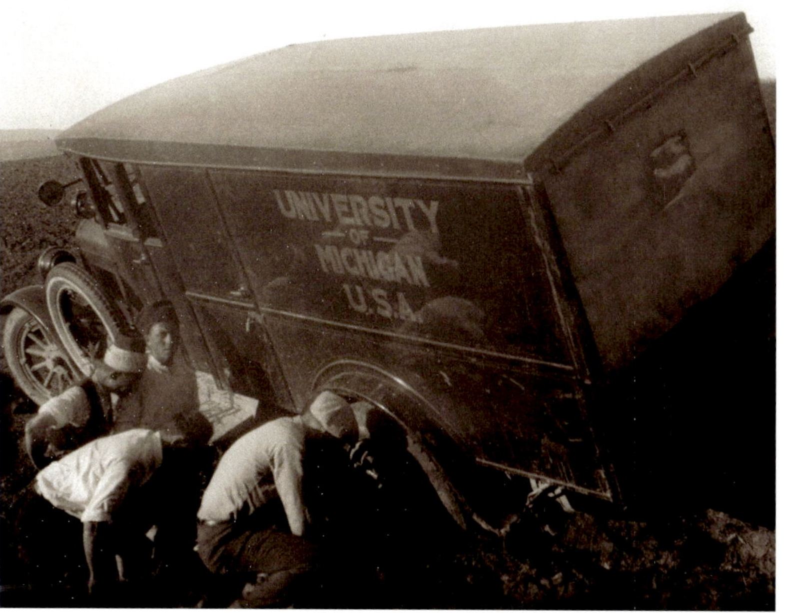

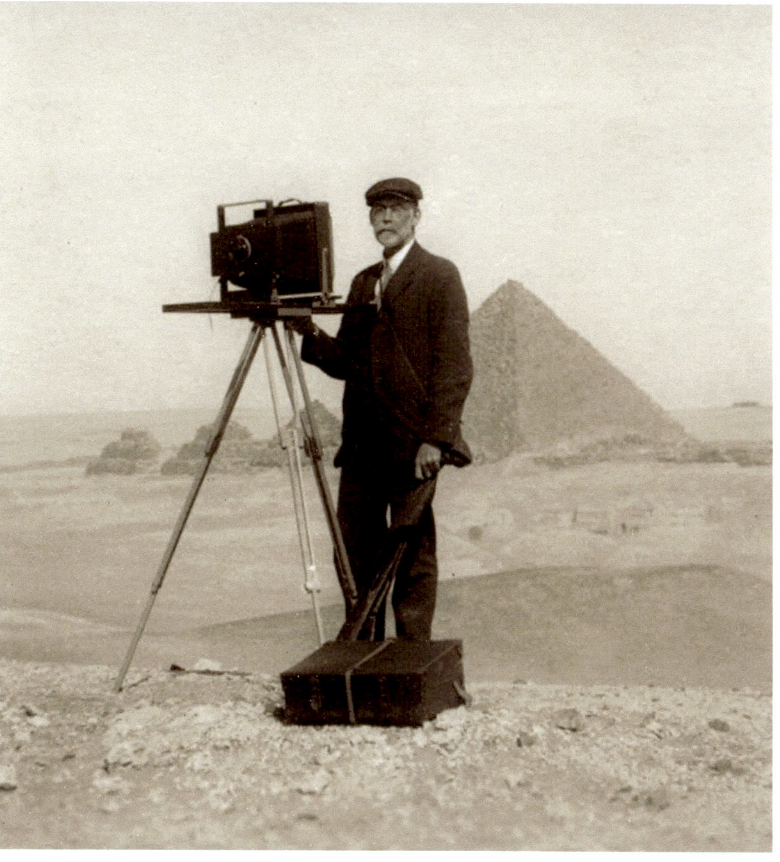

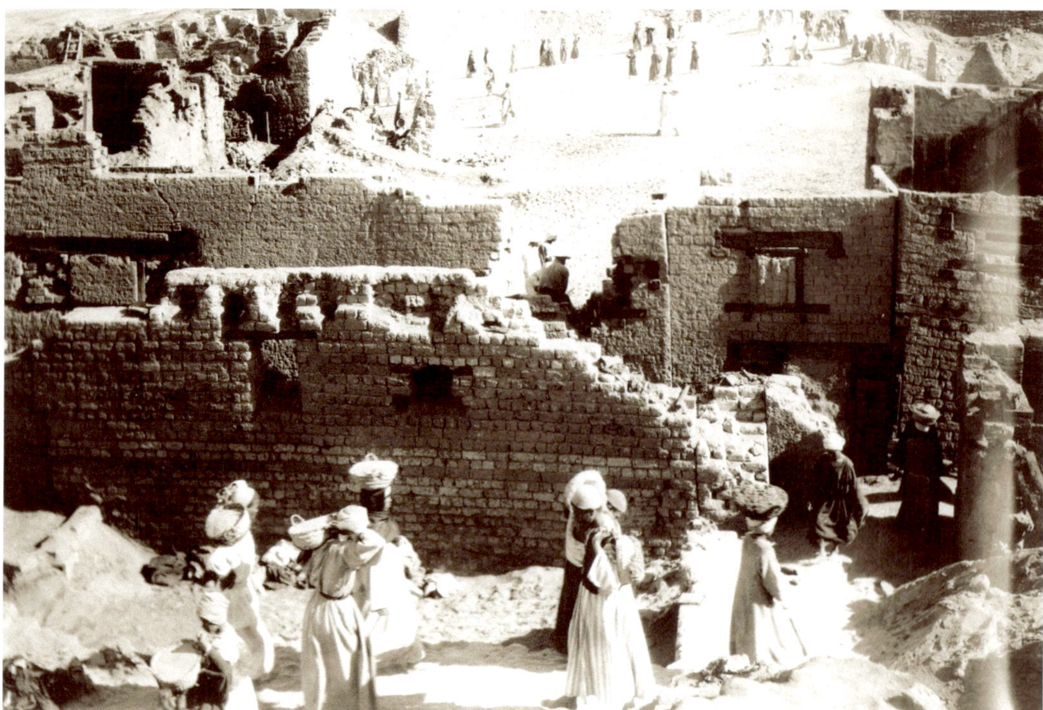

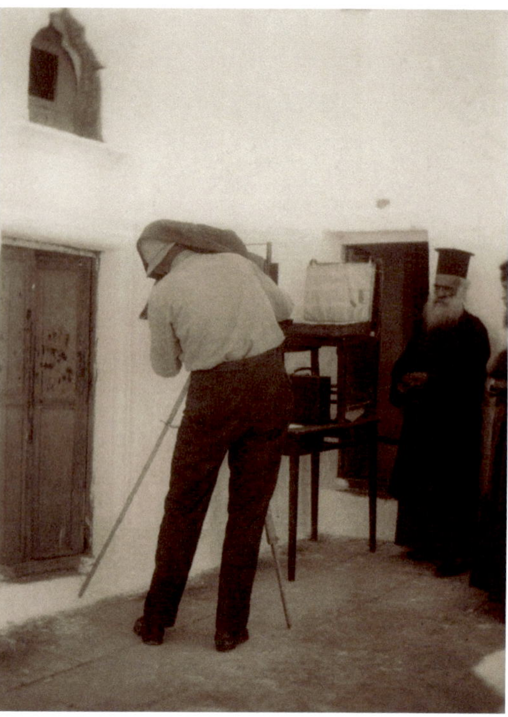

Fig. 6. Excavations in progress, Karanis, Egypt (Kelsey Museum neg. no. 5.2741).

Fig. 7. George R. Swain photographing manuscripts on the roof of a monastery, Patmos, Greece, May 7, 1920 (Kelsey Museum neg. no. KK 195).

hired by Francis W. Kelsey, professor in the Department of Latin at the University of Michigan and the man who would administer all of the institution's archaeological and research missions from 1919 to 1926.[7]

Kelsey and Swain took four trips together during those seven years—sometimes in concert, other times with separate or partially overlapping itineraries. In 1919, Professor Kelsey was granted a two-year research leave from the University of Michigan (September 4, 1919–September 7, 1921) and began a program of intertwined objectives that continued throughout the ensuing years. His goals were multiple: to study manuscripts, particularly biblical examples in European libraries and monastic collections; to buy or produce photographs of ancient sites for teaching purposes; to scout out possible archaeological sites to excavate in the future; to restudy Caesar's battlefields; to purchase both artifacts and papyri for the burgeoning collections at the university; and to investigate the conditions at several foreign missions in Turkey and Syria. While the later trips (1924–1926) continued many of these objectives, they also involved excavations in Turkey, Tunisia, and Egypt.

All the Kelsey-Swain trips were extensive and arduous, traveling from big cities in Europe to small towns in the Mediterranean region—where vermin and bedbugs were unpopular team members—and villages at the edge of the Sahara. Although a 1924 *Detroit News* reporter's warning that Kelsey and his crew were heading into the "turbulent, almost anarchistic regions of Asia Minor and perturbed Egypt . . . [facing] the possibility of violence and bloodshed around them every minute" was likely journalistic hyperbole, the regions were certainly unstable and could be perilous.[8] Indeed, several of Swain's photographs from central Turkey depict armed guards accompanying the vehicles and crew.[9]

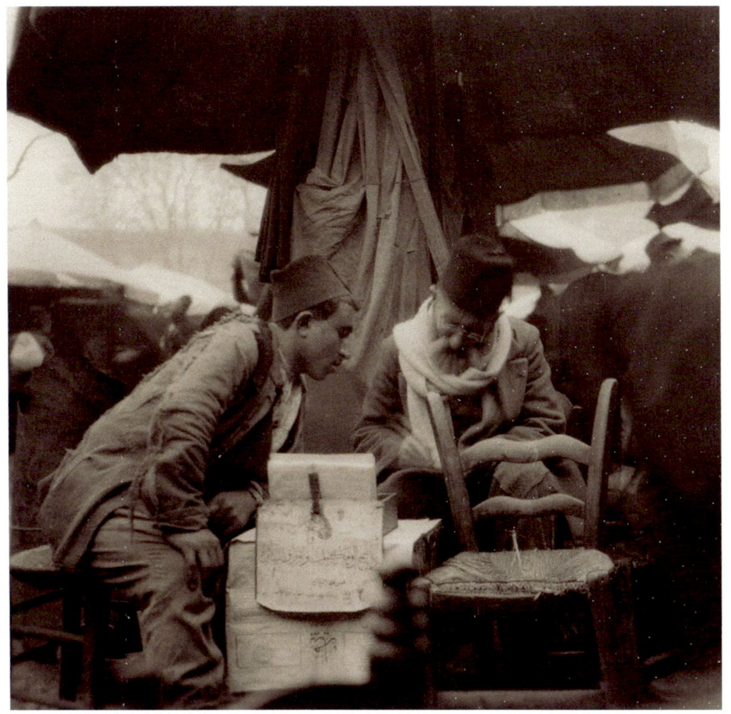

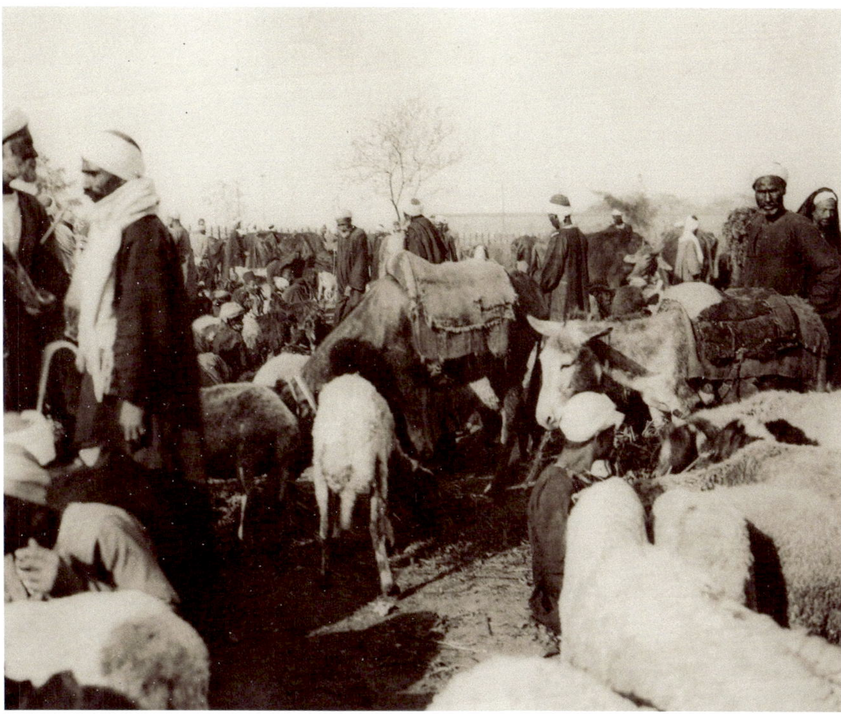

Fig. 8. A young man dictating a letter to a public letter writer, Constantinople, Turkey, December 9, 1919 (Kelsey Museum neg. no. KS 047.10).

Fig. 9. Giza bazaar, Egypt, April 6, 1920 (Kelsey Museum neg. no. KS 165.08).

The first Kelsey-Swain expedition lasted approximately one year, from September 1919 to August 1920. The second, starting in March 1924, stretched over eight months; although the two men were not always in the same location, they kept in contact via letters and cables. The third and fourth trips, where their itineraries again diverged, spanned from February to September 1925 and from March to August 1926, respectively. While the cast of specialists, scholars, and assistants changed from year to year, two "companions" remained constant during the last three trips (1924–1926): the sturdy American vehicles that carried Swain and his fellow travelers from Europe to the Near East and North Africa, often encountering nightmarish roads of "sand, rock, ledges, [and] gulches" in the hinterlands of a post–World War I landscape.[10]

Lanky at six feet, three inches, Swain provided a striking contrast to the slightly portly Professor Kelsey, whom one reporter described as looking like "a grave senator of the Roman Empire" (fig. 10).[11] Both men, however, were inveterate letter writers, habitual notetakers, and devoted family men. Swain wrote almost daily to his wife and children back in Michigan (fig. 11). An aspiring journalist, he also composed a series of essays entitled *Notes and Comments of a Wolverine Abroad*. That title would have resonated with a Michigan audience—the Wolverine was (and still is) the mascot of both the University of Michigan and the state. At least seven of Swain's essays appeared in the *Detroit News*.[12] Given his meticulous (and journalistic) nature, every one of his photographs is also accompanied by an informative caption, some of which are quite detailed.[13]

Like his photographs, his letters and essays cover an impressive range of topics—from politics, local villagers, and landscapes to food (often noted in detail) and intriguing folk traditions. Some entries take a quasi-scientific turn, describing technologies and crafts that

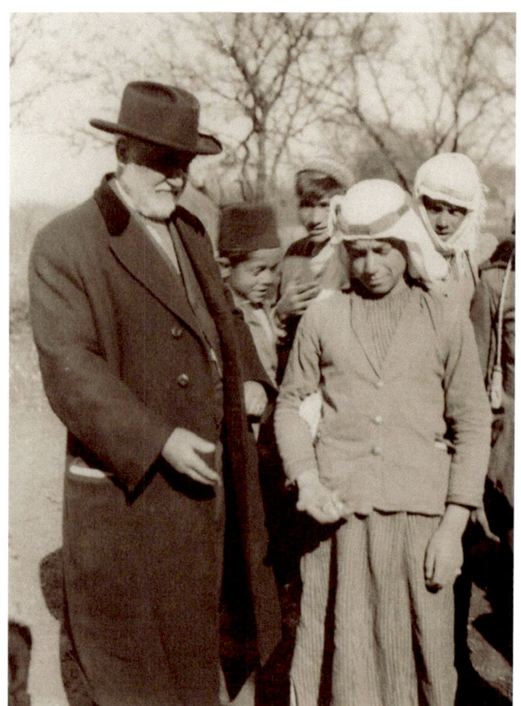

Fig. 10. Francis W. Kelsey buying knucklebones, Baalbek, Syria, June 14, 1920 (Kelsey Museum neg. no. KS 094.04).

Fig. 11. One of George R. Swain's many letters home to his family, March 6, 1926 (scan courtesy of the Harlan Hatcher Graduate Library, University of Michigan).

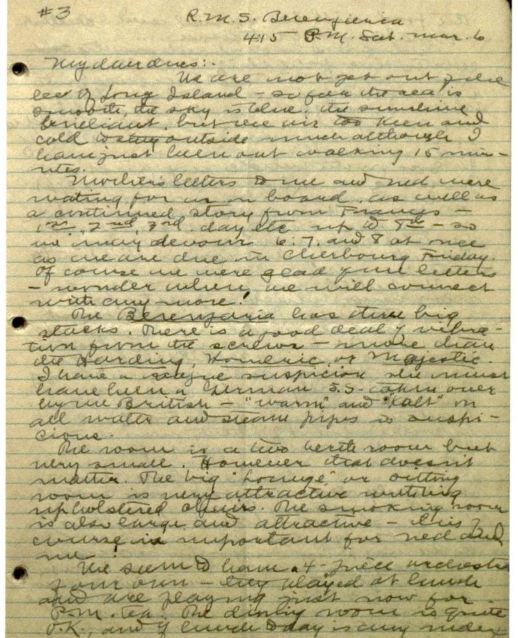

#3 R.M.S. Berengaria
4:15 P.M. Sat. Mar. 6

My dear ones:

We are not yet out of the lee of Long Island — so far the sea is smooth, the sky is blue, the sunshine brilliant, but the air too keen and cold to stay outside much although I have just been out walking 15 minutes.

Mother's letters to me and Ned were waiting for us on board, as well as a continued story from Frances — 1st, 2nd, 3rd day etc up to 5th — so we may devour 6, 7, and 8 at once as we are due in Cherbourg Friday. Of course we were glad of the letters — wonder when we will connect with any more!

The Berengaria has three big stacks. There is a good deal of vibration from the screws — more than the Harding, Homeric, or Majestic. I have a vague suspicion she must have been a German S.S. taken over by the British — "warm" and "kalt" on all water and steam pipes is suspicious.

The room is a two berth room but very small. However that doesn't matter. The big "lounge" or sitting room is very attractive with its upholstered chairs. The smoking room is also large and attractive — this of course is important for Ned and me!

We seem to have a 4-piece orchestra of our own — they played at lunch and are playing just now for P.M. tea. The dining room is quite O.K., and if lunch today is any index

would ultimately become dying arts (figs. 12–13). Others highlight Swain's impatience with what he regards as the region's byzantine bureaucracies and "native" mindsets. But Swain also comments sympathetically on the plight of marginalized and refugee populations (fig. 14) and muses about what he hopes will be better conditions for women. In addition, his letters often paint colorful word pictures of countrysides that he could only capture in black and white. Swain was even inspired by a trip down the Nile and a visit to the top of the pyramids at sunset (fig. 15) to pen a collection of poems (fig.16).[14]

As an American abroad, Swain was ever alert to the differences, both superficial and profound, between Western and Eastern ways of life: "We saw East meets West," he writes from Smyrna, Turkey, in 1924, "when two Fords had to swerve up to the curb to let five heavily laden camels swing by and a group of black-veiled women suddenly scattered at the honking approach of a truck filled with Standard Oil gas."[15]

Swain's letters also reveal that he was acutely aware of the growing sociopolitical changes and disruptions of identities that roiled the Mediterranean and the Near East. Writing about Turkey (fig. 17) for one of his articles published in the *Detroit News*, Swain observes:

> Turkey is in the ferment of violent readjustment—religious, social, economic. A serious attempt has been made to separate church and state. Personally I can't not but think that this is based not only on a political conviction that this should be done, but also on the fact that religious beliefs on the part of the younger educated class is [*sic*] becoming less violent.
>
> In some sections women are being given far more freedom socially, more opportunities for education, and are beginning to be treated as if they might have some brains. . . . Economically, the transition is . . . more convulsive, owing to the sudden withdrawal (or expulsion) of the Armenians and Greeks who transacted a very large per cent of the business of the country.[16]

As we will see, although Swain strongly supported the emerging emancipation of women, the growing separation of church and state, and the expansion of meaningful education in Turkey, he was still a product of his time—not immune to the prevalent colonial attitudes of the early 1900s.

Since Swain lived during a momentous time in history, it is useful to situate his travels in the context of the world's stage. The immediate aftermath of World War I left Europe with crippling debt, bloody revolutions in Russia deposed a long-standing monarchy and established a socialist government, and China suffered not only devastating famine but also internal rivalries that forever altered the political terrain in that part of the globe.

Cataclysmic events were reshaping societies elsewhere as well. Despite the King-Crane Commission Report, much of the Near East was parceled out between Britain and France, Turkey (which was in conflict with Greece) abolished the sultanate and created a republic

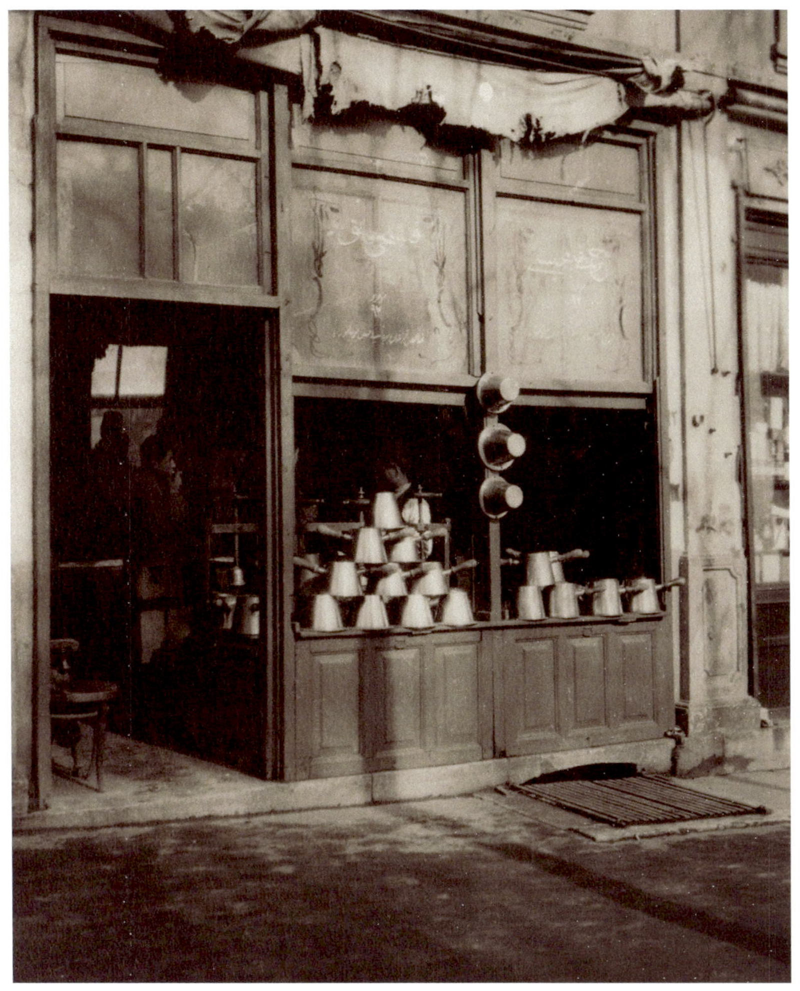

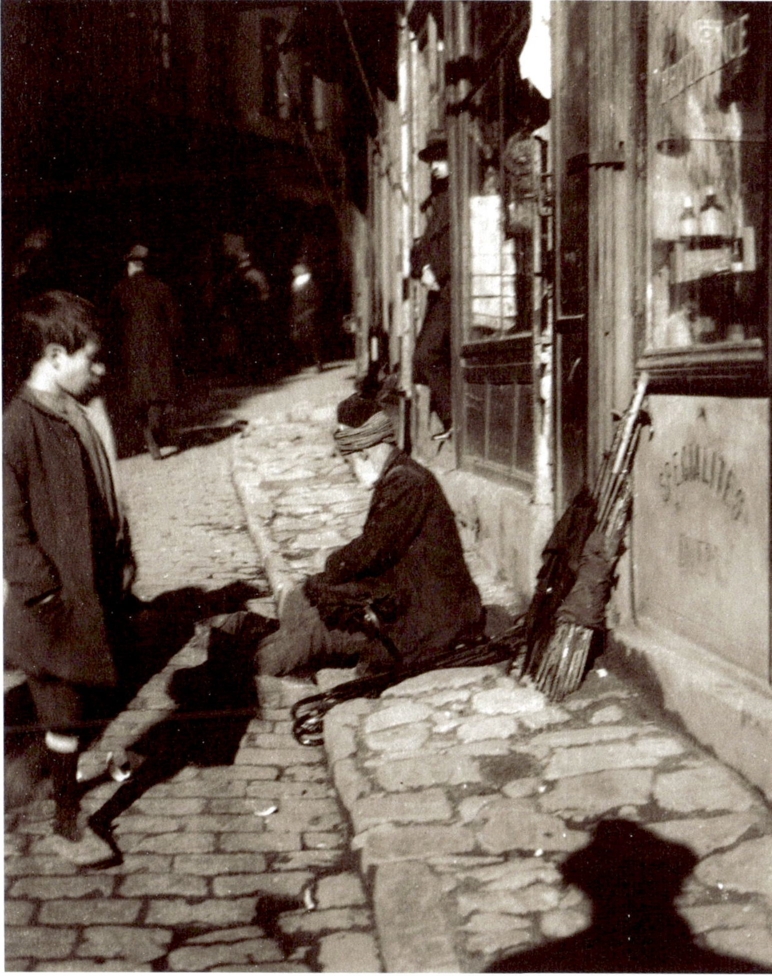

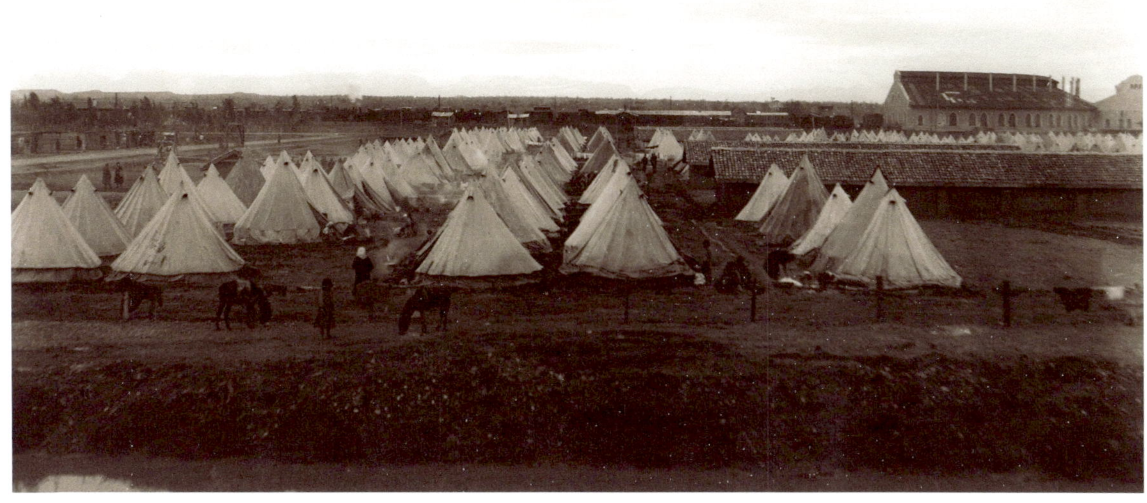

Fig. 12. A shop for pressing Turkish fezzes, Constantinople, Turkey, December 9, 1919 (Kelsey Museum neg. no. KS 046.10).

Fig. 13. An umbrella mender sitting on a sidewalk, Constantinople, Turkey, December 5, 1919 (Kelsey Museum neg. no. KS 043.04).

Fig. 14. An Armenian refugee camp, Adana, Turkey, December 31, 1919 (Kelsey Museum neg. no. 7.0156).

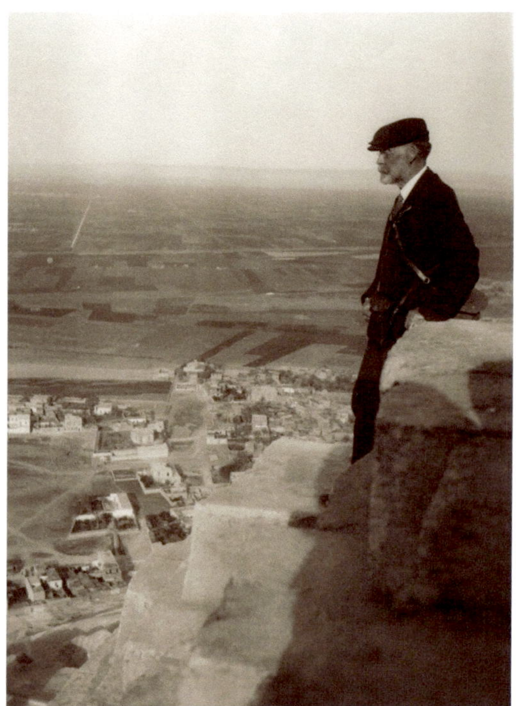

Fig. 15. George R. Swain on the top of the Pyramid of Cheops, with the Nile River Valley visible below, April 1, 1920 (Kelsey Museum neg. no. KS 164.04).

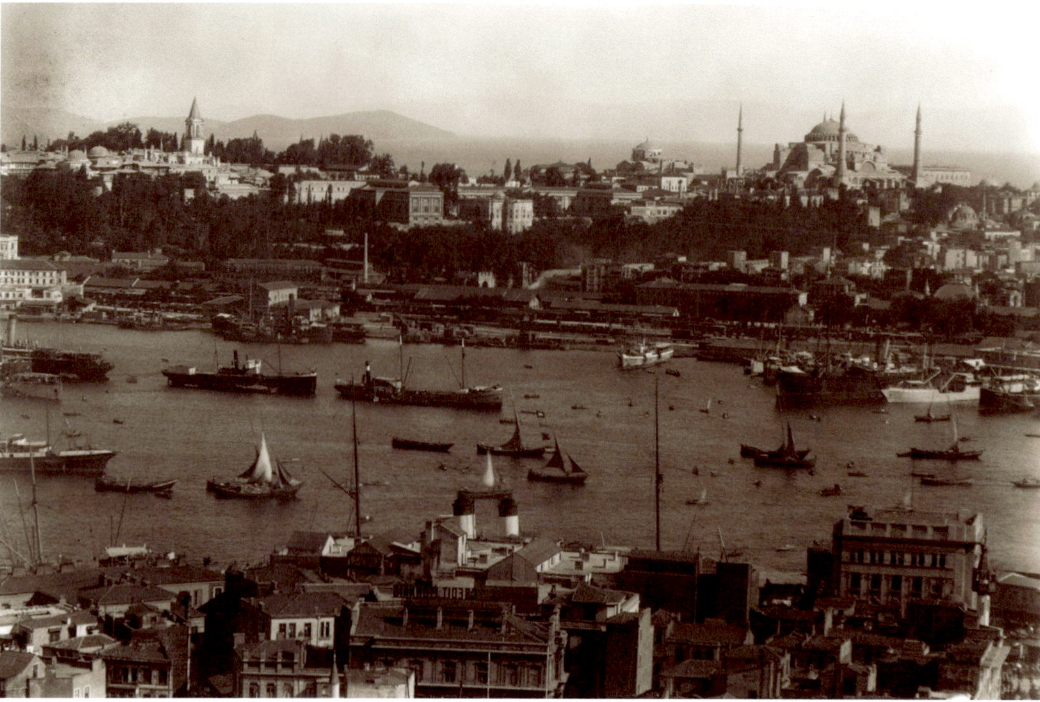

Fig. 17. The Golden Horn, Constantinople, Turkey, June 17, 1924 (Kelsey Museum neg. no. 7.0610).

under Mustafa Kemal Atatürk, and Mussolini (whom Swain mentions in one letter) instituted a fascist government in Italy.[17]

It was also a momentous time in the United States, which was in the throes of widespread social and cultural changes, both positive and negative. The Great War had not blighted the United States' economy as much as Europe's; indeed, the country experienced unprecedented economic growth and runaway consumerism. Automobile and appliance ownership skyrocketed; Americans embraced mass entertainment, including "talking pictures"; the Jazz Era and flappers flourished; the "Lost Generation" and "Harlem Renaissance" produced books that marked a turning point in American literature; and white women were given the vote in 1920. Swain's home country was embracing progress, experimentation, and efficiency.

But not too far below this rosy surface in America were deep sociopolitical conflicts and divisions. The trial and execution of Sacco and Vanzetti (1921–1927) cast a harsh light on rising anti-immigration; the Scopes trial (1925) pitted science and reason against theology and faith; an ever-growing Red Scare was rarely far from the minds of many; the resurgence of the Ku Klux Klan added the persecution of Jews, Catholics, and immigrants to its historic discrimination against Black Americans; and Prohibition fueled the increase of organized crime.

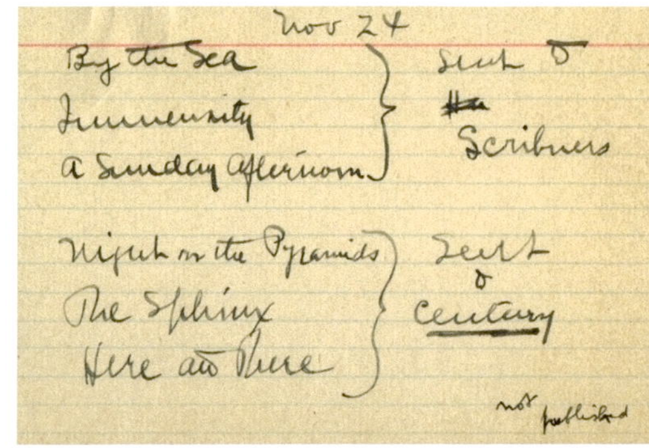

Nov 24
By the Sea
Immensity
A Sunday Afternoon
sent to ~~the~~ Scribners

Night on the Pyramids
The Sphinx
Here and There
sent to Century

not published

Fig. 16. Small slip of paper (date unknown) noting the poems that Swain sent to two publishing houses, Scribners and Century (George Robert Swain Photographs and Papers, Bentley Historical Library, University of Michigan).

A few of Swain's letters lay bare some of his "American" attitudes: "Natives" are not to be trusted, and the Mediterranean is plagued by inefficiency. Swain even suggests that some problems in Greece could be solved by American intervention and entrepreneurial expertise. But Swain is also clearly moved by the horrors of post–World War I Europe and the Near East. His photographs vividly capture landscapes ravaged by war and the tragedy of widespread poverty. In addition, he writes insightfully about the complexities that confronted places like Turkey that were struggling to modernize and reform (see p. 68). In the final analysis, we cannot divorce his images and letters from a world in flux—and the filters through which he viewed those global forces.

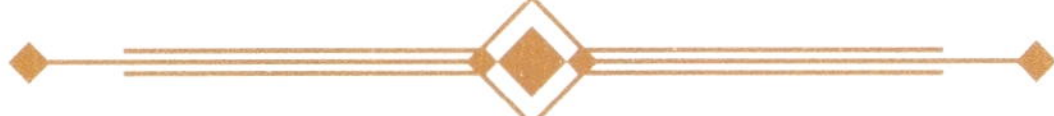

Given the rich and varied nature of the sources I uncovered, this book presented both conceptual and structural challenges. I debated how best to focus a lengthy text that drew from many disparate subjects, people, and themes. Should the vehicles take center stage? Would it be better to spotlight Swain's many photographs and commentaries? Where would the important topic of colonialism fit in? Just as critical, did I want to write an academic book or one that targeted a broader readership?

In the end, I decided to write an accessible book that uses the vehicles as a literary device, escorting the reader from the United States to remote parts of the world. The book is also constructed in a quilt-like fashion and is, consequently, more than the sum of its parts. The subjects and themes are varied—ranging from cars and photography to social history and life on archaeological excavations in the early 1900s. Readers are just as likely to find discussions about the complexities of colonialism as they are to learn about the history of the horseless carriage or the local Turkish tradition of warding off Satan by firing a gun at a lunar eclipse. Each square in the quilt recounts a different story, but the overarching effect is a broad view of life around the turn of the last century in parts of America, as well as in various regions of the greater Mediterranean.

As indicated in the table of contents, the book is divided into four parts: the earlier sections focus on the vehicles and Swain, while the later ones concentrate on the anthropological vignettes detailed in Swain's writings.

Part I offers a brief history of the automobile until the 1920s, a short profile of the men—the Graham and Dodge brothers—who designed and manufactured the two University of Michigan vehicles, and specs for both the truck and sedan.

Part II gives a concise biography of George R. Swain and a summary of his photographic techniques, so different from today's instant image taking.

Part III describes the 1924, 1925, and 1926 expeditions, highlighting Swain's narratives about the worlds he encountered with his automotive companions. Although Swain occasionally records some of the locals' reactions to the university campaigns, for the most part, Swain's voice and agency predominate.

Finally, in Part IV, I take a retrospective view of Swain's work, exploring what motivated his ethnographic interests, how best to parse the narrative power of his images, and how colonialism shaped his work.

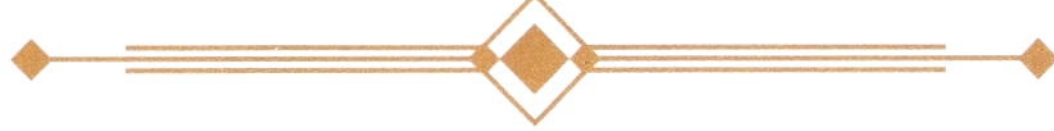

Just as Swain's photographs froze time, so did his letters and reports. Each offers a selective depiction of places and events in the past that we refract through a contemporary lens. By so doing, we participate in what one scholar has famously labeled the temporal slippage between "the here-now and the there-then."[18] Archaeology, too, is a highly selective practice that attempts to immobilize time and levy a modern overlay on times past. If photography can be said to capture and freeze the fleeting moment, so, too, can archaeology. As recently noted, the discipline arrests "the social life of things, buildings and objects, and [attempts to] reconstitute them into an idealized, original state."[19]

While Swain did not set out to conduct documentary or anthropological investigations of the 1920s, he did, in fact, produce an invaluable body of ethnographic work on the "complexity of observable life" in circum-Mediterranean countries.[20] Admittedly an outsider whose concerns were officially archaeological, he offers us glimpses into various behaviors and events in regions struggling with poverty, nation building, empowerment, and social change. Aided by his vehicles and armed with his cameras and curiosity, Swain's documentary impulses provide a unique and personal view of the region in the years following the Great War. He gives voice to small moments from the past, spoken from time's seeming silence.

Part I

THE AGE OF AUTOMOBILES

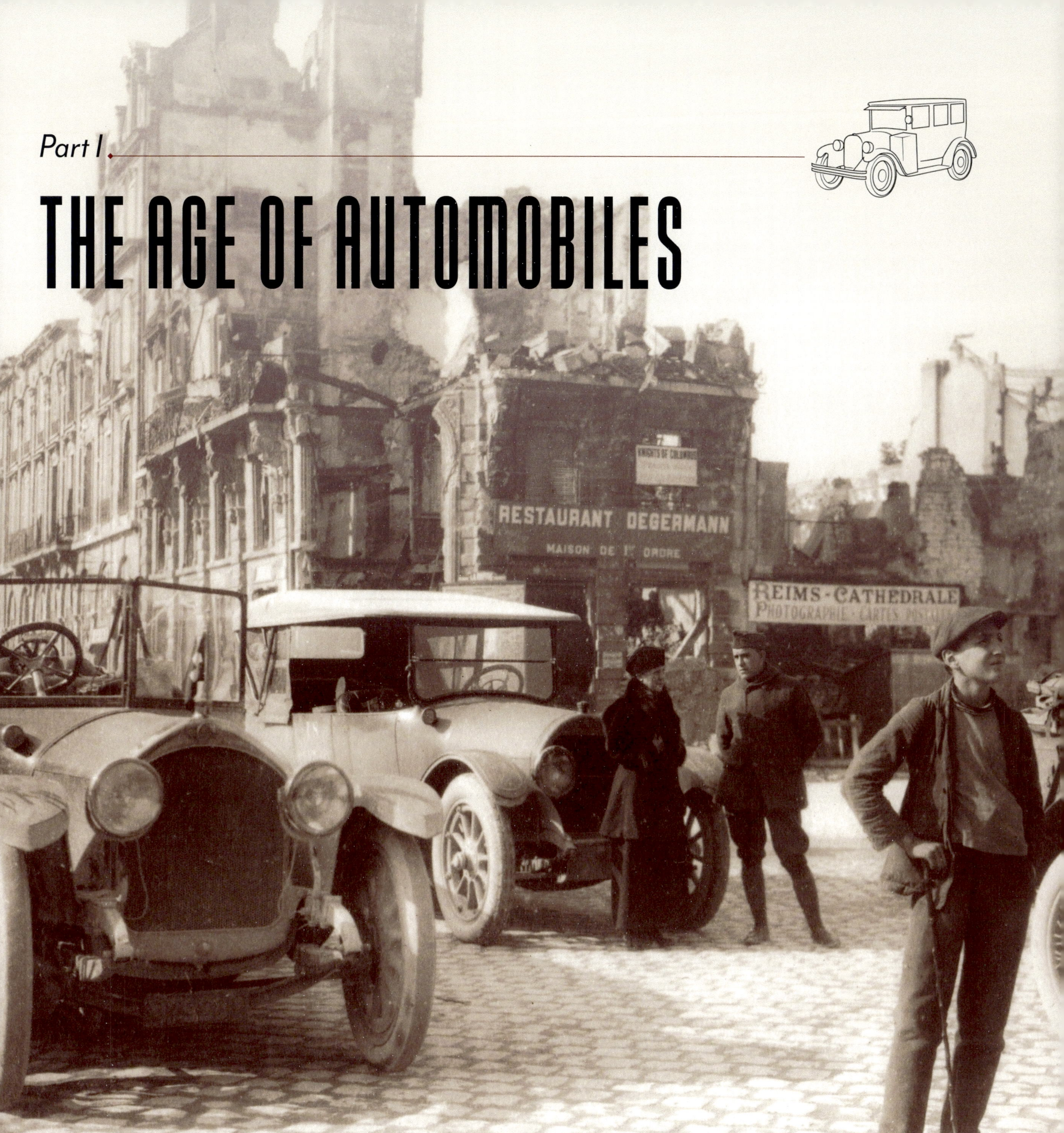

Chapter 2

HORSELESS CARRIAGES AND THE MICHIGAN CARS

Exactly what qualifies as the world's first car remains a matter of debate. Scholars and specialists agree, however, that by the mid-1700s and early 1800s, an impressive list of inventors and tinkerers were experimenting with steam-, electric-, hydrogen-, and gas-powered vehicles of one sort or another (Side Car 1). There was no shortage of aspiring hopefuls, ranging from a blacksmith, a mining engineer, a professor, and a patent lawyer to a plumber, a jeweler, and even a minister. Despite a good deal of resourcefulness, it wasn't until the 1880s that the first practical automobiles were produced by two Germans, who were apparently working independently. Karl Benz, a mechanical engineer, and Gottlieb Daimler, an engineer and industrialist, are usually credited with designing the first gas-powered vehicles propelled by an internal combustion engine.[22]

One of Benz's vehicles was the Motorwagen III (fig. 18), a three-wheeled automobile with a rear-mounted engine that could whip along at 10 miles per hour. The fate of the "wagen" changed unequivocally on August 5, 1888. On that day, Bertha Benz, Karl Benz's 39-year-old wife (and an automotive pioneer in her own right), decided to field-test her husband's car—without his knowledge. She left Mannheim around dawn, with her two teenage sons in tow, ostensibly to visit her mother in Pforzheim.[23] The distance was approximately 65 miles, and she reached her mother's place after dusk (today, the trip would take about an hour). At the time, her journey was considered illegal: written permits were required to operate cars on public roads, and Bertha apparently had never acquired one. Her trip created a stir for another reason as well. Not only did she travel on roads where no one had ever seen a car—and cover more miles than any automobile to date—but the newfangled contraption had a woman at the helm.

Although Bertha encountered several problems along the way, her solutions proved ingenious. Reportedly, she used her hatpin to clean a clogged fuel line, resorted to her garter to plug a leaky valve, and found a cobbler to install leather brake pads (the first of their kind) when the wooden brakes began to fail. Other problems were harder to solve. When the car's two gears couldn't ascend steep inclines, her sons were pressed into service, pushing the Motorwagen from behind.[24]

As soon as Bertha reached Pforzheim, she cabled her husband about the historic journey (the Bertha Benz Memorial Route, which follows her 1888 journey, was officially designated a part of the European Route of Industrial Heritage in 2008). Her trip was

Side Car 1: Da Vinci's Cart

In 1478, long before the efforts of the mid-1700s, Leonardo da Vinci sketched designs for what some consider the first self-propelled cart or wagon. His detailed drawings can be viewed on folio 812r of the Codex Atlanticus. Apparently, da Vinci's machine was never built, and some scholars suspect it was only intended for theatrical use. In 2004, after years of failed attempts, specialists succeeded in constructing a wooden model of da Vinci's cart, which operated like a spring-propelled toy, with gears, limited steering, and a brake. It could travel around 130 feet.[21]

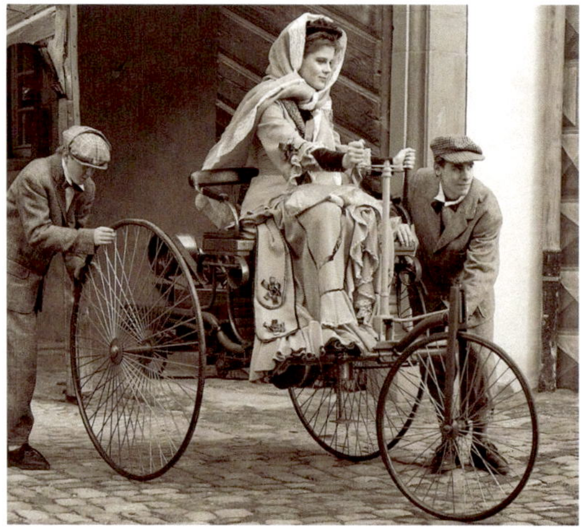

Fig. 18. There are no known photos of Bertha Benz's expedition in the Motorwagen. This image depicts a recreation of the 1888 road trip (Daimler AG, Germany).

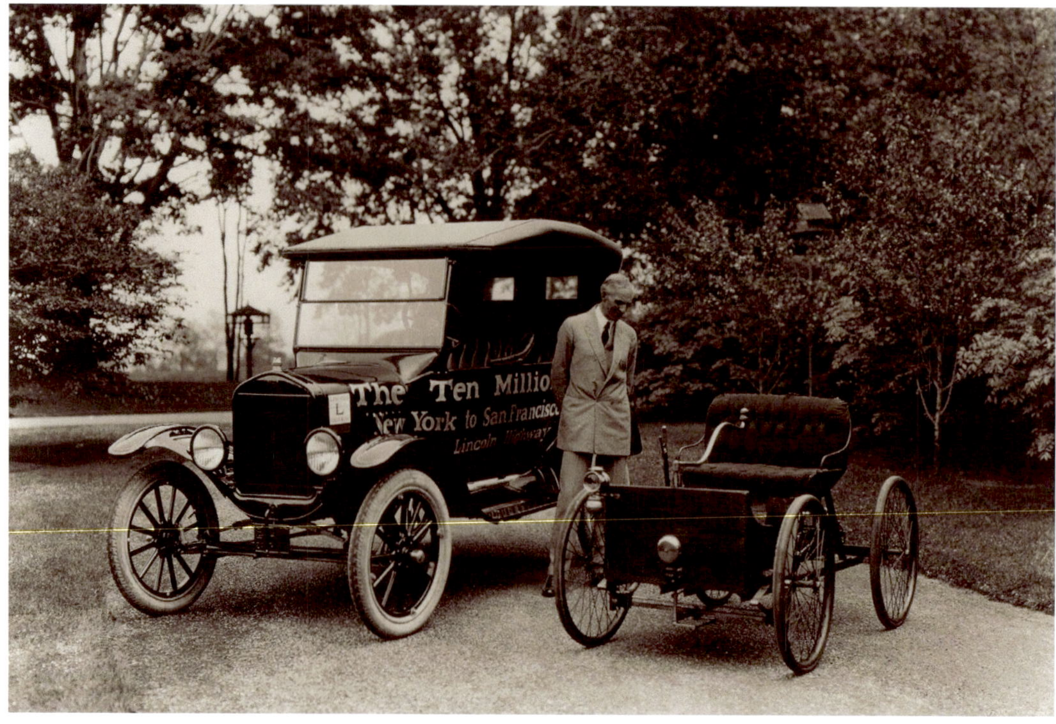

Fig. 19. Henry Ford standing by two of his cars. On the right is his first experimental horseless carriage, the Quadricycle of 1896. The left shows a much later Model T touring car (marked on the side as "The Ten Millionth"). Model T production began in 1908, with the 100 millionth one rolling off the assembly line in 1924 (National Automotive History Collection, Detroit Public Library, na042812; caption courtesy of Michael E. Keller).

enormously successful, not only garnering the kind of publicity she had hoped for but also serving as a test drive to identify problems. Soon after her trip, Benz cars were outfitted with an additional gear for uphill climbs as well as brake linings for increased durability.

Early automobiles like the Benz Motorwagen were the purview of the rich—emblems of prestige and status. In 1885, for example, the Benz prototype cost 600 imperial German marks.[25] The average German earned 581 marks annually at the time.[26] But as production increased both in America and overseas, cars became more affordable. By the second decade of the 1900s, the cost had decreased significantly, in large part due to the inventions of Henry Ford. In the United States, the initial cost of the Ford Model T (fig. 19), which was first manufactured in 1908, was $850 (approximately $27,500 in today's dollars); by 1915, the car cost $390; and by 1916, the price had dropped to $260 (roughly $7,100 in current dollars).[27] Although cars were still out of reach for many Americans—the average American male was earning $687 annually in 1915—by the next decade, vehicles like the Model T were an ever-growing part of US households.[28]

Building on the concept of assembly-line mass production and the use of standardized parts that fit various models (interchangeable parts), Ford was able to produce cars quickly. His reliable and easily maintained models exited the assembly line in 15-minute intervals, and by the 1920s, mass production was common in both America and Europe. In 1917, a little less than a decade after the first Ford Model T was sold, 1 in 13 American households had cars (approximately 5 million vehicles were registered in the United States that year). By 1927, approximately 23 million vehicles were registered nationwide, and an astounding 15 million American families owned Ford's Model T, affectionately known as the "Tin Lizzie" (Side Car 2).[29]

Ford's Model T was not just relatively affordable; it was also easy to fix. The average person could often repair what ailed a Model T "by resorting to twine, baling wire, clothespins, chewing gum, or barbed wire taken from roadside fences." In fact, all one needed was a hammer, a screwdriver, pliers, and a monkey wrench.[31] It took only a little ingenuity to MacGyver the seemingly complicated machine.

America's love affair with the Model T was in a class by itself. After the last of its kind rolled off the assembly line in 1927, an outpouring of eulogies flooded American newspapers.[32] Perhaps the most famous and eloquent eulogy, "Farewell, My Lovely!" appeared in the *New Yorker* in 1936—nearly a decade after the final Model T was produced—attesting to its still-cherished status. Written by the legendary editor and author E. B. White (perhaps with a coauthor), the tribute christened the car as "the miracle God had wrought." In White's estimation, the Tin Lizzie "was like nothing that had ever come to the world before. Flourishing industries rose and fell with it. As a vehicle, it was hard-working, commonplace, heroic; and it often seemed to transmit those qualities to the persons who rode in it."[33]

Regardless of its brand, the automobile generated radical changes in America, in Europe, and beyond, allowing society to become truly mobile. Whether it was a Ford, Dodge, Cadillac, Lancia, Rolls-Royce, or Oldsmobile—all of which were manufactured by the 1920s—the automobile connected the world in new ways, forever altering people's lives. In the United States, suburbs grew exponentially, now that they were only a short drive from big cities; graded roads slowly began to replace routes rutted by wagon wheels; and doctors could travel more quickly and easily to farmers and their families. In fact, the first cars in many rural communities were driven by doctors, who benefited from a mode of travel infinitely quicker than the horse-drawn carriage. According to Henry Ford, country doctors were among his earliest and most enthusiastic customers.[34]

By the 1930s and 1940s, leisure travel changed as well, with families no longer at the mercy of railroad destinations and schedules. Roadside accommodations began to sprout along the landscape. A series of small, attached apartments known as motor hotels—the precursor to the American motel—dotted the United States. Parking was often available outside each unit, and laundry facilities, a grocery store, a restaurant, and a filling station were frequently nearby. The enormous suite of transformations across the country prompted an American sociologist to comment in 1928 that the automobile was "the most revolutionizing force yet experienced by rural society."[35] Following the horseless carriage's first fits and starts in the 1880s, it hadn't taken long for the world to embrace a romance with the automobile—a love affair that continues to this day.

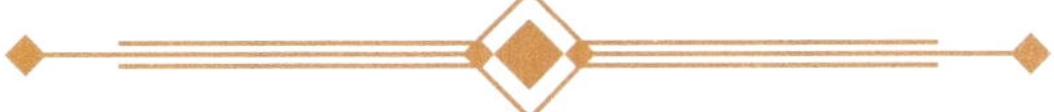

By the time Swain and company traveled overseas, cars were a familiar sight in many major cities (fig. 20). "With any half reasonable care," Swain wrote in 1924, "no one need fear being unable to purchase 'gas' when motoring in France—you will find motoring stations almost everywhere . . . [and] gas is uniformly 52 cents a gallon."[36] Even in recently devastated Smyrna,[37] Swain notes the presence of Oldsmobiles, Buicks, and "squawking Fords"

Side Car 2: Tin Lizzie

The "Tin Lizzie" apparently owes its name to a car race in 1922. One of the entries was a ramshackle Model T. Unpainted and lacking a hood, it was named "Old Liz" by its owner and compared to a tin can by many of the spectators. The car was affectionately christened with a new nickname—"Tin Lizzie"—before the start of the race. Much to everyone's surprise, the car won, beating out the more high-end cars of the day. It was a great victory for Ford, validating the speed and resilience of the Model T.[30]

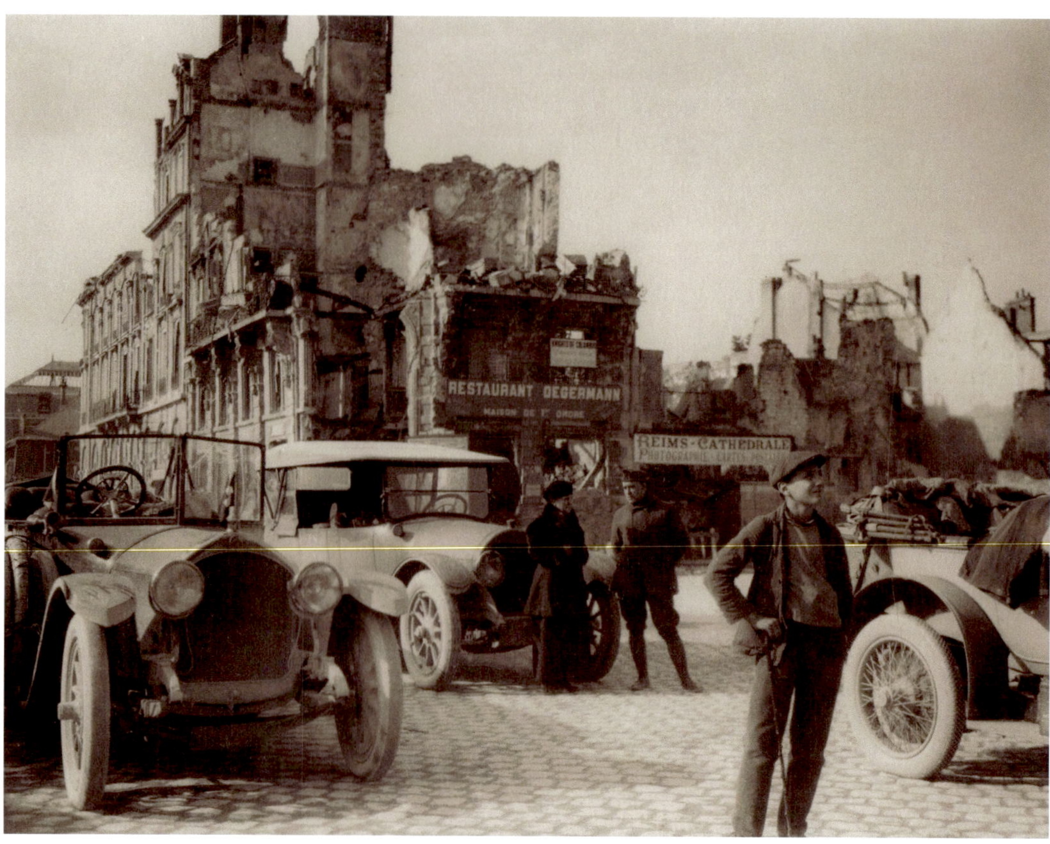

Fig. 20. "In the square in front of the cathedral. Mrs. Kelsey and Rediger, our chauffeur, and the army Cadillac," Reims, France, October 17, 1919 (Kelsey Museum neg. no. KS 019.10).

on the city's narrow streets, as well as vehicles in the streets of 1924 Constantinople, which boasted luxury Cadillacs and the ever-dependable Fords.[38] A year later, Swain would comment on the crush of wheeled vehicles in Greece's capital city: "Athens is saturated with Ford jitney buses; of passenger cars, Dodges easily rank first by a long way, although you may find specimens of most other well-known American cars, including a surprising number of Cadillacs. Some French, English, and Italian cars are there too."[39]

Swain had yet, however, to see another Graham Brothers truck (one of the vehicles in his care). He was therefore pleasantly surprised by what he witnessed in 1925 while idly watching the unloading of a neighboring ship from the deck of a steamer anchored at Piraeus, Greece. As Swain reports, "Up from the hold, over the rail, and down on to the inevitable lighter swung a huge box, and stencilled in big letters on its side was the legend 'Graham Bros. Truck.'"[40]

Although automobiles were a common sight in bigger cities, they were rarely seen in more remote areas. At Gafsa, Tunisia, for example, Swain observed that motorized vehicles count as one of the wonders of the world, noting that only two other cars had passed by the town in six months.[41] In other regions, travel by car was actively discouraged. When Swain traveled to central Turkey in 1924, he heard stories of native carriage (*arabas*) drivers scattering nails on roads to deter these new machines. While Swain rarely experienced this particular inconvenience, two of his colleagues sustained three punctures over the course of a 37-mile trip within Turkey, possibly the consequence of such sabotage.[42]

A Plucky Sedan and an Intrepid Truck

While researching the two University of Michigan vehicles—the Dodge Brothers sedan and the Graham Brothers truck—I wondered why these two models had been selected and how the university obtained them. I found part of the answer in a short document buried in the Kelsey Museum files. The original intent of the paper is not clear—it may have been a status report to the university. Written by Swain and dated November 5, 1925, it is entitled "Travels of Two Dodge Motors" and provides a summary of the trips taken between 1924 and 1925, as well as information that helps flesh out the background of the two vehicles.[43]

According to Swain's report, in December 1923, Howard R. Bloomer (a Detroit lawyer, a well-known philanthropist, and legal counsel to the Dodge brothers) and his wife donated a Dodge Brothers Type B sedan to the University of Michigan "in order to facilitate the work abroad of the Near East Research of the University of Michigan" (fig. 21). The Near East Research initiative had been formed at the urging of Professor Kelsey in 1923, the same year as the Dodge donation. The mission of that initiative was to commence new expeditions overseas and guarantee the timely publication of any subsequent work. Swain was appointed as "Associate Director in Charge of Transportation and Photography." An initial list of objectives stipulated that Swain take "no fewer than four cameras" with him.[44]

Swain's report also notes that the Graham Brothers firm presented another vehicle to the university—a one-and-a-half-ton truck with a panel body, which had the advantage of being larger and sturdier than the Dodge sedan. Both vehicles were to be shipped across the ocean and "begin work" in the spring of 1924.

The transatlantic shipping of cars for American archaeological concessions in the Mediterranean and Near East was far from standard protocol at the time. Cars were usually rented, purchased, or borrowed overseas. Kelsey and Swain, however, seem to have hatched an alternate plan.

A letter from Kelsey to Swain, dated August 24, 1923—approximately five months before their departure for excavations in Turkey—reveals that Kelsey had met with a representative from Dodge who was "interested in your [Swain's] plan, and the engineers in charge of the construction of the Dodge cars and Graham trucks will be consulted upon our problem." Veiled as the comment is, it suggests that negotiations were already afoot to convince Dodge that a donation, perhaps of specially designed vehicles, would have advantages, not least for the publicity it might accrue for the company as well as its standing with the University of Michigan. The same letter mentions that Easton (Professor Kelsey's son, who accompanied him on several expeditions) had just finished his "service at the Ann Arbor Garage," further noting that the Dodge representative had offered "to take Easton into the factory in order to learn what he can of the construction" of Dodge vehicles. Apparently, Kelsey had in mind that Easton might help with the maintenance of the vehicles.[45]

A much longer letter, dated seven weeks earlier (July 3, 1923), indicates that Swain had given much thought to what kind of vehicles would best suit the journey. He argues the merits of various models, weighs the virtues of a Cadillac versus an REO Speed Wagon, tries to gauge wear and tear on tires, and evaluates the vehicles' accelerations and gasoline mileages. Swain finally votes for a Dodge car and the Dodge-Graham Brothers truck,

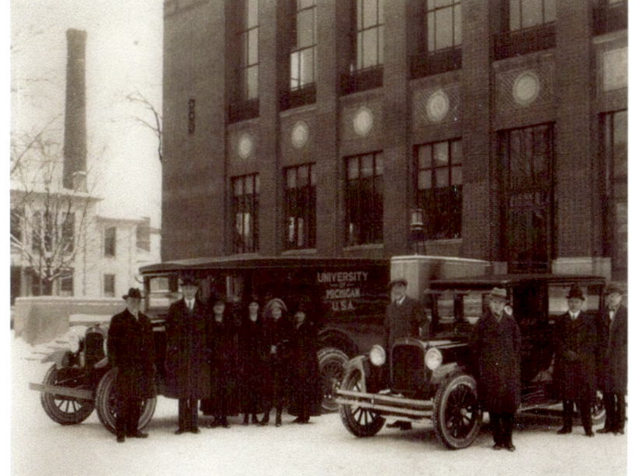

Fig. 21. Francis W. Kelsey (left) and various individuals posing with the Graham Brothers truck and the Dodge sedan in front of the University of Michigan Graduate Library, Ann Arbor, Michigan, 1924 (Kelsey Museum neg. no. KAP 00001).

swayed in part by the reliability of his own car—a Dodge—and the wisdom of having both vehicles manufactured by a single company.[46]

Although I could not determine precisely how the donations were secured, it would come as no surprise that the enterprising and indefatigable Professor Kelsey was the principal financial negotiator.[47] He had been dogged in his fund-raising attempts for the University of Michigan and, over the years, had procured hundreds of thousands of dollars from various donors to underwrite multiple university projects, ranging from archaeological excavations and scholarly publications to the purchase of valuable manuscripts, papyri, and ancient artifacts. Kelsey was intimately involved in other ambitious projects as well, including dreams for a museum of art and a school of humanities. Kelsey certainly knew Bloomer and was successful in garnering money from him on several other occasions; it seems more than likely that Kelsey's skillful powers of persuasion launched the two vehicles on their adventures.

These two gifts were not insignificant in terms of their value. The basic Graham Brothers truck sold for approximately $1,325 in 1924 (approximately $23,000 in today's dollars), and the standard Dodge sedan went for roughly $1,250 (a little more than $21,400 in current dollars).[48] The indispensable vehicles were not just modes of transportation; they also served as overseas storage units, chock full of equipment, including approximately 500 kilos of photographic apparatus as well as supplies, books, baggage, and camping gear. Both were furnished with an array of extras: "spot lights, dash clocks, chains, running board trunk, power air pump, etc. . . . and a formidable list of spare parts . . . gears, springs, axles, etc." in case of emergencies. Every contingency seems to have been anticipated, although the remarkable sturdiness and dependability of the vehicles rarely required the use of these parts. After two seasons, when both automobiles had been tested to their limits, Swain humorously quipped, "I may say that the only use of these . . . spare parts has been to intrigue custom officials."[49]

Chapter 3

THE PIONEERING BROTHERS

Early pioneers in car production were a breed apart, with intriguing histories of their own. This was certainly true of the Graham and Dodge brothers, who developed the vehicles that mobilized the University of Michigan's 1924–1926 excavations in the Mediterranean region. Although they were radically different in many ways, both sets of brothers exemplified the ingenuity, perseverance, risk-taking, and (at times) stubbornness that made their ventures so successful.

The Graham Brothers

Joseph (b. 1882), Robert (b. 1885), and Ray (b. 1887) Graham (fig. 22) were exceptional and talented young men who inherited a tireless work effort and a curiosity about the world from their father, Ziba F. Graham. Although earlier generations of Grahams hailed from humble Kentucky beginnings, a move to Indiana in the 1820s changed the family's fortunes. By the time the three Graham brothers appeared on the scene, Ziba owned one of the largest farms in an area just north of Washington, Indiana (approximately 95 miles southwest of Indianapolis), had purchased Washington's first power plant, and had started the Ziba F. Graham Railway Company, a pioneering local transit system that endeared him to the community and became a source of local pride.[50]

Although the young brothers eagerly pitched in on the sprawling family farm, they harbored other ambitions as they grew older. All three graduated from college, with Joseph receiving a degree from Christian Brothers College in St. Louis; Robert, a degree in chemistry from Fordham University in New York; and Ray, an agricultural degree from the University of Illinois. Shortly after college, the brothers joined forces and, with financial backing from their father, transformed a small, local glass bottle company into an international success. The company was eventually bought out by Libbey-Owens.[51] Their experience with the glass factory cemented their bond not only as brothers but also as partners in business—a relationship that continued throughout their lives.[52]

Joseph (Joe), Robert, and Ray were well suited as a team, each possessing distinctive and complementary talents.[53] Joe, who started earning money at the age of eight, was the more serious brother, full of business and practical ideas.[54] Every Saturday morning, young Joe could be found in the basement of his grandfather's grocery and general retail

Fig. 22. Robert, Joseph, and Ray Graham (Michael E. Keller Collection).

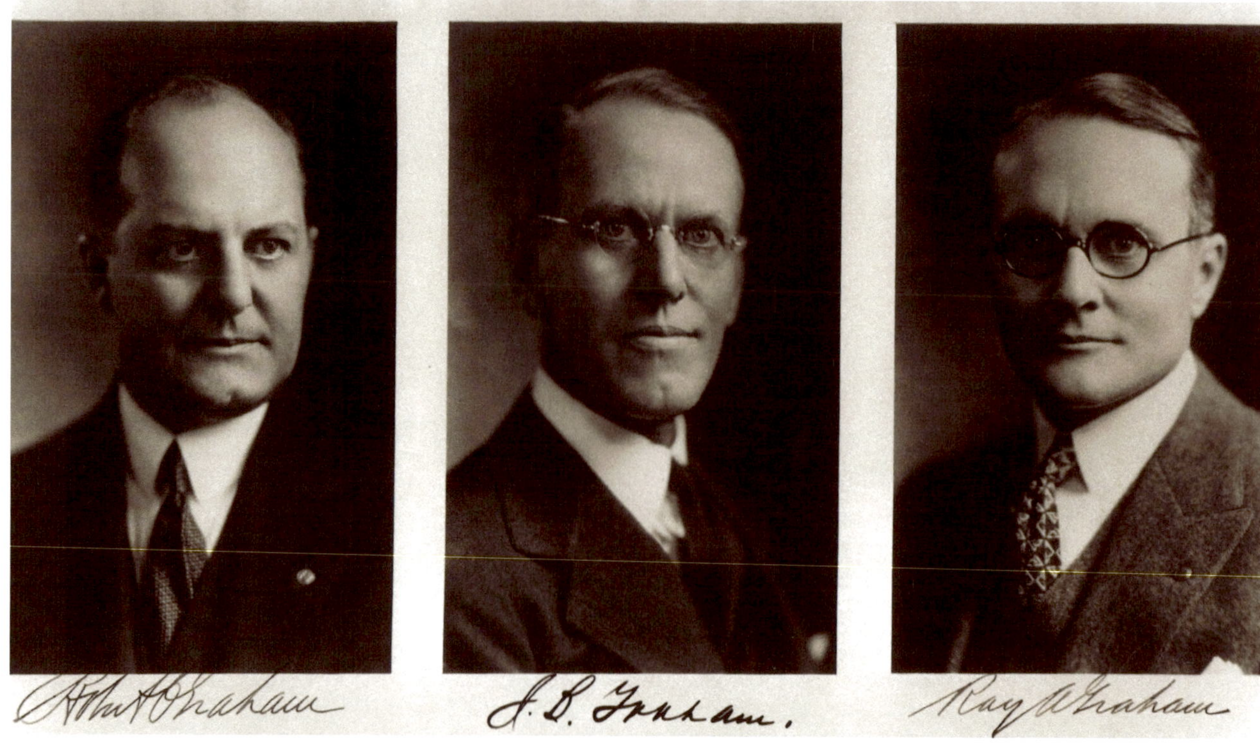

store, which also served as a clearinghouse for local poultry producers, carefully counting hundreds of eggs for the store's inventory.[55] Robert, on the other hand, was the family bookworm, who—unlike Joe—loved school and pondering theoretical ideas.[56] Ray was altogether different: mechanically minded, he was the family handyman, inventor, and general tinkerer.[57] Later in life, Joe would shine as an adept manager in charge of production; Robert, an able salesman; and Ray, the family financier.[58]

While Washington, Indiana, may not have been a bustling metropolis in the early 1900s, it was a popular stop along the Baltimore and Ohio Railroad line. According to Ed Klingler, a veteran reporter for the *Evansville Press* in Indiana, when trains pulled up to the Washington station, passengers would crane their necks out open windows in hopes of seeing an automobile, probably for the first time. Although Klingler's report (below) is seen as fanciful by some scholars, it captures the mood of the times, focusing on Joe Graham at the helm of one of the "newfangled horseless carriages":

> The driver [Joe Graham] was a mere youngster, usually accompanied by one or two others to pick up express packages removed from the train. Sometimes a little excitement accompanied the presence of the automobile. Express wagon horses reared and buckled, while drivers cursed. . . .
>
> Sometimes a train passenger called out, "What kind of car is that?" The youthful driver would answer: "A Graham," and the train passenger came back with "Never heard of it." And the boy's answer: "You will!"
>
> The year was 1901 and hardly anyone owned an automobile.

> When the train passengers were lucky enough to see the boy [Joe Graham] in the automobile, they were seeing half the cars in Washington. The other half was owned by the boy's father, Ziba Graham. Zib [*sic*] Graham bought his car, the boy built his. As a teenager he was probably Indiana's youngest car manufacturer.
>
> [Joe] started his project just as did many other car builders. He removed the wheels from an old buggy, and replaced them with wheels from two second-hand bicycles. Over the rear axle, he mounted a one-cylinder engine originally used to propel a boat. The engine was linked to a rear wheel by a bicycle chain.[59]

In forward gear, the car was steered by a rudder attached to the front axle that snaked up to the dashboard. Unfortunately, the vehicle had no reverse. Not one to be daunted, Klingler writes, Joe apparently suggested that the driver simply get out of the car, pick up the front wheel, and head the vehicle in the opposite direction![60]

The Graham brothers' car "business" took a radical leap forward in 1917, when they launched Graham Brothers, Inc., a small factory in Evansville, Indiana, that produced farm tractors as well as kits for converting automobile chassis into light-duty trucks.[61] By 1919, the highly successful "Graham Brothers Truck Builder" relied almost exclusively on Dodge engines and transmissions, and in 1921, the Graham and Dodge brothers formed a partnership, with the former focusing principally on trucks and the latter on cars. Dodge was committed to selling and servicing Graham Brothers trucks worldwide—a tremendous boon to the Graham organization, given Dodge's international connections and extensive map of dealerships (figs. 23–25).[62]

The Dodge-Graham partnership continued to flourish, and in 1924, Dodge purchased Graham Brothers outright, retaining Joe, Robert, and Ray in high-level managerial positions. Dodge also continued to manufacture their trucks under the well-respected Graham name. The lines between Dodge and Graham remained blurred until 1929, when all trucks that had previously been built with the Graham logo started being produced with Dodge badges.[63]

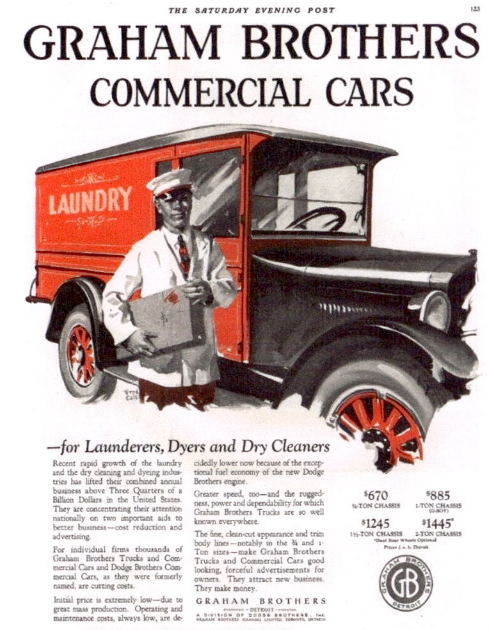

Fig. 23. Advertisement for Graham Brothers trucks and commercial cars, 1927 (*Saturday Evening Post*).

Fig. 24. Cover of a Graham Brothers Motor Truck booklet, ca. 1918 (National Automotive History Collection, Detroit Public Library, na050009).

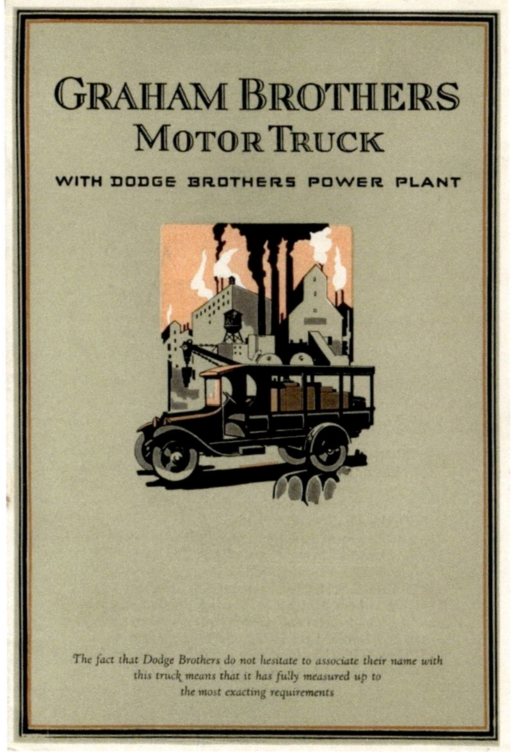

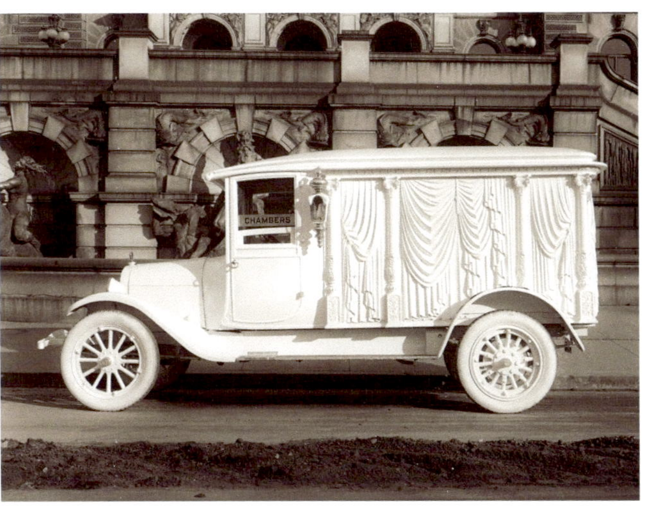

Fig. 25. Graham Brothers hearse (source unknown; public domain).

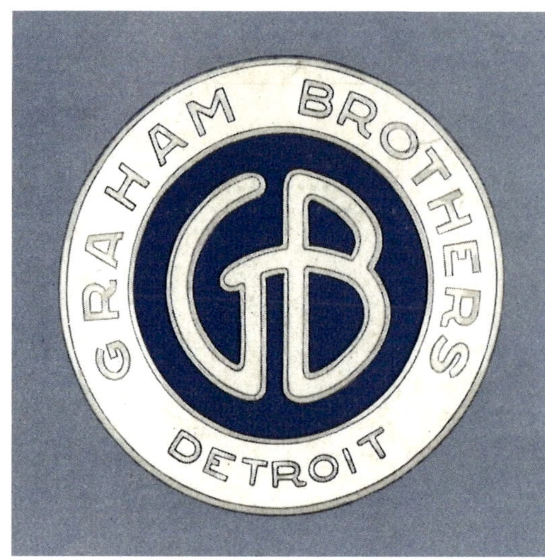

Fig. 26. Graham Brothers truck logo (Michael E. Keller Collection).

Fig. 27. Graham-Paige radiator emblem. The knights represent the three Graham brothers (Division of Work and Industry, National Museum of American History, Smithsonian Institution).

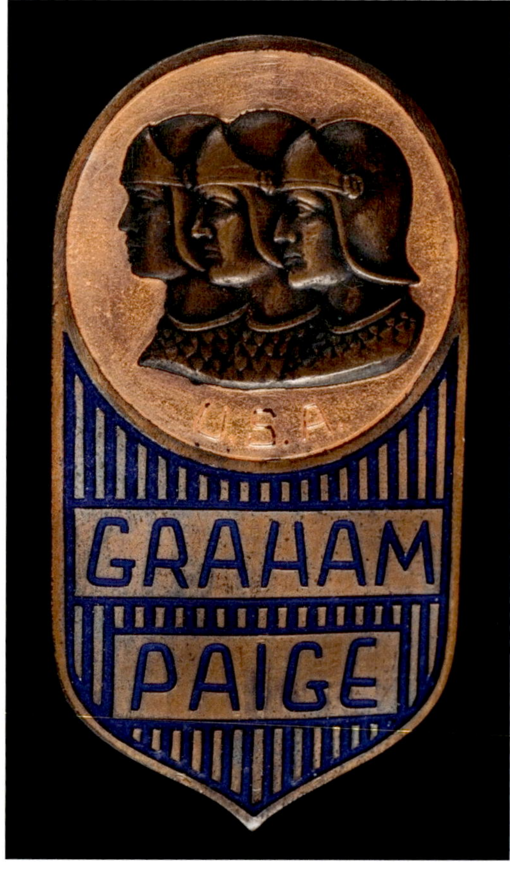

By 1926, the Graham Brothers assembly plants were the "largest exclusive producer of trucks in the world" (fig. 26).[64] Then, somewhat suddenly, in April 1926, the brothers resigned. Precisely why the Graham brothers took such a radical step is debated. Michael Keller, the foremost historian of the Graham legacy, posits that the brothers were at odds with recent changes introduced by the Dodge organization. Dodge, which had been bought out by bankers in 1925, began to institute cost-cutting measures in materials and manufacture, without a commensurate reduction in price. The bankers' philosophies did not align with the Graham brothers' sense of integrity or the customer- and employee-driven values that had long shaped their business principles.[65]

The departure of the Graham brothers from Dodge did not, however, blunt their interest in the automotive industry. They continued to produce trucks in their Evansville plant and eventually launched another car business, acquiring control of the Paige-Detroit Motor Car Company in 1927.[66] The company was rebranded as the Graham-Paige Motors Corporation, which introduced an exciting new series of automobiles, along with a new medieval-inspired logo created by an eminent American sculptor (fig. 27).[67] Promoting its new vehicles, the Graham-Paige Motors Corporation held its initial sales convention in New York in 1928, several days after the prestigious New York Auto Show. The event was an eye-popping extravaganza, conceived around a medieval theme that reflected the company's new logo and the brothers' belief that, like knights of yore, every man had a heroic element and a commitment to integrity in both life and work.[68] Held at the famed Roosevelt Hotel in New York, the convention transformed the banquet hall—walls were covered with medieval scenes, hundreds of two-foot-tall candles illuminated the courtly space, and Graham-Paige banners hung from the rafters.[69] An orchestra provided music, and guest speakers included the heavyweight boxing champion Gene Tunney and the famous Notre Dame football coach Knute Rockne.[70]

Although the brothers indulged in such extravagances and were savvy businessmen who knew the value of innovation, clever advertising, and occasional sensational events, they invested heavily in the welfare and security of their employees. Indeed, the well-being of their workforce was a top priority. Joe's address at the 1929 annual dinner of the Society of Automotive Engineers underscores the brothers' ongoing commitment to their employees. "I have a deep feeling for [the company's employees]," Joe professed. "Our company is not ambitious to be one of the largest concerns manufacturing automobiles—the greatest satisfaction we could desire would come from giving all our men a steady job through all the seasons of the year."[71]

Despite several years of innovation and healthy sales at Graham-Paige Motors, the Great Depression intervened (although the company weathered the first few years of the economic downturn), as did the Second World War's restrictions on auto production. Ultimately, the brothers' business suffered, especially as larger, more robust automotive companies overshadowed smaller enterprises. But ever the optimists and ingenious businessmen, the Grahams invested in other profitable ventures, including real estate management in greater Miami, Florida, partial ownership of Madison Square Garden, and oil and gas drilling.

Unfortunately, except to car buffs and historians, the Graham name is all but forgotten, as are the brothers' significant contributions to the early history of the automotive industry. They did, however, provide a remarkable vehicle for the University of Michigan's expeditions. The 1924 Graham Brothers truck proved to be the workhorse of the University of Michigan explorations, logging more than 4,000 miles during the three years of travel from 1924 to 1926, traversing daunting terrain, and more than once pulling its companion—the Dodge sedan—out of a ditch or a mud-filled trench. The Graham brothers were no doubt rightfully proud of what had become of their first experiments with a car that supposedly had to be lifted up and turned around for reverse.

The Dodge Brothers

The Dodge brothers (fig. 28), John (b. 1864) and Horace (b. 1868), provide a striking contrast to the Grahams. Though both sets of siblings played major roles in the early life of Detroit's automotive industry, the redheaded Dodge brothers were known as much for their rowdy and irascible natures as for their innovations.[72] Horace had a "slow-burning temper" that erupted less frequently than his brother's, but neither shied away from their share of barroom brawls.[73] Hard drinkers, they were inseparable, often dressing in identical suits and insisting that they would only read mail if it was addressed to both of them.[74]

Born in Niles, Michigan, the Dodges moved with the family to Detroit in the mid-1880s. Both brothers worked at a marine boiler factory, then at a machine shop in Windsor, Ontario, just across the border from Detroit. Horace, the younger of the two, tinkered at home and eventually invented the first dustproof ball bearing for bicycles in 1896. The next year, the brothers received a patent for the invention and cofounded a bicycle company (Evans and Dodge). Eventually, they sold their share of the business for $10,000.

With a substantial sum in their pockets, the brothers opened their own shop, focusing on the production of parts for the fledging automotive industry. The success of their business caught the attention of Ransom E. Olds (of Oldsmobile fame), who hired them to produce engines and transmissions for his new Curved Dash cars.[75] The year was 1903, and Olds controlled 30 percent of the car-building industry.[76] Horace and John soon gained a reputation as reliable and dependable suppliers of quality parts.

Ultimately, the brothers decided to work with Henry Ford, but not before they secured agreements with the auto magnate, who had suffered several bankruptcies in the early 1900s. The brothers committed to build and supply all the main components for Ford's cars, provided they could own 10 percent of the Ford company, as well as all rights to Ford's assets in case of another financial disaster. Apparently, neither party was happy with the arrangement, and after a decade of supplying parts for Ford, the Dodge brothers opened their own company, funded by a $25 million buyout from Ford (approximately $740 million in today's dollars). The first Dodge vehicle came off the assembly line in November 1914.[77] By 1915, Dodge was the number-three brand in America, with vehicle sales that year numbering more than 45,000. By 1924, the company had 20,000 employees and was capable of manufacturing 1,000 cars a day (figs. 29–30).[78]

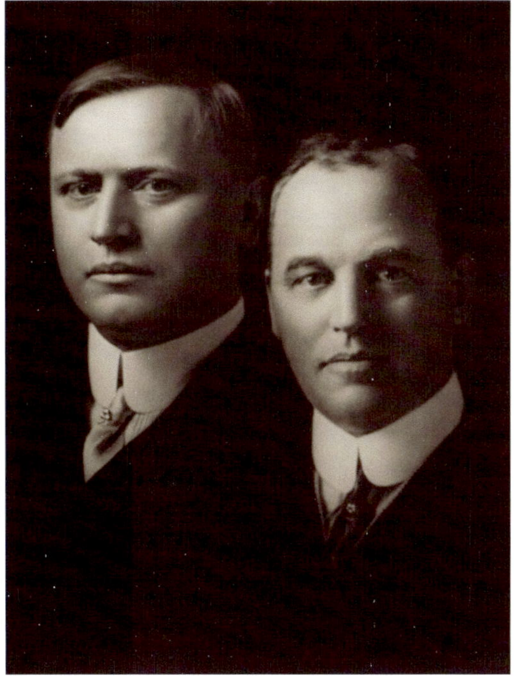

Fig. 28. John and Horace Dodge (Burton Historical Collection, Detroit Public Library, bh023763).

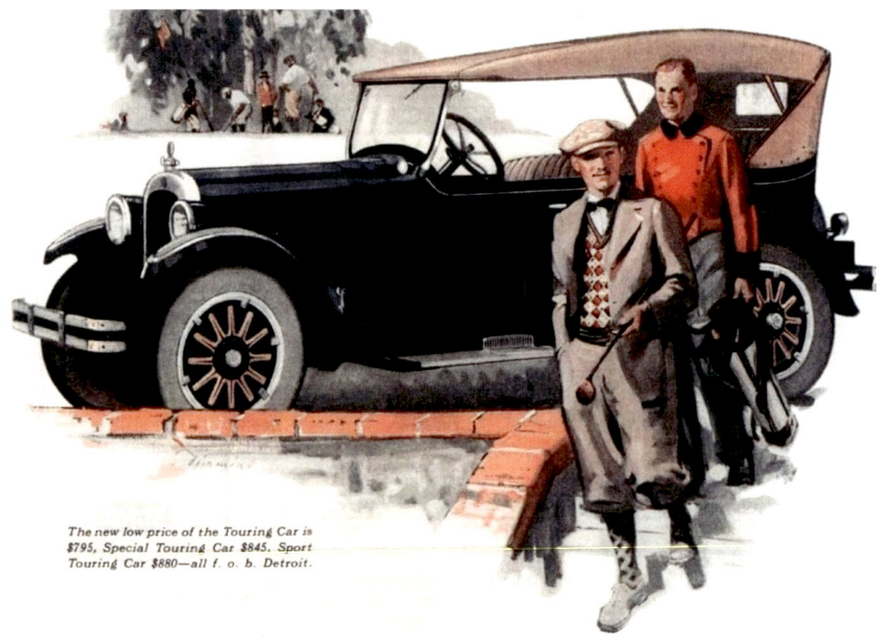

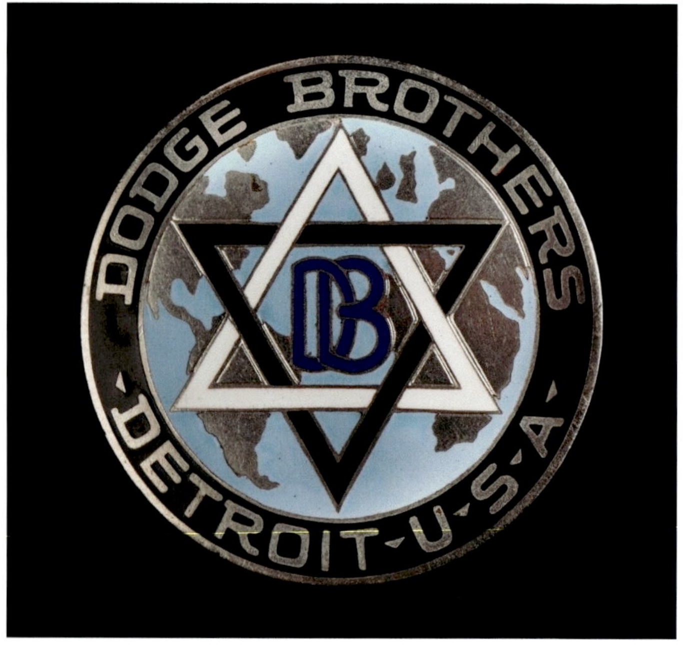

Fig. 29. Detail of a Dodge Brothers advertisement, May 1, 1926 (*Saturday Evening Post*).

Fig. 30. Dodge Brothers radiator emblem, 1920s (Division of Work and Industry, National Museum of American History, Smithsonian Institution).

Dodge cars were known for their toughness and dependability. As early as 1916, then–Brigadier General John J. Pershing selected a fleet of Dodge cars for his pursuit (over difficult terrain) of the Mexican revolutionary Pancho Villa. Dodge was also a major supplier of light-wheeled vehicles for the United States during World War I, as well as special four-wheel-drive trucks and utility vehicles for use as ambulances and command cars in World War II.[79]

Despite the success of the company, the Dodge brothers were often shunned by Detroit's high society. Their rowdy reputations had preceded them. When the tony Grosse Pointe Country Club denied Horace admission, he constructed an enormous mansion facing the club. Outfitted with a 12-car garage, Horace made sure he was a difficult and obstreperous neighbor, much to the annoyance of the country club.[80] The hard-driving reputations of the "bad boys" notwithstanding, the Dodges were also charitable and farsighted. They often gave anonymously to local organizations and donated substantial funds to the Detroit Symphony Orchestra. Some of their business practices were visionary for the times: a fully staffed medical clinic could be found on-site, and daily lunches, consisting of sandwiches and beer, were provided, courtesy of Dodge. Most unusual was a machine room known as "The Playpen," where employees could tinker after their shifts ended.[81]

The untimely death of both brothers put an end to their involvement in a remarkable business. John contracted influenza at the New York Auto Show in 1920, as did Horace, though the latter eventually made a partial recovery. With Horace by his side, John passed away at the Ritz-Carlton Hotel at the age of 55. After John's death, a delegation of workers requested that his body be temporarily transferred to the Dodge Brothers factory so that all 18,000 workers could have the opportunity to pay their respects to their employer.[82] Bereft and still weakened by influenza (and other medical problems), Horace died within the year. The "mechanic with the soul of a poet," Horace was likewise honored by thousands of workers, friends, and colleagues.[83]

By the time the University of Michigan received the gift of the Dodge sedan from Howard Bloomer in 1923, the brothers had been deceased for approximately three years. In 1925, the brothers' widows sold Dodge to an investment bank for $146 million in cash (at the time, the largest cash transaction in the United States).[84] In 1928, the Chrysler Corporation purchased the company for $170 million, making Chrysler the world's third-largest automaker.

The legendary dependability of the Dodge sedan and Graham Brothers truck is on ample display in a letter from Swain. After two years "on the road," Swain wrote to Dodge Brothers, Inc., not only to thank the company for the donation of the two vehicles but also to report on how the sedan and truck fared on their arduous journeys:

> These two motors have given the utmost satisfaction. They have been used in Belgium, France, Switzerland, Italy, Asia Minor, Tunisia, and Algeria. They have driven over everything from the best of highways to the most abject apologies for roads and even over open country with no roads at all. They have encountered mud, rocks, ledges, deserts, and mountain grades up to a height of almost 7,000 feet—grades so heavy as to compel the cars to run in "low" for miles, not to say hours. . . .
>
> Not even a spring leaf has broken—in fact no structural part of either car has even shown any sign of weakness . . . the replacements on the trucks have been two fan belts, two spark plugs, a small gasket or two, and some light bulbs—and the list of repairs for the sedan is hardly longer.
>
> . . . were I now planning anew two years more of equally severe and strenuous work, demanding cars of extreme sturdiness and responsibility, I would unhesitatingly specify the same two machines—a Dodge Bros. Type B Sedan, and a Graham Bros. One and One half Ton Truck with closed body.[85]

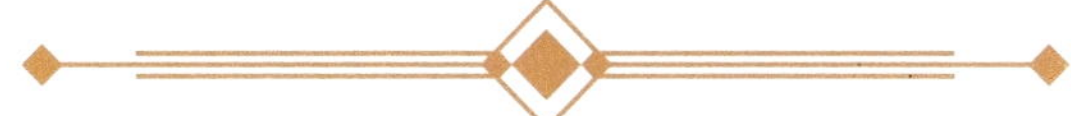

Archaeologists spend much of their lives describing, measuring, photographing, and drawing artifacts. In that vein, and for any gearhead who might read this book, I offer the specs of the two vehicles here (Side Cars 3 and 4).

Side Car 3: Standard Specs for 1924 Dodge Series Sedan B; Chassis No. 994204; Auto No. 68005

The 1924 Dodge Series Sedan B, which originally cost $1,250 ($21,400 in today's dollars), weighed in at 3,050 pounds with a wheelbase of 116 inches. The L-head engine had four cylinders with a displacement of 212 cubic inches. Producing 24 horsepower, it featured a 3⅞-inch bore by 4½-inch stroke, three main bearings, and splash and pressure lubrication. The 15-gallon fuel tank fed a Stewart updraft carburetor. A water pump and tubular radiator cooled the engine. A dry-disc clutch took up the power and fed a three-speed selective sliding gear transmission. Having rear-wheel drive, the Dodge featured a spiral bevel differential with a 4.54:1 ratio. The front and rear suspensions had semi-elliptic leaf springs. The steering gear was worm and wheel. The sedan was equipped with external contracting service brakes on the rear wheels, as well as internal expanding emergency brakes also on the rear wheels. It had artillery wheels, with spokes fitted together then bolted to a metal nave.[86]

Side Car 4: Standard Specs for Graham Brothers One-and-One-Half-Ton Truck with Panel Body; Chassis No. 975540; Auto No. A-37519

The Graham Brothers 1924 Model EB one-and-a-half-ton truck, which originally cost $1,325 ($23,000 in today's dollars), weighed in at 4,000 pounds (including cab and body weight) and featured a wheelbase of 124 inches. The L-head cast in block engine had four cylinders with a 3⅞-inch bore by 4½-inch stroke, putting out a generous 24 horsepower. The oiling consisted of a pump and splash feed, with an eccentric pump driven by spiral gears from the crankshaft. The cooling system had a capacity of 2¾ gallons, a tubular radiator, and a centrifugal pump. The carburetor was a special design with an automatic air valve and heated air intake for easier starting in all weather conditions. Fuel was delivered from a 12.5-gallon tank (with a gauge under the driver's seat). Power was delivered through a dry, multiple-disc-having, ball-thrust release mechanism clutch, which fed into a three-speed transmission. A 17-inch steering wheel drove a worm and wheel steering gear. The truck was fully equipped with both service and emergency internal expanding brakes. The front springs were alloy steel, semi-elliptic, 37 inches long, and 2 inches wide, with 9 leaves. The rear springs were alloy steel, double elliptical, and cantilevered on each side rail. The truck was also equipped with two head lamps with dimmer combination tail and rear signal lights and an instrument board light. The vehicle was sold under the Standard Truck Warranty adopted by the National Automobile Chamber of Congress.[87]

Part II

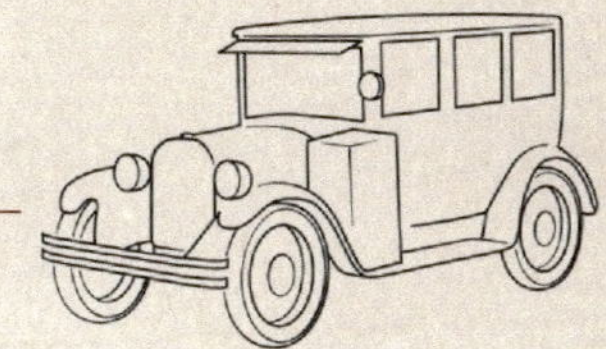

GEORGE R. SWAIN: THE MAN BEHIND THE LENS (1866–1947)

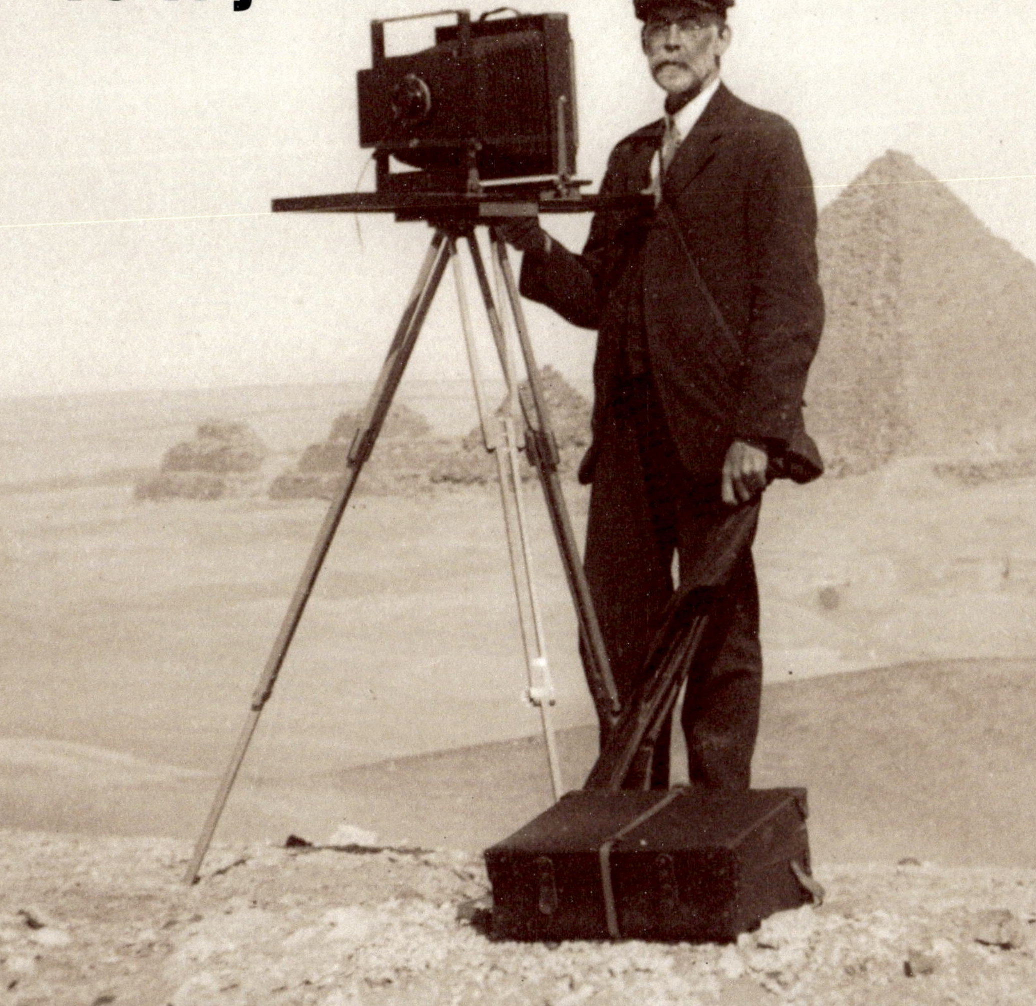

Chapter 4

GEORGE R. SWAIN: A BRIEF BIOGRAPHY

New Hampshire Beginnings and the Call of California

George Robert Swain (fig. 31) was born on July 15, 1866, in Meredith, New Hampshire, a small rural community.[88] His family came from modest means, and—as Swain later noted—he grew up "on an out of the way farm [with] few companions."[89] Little is known about his early education (fig. 32), although his primary schooling was described in his obituary as "catch-as-catch-can."[90] In his late teens and early 20s, Swain spent at least two years at what is now New Hampton School, a well-regarded Baptist-oriented college preparatory school founded in 1821.[91] An avid reader—well-grounded in authors such as Dickens, Hawthorne, Twain, and Hugo—he was, by his own admission, especially drawn to books on travel and adventure.[92]

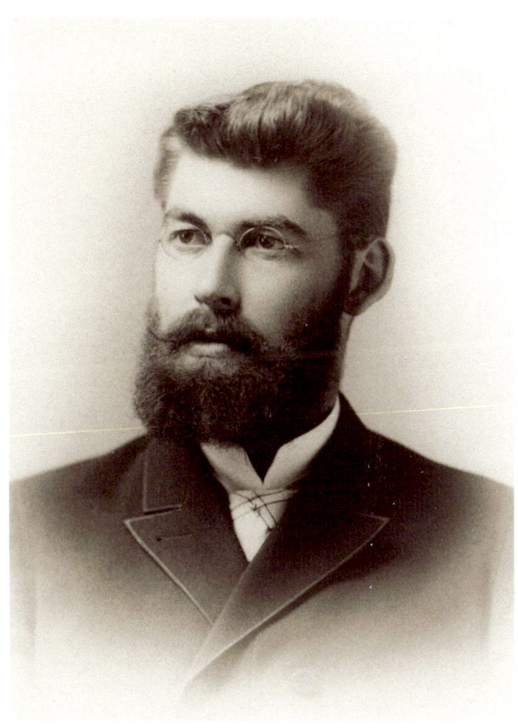

Fig. 31. Portrait of Swain as a young adult (HS19561, George Robert Swain Photographs and Papers, Bentley Historical Library, University of Michigan).

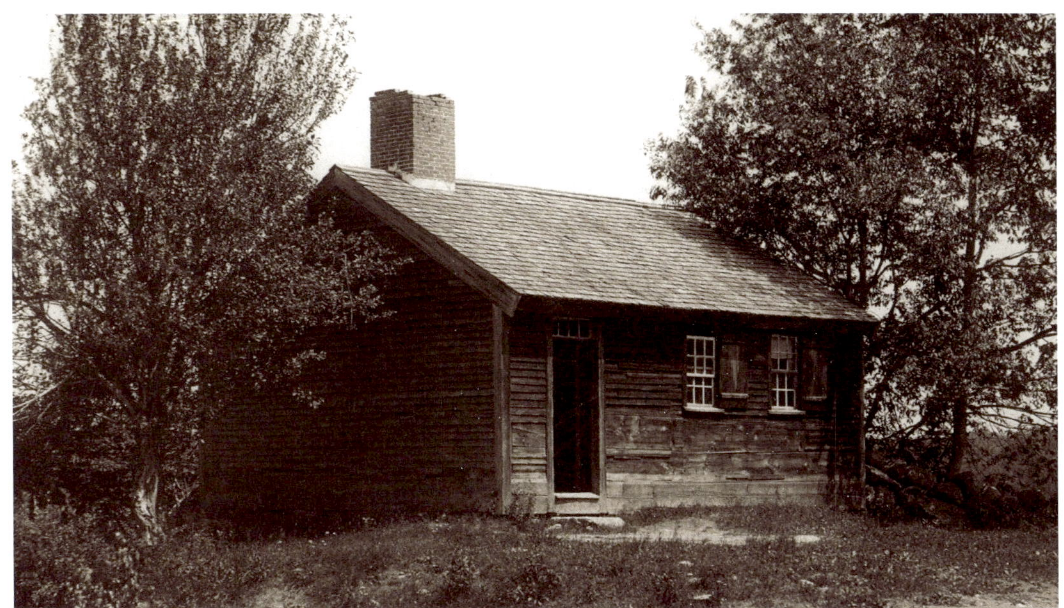

Fig. 32. Swain's schoolhouse in New Hampshire (HS19566, George Robert Swain Photographs and Papers, Bentley Historical Library, University of Michigan).

Once Swain completed secondary school—at the age of 20 or 21—he was eager to set out on his own. Options, however, were limited. In 1887, he began work at a foundry in Lakeport, New Hampshire, that produced heavy wood and iron machinery, including axles for steam locomotives and equipment for sawmills and gristmills. Although the work was hardly inspiring, his apprenticeship likely instilled a lifelong interest in all things mechanical. Casting about for potential professions, Swain began entertaining thoughts of a degree in mechanical engineering, possibly at Cornell University in upstate New York.[93]

In the spring of 1888, his life took an unexpected turn. His sister Edith, a teacher at a small local school, was offered the opportunity to teach English at another institution in Campton, New Hampshire. Although Edith declined the offer, Swain was able to fill the position, embarking on his first teaching experience. While Swain seemed to enjoy his newfound profession, life in New Hampshire held few enticements. Serendipitously, a distant cousin who lived in Fresno, California, came for a family visit soon after Swain started teaching. Long discussions ensued, inspiring Swain, who was reportedly bitten by the "California bug," to discover America's other coast. He was determined to find his way west, with hopes of studying for the teacher's exams. Borrowing $125 from a family member, Swain began the long trip to California in November 1888.[94] Soon after arriving, he started preparing for the teaching exams, which were set for December of that year.

The California exams were arduous, entailing nearly a week of testing. His long hours of study, however, were rewarded: he was one of only a small group of aspiring teachers awarded a county teaching certification. Credential in hand, Swain had broken his last five-dollar bill when he was offered a position at an ungraded school near Borden, a small, mostly Chinese community in central California.[95]

Swain's initial job in his new home paid $80 a week, $20 of which covered room and board. Allegedly, Swain bought his first gun that year (1889) to protect his pay. After only one year in Borden, Swain transferred to a school in Petrolia, a tiny town on the dramatic Pacific coast of northern California. Nearly two years later, Swain moved again, this time to the southern part of the state, teaching math and science at Ventura Union High School, where he became a much-beloved mentor (fig. 33).[96]

California spawned a number of interests for Swain—most importantly, his fascination with photography and his love of the outdoors (he became an inveterate hiker and "shot jackrabbits for the fun of it"[97]). Swain ordered his first camera and lens from a store in San Francisco, traveled to various parts of the state to take pictures, and ultimately started producing his first slides. He also began to have trouble with his eyes during his first year on the West Coast. George Pardee, an "oculist" in San Francisco—who would later become the governor of California—discovered a growth in Swain's eye (possibly caused by metal pieces from working at the foundry in New Hampshire). Part of the treatment included eye surgery—a cut into the edge of his iris and three stitches. Swain bought his first pair of glasses then and was told that he suffered from astigmatism. Given his later career as a photographer, Swain must have appreciated receiving successful treatment in his mid-20s.[98]

Despite the joys of teaching at Ventura and photographing the wonders of California, Swain felt that he needed more education if he intended to craft a meaningful life. He entertained thoughts of applying to Oberlin College in Ohio for a teaching degree rather

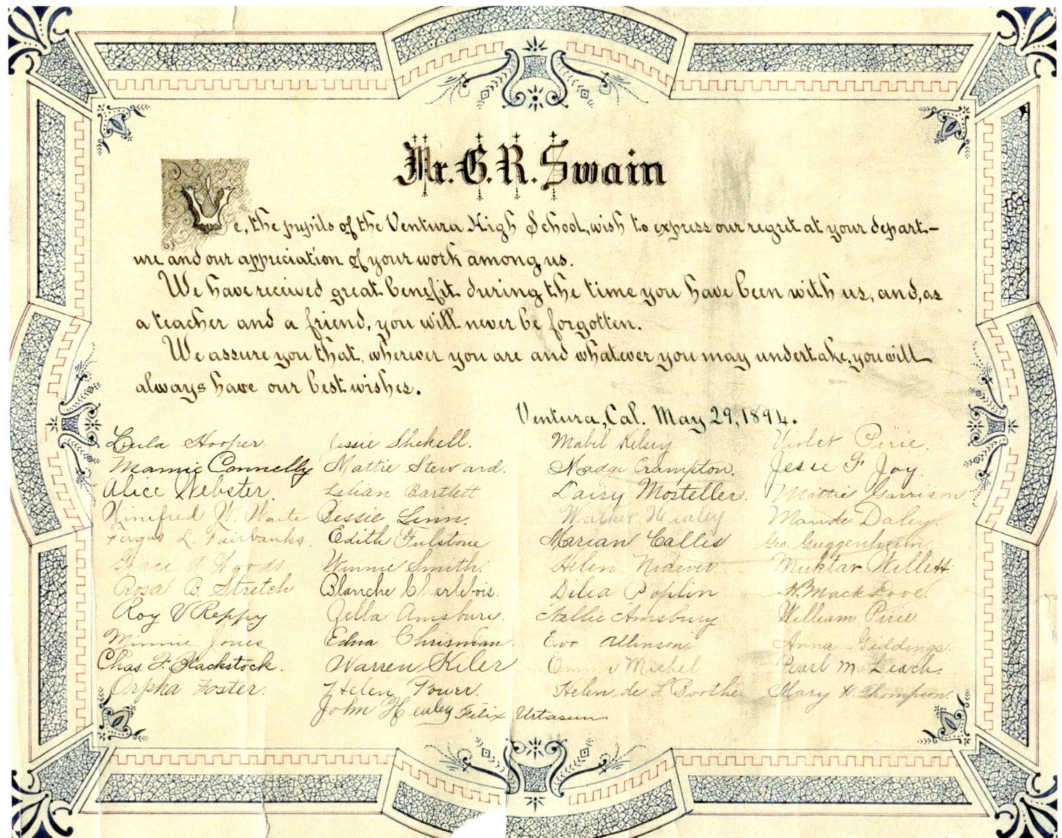
Mr. G. R. Swain

We, the pupils of the Ventura High School, wish to express our regret at your departure and our appreciation of your work among us.

We have received great benefit during the time you have been with us, and, as a teacher and a friend, you will never be forgotten.

We assure you that, wherever you are and whatever you may undertake, you will always have our best wishes.

Ventura, Cal. May 29, 1894.

Fig. 33. A thank-you from Swain's students at Ventura High School in California, 1894 (HS19558, George Robert Swain Photographs and Papers, Bentley Historical Library, University of Michigan).

than seek an engineering degree from Cornell University. Then, in 1893, on a bike trip north along the California coast, his bicycle broke down, forcing him to wait for a train in the small town of Paso Robles. According to family lore, the pharmacy clerk at the station told Swain that if he was serious about college, he should go to a "real school," such as the University of Michigan.[99]

Undergraduate Years at the University of Michigan

Swain heeded the clerk's advice: following nearly six years in California, he uprooted once again and, in 1894, at the age of 27, enrolled in the University of Michigan's College of Literature, Science, and the Arts. His decision to pursue a college degree did not come without some personal anguish. Swain had become engaged in the summer of 1891, while still in Ventura. His fiancée, however, would not consent to a long engagement: if Swain agreed to her wishes, it meant he would have to give up his dream of going to college. As Swain wrote many years later, "It was a bad wrench for me and pretty nearly set my world awry for the time being. I was east six months, returned to Ventura in Dec. '92, went through the rest of the school year on quinine and strychnine (doctor's orders), [and] stayed outdoors the summer of '93."[100] The quinine and strychnine were most likely prescribed for depression.

Swain's six-month leave of absence from teaching in Ventura seems to have been prompted by plans to further his studies and prepare himself for entry into college. He later described this period of his life in a letter to his wife, Edith: "I resigned, going east with the intention of studying, photographing, and some lecturing for a year (I had a lot of entrance work to make up), intending to enter college in '93."[101] However, perhaps due to his mental health struggles and recovery, he did not start at the University of Michigan until October of 1894.

Although the University of Michigan was known for its rowdy social life—no doubt boosted by its recent admission into the Big Ten athletic conference—Swain appears to have been a serious student. Initially interested in mathematics and physics, he found his calling in the middle of his second year, majoring in languages with a special concentration in Latin. It was at Michigan that he first met his mentor, Professor Kelsey. In 1897, at the age of 30, Swain received his AB and Teachers Diploma.

A small but intriguing selection of Swain's undergraduate essays are preserved in the Bentley Historical Library. They reflect assignments from classes on rhetoric and writing, and they offer insights into his interests and somewhat conservative view of the world. The topics are thoughtful and varied, ranging from the current state of universities, the dangers of intercollegiate sports, and immigration (he favored restrictions) to vivisection and the decidedly moral failings of cities such as San Francisco, with its "alluring haunts of sin."[102]

While Swain prided himself on careful, reflective writing as well as precise and logical thinking, not all of his essays adopted a sober tone. One charming story recounts the dangers of bicycle riding from the point of view of a small calf who lives in the countryside. As a postscript, Swain wryly adds that the reader should excuse the "discursiveness of the calf's narrative and occasional lapses into slang" since the calf had not taken the requisite English classes at the university.[103] A humorous poem, "The Possum Hunt," is a clever pastiche written in English and quasi-Latin about a determined dog's stymied efforts to catch a possum. An excerpt reads:

> For hic dog to make a turnus
> Circum self from stem to sternus...
> But cucurrit on, intentus
> On the track and on the scentus
> Till he treed a possum strongum
> In a hollow trunkum longum. . . .[104]

Perhaps his most puzzling and provocative piece is a short story entitled "Because of a Kodak." The work was published in the 1896–1897 volume of *The Inlander*, the University of Michigan's literary magazine for undergraduate students. Cofounded by the progressive educator and reformer John Dewey, the journal not only included creative writing pieces, such as poems and short stories, but also encouraged social commentary.

Swain's submission recounts the experience of a student photographer from "bluest Carolina blood," whose family is described as hardly able to forgive the emancipation of enslaved people during the Civil War. The protagonist in the story encounters, but cannot see, a fellow photographer working near him in a darkroom. They exchange a few comments, and he finds himself seduced by the melodious voice of this unseen woman. The main character is known by his best friends as paying little attention to a woman's physical beauty, instead basing his like or dislike on the quality of her voice. Barely able to concentrate, the man begins to suffer failing grades in his classes and returns often to the darkroom, hoping once again to hear the woman's siren call. He had found "the voice he had been waiting for all his life." At the close of the story, he finally has a chance to see her, as she exits the long corridor of the workroom. The last line reads, "He walked unsteadily back to the darkroom; something in his head had seemed to snap as his eyes fell on her face—for that face was plainly, unmistakably, of African extraction."[105] Interestingly, and perhaps in keeping with his growing engagement with photography, Swain draws the reader into the story via the power of sound, but it is the visual element that becomes the core of the episode.

The last line of Swain's short story invites questions. Was the protagonist simply startled or perhaps repelled, especially given his racist upbringing? Did Swain harbor racist attitudes of his own? And why did Swain write this piece—did he hope to instigate a discussion among fellow undergrads about the place of Black students at the university? Was he also asking a broader question—namely, what happens when you seemingly fall in love with a type of person you were raised to discount or despise?

Growing up in New Hampshire during the late 1800s, Swain had little or no exposure to people of color. The state's Black population was minuscule,[106] and his contact with African Americans at the University of Michigan would have been equally limited. Only three Black students were enrolled during his time there.[107]

Racial discrimination, segregation, and Jim Crow laws were rampant in late-1800s America. Swain's story was published soon after the Supreme Court's landmark decision of *Plessy v. Ferguson* in 1896. The ruling recognized that separate-but-equal facilities did not violate the 14th Amendment, thereby upholding the United States' stance on the legality of racial segregation. The Supreme Court decision was covered in the news, and the issues raised may have motivated Swain to write "Because of a Kodak."

At this point in his life—depending on what he meant to convey by the story's ending—Swain, like many of his contemporaries, possibly held racist opinions. We know that he favored restrictions on immigration and that he left his first job in California at a predominantly Chinese school after only one year of teaching. His resignation, however, appears to have had more to do with the quality of the school rather than its demographics, as well as an initial plan to reassess other opportunities in the state after his first year of teaching.

Swain's perspectives seem to have evolved later in life, as his travels exposed him to different cultures overseas. While he clearly expressed colonial views about some of the groups he encountered, he also wrote supportively about the difficulties confronting the region's underprivileged and underserved. In the final analysis, determining whether his story (published in what was seen then as a progressive journal) reflects Swain's own possible racist attitudes or was written to spark discussion about race in America—or both—remains a matter of debate.[108]

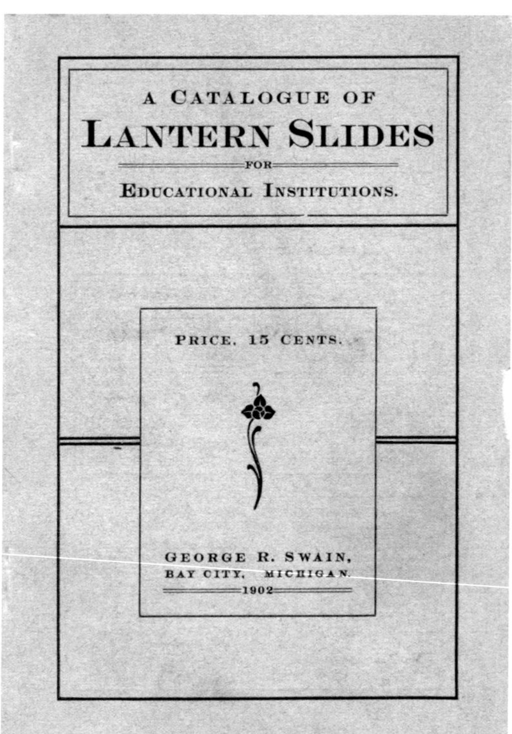

Figs. 34a–b. Front and back covers of Swain's catalog of lantern slides for sale to educators (HS19556, George Robert Swain Photographs and Papers, Bentley Historical Library, University of Michigan).

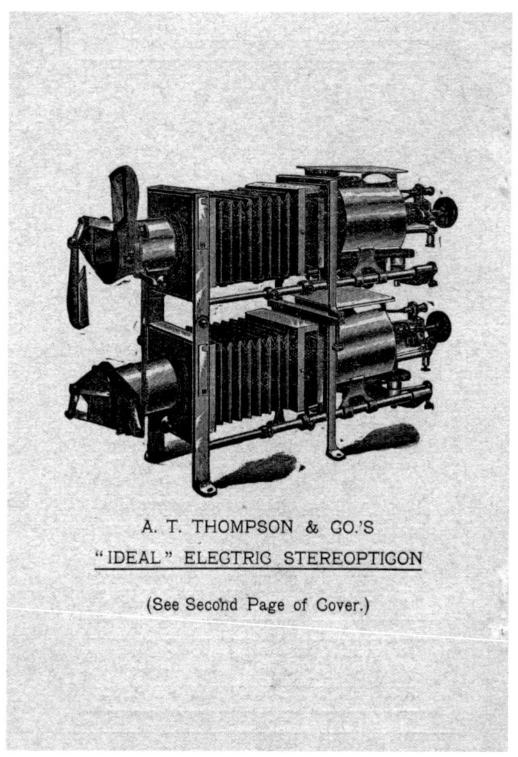

Leaving College and Returning to Ann Arbor

Once school was behind him, Swain was eager to start the next phase of his life. While classics and ancient history continued to remain enduring passions, he was deeply committed to teaching. His first job offer came from Great Falls High School in Montana, in the "wild and woolly west," as Swain wrote his mentor, Professor Kelsey.[109] He served for one year as principal (1897–1898) and also taught Latin and German. Unfortunately, Swain found himself caught in the crossfire of school politics, resigning in 1898 before he (as well as the school's superintendent) would have been dismissed. The details of the Montana debacle are murky, but Swain is damning in his assessment of the school: "This is the result of the meanest school fights that was [*sic*] ever put through by lying, scheming, and duplicity," he writes Kelsey. "I would not advise any decent man to have anything to do with the schools of Great Falls."[110]

As we will see, this was not the only time that Swain became ensnared in school politics. Because the University of Michigan archives contain mostly his perspective, it is hard to form an objective picture of each situation; we know, however, that Swain worked in a profession that was beset with power plays and cronyism during the late 1800s and early 1900s. Even Kelsey comments on the terrible conditions in American secondary schools, especially the unfair treatment of teachers.[111] Given the climate, it is easy to understand how a man of Swain's exacting standards, and perhaps occasional intransigence, could become a target.

Undeterred by the Montana fiasco, Swain accepted a position to teach Latin and ancient history at University School, a private school for boys in Cleveland, Ohio. His tenure there was again brief—not more than two years (from 1898 to 1900)—but this time not caused by unsavory school politics. Rather, there were other reasons, not least that he was consigned to a men's dormitory, precluding the opportunity to live with his new bride, Edith, whom he married in 1900 (see p. 35). Just as importantly, his letters suggest a sense of dissatisfaction, primarily because he fears that some of his "cherished ideals of teaching are liable to vanish" if he were to remain at the school. Swain had long valued the idea of helping young people from less fortunate families, of guiding "the boys and girls that have to 'hustle' for what they get." In Cleveland, however, most of his pupils came from wealthy families, and he worried about becoming "a lower sort of teacher than I had hoped to be."[112] That said, Swain appears to have been an outstanding educator and administrator, claiming a long list of fervent supporters, who characterized him as a man of the "highest ideal . . . conscientious, and possessed of unusual power of organization and administration," "unquestionable integrity," and "sterling ability."[113]

A highlight of Swain's Cleveland years was a six-week summer trip in 1899 to Europe—his first overseas travel—paid for by *Century Magazine*. He covered 2,000 miles by bicycle through France, Switzerland, Belgium, Holland, and Germany, photographing Caesar's battlefields. Swain hoped to turn his photographs into a publication, as well as a set of slides that he could sell to teachers. While the publication never materialized, he produced an impressive collection of slides that became the basis for *A Catalogue of Lantern Slides for the Use of High Schools, Academies, Colleges, and Universities* (figs. 34a–b). His catalog continued to grow over the years, eventually listing over 2,000 slides, primarily of the ancient Greek and Roman worlds. For years, these slides and others he produced on request provided a small, ongoing income stream to supplement his modest teacher's salary (fig. 35).

The Cleveland years were also marked by another highlight: in 1900, Swain married Edith Louise Rice (fig. 36), who had attended Ventura High School in California when Swain had taught there.[114] According to family notes, she spent the last two years of her college education at the University of Michigan, graduating a year after Swain, in 1898. She was 27 when they married (Swain was 34), and they would have three children, Frances, Robert, and Edwin (figs. 37–38), two of whom occasionally traveled with their father on overseas expeditions. Like her husband, Edith Swain had an enduring interest

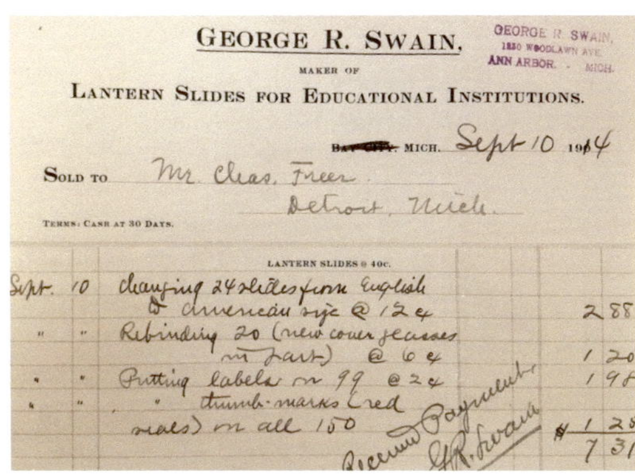

GEORGE R. SWAIN,

MAKER OF

LANTERN SLIDES FOR EDUCATIONAL INSTITUTIONS.

GEORGE R. SWAIN, 1230 WOODLAWN AVE. ANN ARBOR, MICH.

MICH. Sept 10 1914

SOLD TO Mr. Chas. Freer

Detroit, Mich.

TERMS: CASH AT 30 DAYS.

LANTERN SLIDES @ 40c.

Sept.	10	changing 24 slides from English & American size @ 12¢	2 88
"	"	Rebinding 20 (new cover glasses in part) @ 6¢	1 20
"	"	Putting labels on 99 @ 2¢	1 98
"	"	" thumb-marks (red ovals) on all 150	1 25
			7 31

Received Payment G. R. Swain

Fig. 35. George R. Swain invoice for a lantern slide order, September 10, 1914 (George Robert Swain Photographs and Papers, Bentley Historical Library, University of Michigan).

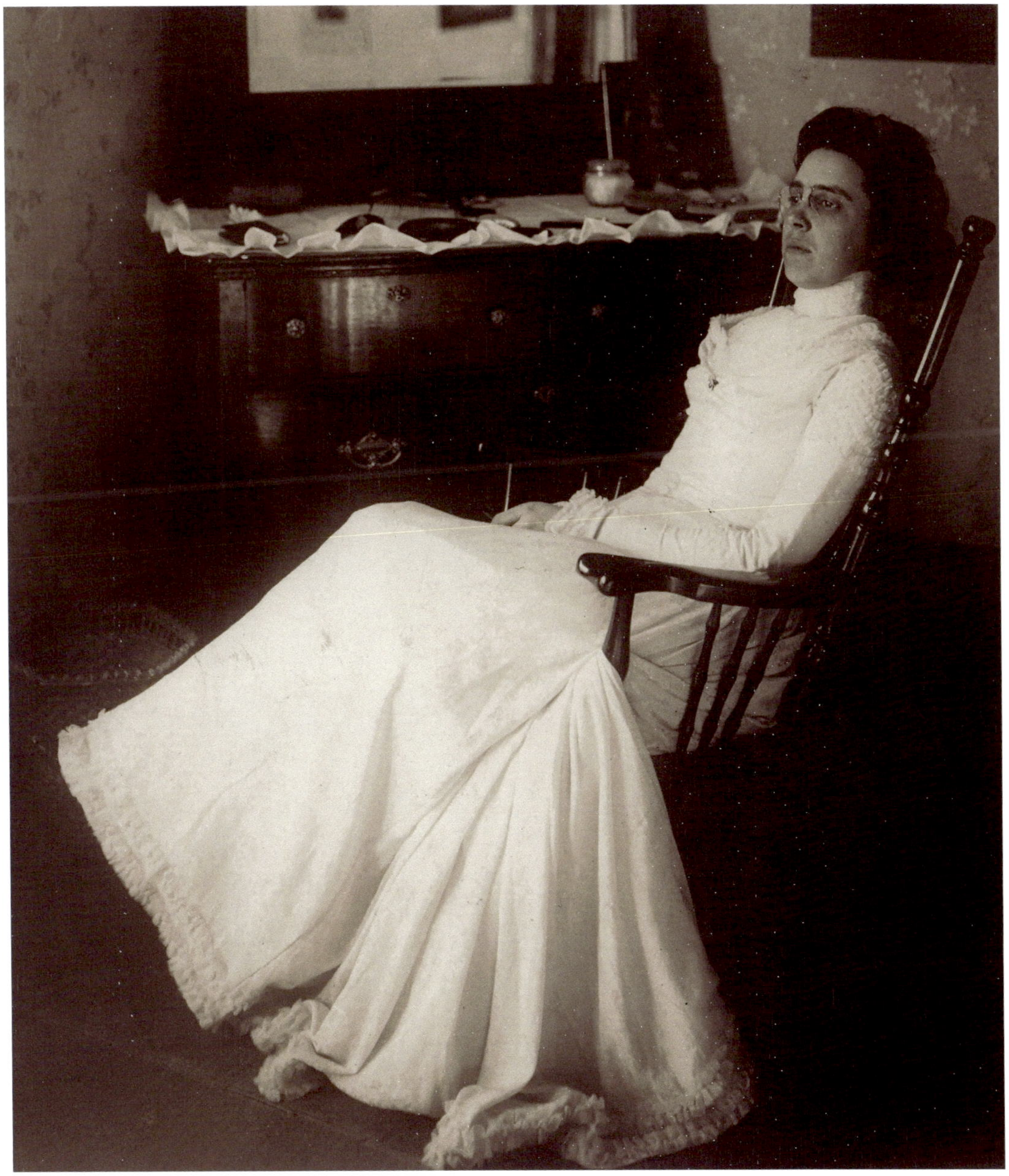

Fig. 36. Edith Louise Rice, George R. Swain's wife (Swain Family Archive).

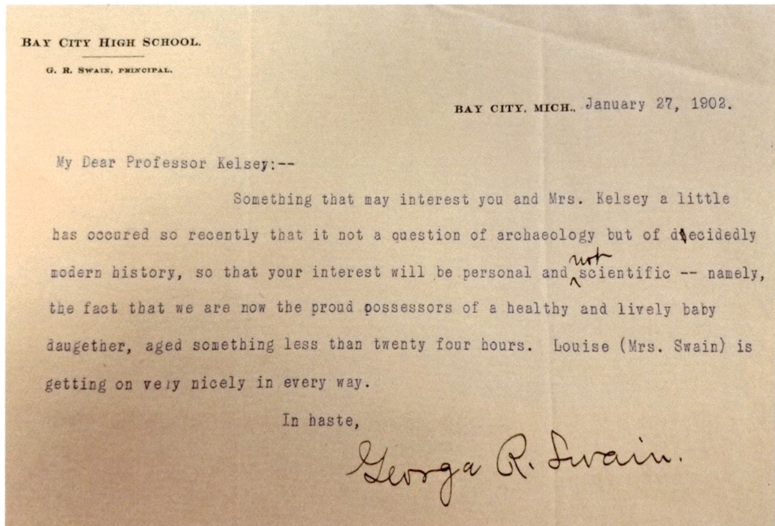
BAY CITY HIGH SCHOOL.
G. R. SWAIN, PRINCIPAL.

BAY CITY, MICH., January 27, 1902.

My Dear Professor Kelsey:--

Something that may interest you and Mrs. Kelsey a little has occured so recently that it not a question of archaeology but of decidedly modern history, so that your interest will be personal and not scientific -- namely, the fact that we are now the proud possessors of a healthy and lively baby daugether, aged something less than twenty four hours. Louise (Mrs. Swain) is getting on very nicely in every way.

In haste,

George R. Swain.

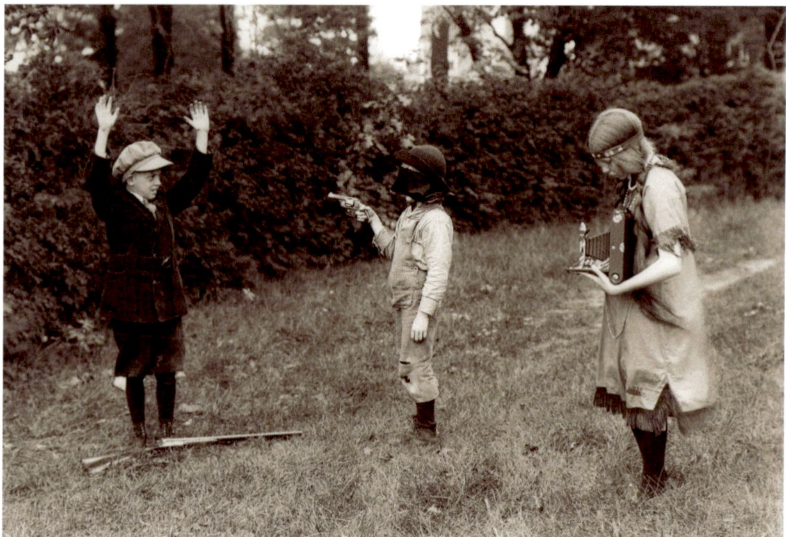

Fig. 37. Swain's note to Francis W. Kelsey, announcing the birth of his first child, January 27, 1902 (George Robert Swain Photographs and Papers, Bentley Historical Library, University of Michigan).

Fig. 38. Swain's three children, Robert, Edwin, and Frances, with Frances taking a photograph (HS19564, George Robert Swain Photographs and Papers, Bentley Historical Library, University of Michigan).

in education and would become head of the kindergarten classes at Ann Arbor's First Congregational Church.

Swain's letters often mention his family; he wrote regularly to his wife and daughter during his travels (letters addressed specifically to his sons were rare). His missives to Edith are filled with professions of love and romantic poems inspired by her. He worries about his young daughter's struggles with self-confidence, encourages her schoolwork, and assures her that he likes her "just as you are" when she broods about not attracting the attention of boys (fig. 39). Even the family cat, Caruso, deserves a line or two: "Too bad Caruso is no more—*resquiecat in pace* [with *cat* underlined]. I suppose sooner or later Ned [Edwin, Frances's brother] will annex another."[115] Edith's death in 1939 at the age of 66 devastated Swain and seems to have induced some degree of depression. His granddaughter, Elizabeth Babcock, remembers a dour and imposing man who rarely laughed—a far cry from the husband and father who wrote charming letters home, filled with humor and erudition.[116]

During part of his first year of marriage (1900), Swain was without a source of income. His letters to Kelsey speak of his concerns, growing dismay, debt, and the deteriorating health of his parents, who still lived in New Hampshire. But by 1901, Swain was offered a position as principal at East Side High School in Bay City, Michigan, where he would remain for nearly a decade (1901–1911). The high school was large—with over 500 students—and Swain appears to have enjoyed many productive years until another controversy struck, this time a power struggle between Swain and the superintendent. Swain was committed to maintaining the highest standards for the school and his students, even if that required some difficult measures. Eventually, he crossed swords with the superintendent, who wanted to lower the bar Swain had set. As the incident became fodder for the local papers, Swain was forced to take a public stance and penned a long letter in the *Bay City Times*.[117] Although he was eventually vindicated, he was no longer comfortable remaining at the school and decided that, if possible, it would be best to move closer to his ailing parents.

Good school positions near New Hampshire, however, were hard to find, so Swain ultimately accepted a principal's position at the Lockport Township High School in Lockport, Illinois (1911–1913). Once again, Swain became embroiled in school politics and eventually resigned. He recounts the details in a long letter to Kelsey: he was falsely accused, among other things, of having an outside job, not showing sufficient interest in the school, and not effectively disciplining his students. Most interesting is Swain's assessment of the social circumstances of life at the school: "I have been a complete social failure," he writes on May 17, 1913. "I do not dance or play cards (the standard social diversions here), and I do not happen to be a Mason, nor do I belong to the strongest church in town—Methodist."[118] Ever his supporter, Kelsey writes to buoy Swain's spirits: "I did not suppose such barbarism would be found in a community of any size near Chicago. It is a hard experience, yet you are too much of a man to be discouraged by it."[119]

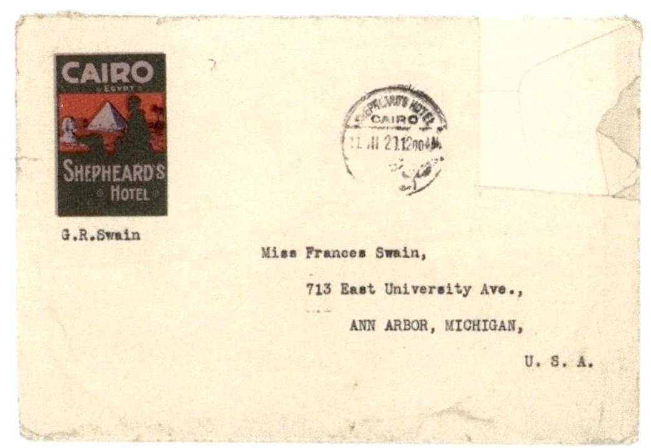

Fig. 39. Envelope from one of Swain's letters to his daughter, Frances, sent from Cairo, Egypt, 1920 (Swain Family Collection).

Financially stressed and worried about his parents' failing physical health, as well as his mother's increasingly poor psychological state, Swain decided that, at the least, he should seek employment in a town he knew well and where his children would receive a good education. In 1913, he moved back to Ann Arbor with his family. Hanging over his head, however, was the difficult decision of whether his mother should remain at home in New Hampshire (mostly under his sister's care) or be moved to an "asylum." Swain's mother appears to have battled bouts of both depression and anxiety. When Swain was a child, he often heard her fret that the family would starve and that she would be the cause. And at one point, she allegedly took to her bed for two or three years. Those were no doubt difficult years for young Swain.[120]

At nearly 47 years of age, Swain was $2,000 in debt and had paid out several thousand dollars over the years to underwrite his parents' care. Given the grim situation, Swain set up shop as a commercial photographer and explored teaching possibilities at the University of Michigan.[121] Fortunately, Swain was hired—most likely with Kelsey's help—as a university photographer in 1913, finished his master's degree (which he had begun in 1900), and was given a small stipend to teach Latin in 1914. For more than two decades, starting in 1922, Swain and his wife also managed Kamp Kairphree, a summer camp for girls that was located in northern Michigan. The camp focused on education, nature, arts and crafts, dance, music, swimming, and canoeing (fig. 40).[122]

Swain had finally found his footing in Ann Arbor. His happiest years were spent there, busy photographing, teaching, raising his children, running the summer camp, and offering a series of lectures to the public on his archaeological travels and work overseas (figs. 41a–b). He served as the university's official photographer for 34 years, until his death in 1947, at the age of 80. His photographs—numbering in the tens of thousands—are an exceptional trove of information. They cover not only his trips with Professor Kelsey overseas but also subsequent archaeological expeditions, university events, slides for lectures, and early 20th-century images of Ann Arbor and other Michigan locations.

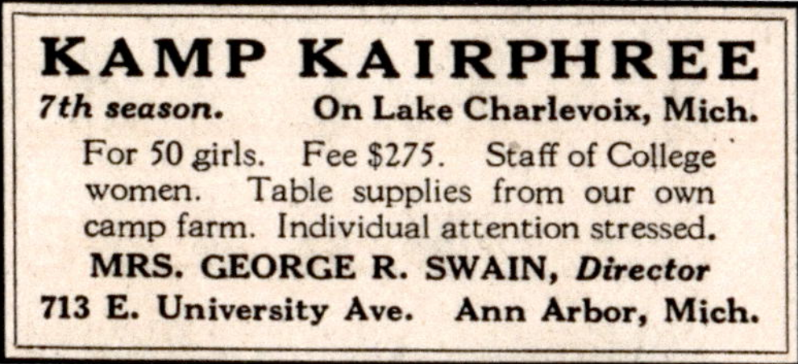

Fig. 40. Kamp Kairphree advertisement (George Robert Swain Photographs and Papers, Bentley Historical Library, University of Michigan).

Swain's commitment to education, his curiosity about the ancient world, and his love of archaeology, travel, and family helped form a strong bond with Kelsey—a bond that lasted until the final day of his mentor's life. Swain was the last person to talk to Kelsey before he passed away on Saturday, May 14, 1927. Surrounded by papers and books in his hospital room, Kelsey wanted to discuss plans for a five-year research program with Swain.

Figs. 41a–b. Brochure for Swain's lecture series, *Travel with Mr. Swain from the Danube to the Nile!* (HS19647, Kelsey Museum of Archaeology Papers, Bentley Historical Library, University of Michigan).

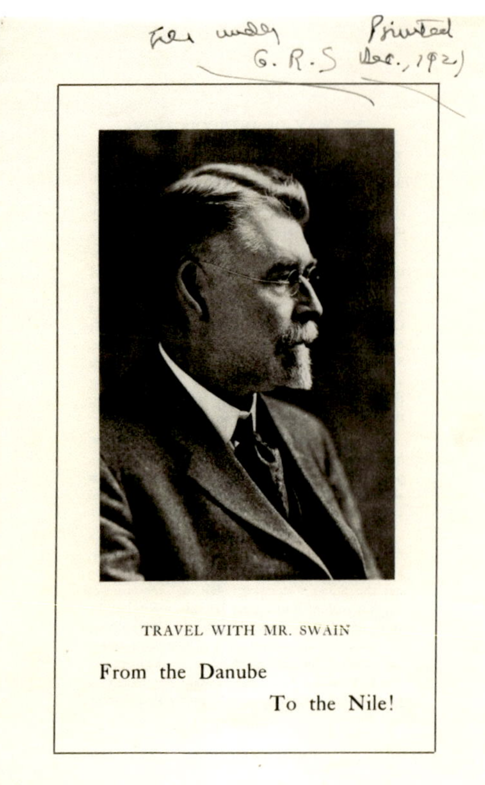

BY WAY OF INTRODUCTION

MR. GEORGE R. SWAIN (A. B., A. M., University of Michigan) is a member of the staff of the Latin Department, and is also one of the extension lecturers, of the University of Michigan.

Before his present connection with this institution, Mr. Swain spent twenty years in public school work (chiefly as a high school principal) in New Hampshire, Ohio, Michigan, Illinois, Montana, and California — so he knows the northern part of Uncle Sam's Farm as most men know their own State. Sent over by one of the leading magazines, he rode a bicycle 2,000 miles in Western Europe during the summer of 1899, studying and photographing the sites of Cæsar's Gallic War.

From both the technical and artistic standpoints, his work in photography is unusual. His skill in photographing old manuscripts is well known, even abroad, while graduate work in Fine Arts has added cultivated judgment to natural talent.

He is a man of commanding physique — "six feet four from the top down," — of strong personality, a keen observer with a Yankee knack of picking out the things that count. His easy command of English enables him to speak informally but fluently. A broad education, varied experience in teaching, unusual skill with a camera, live interest in things and especially in people, — these are some of the factors that enabled Mr. Swain to make the most of a year's travel in Europe, Asia Minor, Syria, Palestine, and Egypt.

After their talk, Swain left his colleague's bedside at 11 a.m.—just moments before his cherished friend and mentor slipped into a coma. An hour later, Kelsey died, with his son, Easton, by his side.[123]

For many years after Kelsey's death, Swain continued to work overseas on projects that Kelsey had initiated. No doubt his dear companion would have been pleased with Swain's ongoing work, which helped further Kelsey's pioneering vision of archaeology and the classical world at the University of Michigan.

Chapter 5

SWAIN AND HIS CAMERAS

Most of us take for granted the ability to create images with our smartphones. We simply point and shoot. Today, anyone can be a photographer, turning digital snapshots into refrigerator magnets and small keepsakes, online albums, or large-format pictures to hang on walls like fine art. We are bombarded daily by a virtual gallery of Internet photographs where, in an instant, the fleeting becomes fixed.

When Swain became interested in photography during the last decade of the 19th century, nothing was instantaneous; indeed, taking a photograph was anything but a passing event. Unlike today, only a small number of cameras and techniques were available to him. The "dry plate" was popular (a glass plate coated with a gelatin emulsion of silver bromide), and the first Kodak, which revolutionized photography, had just been invented (see p. 43). As the century turned, more camera types and methods came on the market, but Swain was a staunch advocate of large-format view cameras (with glass plates) for most of his archaeological images (fig. 42), preferring the Kodak for more spontaneous photographs. He used both during his expeditions with Kelsey from 1919 to 1926 (figs. 43–44). Starting in 1904, an ingenious panoramic camera—known as a Cirkut camera—was manufactured, which Swain also took on his travels from 1924 to 1925 (see figs. 50a–b, pp. 43–45).

During his earliest ventures into photography, Swain often turned his lens toward local landscapes. Given his passion for hiking and canoeing, it is not surprising that he found inspiration in nature. Outdoor photography helped him develop, as he writes in one essay, "a strong liking for pictures, and sharp observation in noting effects in light and shade—I might almost say it has opened a new world of enjoyment to me."[124] This interest in light and shade would become a hallmark of his later images (figs. 45–47).

Swain had a meticulous eye, which was essential for maintaining proper and detailed records. He was well aware of how critical photographic documentation was for archaeology, especially given the destructive nature of the discipline—each layer that was uncovered was ultimately destroyed by digging deeper into the underlying level. His photographic work, therefore, was an indispensable part of the mission and, in many cases, remained the only visual record of contexts and finds that would be gradually obliterated.

Whether Swain was photographing inscriptions, architectural elements, manuscripts, papyri, or artifacts in situ, his images needed to be crisp, informative, and filled with details

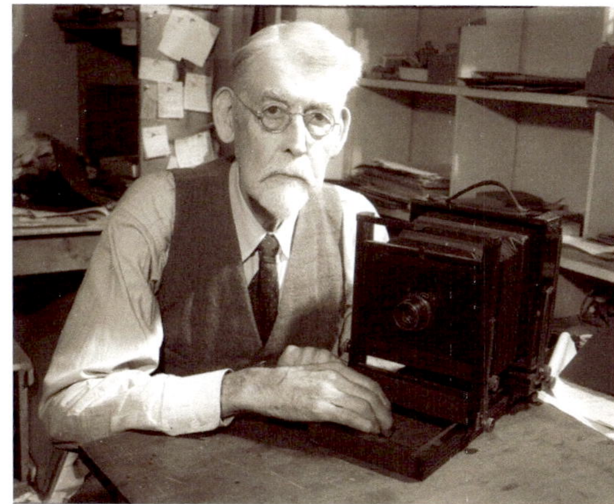

Fig. 42. George R. Swain with one of his cameras, October 1945 (courtesy of the *Ann Arbor News*.).

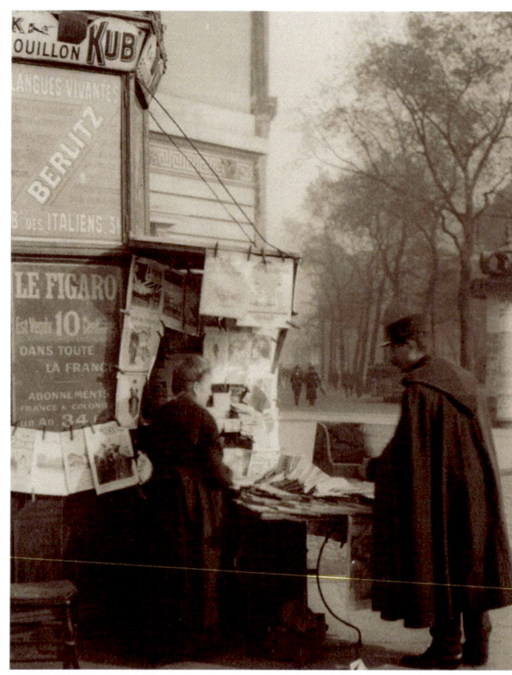

Fig. 43. A French newsstand operated by a woman in Paris, France, October 12, 1919 (Kelsey Museum neg. no. KS 014.09).

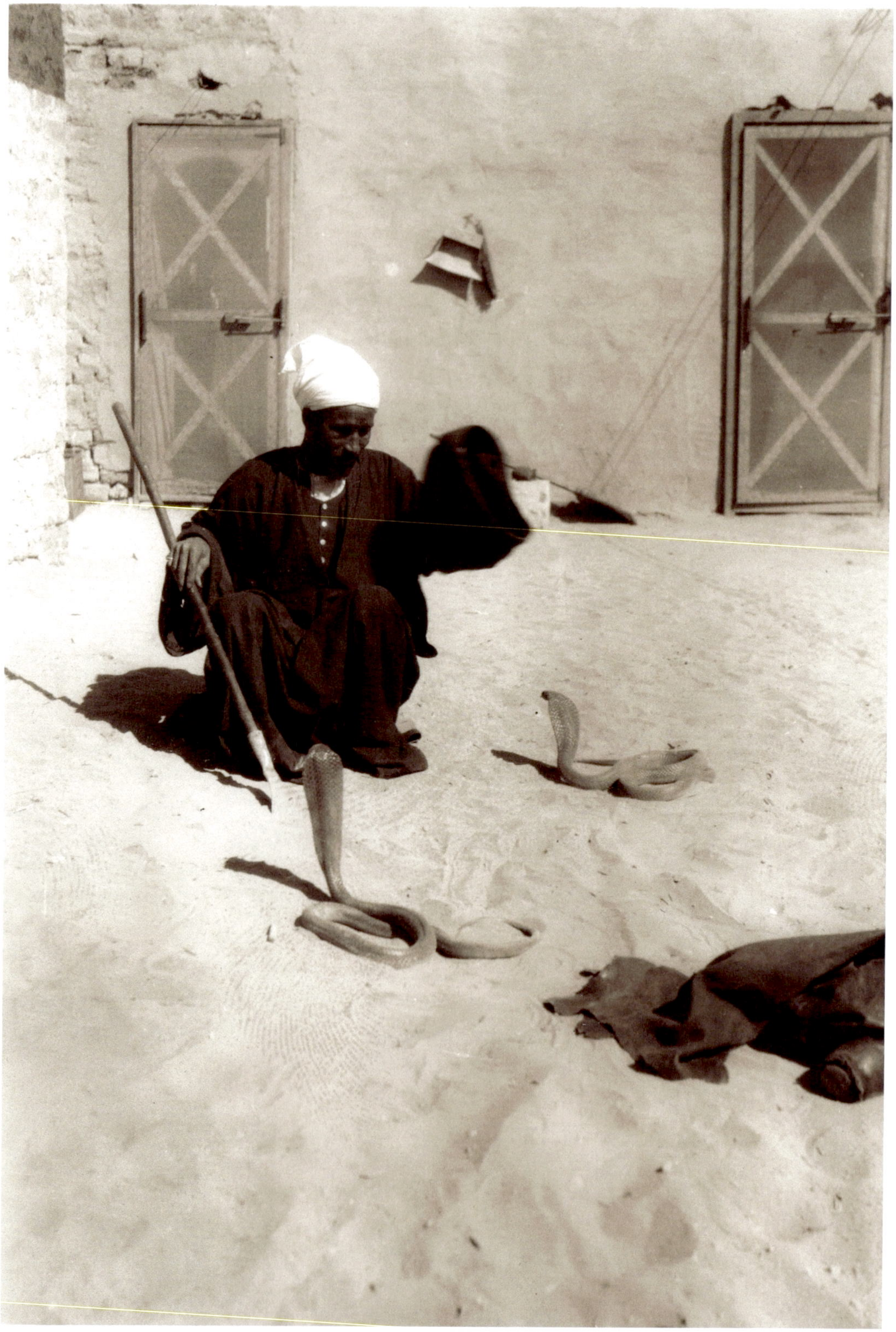

Fig. 44. "The snake charmer at Kom Aushim. The charmer later died from a cobra bite," Karanis, Egypt, 1920s (Kelsey Museum neg. no. 0652).

that could be studied later by specialists who were not on-site. Since many objects uncovered during these campaigns remained in the host country, Swain's photographs served as vital and irreplaceable sources of information for scholars. His ethnographic photos display the same attention to detail. Although they were not intended to be studied by scholars, they, too, provide an invaluable form of documentation.

This precision and attention to minutiae was typical not only of his photographs but also of his recordkeeping: many of his images have long and informative captions. Swain's proclivity for exactitude appears almost comical when he writes to his wife about riding the "lusso" (deluxe) rail line from Rome to Paris, a train that Kelsey cautioned was "dangerously fast":

> I never travelled 903 miles (distance Rome to Paris) in greater comfort. The total time scheduled is 28 hours and 25 minutes. Subtracting the total amount of stops, the actual running rate averages 36 miles an hour, and they maintain a remarkable even average speed. From Bourg into Paris, some 280 miles, the train halted twice for few seconds at block signals, and made but two station stops. In Italy the average of 22 stops at 6½ minutes each, and of 7 stops in all in France, the average is but 3½ minutes each. This looks pretty good railroading even to an American. I forgot to say that the dining car service was beyond criticism.[125]

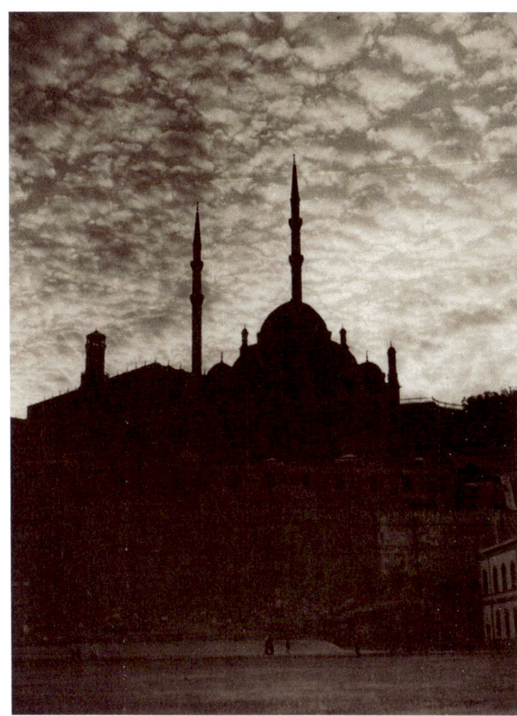

Fig. 45. The Mosque of Ali seen in the morning, Cairo, Egypt, March 28, 1920 (Kelsey Museum neg. no. KS 161.01).

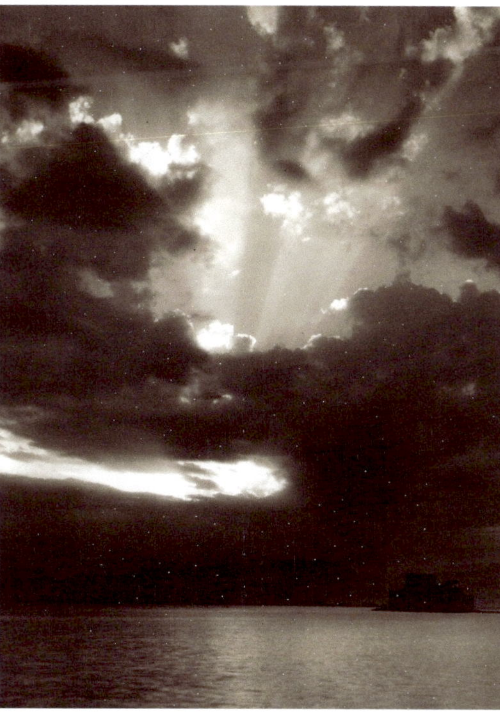

Fig. 46. The Gulf of Argos as seen at sunset, Nauplia, Greece, August 18, 1925 (Kelsey Museum neg. no. 8.0401).

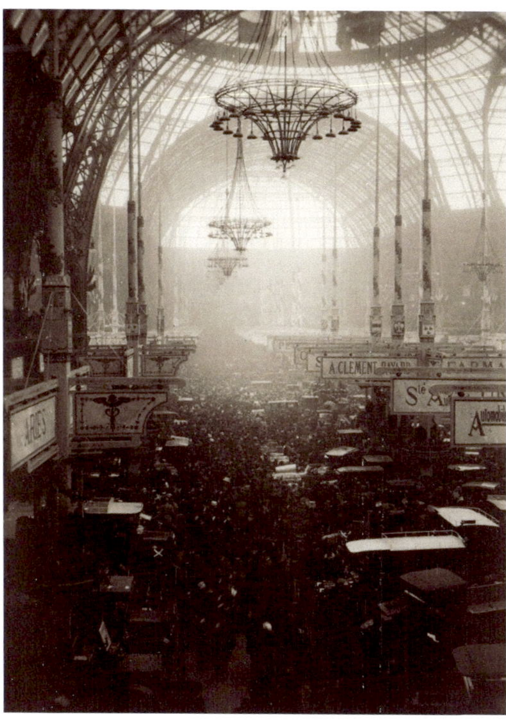

Fig. 47. The auto show at the Grand Palais exhibition hall, Paris, France, October 13, 1919 (Kelsey Museum neg. no. KS 015.09).

The Science and Art of Swain's Photographs

For most of his professional career with Professor Kelsey, Swain favored several types of large-format cameras: a 5 by 7, an 8 by 10, and a 7 by 11 (the numbers refer to inches). He also used an 11 by 14 that was especially well suited for photographing ancient manuscripts. These cameras produced substantial-size negatives resulting in sharp images with high resolutions. In Swain's day, the large-format cameras consisted of two panels—one in the front and one in the back—connected by lightproof bellows. The front panel held the lens, while the back panel held a ground glass plate onto which the image was set (fig. 48). Cameras, plates, and lenses formed only a part of his overall photographic assemblage, however. His work required a large, dark cloth to drape over his head while he composed the photograph, light meters to establish exposure, and tripods to steady these hefty machines. Sturdy tripods were particularly vital, and Swain, ever the tinkerer, delighted in reporting to his son one of his latest photographic inventions: "I have concocted a tripod for the 8 x 10 that is rigid, light, and strong enough to sit on, and that should last about 10 years. It is really a cine-kodak tripod with part of the top taken off and a regular tripod head substituted."[126]

Given the weight of the cameras, multiple glass plates, and requisite paraphernalia, Swain depended on the Dodge sedan and Graham Brothers truck to serve as oversize storage units for his "photographic family," proving the vehicles' value as more than just transportation. Traveling between home base and archaeological sites was often a Sisyphean task, maneuvering along trails or precarious mountainsides. In those instances, Swain

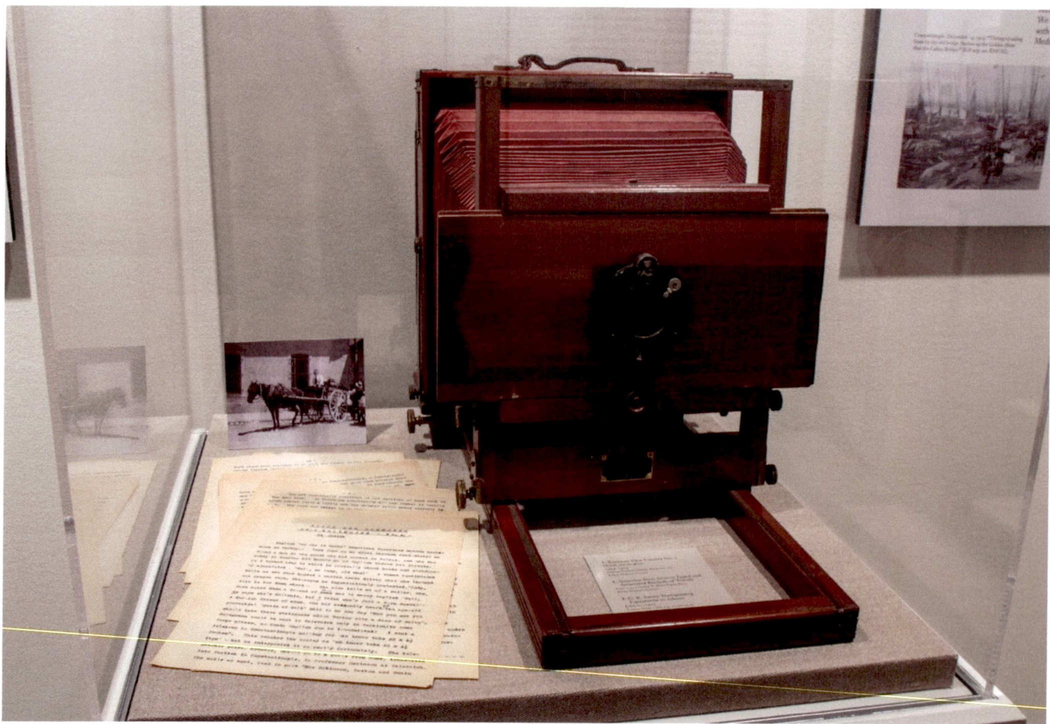

Fig. 48. One of Swain's glass-plate cameras, Eastman View Camera No. 2, on display with typed records of his travels and one of his photographs (Kelsey Museum Archives).

commandeered mules to transport the bulky equipment from his archaeological residence to off-the-beaten-track sites (fig. 49).

Unlike today, the lens in Swain's large-format cameras formed an inverted image onto the glass plate. The photographer, therefore, composed his image upside down. At one point, Swain wrote to his family about the confusion of his Turkish assistant, who had discovered the topsy-turvy world of modern photography: "I have an assistant to help carry camera stuff—named Hassan (accent last syllable) so I am doing little lugging and don't expect to. I let him look through the ground glass once this morning—at first his head came out pop-eyed, then looked again, then held his hands one above the other, then flipped them over to indicate things were down side up, and grinned for five minutes."[127]

In addition, Swain traveled with the less cumbersome Kodak for more impromptu shots. The Kodak camera was lighter and more portable, used paper rolls rather than glass negatives, and had a fixed focus. The first Kodak, invented in 1888, changed the face of amateur photography. These early box cameras came loaded with 100 exposures in a roll, and when the roll was finished, the camera was mailed back to the factory, reloaded, and returned to the customer while the old exposures were processed. The company's slogan boasted, "You press the button, we do the rest."[128]

The rolls that Swain brought with him did not include the standard 100 exposures but instead had 12 exposures each, likely making it easier to keep track of and ultimately develop images in small batches. The Kelsey Museum archives include 3,915 Kodak captions by Swain, but only 2,985 of the actual photographs exist (there are no surviving negatives). All the Kodak images were taken during Swain's travels with the university expeditions from September 4, 1919, to August 28, 1926, and a number of them—labeled with the prefix KS, standing for Kodak Swain—are reproduced in this book.

Swain also owned a Cirkut, one of the earliest rotating panoramic cameras. Manufactured from 1904 to 1949, it could produce large, full-scale, full-circle panoramic images by pivoting horizontally along a vertical axis. The final images could be quite impressive, varying in length from 3 to 20 feet. Although Swain's captions from the panoramas include 111 entries, only 78 images currently exist in the Kelsey Museum archives. They were all taken in 1924 and 1925, during his travels to Europe, the Mediterranean, and North Africa (figs. 50a–b).

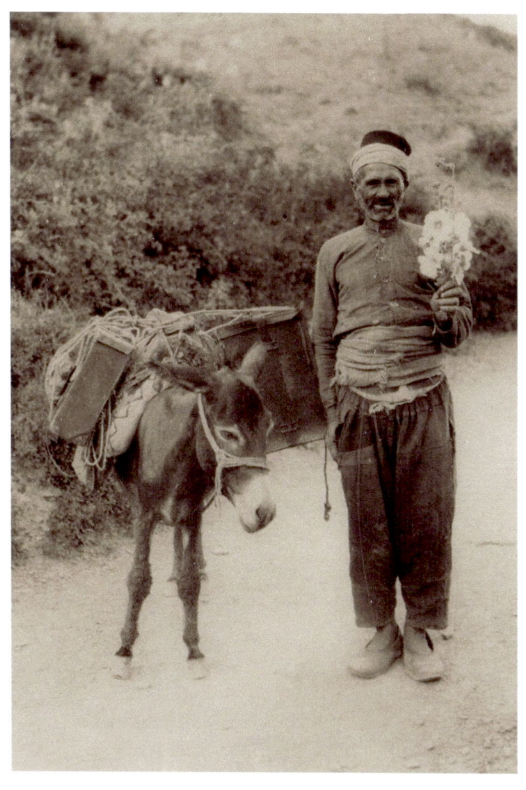

Fig. 49. Omar—holding wild pink hollyhocks—and his donkey with camera equipment, Antioch, Turkey, July 12, 1924 (Kelsey Museum neg. no. KS 279.05).

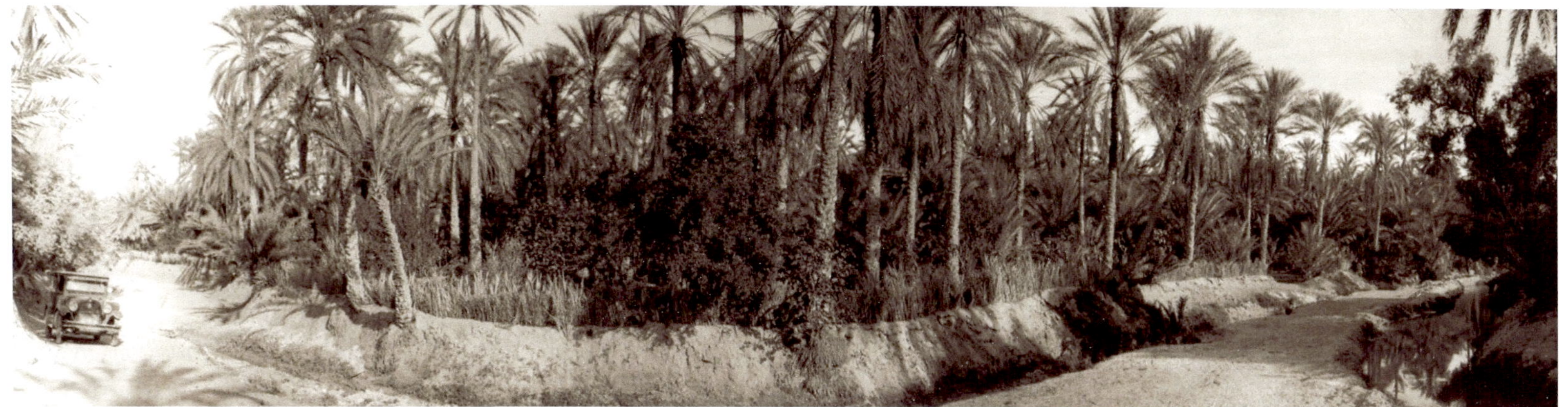

Fig. 50a. Panoramic view of the Tozeur oasis, Tunisia, with the Dodge sedan on the road at left. The center shows date palms and fruit trees, April 18, 1925 (Kelsey Museum neg. no. Cirkut 096).

Taking photographs was only one aspect of Swain's remit. Developing the negatives was an entirely different, perhaps more challenging, enterprise. Swain did not have ready access to darkrooms overseas, and even when he was able to construct makeshift facilities, technical issues prevailed.[129] Glass plates, like Kodak film, had to be processed in chemical solutions, including developing fluid, fixing solution, and clean water. Because many of the negatives could not be developed overseas, Swain often had to wait months before he could see the final results of his work—and only then after he had returned to Ann Arbor. He reportedly exposed 1,200 heavy glass plates on one trip, all of which had to be transported back to Michigan. Once back in Ann Arbor, he could not develop his negatives on campus, since his office was housed in the campus library, where chemicals were strictly forbidden. Instead, he had a darkroom at home, where he worked long hours, undoubtedly well into the night.[130]

Reading through Swain's many letters and reports, one is repeatedly struck by his painterly sensibilities and his constant focus on form, composition, detail, and even sound (figs. 51–54). His written descriptions—whether about ports of call, mosques, monasteries, quaint shops, or local customs—readily summon scenes to the mind's eye. For example, Swain paints a vivid word picture of a port in Piraeus, Greece, where he had just witnessed hundreds of condensed milk cases hoisted from the hold of a steamer:

> A U.S.-lines freight steamer is belching smoke and steam. Row boats are darting around apparently helter skelter, a man is enjoying a swim . . . in the center of the tiny harbor, the harbor [rimmed] almost literally by a forest of masts and smoke stacks. Ships anchor stern to shore bow straight out . . .

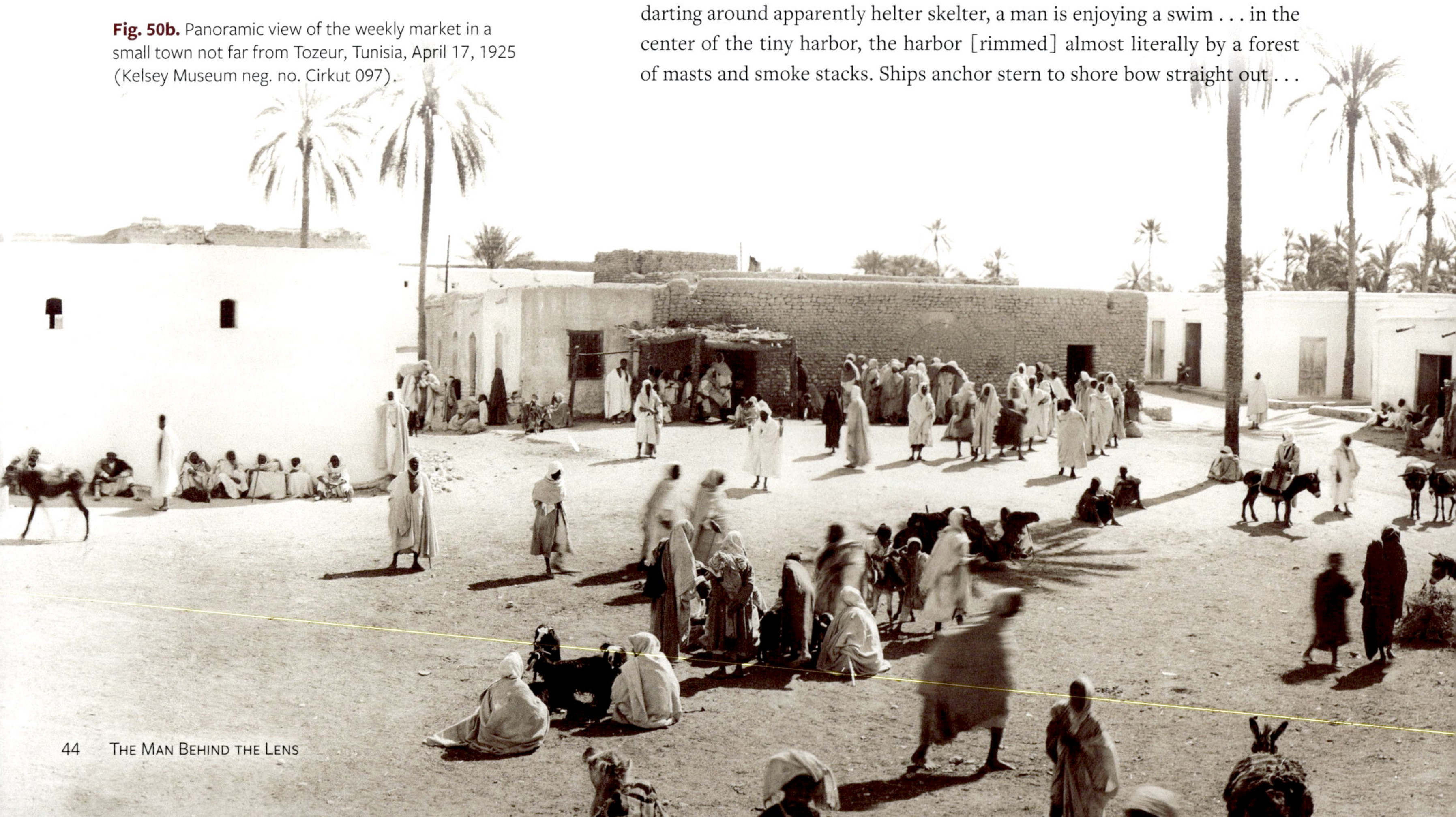

Fig. 50b. Panoramic view of the weekly market in a small town not far from Tozeur, Tunisia, April 17, 1925 (Kelsey Museum neg. no. Cirkut 097).

> while the shore is a general mélange of sunshine, carriages, custom house, dust, bipeds assorted as to [nationality], age and sex, trolley cars, carts, a babel of tongues and then more sun and more dust.[131]

While Swain was surely frustrated by his inability to capture the fullness of colors through his lens, he often commented, sometimes floridly, about the richness of the palettes he encountered. Writing about the Gulf of Tunis, he muses on the chromatic display of the water:

> . . . all shades of blue from warm purplish through chilly cobalt to greenish, and even shades of green—it is never twice alike and would, I think be the inspiration or despair of a marine painter. Nor is color confined to the water, for in March and April the fields are dazzlingly gorgeous with crimson poppies, yellow daisies, and blue flowers. . . . These flourish in such profusion that green becomes the minor note in an incredible polychromy display. The amount of raw color, so to speak, in the landscape at times is simply incredible, not to be imagined by anyone who has not traveled outside the central west.[132]

As we will see in the following sections, Swain's keen eye and talent for composition, light, and texture provide striking views of life in the Mediterranean and beyond. In the absence of the color he so loved to describe, Swain offers us black-and-white images that encourage us to look closely and to delight in all the small details and hidden surprises captured by his lens.

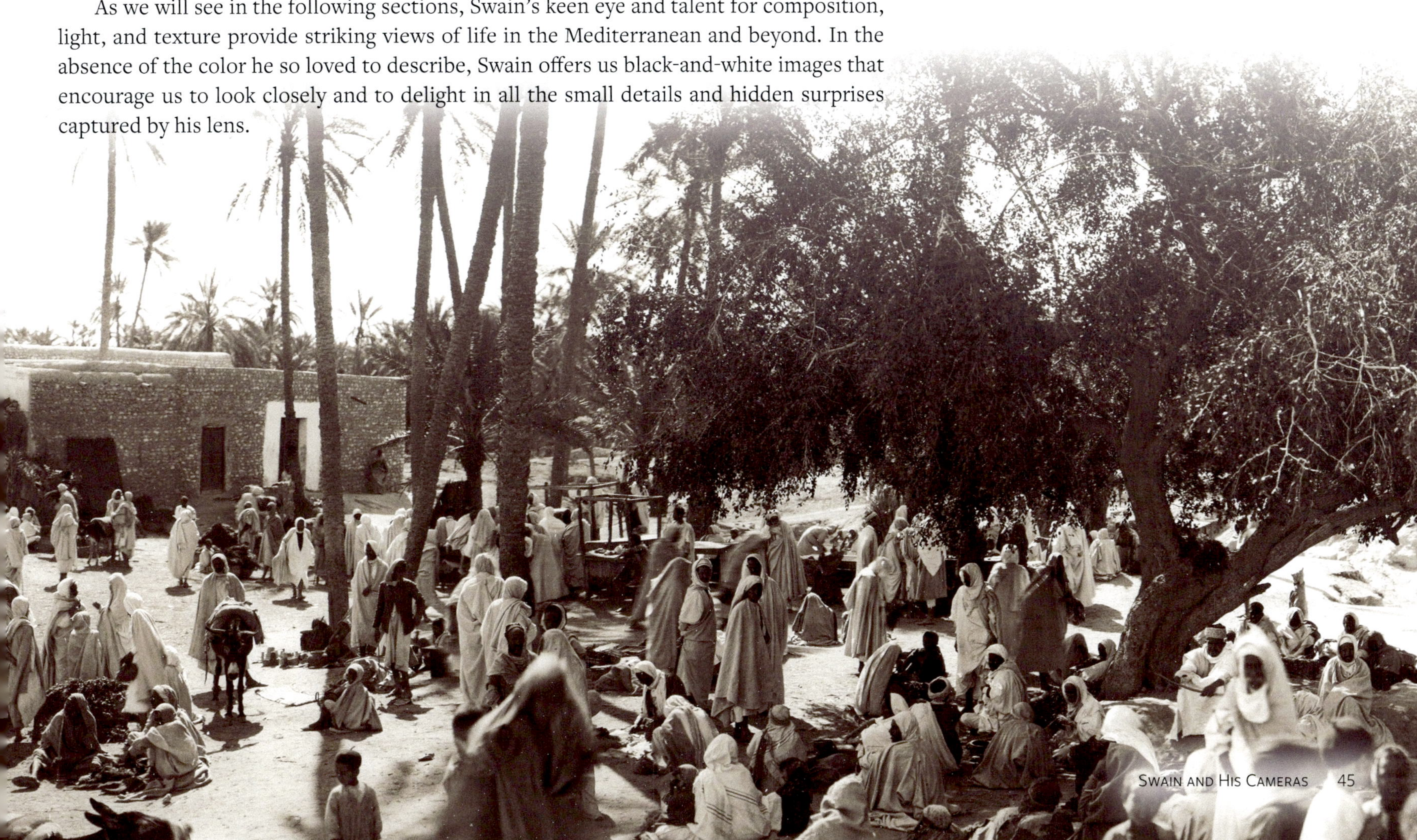

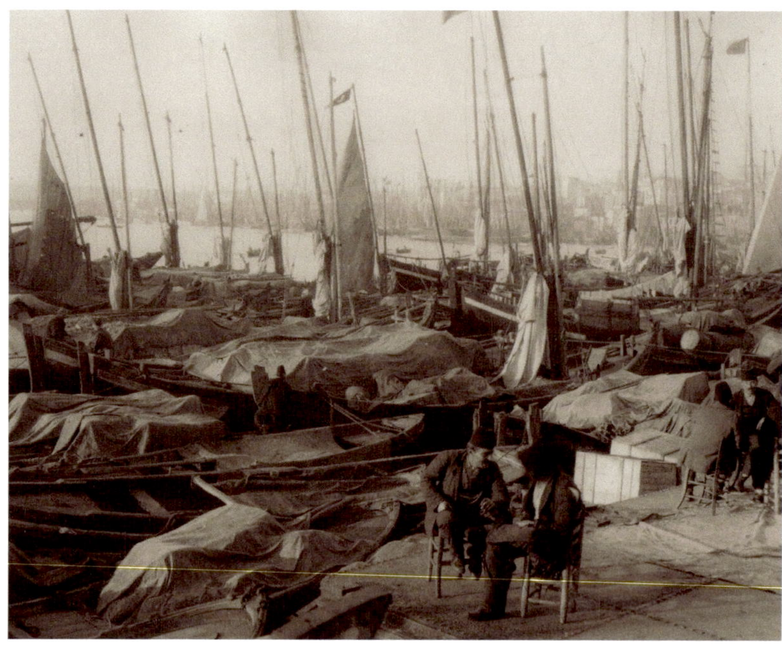

Fig. 51. Sailing boats by the old bridge on the Golden Horn, Constantinople, Turkey, December 5, 1919 (Kelsey Museum neg. no. KS 045.02).

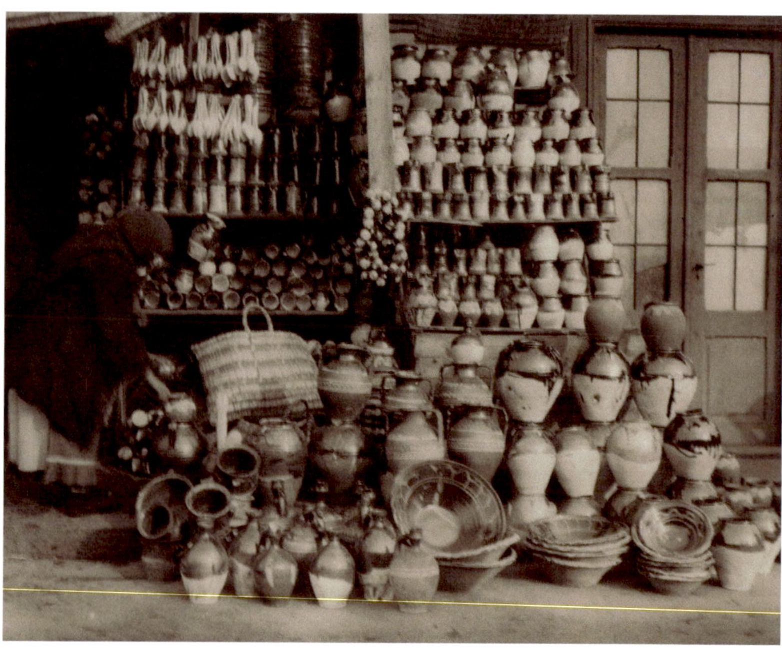

Fig. 52. Stall selling jugs, jars, and pots, Bucharest, Romania, November 25, 1919 (Kelsey Museum neg. no. KS 035.11).

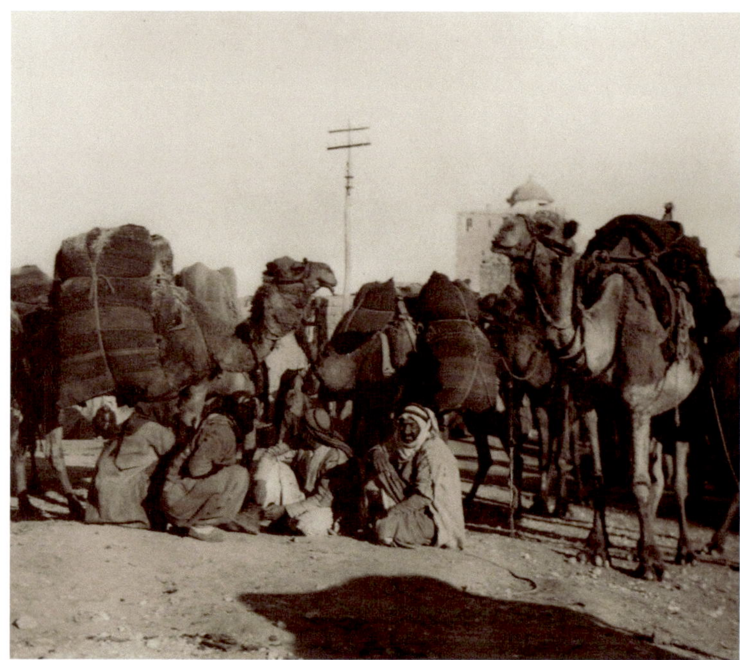

Fig. 53. "Loaded camels, Arabs seated on the ground," Aleppo, Syria, January 7–8, 1920 (Kelsey Museum neg. no. KS 081.04).

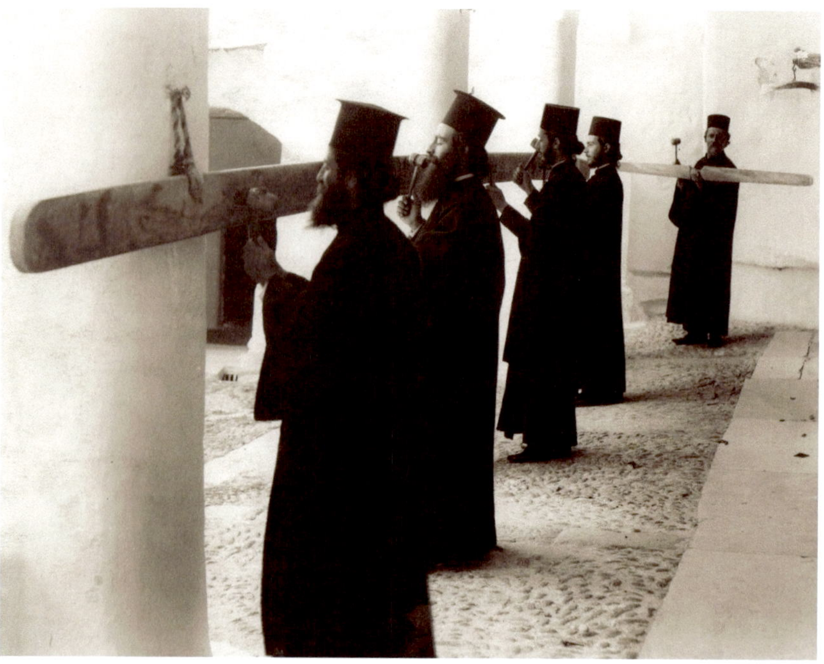

Fig. 54. "Monastery of St. John. Four monks playing with mallets on the rear 'semandron' in the court. A fifth monk beyond with a small semandron in his hand. The use of these wooden bars is said to have originated in a time when the use of bells was forbidden to monasteries. The great semandron is a bar of oak (25′ 9″ long, 2′ 6.5″ section). One wonders if it is some old ship timber," Patmos, Greece, May 1920 (Kelsey Museum neg. no. 7.0422).

Part III

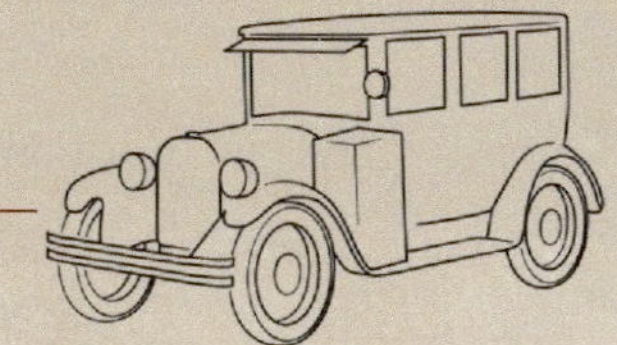

BACK ROADS, LOTUS EATERS, AND MONASTIC LIFE: THE 1924–1926 EXPEDITIONS

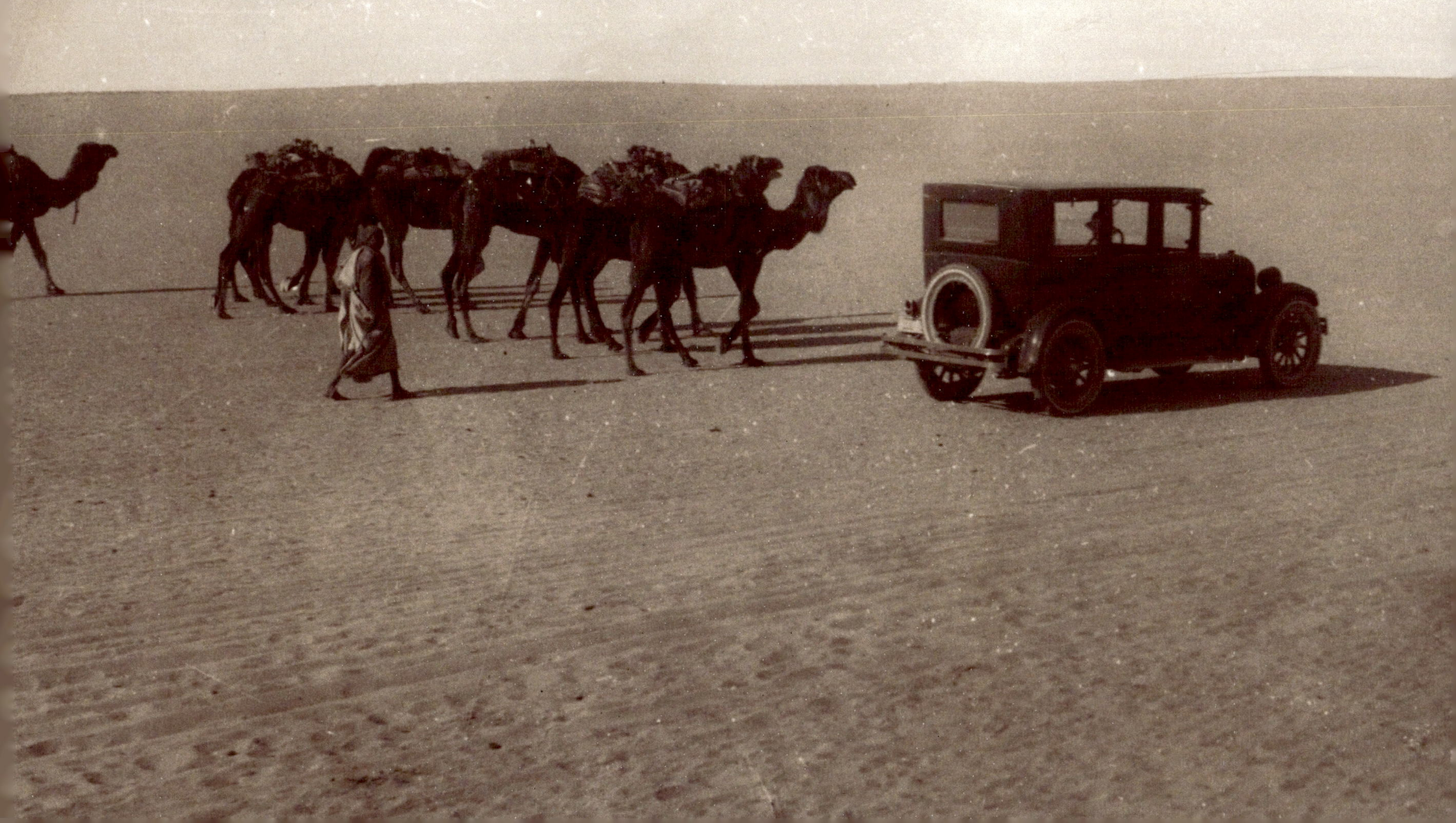

Chapter 6

LIFE ON THE ROAD: OVERVIEW OF THE 1924–1926 EXPEDITIONS

Although the expeditions of 1924, 1925, and 1926 were all principally archaeological in nature, each had distinct objectives and involved travel to different parts of the Mediterranean and North Africa. The trip of 1924 focused primarily on Turkey; the 1925 campaign targeted Tunisia, Algeria, and monastic life in Greece; and the final expedition in 1926 consisted of trips to a range of towns and sites throughout Italy and back to Greece. Despite their differences, they were all conducted in regions experiencing political and social upheaval generated, in part, by the dissolution of the Ottoman Empire and the aftermath of the Great War.

The initial campaign of 1924 centered on excavating and documenting the site of Antioch of Pisidia, an important Roman town in the interior of Turkey (fig. 55). Although Swain was the official expedition photographer—responsible for creating a detailed visual record of the site's finds and architecture—he became increasingly intrigued by life in and around Yalivadj, the small town serving as home base for the expedition crew. He often enlisted his camera to capture daily activities in this remote village, which was on the cusp of various changes. Atatürk had come to power in 1923 and was instituting radical reforms in the new republic.[133] Both Swain's letters and his photographs document the customs and struggles of this secluded village during a critical time in Turkey's history.

The aim of the 1925 expedition was quite different—namely, excavations at the site of Carthage, a famous ancient city on the coast of modern Tunisia. Carthage was one of Rome's greatest rivals in the Republican period (509–27 BCE) and home to the legendary, ill-fated Queen Dido.[134] The city was destroyed and leveled by the Roman army, which reportedly salted the earth to discourage reoccupation. Over the years, both sanctioned and illicit excavations at the site had uncovered a rich collection of artifacts, including a number of unusual stelae (freestanding markers often serving as gravestones) associated with the Punic goddess Tanit (fig. 56). Many of these curious stone markers began surfacing on the antiquities market, capturing the attention of both buyers and archaeologists, most notably the swashbuckling "Count" Byron Khun de Prorok—a wealthy adventurer, an amateur archaeologist of questionable character, and a fake count to boot. He ultimately purchased land at the site and launched a hasty excavation in 1924 (figs. 57–58). In need of more funding and an academic imprimatur, de Prorok joined forces with Kelsey (who seemed "undeterred by de Prorok's reputation") and several French scholars.[135] The

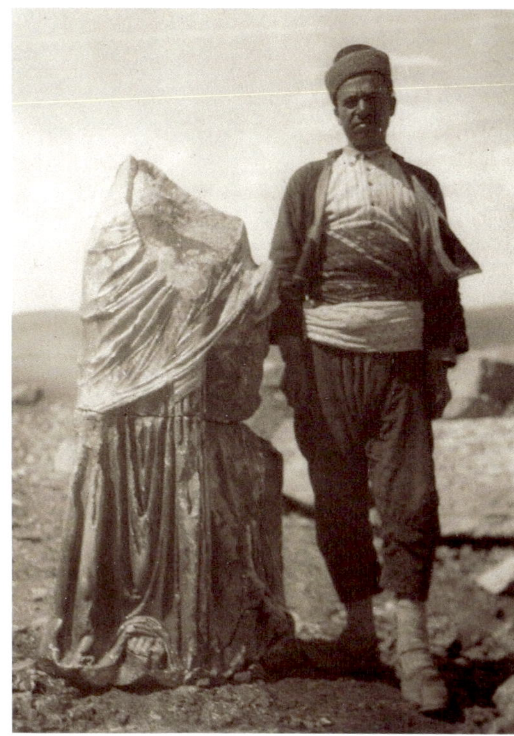

Fig. 55. Hussein standing by a female statue uncovered at U-M's Antioch excavations, May 17, 1924 (Kelsey Museum neg. no. KR 015.11).

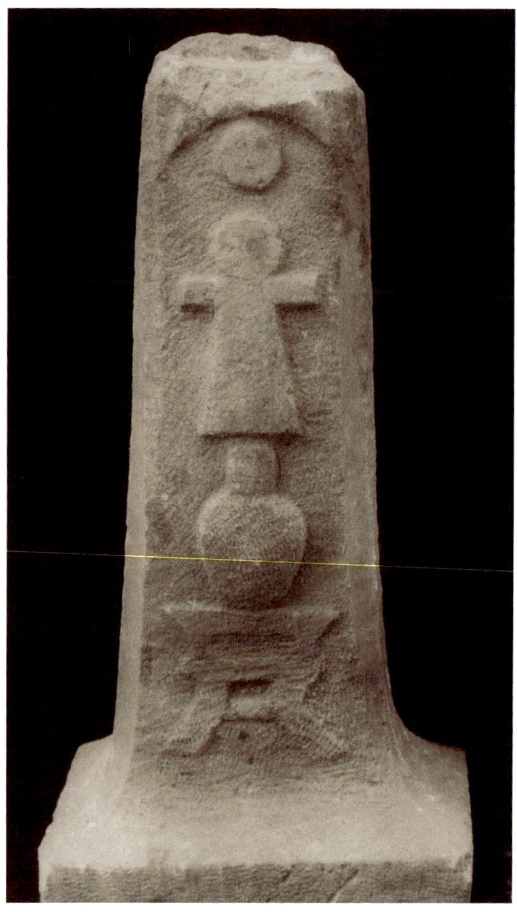

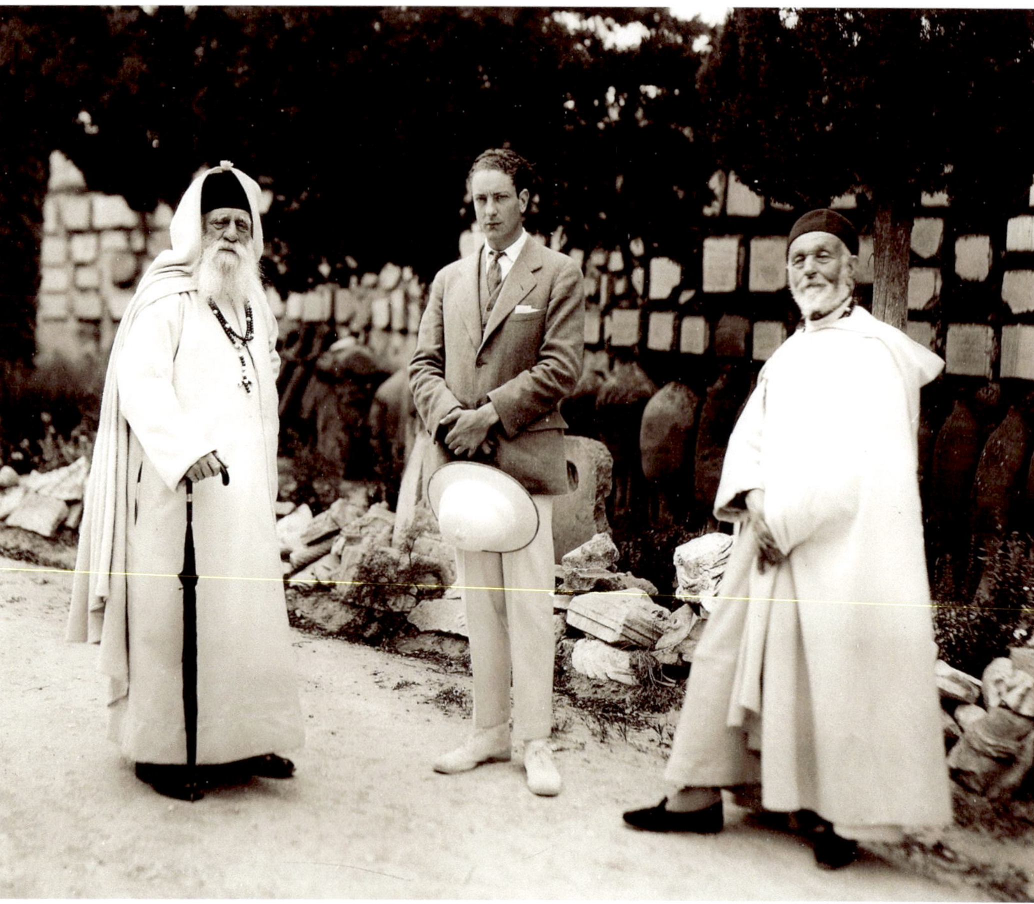

Fig. 56. Stone stela from the Tophet, a sanctuary of the goddess Tanit, Carthage, Tunisia, 1925 (Kelsey Museum neg. no. 5.0680).

Fig. 57. From left to right, Pere Delattre, Count de Prorok, and Pere Hugenot in the Cathedral Gardens, Tunisia, May 1–12, 1925 (Kelsey Museum neg. no. 7.2050).

Franco-American project lasted three months in the spring of 1925, with Swain hired as the photographer. The count had other plans as well for that season: he was intent on exploring the "lost worlds" of southern Tunis and Algiers, where he hoped to uncover buried cities and a mysterious race of people. For 23 days, Swain, the Graham Brothers truck, and the Dodge sedan accompanied the count, his crew, and a filmmaker from Pathé News (the famous film production company) in search of these lost civilizations. Traveling approximately 2,000 miles in Tunisia and Algeria, they documented several curious villages hidden amid the gigantic sand dunes of the area. Swain's photographs and letters remain an invaluable source of information on these towns that were largely unknown and unseen by the outside world.

Unlike the earlier two trips, the 1926 campaign did not focus on a particular excavation, although the initial plan had included archaeological work in Egypt. Much to Swain's disappointment, Kelsey canceled the latter part of the Egyptian project, stranding Swain (and his son Ned) in Italy. Ultimately, Kelsey reconfigured the 1926 trip, arranging for Swain to photograph valuable manuscripts in Greek libraries and monasteries (fig. 59). After a frustrating three months in Italy, Swain and Ned finally traveled to Greece, spending approximately six weeks documenting biblical and religious manuscripts, each stop an adventure unto itself.

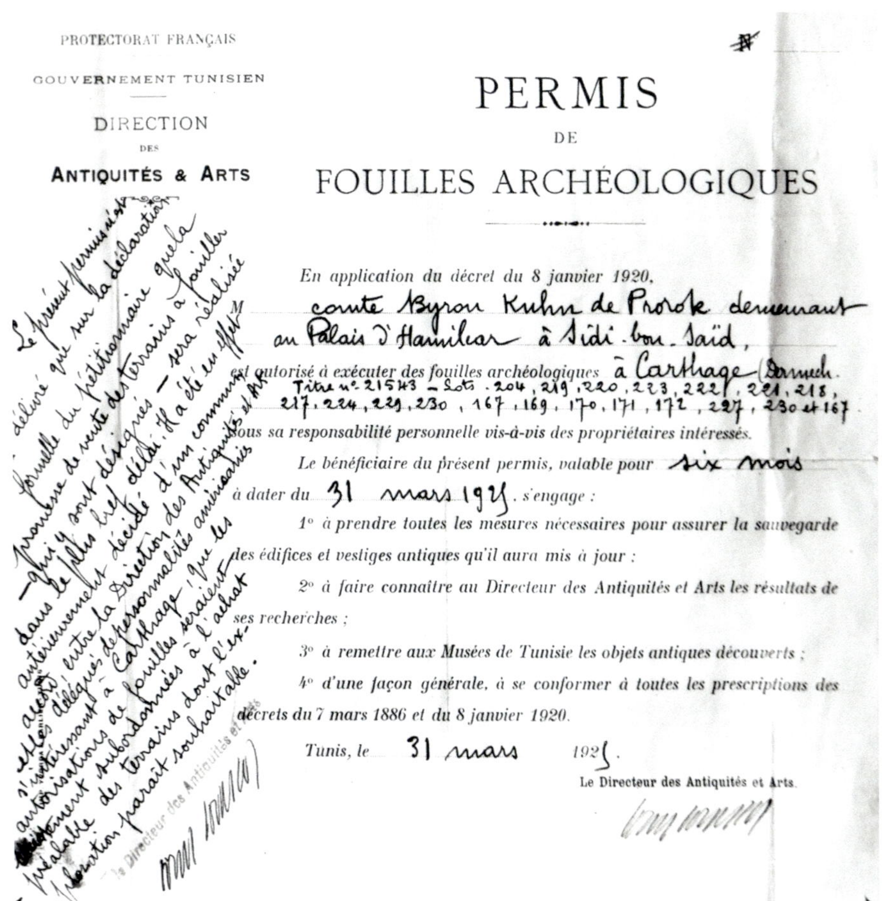

PROTECTORAT FRANÇAIS

GOUVERNEMENT TUNISIEN

DIRECTION DES ANTIQUITÉS & ARTS

PERMIS DE FOUILLES ARCHÉOLOGIQUES

En application du décret du 8 janvier 1920,

M comte Byron Kuhn de Prorok demeurant au Palais d'Hamilcar à Sidi-bou-Saïd,

est autorisé à exécuter des fouilles archéologiques à Carthage (Dermech. Titre n° 21543 – Lots 204, 219, 220, 223, 222, 221, 218, 217, 224, 229, 230, 167, 169, 170, 171, 172, 227, 230 et 167 sous sa responsabilité personnelle vis-à-vis des propriétaires intéressés.

Le bénéficiaire du présent permis, valable pour six mois à dater du 31 mars 1925, s'engage :

1° à prendre toutes les mesures nécessaires pour assurer la sauvegarde des édifices et vestiges antiques qu'il aura mis à jour ;

2° à faire connaître au Directeur des Antiquités et Arts les résultats de ses recherches ;

3° à remettre aux Musées de Tunisie les objets antiques découverts ;

4° d'une façon générale, à se conformer à toutes les prescriptions des décrets du 7 mars 1886 et du 8 janvier 1920.

Tunis, le 31 mars 1925.

Le Directeur des Antiquités et Arts.

Le présent permis n'est délivré que sur la déclaration formelle du pétitionnaire que la promesse de vente des terrains à fouiller – qui y sont désignés – sera réalisée dans le plus bref délai. Il a été en effet antérieurement décidé d'un commun accord entre la Direction des Antiquités et Arts et les délégués des personnalités américaines s'intéressant à Carthage, que les autorisations de fouilles seraient uniquement subordonnées à l'achat préalable des terrains dont l'expropriation parait souhaitable.

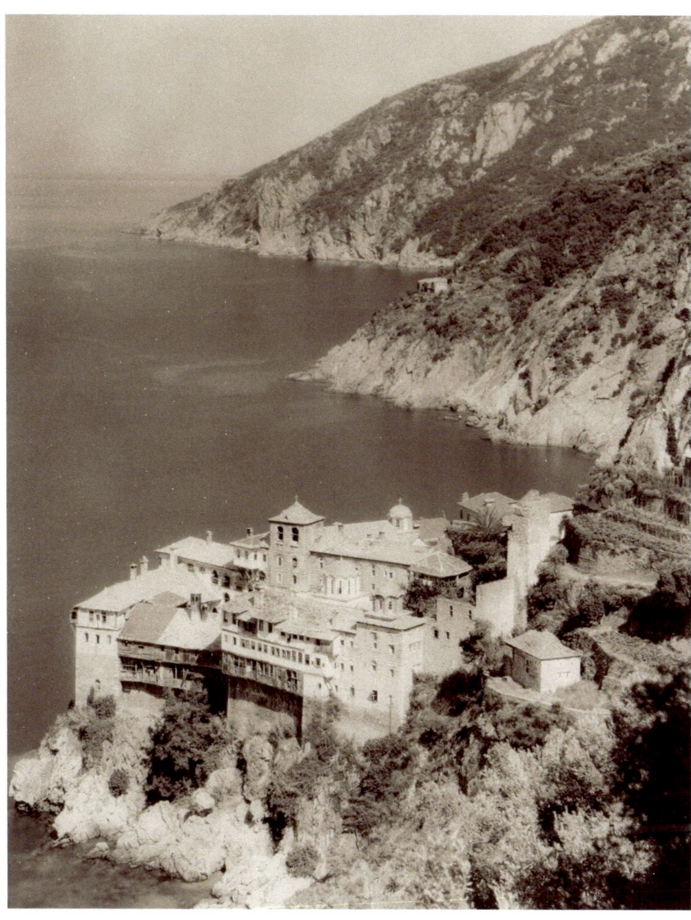

Fig. 58. Permit to excavate the Dermech concession, Carthage, Tunisia. Issued to Count de Prorok on March 31, 1925 (Kelsey Museum neg. no. 7.2038).

Fig. 59. Looking down over the monastery of Gregoriou, Mount Athos, Greece, July 10, 1925 (Kelsey Museum neg. no. 8.0227).

In total, the two University of Michigan vehicles covered more than 8,000 miles in their 1924–1926 campaigns. The ensuing three chapters document those travels: Each chapter begins with a map providing a visual snapshot of the year's routes, followed by a table containing a detailed itinerary. The remainder of each chapter includes discussions that highlight Swain's observations on the archaeology and sociopolitical landscape of the regions he visited.

Despite Swain's well-captioned photographs and his many letters, it was sometimes difficult to ascertain the exact date and location of an event, or whether one or both of the vehicles were "in attendance." In addition, occasional contradictions occur. These problems notwithstanding, the tables and discussions are as accurate as possible, given the available data.

Chapter 7

TRAVELS OF 1924

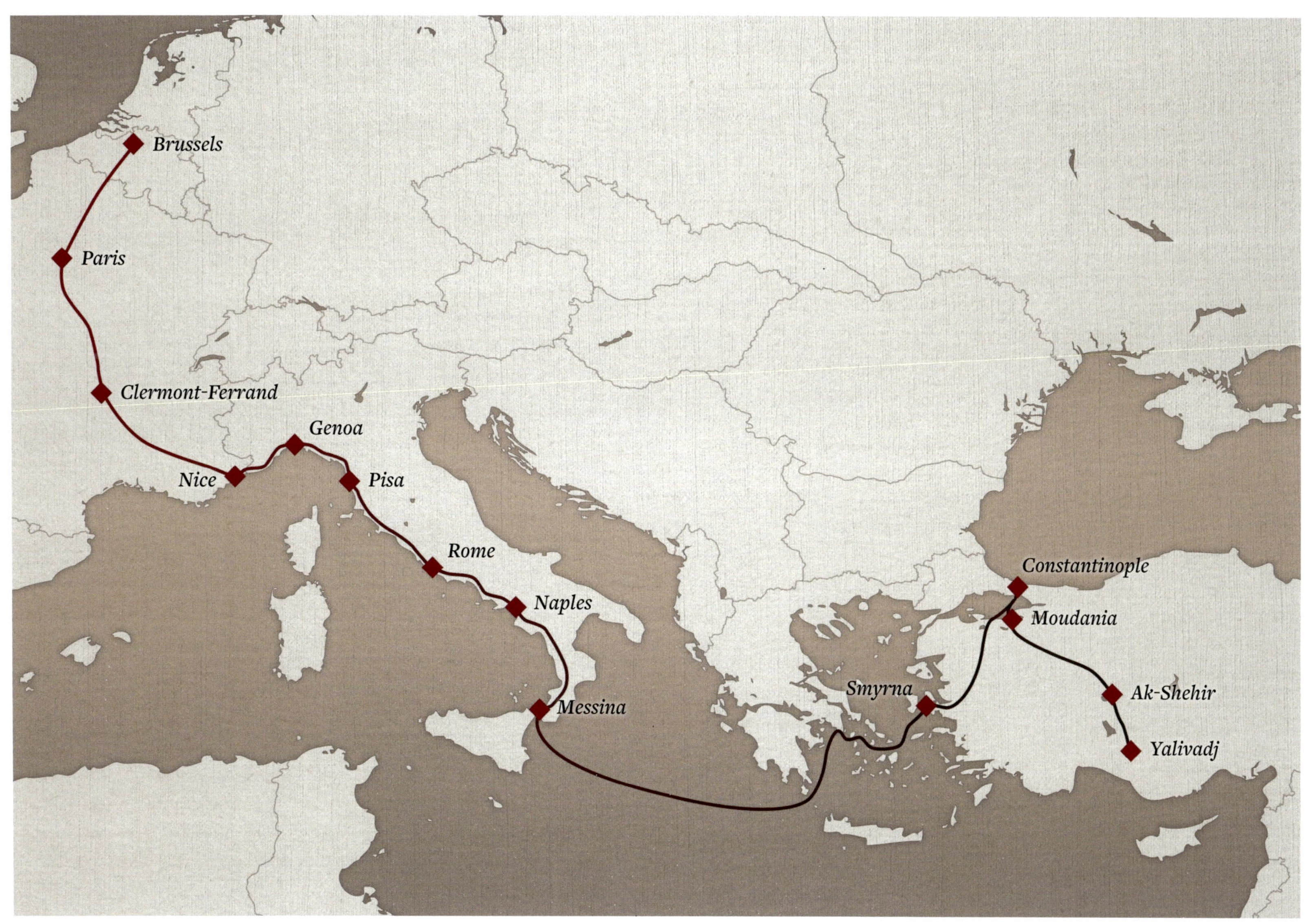

Approximate outbound route of the Graham Brothers truck and Dodge sedan from Brussels, Belgium, to Yalivadj, Turkey.

Date	Location	Notes
March 1	Swain and Easton Kelsey leave New York	SS *President Harding*
March 5	Vehicles were supposed to be shipped from New York but encounter major delays	
March 9	Swain and Easton arrive in England	
March 16–April 6	Paris, France, and environs	Sightseeing and purchase of supplies while Swain and Easton await the arrival of the two vehicles destined for Brussels
April 14	Vehicles finally arrive in Brussels, Belgium	Truck and sedan picked up by Swain and Easton in Brussels
April 16–May 27	Vehicles driven from Brussels to Naples, Italy (ca. 1,200 miles); relatively leisurely trip of approximately 40 days	Route: Brussels to central France, along the French and Italian Rivieras, west coast of Italy to Rome, and finally to Naples
May 28–June 5	Vehicles loaded onto steamer in Naples for a short trip to Sicily, then via Greece and the west coast of Turkey to Constantinople	SS *Costantinopoli*
June 7	Swain and vehicles arrive in Constantinople	Swain delayed in Constantinople for ca. 17 days, due to bureaucratic complications
June 24	Vehicles loaded onto steamer in Constantinople for port town of Moudania, Turkey, on the south side of Sea of Marmara	More direct route from Constantinople to Yalivadj hindered by roads destroyed during the war
June 26–July 1	Vehicles driven from Moudania to Broussa, then via Ak-Shehir to Yalivadj, Turkey (300 miles)	Ak-Shehir is a station on the Berlin–Baghdad Railway
July 2–September 1	Antioch excavations: work had begun in early May; Swain and Easton arrive July 2; crew based in modern town of Yalivadj; Antioch excavations completed September 1	Vehicles used for local trips and ferrying the crew back and forth to the dig site
Mid-September	Vehicles shipped to Constantinople via rail in mid-September	Swain busy with post-excavation activities—packing supplies, arranging photographs, and preparing for a possible return to Antioch in 1925
September 23–28	Swain and vehicles travel by steamer from Constantinople to Naples	SS *Albania*. Vehicles held up in Naples, awaiting permit to enter the country
Early October	Vehicles stored in Rome for the winter	Swain photographs in Pompeii for Professor Kelsey
October 25	Swain and company leave Rome for Paris	
October 29	Swain on board ship for New York	SS *Majestic*
November 4	Swain arrives in New York	

Summary of the 1924 Expedition

Several weeks before Swain, Kelsey, and their crew embarked on the 1924 trip, the *Detroit News* painted a somewhat overstated picture of the potential dangers that lay ahead for the expedition. According to the journalist, Professor Kelsey's travels were "no small task in this period of international suspicion. . . . He must convince the authorities of the countries where he hopes to gain his ends that he is not a spy of some inimical government, and also that he is not attempting to find or pilfer hidden wealth. He will never know what day will bring forth a revolution . . . or an invasion of the country in which he may be, and must be on the lookout for danger continually." The crew would also have to contend with "the scorching heat of Egyptian deserts, as well as the bitter cold of the plateaus of Asia Minor in the dead of winter."[136] The reporter's dramatic tone notwithstanding, several archaeologists did, in fact, serve as spies for the United States Office of Naval Intelligence during World War I. Their archaeological work provided good cover for espionage activities.[137]

On March 1, Swain and Kelsey's son, Easton (fig. 60), left New York (fig. 61) aboard the SS *President Harding* (fig. 62). The ship boasted one of the fastest transatlantic crossings in the early 1920s, and its lavish brochure claimed that if the vessel were cleaved in

Fig. 60. Easton Kelsey, Patmos, Greece, May 8, 1920 (Kelsey Museum neg. no. KK 204).

Fig. 61. View of Manhattan from the deck of the SS *President Harding*, March 1, 1924 (Kelsey Museum neg. no. KS 231.06).

Fig. 62. Postcard of the SS *President Harding* (George Robert Swain Photographs and Papers, Bentley Historical Library, University of Michigan).

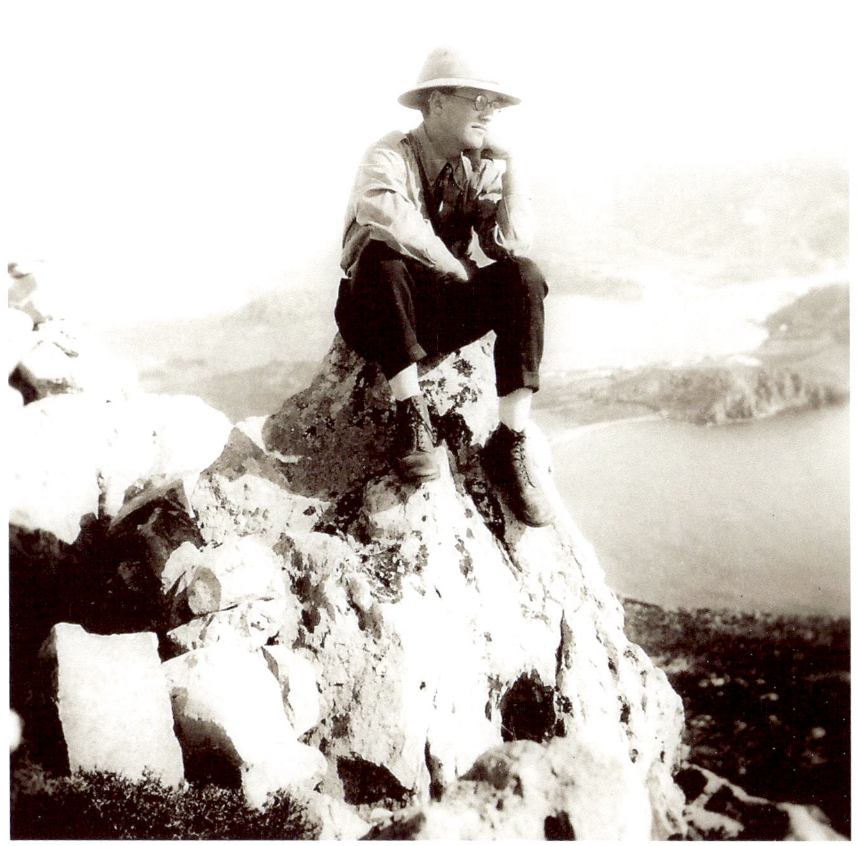

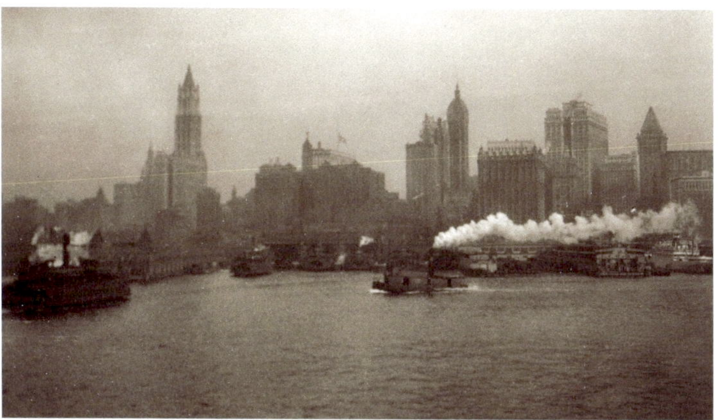

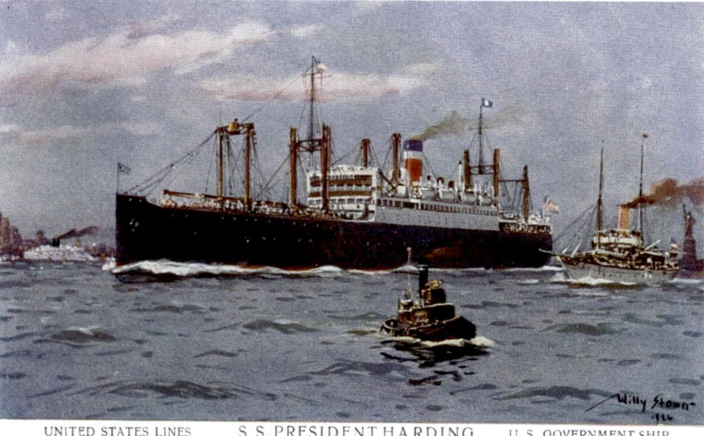

half, both sides would float—perhaps an assuring reference to the still-searing memory of the *Titanic*'s 1912 disaster.[138] On March 9, just eight days after leaving New York, they arrived in England.

The two vehicles, which were transported on another vessel, encountered delays in New York and then problems clearing customs in Belgium. Swain and Easton would have to wait almost a month after their arrival in England to retrieve the Graham Brothers truck and Dodge sedan in Brussels, where the automobiles had been "tuned up to concert pitch."[139] The next leg of the journey—from France to Italy—lasted nearly seven weeks, with Swain and Easton driving through the central regions of France (figs. 63–65), onward to the Italian Riviera, and then to Rome. Following a short stay in Naples, the vehicles traveled as "deck passengers" on a steamer to Constantinople, arriving on June 7 (fig. 66).[140] After a frustrating 17-day delay in Constantinople, Swain, Easton, and the two vehicles were finally able to start the trek on horrendous roads to Yalivadj, the small town that would serve as their base during the excavation season at Antioch of Pisidia. At the conclusion of the dig season, the sedan and truck were transported by rail to Constantinople, then by steamer to Naples, and eventually to Rome, where they rested happily over the winter.

Antioch and Delays in Constantinople

Antioch, the focus of the University of Michigan's 1924 campaign from the middle of May until early September, was a Hellenistic town refounded by Augustus as an important Roman colony in 25 BCE and later visited by Saint Paul as part of his extensive missionary activities. Located approximately 3,800 feet above sea level and dominated by the lofty heights of the Sultan Dağ mountain range, the town contained a large, sprawling, easily

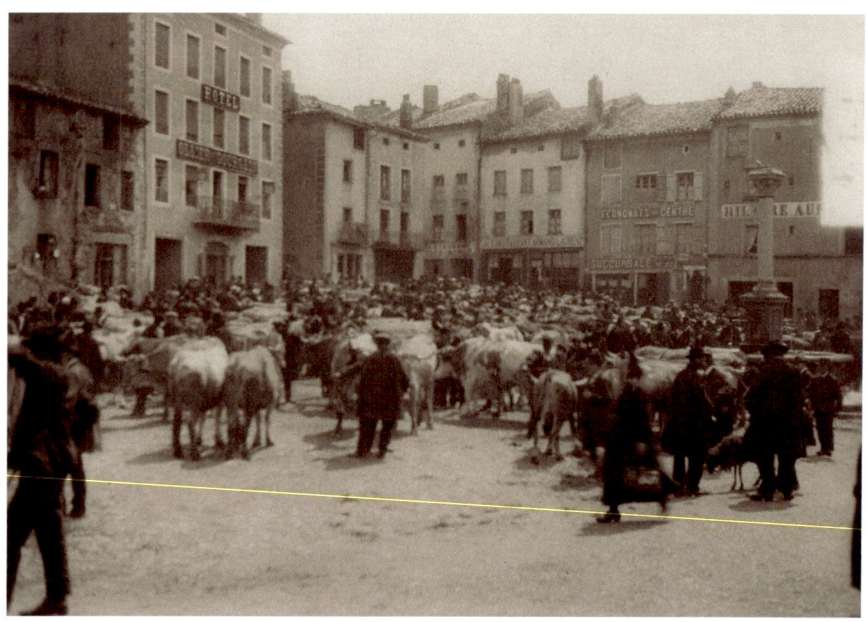

Fig. 63. Cattle market between Le Puy and Orange, France, trip from Paris to Constantinople, April 23, 1924 (Kelsey Museum neg. no. KS 240.12).

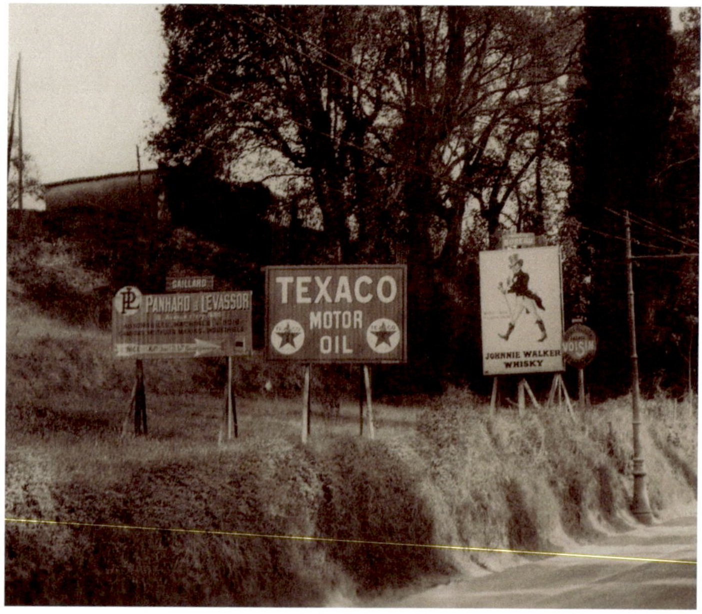

Fig. 64. "Cannes and vicinity. Again the billboard nuisance—autos, motor oils, and whiskey," Cannes, France, trip from Paris to Constantinople, April 27, 1924 (Kelsey Museum neg. no. KS 248.08).

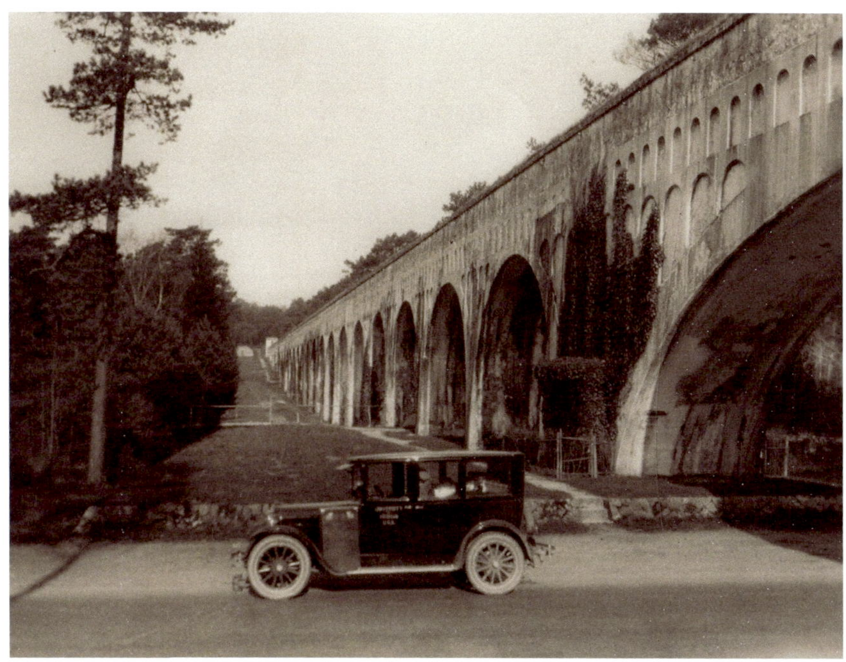

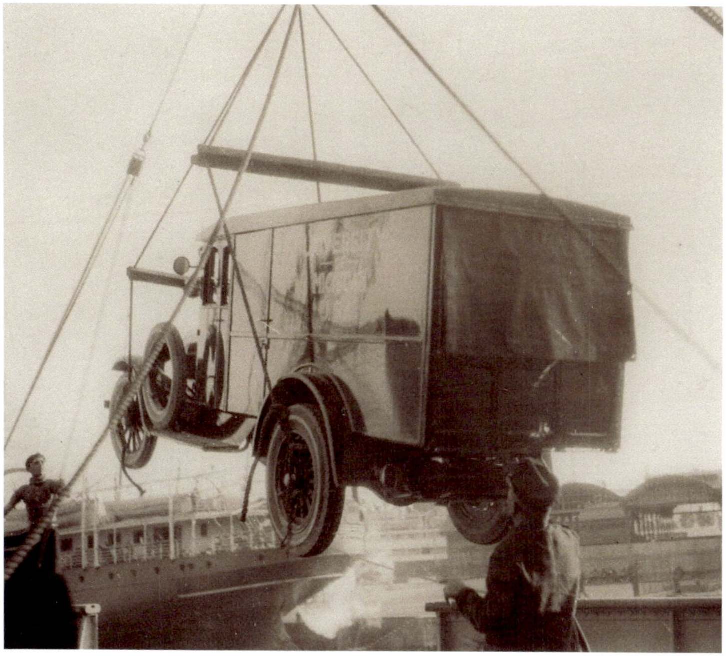

Fig. 65. The Dodge sedan by an aqueduct, Forest of Fontainebleau, France, April 20, 1924 (Kelsey Museum neg. no. KS 237.12).

Fig. 66. The Graham Brothers truck hoisted onto the SS *Costantinopoli* at Naples, Italy, bound for Constantinople, May 28, 1924 (Kelsey Museum neg. no. KS 262.12).

defensible settlement. First identified in the early 1800s, Antioch became the focus of several excavations, most notably in the early 1900s.

By the time Swain and company arrived in Antioch on July 2, work had already begun under the direction of David M. Robinson, a classical archaeologist from Johns Hopkins whom the University of Michigan had hired. His crew included nearly 200 local workmen. By the end of the season, an impressive array of inscriptions and architecture had been unearthed, including one of the few surviving copies of the *Res Gestae Divi Augusti* (a famous text on the accomplishments of the emperor Augustus[141]), an imperial cult sanctuary, an elaborate gate, a theater, and a bath complex serviced by a massive and extensive aqueduct (fig. 67).[142]

Although Swain and Easton were not scheduled to join the Antioch crew until well into the season, they arrived even later than expected because of both bureaucratic difficulties and disastrous roads. In fact, the trip from Constantinople (their first major port of call in Turkey) to Yalivadj could not begin until officials granted the two vehicles proper permits. As we will see, obtaining those permits proved a Herculean task for Swain.

Permits were only one of Swain's challenges. Driving the cars to Yalivadj presented another set of complications. The most direct roads from Constantinople to the interior of Turkey had been devastated by war and never repaired. Given no choice, Swain had to devise an alternate route; he finally decided to drive from Constantinople to the port of Moudania on the south side of the Sea of Marmara, disembark at the town of Broussa, and then follow inland roads, reportedly in better condition (see map, p. 53).

But the drive to Moudania would have to wait while Swain dealt with officials in Constantinople. The local embassy had made no advance preparations for the vehicles' permits, and the embassy's workdays were limited. The city was, in Swain's words, "a

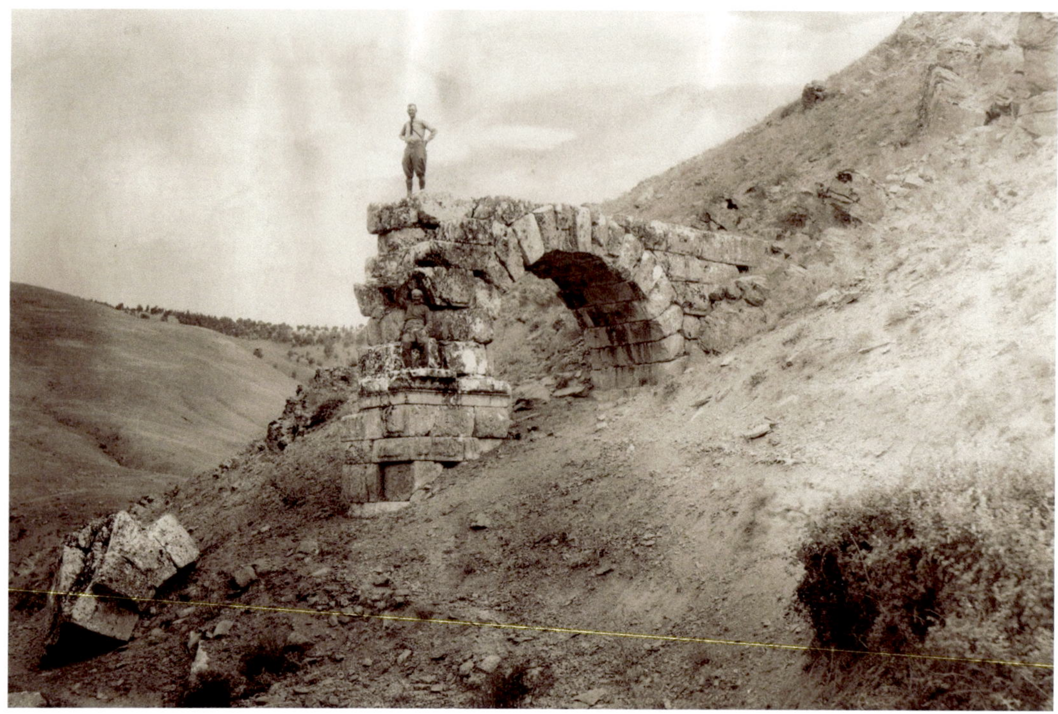

Fig. 67. Field director Enoch E. Peterson standing on the aqueduct that brought water to ancient Antioch, Turkey, July 12, 1924 (Kelsey Museum neg. no. 7.1358).

town of three Sundays a week. Friday Moslem, everything closed up, compulsory now; Saturday, Jew, optional but a few closed; Sunday Greeks and some others, optional, but . . . many stores had shutters up."[143] Mincing no words, Swain vents that "there were various times . . . when a permissible vocabulary could hardly express my feelings."[144]

In a letter to his wife dated June 19, 1924, Swain offers details about the delays and his exasperation, reflecting a decidedly Western perspective on Near Eastern attitudes toward time, efficiency, and a set work schedule:

> In a.m. we got nowhere at custom house . . . office hours seems to be a nebulous hypothesis. . . . But at 2:25 . . . till 5:30 (closing hour) we really got a lot done, but I wouldn't like to try to estimate how many miles we walked in the maze of offices that make up the Stamboul Custom House—O.K. here, stamp there, certificate somewhere else, see somebody for this order, another for that, go back and see some of them a second or third time etc. etc. ad nauseum. . . . Once we were told we had to drive the cars out a mile or two to have them weighed (no scales here with platform large enough to drive on), but in the end they decided to accept my statement as to weight of cars and parts. . . . [W]e shall have accumulated a total delay here of almost 15 days—of which the embassy should have saved at least half.[145]

Swain's frustration with what he viewed as endemic incompetence surfaces in other letters as well. "I should have had some mail tonight, but didn't," he writes, "[b]ecause of some military performances—maneuvers or something—all mails were suspended for four days. Imagine it in the U.S.!"[146] Although the topic of "eastern" attitudes and incessant red tape proved endlessly trying for Swain (Side Car 5), his inimitable humor materialized periodically when faced with the inevitable. "The regular recurrence of the irregular," he observes, "may confidently be predicted—especially in the Near East."[147] And at one point, while sailing on the west coast of Italy, he muses, "Here sailed crafty Odysseus (did delay in passport visas have anything to do with the length of his journeys?)."[148]

By June 24, after more than a two-week delay in Constantinople, the matter of vehicle permits was finally resolved. But the next venture—maneuvering the truck and sedan on board a steamer for Moudania—was not without its own drama (fig. 68):

> Yesterday (Tuesday) morning we arrived at the steamer about 8:15 a.m. to find sailing had been postponed for 24 hours, but they were going to load the cars at once. Easton and I were on the dock till 1:15 when the operation was completed. Their hoist was small and the boom was too short to reach over and pick up the cars bodily. They put gang planks down at an angle of 45° and yanked the cars up these. With the hoist. The two gang planks were of different lengths. On the dock below the planks, in case they broke were huge bales of—guess what—silk cocoons! I was steaming hot on the docks. I wonder the cars were not damaged by the way they were handled. Fender and some other sheet steel parts got some bent. At last the cars were on deck and lashed. I was about as wet as if I had been in the water.[149]

Side Car 5: Swain's View of Turkish Bureaucracy

"You are subjected to considerable red tape when traveling in Turkey. Before entering Turkey you get a visa on your regular U.S. passport, but this visa is good for 15 days only and merely admits you to the country. Arrived in Constantinople you must get a police permit or local passport on which your photograph is pasted. If going to the interior, as I was, you must obtain another police permit, also with your photograph, which states the places you expect to visit. Theoretically, this is stamped by a police agent at every place you stay all night, and if you stay longer it is left on deposit with the police until you depart and is stamped with the statement that you are leaving. Then before coming over in the ferry from Haidar Pacha you have to 'check out' of Anatolia. On leaving Constantinople you must again have your passport stamped with permission to leave, surrendering your police permits."[150]

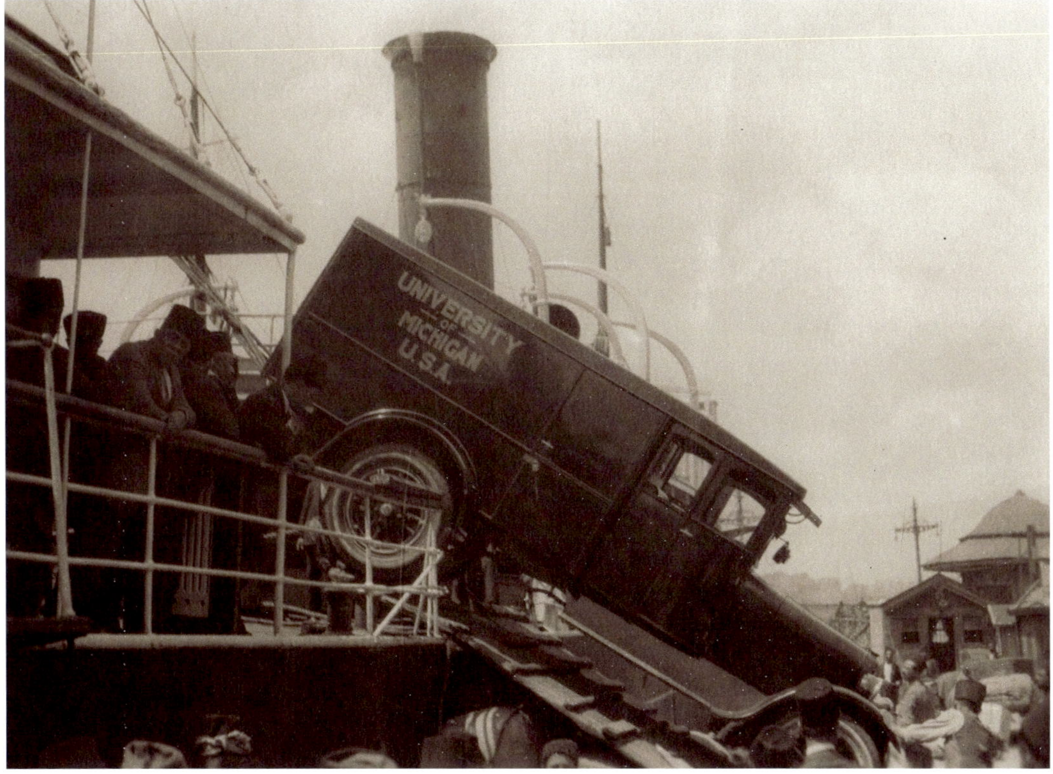

Fig. 68. The Graham Brothers truck hauled backward onto a steamer at the port town of Moudania, Turkey, June 25, 1924 (Kelsey Museum neg. no. KS 272.10).

The Sardis Affair

While most of the delays were caused by bureaucratic ineptitude and an overburdened system, one letter suggests more troubling events—namely, the dark shadow of traffic in illicit antiquities. A letter from Kelsey, dated approximately a month before the start of excavations at Antioch, indicates that the project at Antioch would be refused a dig permit if a longstanding and contentious argument between the Turkish government and New York's Metropolitan Museum of Art was not resolved. Kelsey and the University of Michigan found themselves caught in the vortex of the so-called Sardis Affair, a complicated and revealing story about colonialism, nationhood, and the struggle for ownership of Anatolian antiquities.[151] A slight detour, summarizing these convoluted events, is needed to appreciate the difficulties facing Swain at the time.

Following World War I, powerful nationalistic movements began to emerge in both Anatolia and the Near East, resisting Western attempts to control the region. Italy, France, Greece, and Britain all had territorial claims to the extensive areas once ruled by the Ottoman Empire. Tensions played out starkly in archaeology, with good reason. As one scholar notes, "Disputes over ancient sites and the antiquities they yielded went to the heart of the nationalist struggle; whoever controlled them obtained a useful tool for shaping the history and ideology of the nation."[152] Although the United States' presence in Anatolia was limited to a few businesses, missionary schools, and relief organizations, there were a number of ongoing American excavations in the region, none more successful than the site of Sardis, home of the legendary King Croesus.[153]

The Ottoman government had granted permission to Professor Howard Crosby Butler of Princeton University to excavate Sardis in 1908. He had received substantial financial backing from wealthy American donors (including J. P. Morgan), many of whom had close ties to the Metropolitan Museum. Butler's discoveries at the site were exceptional, and his backers were eager to reap the rewards of owning and displaying some of the more spectacular finds in New York's premier museum. Despite a 1906 Ottoman antiquities law that prohibited foreign concessions from retaining any finds, foreign excavations often received a share of the excavated material.

Some of Butler's donors, however, were not only impatient but also unscrupulous. One trustee of the Metropolitan Museum brazenly suggested that Butler spirit out what he could to impress donors who "were not interested in what was found, but in what the museum would receive." Allegedly, it was even suggested that Butler encourage anyone who visited Sardis to smuggle out fragments, thus circumventing the Ottoman authorities.[154]

The outbreak of World War I obviated further discussion, but matters grew more complicated after it ended, with the Metropolitan Museum demanding, once again, a share of the finds. Heated discussions, failed negotiations, and frayed tempers between Turkey and representatives from both the American government and trustees of the Metropolitan Museum ensued. In the midst of these negotiations, 58 crates of Sardis artifacts were hurriedly shipped to New York in 1922.[155] Not surprisingly, Turkey demanded the return of the Sardis antiquities, threatening that no foreign country would ever again be granted permission to excavate in the country. Hostile communications flew back and forth among the various players, with the Americans labeled a "bunch of crooks"[156] and the Turkish representatives finding it nearly impossible to escape long-standing perceptions of them as unruly, unreasonable, "terrible Turks."[157] Even Kelsey felt compelled to voice his opinion, writing to the president of the Metropolitan Museum and urging it to return the finds. Kelsey poetically wrote, "In the case of an Institution, as of a man, 'A good name is rather to be chosen than great riches.'"[158]

Eventually, matters were settled: all of the Sardis material, except for the heaviest pieces, were to be returned to Constantinople and there a negotiated division with the Americans effected, with the Metropolitan Museum receiving a share.[159] Kelsey notes in his diary of May 19, 1924, that he received a telegram while he was in Naples stating, "Sardis matter adjusted. Granting of your permit to be facilitated and expedited."[160]

Although the Sardis Affair was brought to a satisfactory conclusion, at least for the Metropolitan Museum, it laid bare colonial attitudes of Americans working in the Mediterranean and Near East. Not least were the notions that local populations cared little for their antiquities; would probably steal their countries' treasures to sell them on the black market; and, unlike the West, lacked the facilities to properly house the jewels unearthed from their archaeological backyard. We will see this colonial attitude surface in Swain's writings as well.

The Russian Refugees

Soon after Kelsey received the good news about the university's permit, excavations commenced at Antioch. Swain and Easton were still en route from France, unaware that they would encounter a long delay in Constantinople. Fortunately, Swain used his stay there to discover the city; his letters provide picturesque descriptions of "Stamboul" (the central parts of the historic city) and insights into a country struggling with change and financial turmoil. On one leisurely day, he strolled the waterfront, describing the sights and smells (fig. 69): "The most prominent thing . . . was a lot of dried fish . . . about 7–8 inches long shipped in bulk in the small boats, and stacked up in heaps directly on the sidewalks, and the air filled with the penetrating archaic ichthyological—shall I say perfume?"[161]

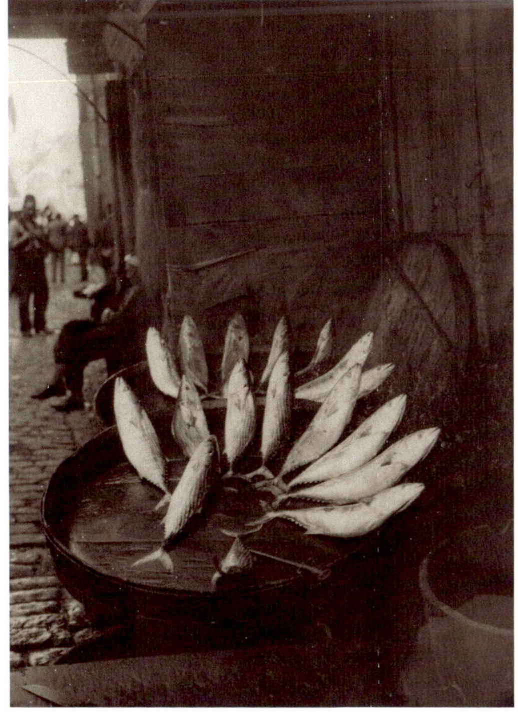

Fig. 69. Large mackerel for sale in the street, Constantinople, Turkey, June 14, 1924 (Kelsey Museum neg. no. KS 270.04).

In a letter to his wife, Swain describes the bustling bazaars, filled with "cheap, gaudy, meretricious international stuff—not all of course, but far too much. The amount of handiwork is interesting—hammering out copper and brass bowls, making slippers and low shoes by hand, tiny brass foundries, making furniture all by hand. . . . Some filigree silver work is good, and some amber beads. . . . Some of the lingerie would have probably interested you, but Paris can beat it a mile."[162]

The financial struggles of the city did not go unnoticed by Swain. Businesses are "about dead," he notes in one letter, since many of the Armenians and Greeks, who were largely in charge of the city's commerce, had been forced out several years earlier.[163] The city still had a fair number of immigrants, however, and on the evening of June 14, 1924, Swain dined at a restaurant run by Russian refugees who had fled to Constantinople. His rather class-conscious and ethnically biased comments are of interest, offering insight into the difficulties faced by Russian refugees, as well as observations on the remaining Armenian population:

> When [?] army came out of the Crimea, a lot of Russian aristocrats came out as refugees here to Const., in some cases with nothing . . . These were women who had never worked in their lives, but instead of whining . . . rolled up their sleeves and went at it. Some of the young women went into a restaurant as waitresses. . . . Later, dissatisfied with wages five of them rented a place and went at "on their own." The food was excellent and the prices about half the rates here at the hotel. The service was swift, deft, courteous—of course they all speak French. They were not in uniform, but did all wear white, and except one, plainly an Armenian, they were all Russian aristocrats. There were blondes and brunettes—I couldn't detect anything you could call a racial type. The head waitress, perhaps 30 (strictly but politely "on the job") had patrician written all over her. The waitresses were perhaps 18–20 years old. Dress them up in society cloths, and you would have a group that for apparent intellectual charm, grace of carriage, beauty of face and figure—a group that need fear no comparison with any American group from any stratum of society—even college seniors. Query, on the mass of masculine international drift wood that eddies around Const. whom are they going to marry?—except possibly members of the diplomatic set, who would seem to be their only equals—and how would they meet them? By the way, relative to some of my last comments on the Armenian unattractiveness, Miss Stanley says there exists a patrician Armenian type, mostly killed off however, but with slim long fingers, finely cut features, and slender wrists and trim ankles—but you would be lucky to find one of this type now in sixty others, the peasant type. These last mature at 12, marry at 14, bear children at 15, work in the fields, and are old at 30. And yet given a chance they are keen and ambitious intellectually.[164]

The Road to Yalivadj

By the end of June, Swain and Easton finally embarked on the 300-mile trip from Broussa (20 miles south of Moudania) to Yalivadj, in the interior of Turkey. Swain had managed to obtain maps of Asia Minor: "24 large sheets (20 x 24 inches) on a scale of 10 km per inch, or about 6 miles to the inch." They had been produced in Germany before the war and showed "everything with German thoroughness."[165] Detailed as they were, they were out of date, and Swain anticipated that the trip would be challenging—not least because the vehicles, which were heavily loaded, would have to scale several mountain passes and traverse poorly maintained roads. In addition, town names presented a conundrum. "There is no standard transliteration of Turkish and Arabic names," Swain indicates in a letter to his family, "so if you look on other maps (as in the big Rand & McNally atlas at the library) you will have to look for anything that resembles anything I write. Yalovatch, Yalivaj, and Jalovatsch are all the same place, but from different maps—slightly confusing in view of our exactitude in names of places."[166]

Swain's initial assessments of the roads would presage the rest of the trip: "We were soon in a position to furnish museum specimens of every sort of road, past, present, and future."[167] Swain and Easton had to maneuver "through sticky mud, ford streams, cross shaky bridges (one settled a foot as the truck went over), do 'switch back act' on side hills, follow barely discernable cart tracks under the guidance of natives, [and] feel our way along roads hidden with reddish flood water. . . . One rear wheel of the truck crushed through the rotten top of a hidden culvert and had to be pried out with a telegraph pole."[168] Although driving was a challenge, Easton writes about the journey with youthful enthusiasm: "Few roads, almost no bridges, and deep mud combine to make it a great adventure. In the rainy season, being pulled out of the mud is sometimes an hourly occurrence."[169]

Projecting a more serious tenor, Easton, who was barely 20 at the time, also shares his perspective on the devastations caused by the Greco-Turkish War:

> For 200 miles after leaving Brusa . . . the ravages committed by the Greeks in the Turko-Greek war of 1921–22 met one everywhere. The Greeks made a clean sweep, destroying thoroughly every village they came to. Although most of these have been rebuilt, since the majority of buildings were of mud-brick, an easily replaceable material, we passed several villages where, when the Greeks in turn were driven out by the Turks not a wall over five feet high was left standing in the Greek retreat. Crops were destroyed, cattle carried off, orchards cut down and irrigation ditches broken. Most of the destruction was apparently unnecessary for military reasons, but since it was committed by an ostensibly Christian nation, the western press of course remained silent.[170]

Swain similarly writes about the scourges of war and how "utterly wrecked the villages were by the Greeks on their disastrous rout back to Smyrna and the sea." The burning of Smyrna in 1922 left him with searing images. After his visit there, before his stay in Constantinople, Swain writes, "I must own I was glad to leave Smyrna—I couldn't quite put out of my mind the horrors of the debacle scarcely 20 months ago" (Side Car 6).[171] And his notes about the squalid and crowded conditions in Mytilene on the island of Lesbos cast a foreboding shadow on today's world politics. "The normal population of the island is something like 100,000, town 20,000, and there are still some 60,000 refugees on the island," he writes home. "The few thousand Turks [that were] here of course had to go and the two mosques in the town of Mytilene are now camping grounds for refugees, curtained off by burlap screens in an attempt at privacy—must make Allah squirm!"[172]

Commenting further and sympathetically, he notes, "Unavoidably all the efforts of the people, poverty stricken now if not before, have been devoted to reconstruction of hovels and houses, and they have been utterly unable to pay taxes, so there have been no funds for road repairs in most districts."[173] In a letter later that year, Swain strikes a similarly compassionate tone, writing that the money paid to the local laborers at the dig "had the effect of a relief fund, for some of the people were facing starvation."[174]

Side Car 6: The Burning of Smyrna

The results from the ferocious burning of Smyrna in September 1922 still lingered when Swain visited in 1924. He described what he saw in a letter to his family: "[The] wide quai . . . ran over a mile along the shore. The fire destroyed not over 1,000 feet of this front, but made a clean sweep in the back from some 3 km.—how wide at the back I do not know—it was the entire Greek-Armenian foreign quarter. The former population was some 300,000, now 90,000 as an estimate. Practically no rebuilding has been done yet—enough of the city left for the people here perhaps! The burnt area seems to me to be possibly a half mile by perhaps three quarters. . . . It is absolutely wrecked however as far as it goes and was almost the commercial heart of Smyrna—was mostly two-story buildings except the narrow edge where it touched the water where some were higher."[175]

On June 30, 1924, a few days after they had disembarked at Broussa, Swain and Easton reached Ak-Shehir, the nearest rail station to Yalivadj on the Berlin–Baghdad Railway (fig. 70). The railway had provided a strategic military lifeline during the Great War. It was just as important to archaeologists, who were now traveling the rails in search of previously inaccessible sites.[176]

The Broussa–Ak-Shehir stretch of road was approximately 115 miles, which took 14.5 hours of driving. Swain and Easton took a wrong turn that cost them an extra 25 miles; the sedan became stuck in a wheat field; and the last 45 miles, once consisting of narrow roads and bridges, had been reduced to several small streams. Ten feet from the hotel in Ak-Shehir, the truck lurched and came to a sudden stop: a concealed drain had given way under one of the hind wheels. The vehicle was left until morning, when several locals were commandeered; they used rope, telephone poles, and planks to rescue the abandoned vehicle. Having endured several near disasters since their arrival overseas, both the truck and sedan must have felt like veterans of the unexpected.

Although no doubt happy to settle into a night at Ak-Shehir, Swain and company discovered that their ramshackle hotel housed some unexpected occupants. "The hotel breakfast was served to us in the 'mezzanine' floor," writes Swain. "The windows were mostly missing, and there were swallows nests over head with young ones in them. Two were at one side, and one over the table—but some particular person had suspended a board under this nest over the table. Outside several storks' nests were visible on nearby roofs."[177]

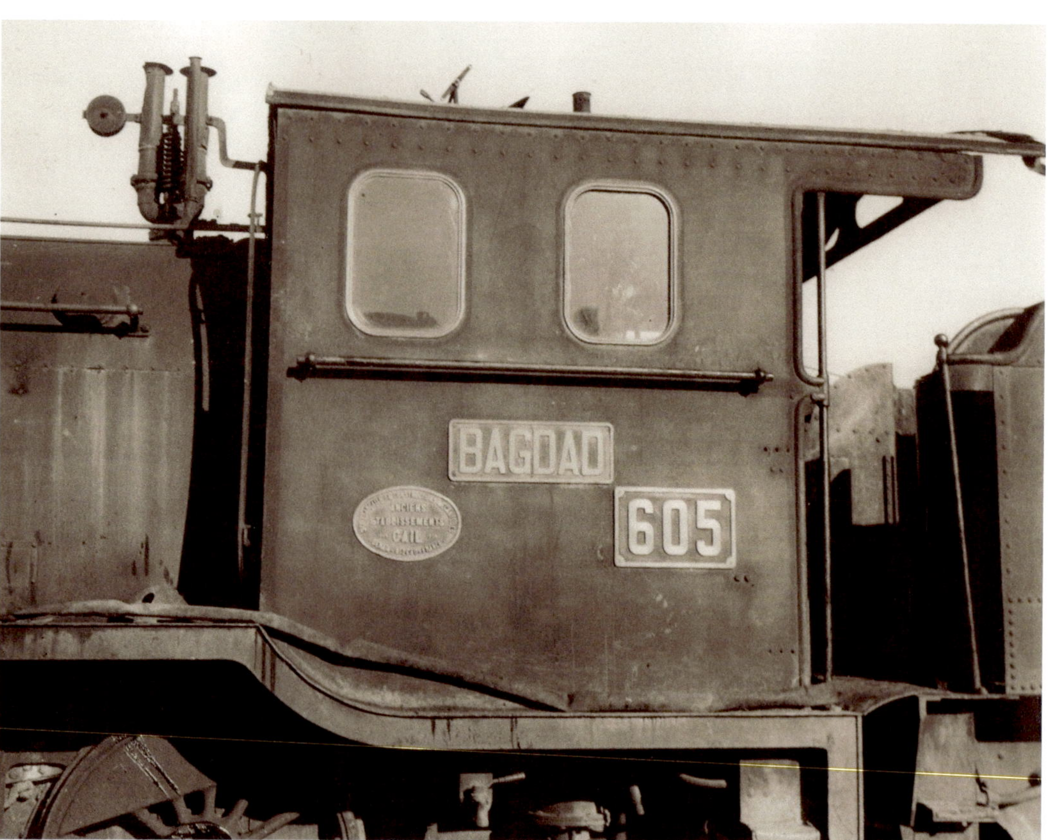

Fig. 70. Railway car with a metal placard reading "BAGDAD," Adana, Turkey, December 31, 1919 (Kelsey Museum neg. no. KS 063.02).

The last stretch of roads was “abominable,” and the truck nearly tipped over three miles from Yalivadj. David Robinson (director of the Antioch excavation) and some of his crew came from town, working four hours in the dark as they stood in mud and water. The only illumination was provided by the headlights of the sedan, which had been pressed into service to help its companion. It took a good deal of ingenuity, accompanied by “yells and cuss words” to rescue the hefty truck.[178] “A long heavy pole was gotten under the frame of the car ahead of the wheel, and four men lifting on that could prevent any tipping so an inch or less at a time we had to jack the thing up some two feet, and shove the back of the car over at the same time.”[179] Finally, the truck was righted and on its way. As Swain observes, “I did not suppose cars could be built to stand the strains we have put on these two coming, and have nothing give way.”[180]

Life in Yalivadj

Swain spent several months in Yalivadj, photographing the valuable material and important structures unearthed by the Antioch excavations. Busy as he was, he still carved out time to photograph and discover the town and its environs. Yalivadj was small, situated in a fertile plain between rolling hills and a deep gorge. The summer landscape boasted “slim poplars . . . and almost countless pear, apple, quince, plum, and walnut trees.”[181] The population stood at 14,000 (housed in modest mudbrick houses), with an outlying population of another 14,000. After all the tribulations the truck and sedan had endured, the two vehicles must have hoped that the town roads would offer a welcome respite. Quite the contrary: Yalivadj’s roads had their own trials. As Swain notes, “The streets were so narrow and crooked, it was an even bet whether you could drive around a corner without . . . taking off an awning or overturning a tradesman’s bench.”[182]

Easton provides a good summary of the village and the crew’s accommodations:

> Yalovatch itself is thoroughly oriental. Streams from the nearby mountains water it so plentifully that from a distance one sees only trees. The “civic center,” as it were, is a space surrounded by coffee houses and shaded by a centuries-old plane tree. On warm days, the enterprising hosts put benches in the shade of the great tree where one may sip thick coffee, tea, or sherbert made from snow brought from the nearby summits. The coffee house is the movie, the lecture hall, the library, and the club of Yalovatch. Adjoining the plaza of the plane tree are the bazaars—narrow covered streets, which are lined with little shops where merchants sit surrounded by their wares or where craftsmen fashion shoes, plows, and pots. Farther away are houses and luxurious gardens. . . . The public buildings include eight mosques . . . two public baths, several elementary schools, and a high school, a post office and . . . a governmental building. The one hotel, if one may grace it with that name, was leased . . . for the Michigan party. The ground floor was occupied by Yalovatch’s one club, a large hallway, and a coffee house, which was soon closed when we threatened to move out unless the riotous evenings ceased.

On the second floor were four bedrooms, a storage room . . . a very large room which was used as a combination kitchen, dining room, library, cardroom, [and] photographic dark room [figs. 71–72].[183]

Swain's observations of the local population, dress, day-to-day behaviors, and special events echo Easton Kelsey's and add a few more details that help envision life in the town:

In Yalovatch: Nine-tenths of the men wear the native Turkish costume, the rest European [fig. 73]. . . . In the middle of the town is a perfectly enormous plane tree—shading an outdoor coffee house—masculine gossip exchange. Mail is received and dispatched twice a week. Telegrams may be sent and received, but in Turkish only and the things that happen to English proper names are fearful and wonderful.[184]

The women here go veiled almost always—unless under 12 or over (apparently) 75. They wear—when at work at least—a sort of trousers fairly close at the ankle and getting larger and larger as you go up till they are voluminous at the hips. If a veil by any chance is not at hand, or cannot be put on quickly enough, [then] they face a wall or a corner of two walls [fig. 74].[185]

Fig. 71. Plane tree and café in the center of Yalivadj, Turkey, August 1924 (Kelsey Museum neg. no. 7.1621).

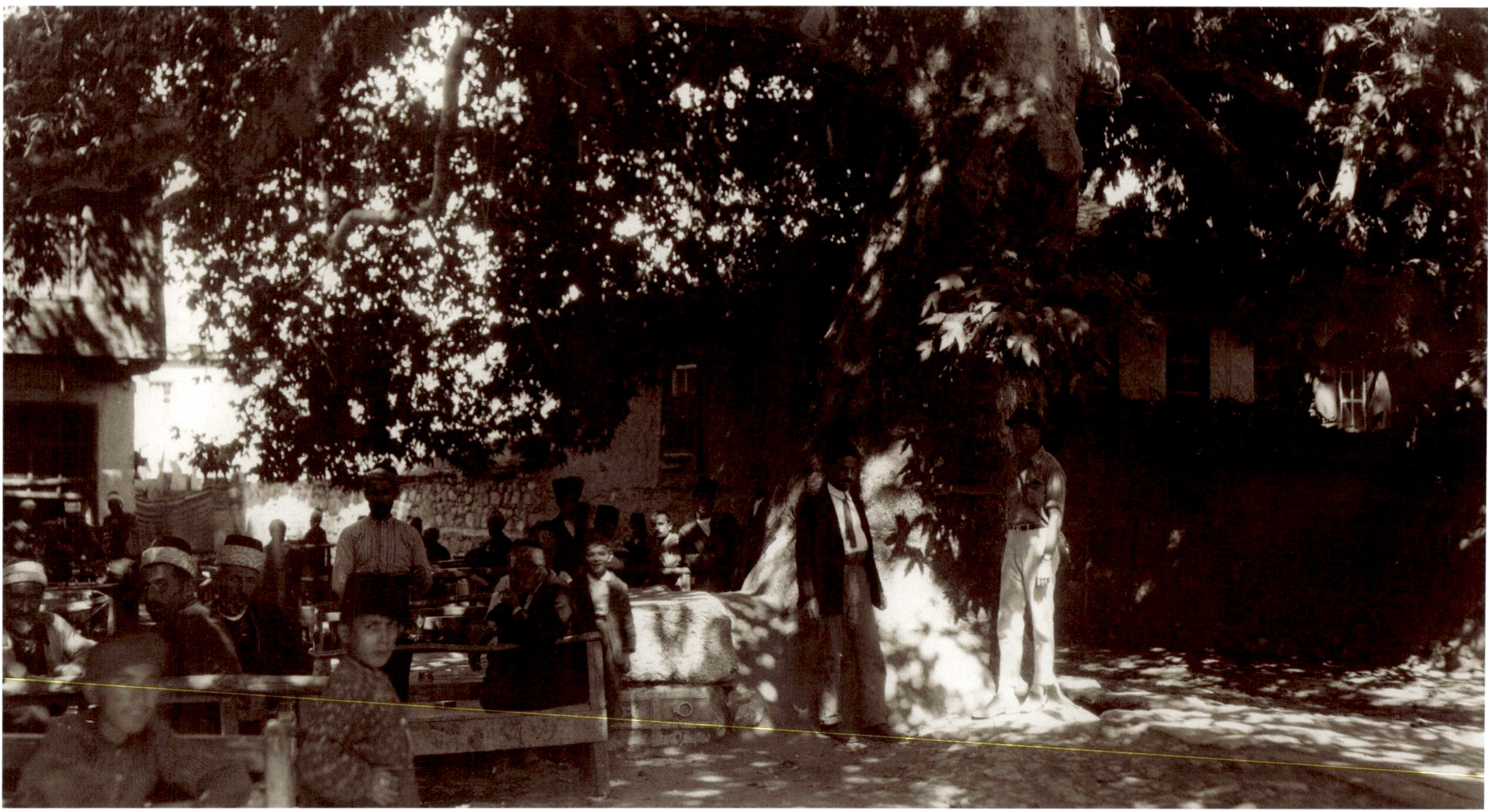

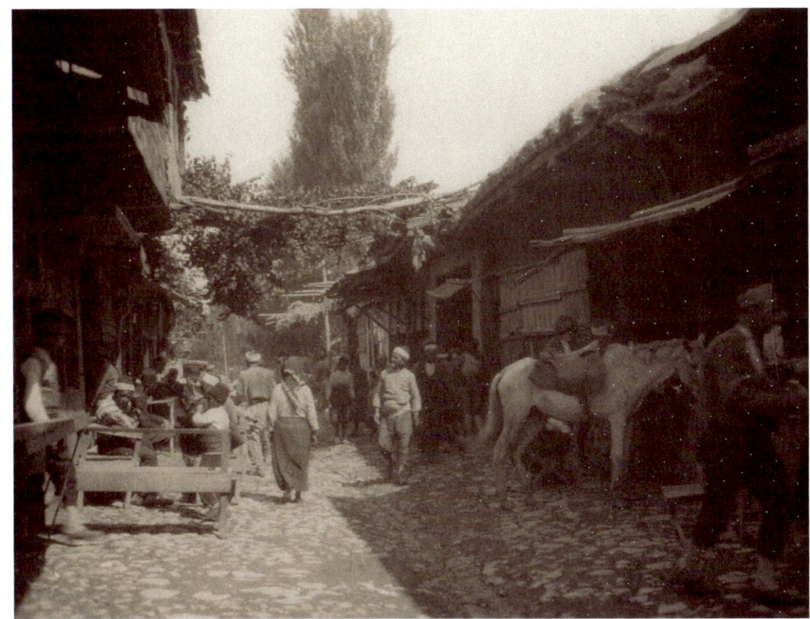

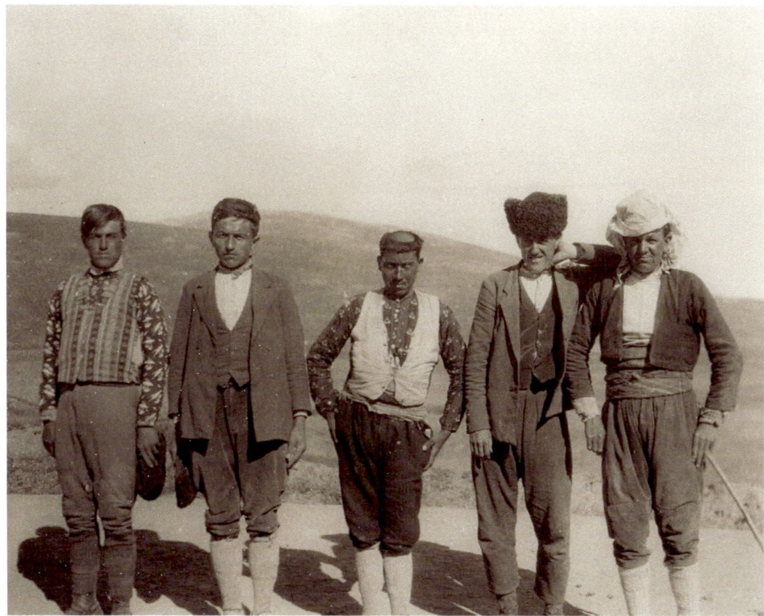

> By the way, the horse trail to Ak-Shehir goes up [a] valley. . . . By the trail in some places bits of colored string and cloth tied on the bushes propitiate some saint who is supposed to live below and help heal diseases.[186]
>
> A four-day religious festival began yesterday—Feast of Byram, so we may be unable to do much till Tuesday. One of the features of the program is that each family is supposed to have a sheep and give away ¼ of it to the poor. If they are all as fresh as the specimens from which some sections were served us last night I'd be willing to give all my share to the poor![187]

Fig. 72. View of a typical street in Yalivadj, Turkey, August 17, 1924 (Kelsey Museum neg. no. KS 288.03).

Fig. 73. Hassan and four Turkish workers, Yalivadj, Turkey, July 2, 1924 (Kelsey Museum neg. no. KS 276.10).

One of Swain's more unusual stories about life in Yalivadj centers on an event during the night of August 13, 1924. His short narrative not only highlights local superstitions but also hints at the relationships between the expedition crew and the town's residents:

> As the heavy shadow moved over onto the silver disc of the moon a stray shot or two cracked out in town. As the area of the shadow increased so did the fusillade of shots. . . . Tradition has it that the cause of the darkness is Satan drawing a curtain over the moon and that shooting frightens him away. The literati of the present day scoff at this and say the shooting is merely for fun and to announce the eclipse. But I have a sneaking suspicion that more than one of the people think that shooting can do no harm—and really it is just as well to be on the safe side! But the people are not wholly lacking in a sense of humor. Woodbridge (architect of the Near East Research) has a wee pistol of .10 caliber or smaller, about the [size] of a fraternal watch charm, but actually fires a cartridge well nigh microscopic—a weapon with which you would have a

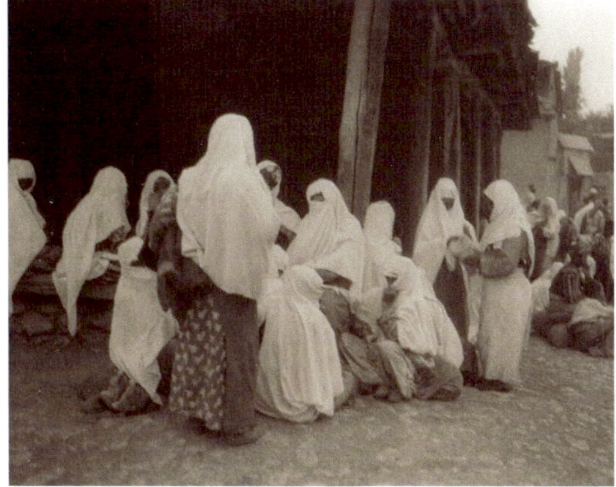

Fig. 74. A group of veiled women at the Monday bazaar, Yalivadj, Turkey, August 17, 1924 (Kelsey Museum neg. no. KS 287.11).

> 50-50 chance of defending yourself from a half grown mouse, and with a report almost as loud as a paper cap. But when, at the height of the eclipse bombardment, he stepped out into the street in front of our "hotel" and, gravely pulling this from his pocket, carefully sighted at the moon and fired, the performance was greeted with roars of laughter, and he was virtually compelled to give two or three encores.[188]

While all of these descriptions offer invaluable commentary on the daily activities in and around Yalivadj, it is Swain's photographs that best transport us to this remote village of 1924. The concept of "how one spends one's days is how one lives one's life" is fully captured by his fine black-and-white images.[189] Particularly evocative are his photos of the Monday bazaar, with its sellers of yogurt, vegetables, water jars, and cloth; views of typical streets and local shops; hides being tanned in the countryside; men hunting partridge with decoys; and sheep sleeping in the shade of midday (figs. 75–80).

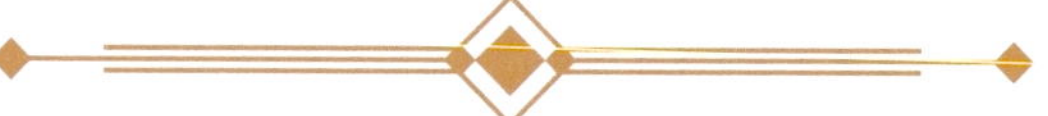

The country of Turkey that Swain experienced in 1924 was in the throes of massive transitions. Once Mustafa Kemal Atatürk came to power in 1923, he undertook sweeping reforms, pushing the country to become a modern, industrialized, and secular nation-state. As a teacher, Swain was particularly curious about the educational reforms of Atatürk, questioning how successful his ambitious programs might be:

> Whether Turkey solves her problems of readjustment successfully and makes a republic grow in a soil 90 per cent illiterate, only the future can disclose, but in some things a great beginning has been made—as in education. They

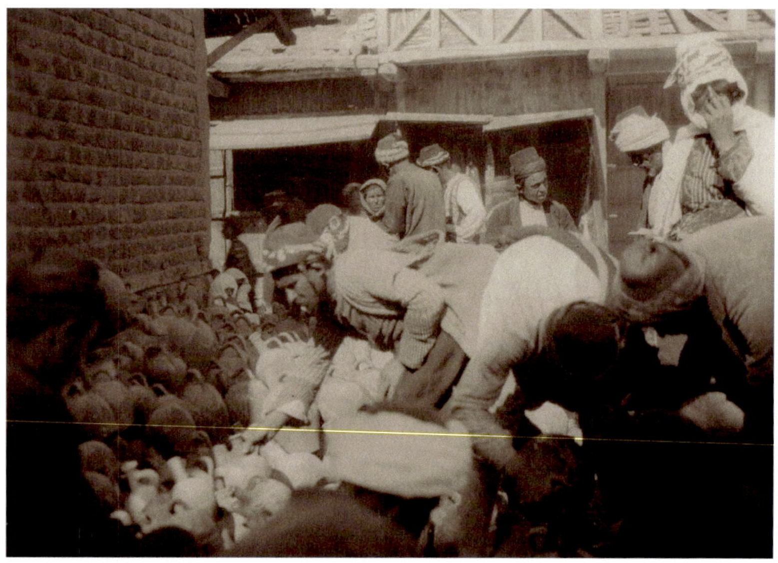

Fig. 75. Water jars for sale at Monday's bazaar, Yalivadj, Turkey, July 28, 1924 (Kelsey Museum neg. no. KS 283.06).

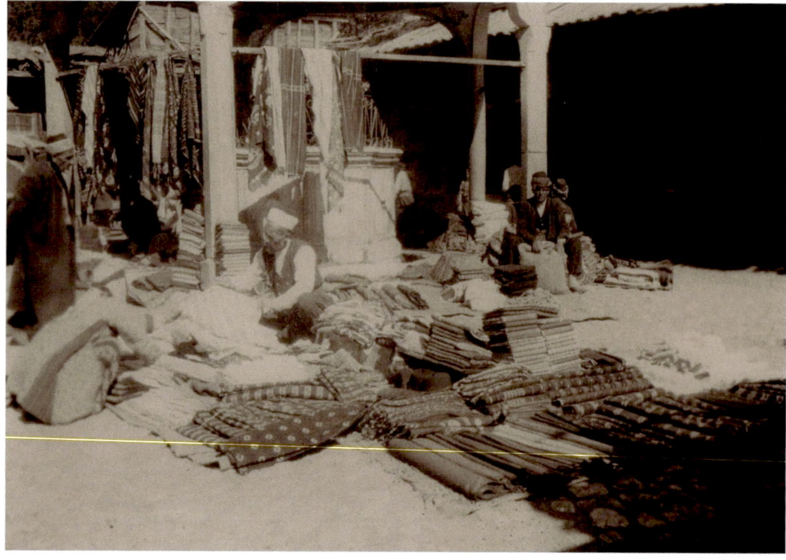

Fig. 76. The cloth market at Monday's bazaar, Yalivadj, Turkey, July 28, 1924 (Kelsey Museum neg. no. KS 283.03).

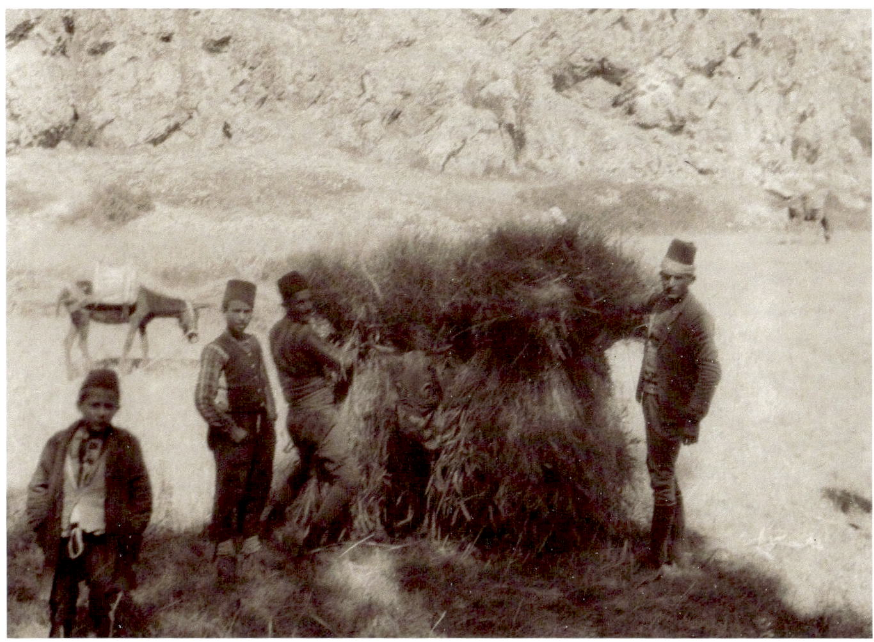

Fig. 77. Men loading a donkey with grain, Yalivadj, Turkey, July 18, 1924 (Kelsey Museum neg. no. KS 280.06).

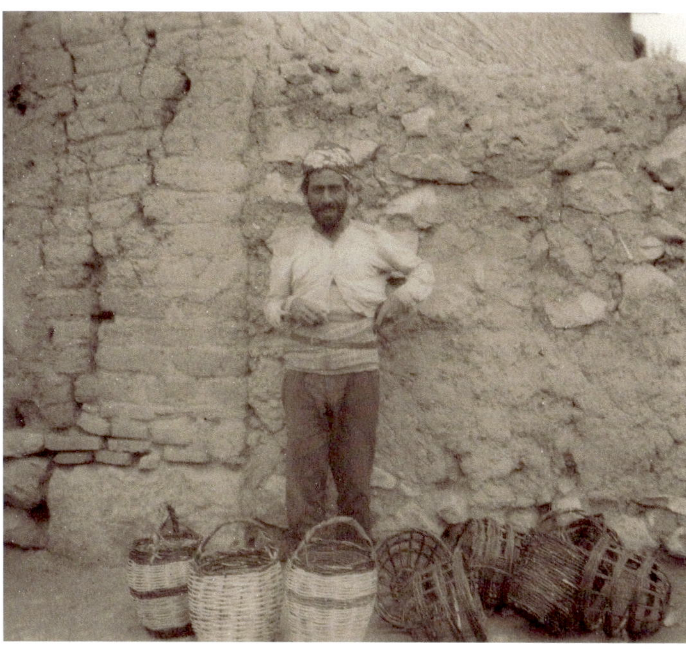

Fig. 78. Man selling baskets at Monday's bazaar, Yalivadj, Turkey, August 17, 1924 (Kelsey Museum neg. no. KS 287.12).

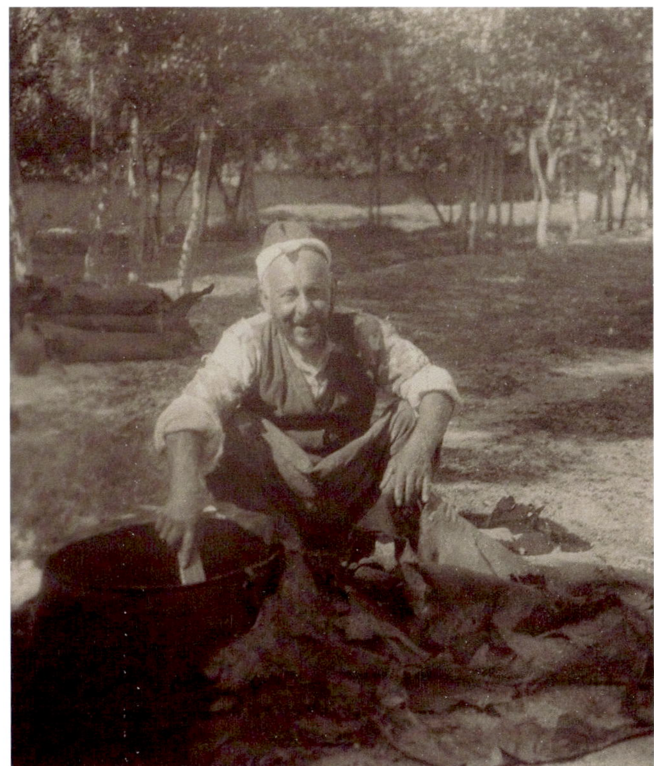

Fig. 79. A man tanning hides, Yalivadj, Turkey, July 20, 1924 (Kelsey Museum neg. no. KS 281.09).

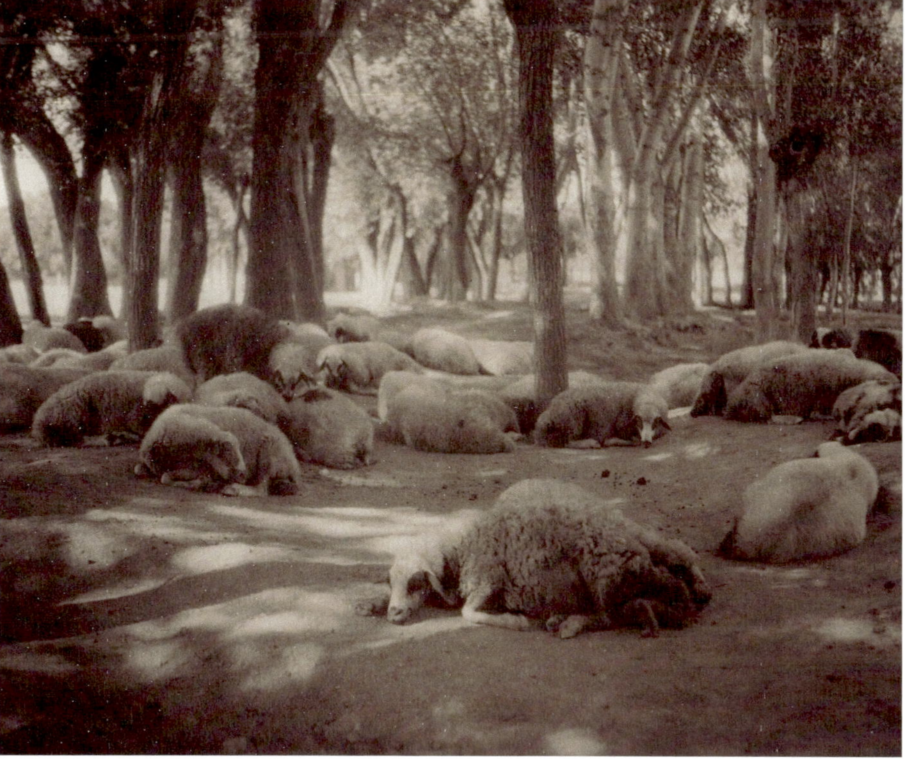

Fig. 80. Sheep seeking shade in the middle of the day, Yalivadj, Turkey, August 17, 1924 (Kelsey Museum neg. no. KS 288.10).

> are trying to establish a normal school at the center of each vilayet (local area corresponding to counties in a state). In Yalovatch . . . [there] are 50 elementary schools, each with 50 to 150 pupils. Most teachers are men but there are already five or six women in these schools. New school buildings are going up. In Yalovatch is a lycée (high school) in a fine new building (partly erected by Greek prisoners of war) with, for this part of the world, a surprising amount of scientific apparatus.[190]

Swain was also interested in the local economy and intrigued by the process of taxation, which he likens to ancient Roman laws—both equally corrupt in his estimation:

> They collect various sorts of taxes here. The grain tax is in a class by itself. It is farmed out in the good old Roman way. An area—village or district—is put up at auction, the successful bidder paying the government a lump sum. Then, legally he goes out, collects and sells one eighth of the threshed grain. If the one-eighth in the area sells for more than he paid the government, he is entitled to the gain, if less he must pocket the loss. Practically, according to Avney Effendi (the Turk who was ten years in the U.S.) it leads to all sorts of abuses as some of the tax collectors are bullying scoundrels who may take anything up to half of the crop of a poor peasant whom he thinks cannot kick about the procedure—or who wouldn't dare to. Lovely situation.[191]

Occasionally, Swain comments on the personalities, foibles, and habits of his coworkers, as well as some of the local inhabitants. His observations about the "Yalivadjites" vary; some, like the following, are sympathetic (and inform readers about inheritance practices), while others (see p. 72) berate the attitudes of locals toward antiquities in their own backyard:

> I think Avney Effendi [local representative of the Turkish government stationed at the site] is at times lonesome—he was ten years in the U.S. partly in school, partly working (once as a proof reader for a magazine firm) was summoned back here by his father on the death of his brother (killed in the war) to marry his brother's wife in order to hold some property in the family. He had to serve a year in the army first and has now been out of that a year. I don't know what he ultimately plans doing—except that he wants to get back to the U.S.A. He is well educated, intelligent, good looking, rather broad minded.[192]

Talk about a Bad Day

On August 19, 1924, while still in Yalivadj, several crew members needed to travel to Ankara—a distance of approximately 180 miles—for business reasons. The Ankara contingent included Easton Kelsey, Enoch E. Peterson (a student at the University of Michigan), David Robinson, and a Mr. Woodbridge (the project's architect). A Turkish student at the

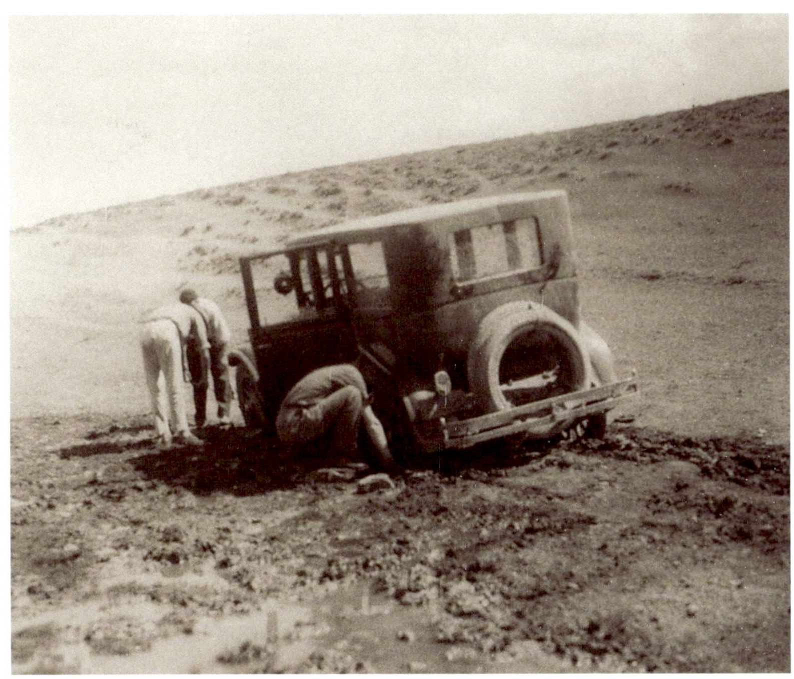

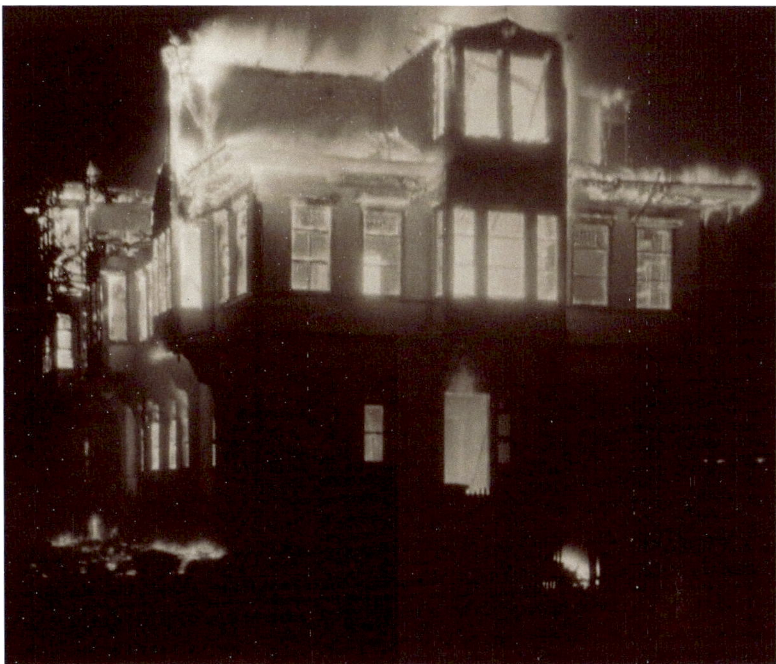

University of Michigan, Hussein Shefik Feizy, whose brother was the chief of police in the city of Konya and served as interpreter and surveyor for the Antioch project, was also part of the group.

The trip was doomed from the start. First, the sedan nearly ran out of gas (fig. 81), then later that night, after finding fuel and settling into a hotel, they all had to flee for their lives (fig. 82). Both Swain and Robinson wrote about the night's disaster. The following is a firsthand account from Robinson and Peterson's *Journal of Antioch Excavations*:

> About 10:45 p.m. I was awakened by a peculiar noise and noticed that the electric wire in my room was red hot. In a moment the woodwork was afire. I got up in my pajamas and called the hotel men who could have put the fire out in a few moments if they had kept their heads. A panic ensued and all the hotel was in complete darkness. I got dressed with difficulty, packed up my things which were all scattered about my room. Even so I found I had forgotten some things and went back a second time to get them, and even a third time to rescue my gold watch and my collar box with studs. I never realized for one moment that the fire would spread beyond my room, but when I saw the inefficiency of the firemen who were even battering down the staircase, I concluded that I had better get out of the hotel. I then broke open the door of the sedan and with the help of some men backed it out of danger. There was no time to rescue the belongings of Mr. Woodbridge or Mr. [Easton] Kelsey or Mr. Feizy. And they lost nearly two hundred fifty dollars worth of things including valuable documents and the keys to the automobile. The hotel burned to the ground and also the surrounding buildings. . .[193]

Fig. 81. David Robinson provided the following caption for this image he captured: "On August 19, 1924, members of the excavation team embark on a trip to Ankara, Turkey. On this inauspicious day the 'dig car' gets stuck in the mud, gas runs dangerously low, and the night in the hotel at Ankara ends with a blazing fire that burns the hotel to the ground" (Kelsey Museum neg. no. KR 097.02).

Fig. 82. Robinson's photograph of the hotel burning, Ankara, Turkey, August 19–20, 1924 (Kelsey Museum neg. no. KR 097.09).

While Swain was not part of the trip, his letter home corroborates the events, adding a negative appraisal of the local inhabitants: "The natives all lost their heads. . . . Easton and Woodridge [*sic*] lost a lot, not so much by fire as by looting—fire was a signal to steal all you could apparently. Among other things was Easton's Kodak (his personally) a brand new one like mine. Woodbridge had an automatic revolver belonging to Feizy. After about everything had been stolen that could be, a cordon of police was formed. From all accounts it must have been a fair sample of pandemonium for a time."[194]

Archaeological Destruction and Western Colonialism

Although Swain voices both positive and negative comments about the local population in Yalivadj, he is especially vocal about what he perceived as the villagers' disturbing treatment of their antiquities, a common perspective of Western archaeologists working in the Mediterranean and Near East during the 20th century. While several of Swain's condemnations were legitimate (e.g., the destruction and looting of ancient artifacts by some village residents), what developed among many archaeologists (and Western government officials) was a wholesale trashing of local populations and foreign governments. Painted with a broad brush, these groups were viewed as neither caring for their heritage nor capable of curating and protecting it. Western colonial powers believed they had a mission to rescue the world's heritage from neglect and destruction—although some of their motives were clearly less noble, spurred by greed and profit. As discussed in Part IV, the history of archaeology is littered with such colonial attitudes.

Swain's perspective is best summarized in a *Detroit News* article of November 12, 1924, written by reporter Allen Shoenfield:

> Mr. Swain smiled as he recounted difficulties experienced by the excavators in preventing their Turkish workmen from wantonly destroying priceless mosaic floors, valuable inscriptions and the rare vases and bits of sculpture uncovered from the debris of the ancient city, often at a depth of 15 to 20 feet.
>
> "It is said that the Turks delight in destroying whatever may partake of Christianity and it is certain that Antioch of Pisidia, one of the 16 cities of that name built by the son of Antiochus, was an early seat of the church. . . . It is certain, too, that this is the very Antioch mentioned by Paul in the XIIIth Chapter of the Acts of the Apostles, and that he and Barabas trod the pavements, the squares and the stone flight of stairs we uncovered. And yet, I do not think any religious feeling actuated the Turks. They had just had a very poor harvest and were eager to work for us at about 40 cents a day each. We established the usual system of 'baksheesh' or bonus for every find brought to us, and this proved of value. But the Yalovatchians are apparently imbued by a spirit of pure cussedness which moves them to destroy whatever they cannot put to immediate use in their own building operations.
>
> For centuries the site of Antioch has been used as a quarry and it is a common sight to see embedded in the foundations of the brick or mud

houses of Yalovatch great stones bearing Latin inscriptions of the greatest significance to archaeologists. One never knows, in seeing a stone set into a wall whether the inner side, concealed forever, may not hold some inscription of high historical significance.

The expedition unearthed a magnificent triumphal city gate, part of which was missing. Later we found one of the missing blocks being used as a stepping stone across a small stream near the village and had to get permission of the city authorities to take it up.

At another time we discovered part of the vast drainage system of the city and found sections of terra cotta piping in an excellent stage of preservation, flanged exactly like our modern pipes. With infinite care the excavators piled up 60 feet of this pipe, but on looking for it later, saw it had disappeared. The city fathers had calmly appropriated it, and built it into a drain. With some difficulty we got it back again."

Mr. Swain stated that the Turkish government, although rendering the expedition every courtesy steadfastly refused to permit the export from the country of any of the relics except in rare cases of unimportant duplication of finds.[195]

Swain reiterates his sentiments about the local disregard of antiquities in several letters to his family; one in particular recounts the discovery of a large, ancient inscription built into a local mudbrick wall (fig. 83):

Yesterday p.m. a barber paid me a much needed visit, then later I went up on a hill with camera for some general views—with Omar and his donkey to carry things [see fig. 49, p. 43]. Coming back by a narrow, crooked street on the edge of a patch of hovels, as a part of the door frame of a mud-walled yard, we found an inscription new to all of us now here. It is a section of the marble architrave in two bands surrounded by a pretty good Greek moulding—egg and dart stuff. The two bands carrying a Latin inscription in letters 5–6 inches high. It must have been a big slab, for the top (upper end) was gone, and although we dug down some two inches the slab and inscription kept going down. The slab must be six or seven feet long. I think it is rather late, judging by the character of the letters—or rather the cutting, and it may be of no particular importance but it is interesting as a sample of what you run into at any time here abouts.[196]

Given Swain's comments, it is no surprise that he worried about the ultimate fate of material exposed by the excavations. Voicing his fears, he writes in a letter home, "Probably many of the fine architectural marble carvings we have found here at the 'dig' this year will be hopelessly splintered before next year—one reason why I have made so many photographs." He continues:

Apropos of destroying things—up to the dig, one building called for convenience the Basilica (maybe an early cathedral) was found to have below

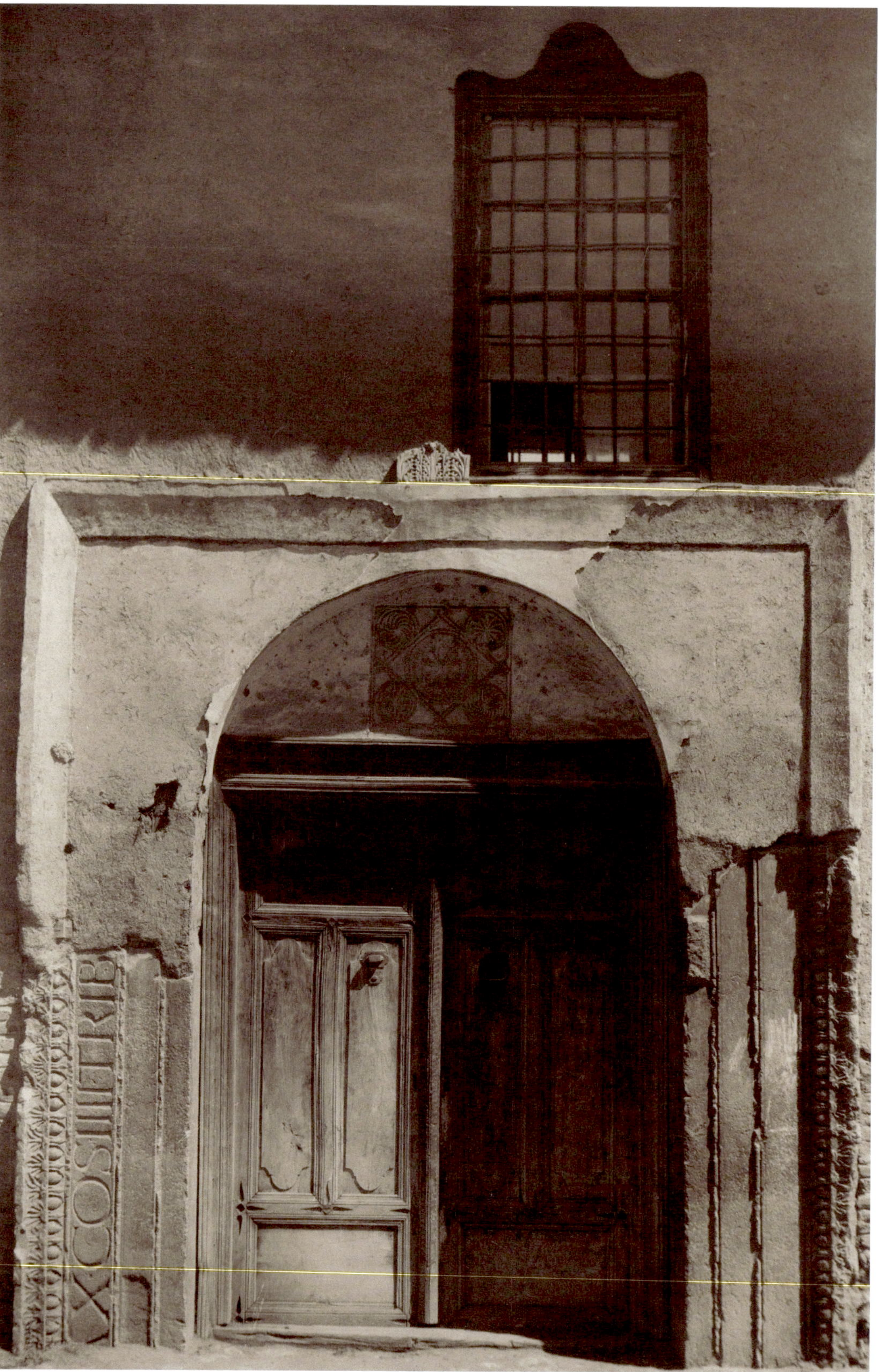

Fig. 83. "Doorway of Avnee's house. Old Roman architraves on right and left, vertical, one with inscription," Yalivadj, Turkey, August 1924 (Kelsey Museum neg. no. 7.1619).

> what seems to have been the floor of the later building, a fine Roman mosaic floor, of a still earlier church or public building. Quite large parts of this is—or was—intact. As fast as we covered and cleaned, I photographed sections showing different patterns—it is in four colors. Watchman were supposed to be on guard day and night at the dig—we paid one or two. When we're all through the remaining mosaic was covered ten inches deep with dirt. But in the interval probably 15%, perhaps 20%, had been deliberately pounded to pieces by natives. I don't pretend to know why. This is another reason why some of the best pieces, including almost all sculpture, has [*sic*] been brought down to the school here in town—it is a mile up to the dig.[197]

Misadventures in Italy and Returning Home

Excavation and study began to wind down by the end of August 1924. Swain, several of his colleagues, and the two vehicles left Yalivadj in the middle of September. The sedan had covered approximately 2,500 miles in Anatolia, with the truck logging 750 miles. Swain had taken 700 to 800 photos, excluding Kodak images. It was a hectic last few weeks in Yalivadj, as Swain decided what to pack, what to leave for a potential return visit in 1925 (which never materialized), and how best to organize the mass of photos, negatives, data, notebooks, and drawings that had emerged from the project. Equally important was organizing the protocols for the trip back to Europe: securing permits and visas for both people and cars, as well as plotting the final journey home, which would include the train from Konya to Ak-Shehir and Eski-Shehir; transport to Constantinople, Smyrna, Naples, Rome, and Paris; and ultimately, the transatlantic voyage back to the United States.

Swain, who often found humor in the smallest details, provides an informative description of the train from Konya to Ak-Shehir, taken on September 12, 1924:

> The station buildings are all good, usually two-story (station master lives up-stairs), stone or stucco, tile roofs, with well-kept grounds. Starting a train after a station stop is a junction—first a dinner bell is jangled; about four minutes later [it] is jangled again somewhat more intensely; then somebody blows a penny whistle, somebody else answers with a tin toy trumpet. The engine toots twice—and then you move off with impressive (?) slowness. Coming in to a station, trains slow down some two hundred yards away, and romp into the station at a reckless rate of perhaps four miles an hour—any way ducks, hens, and geese have no trouble getting out of the way with no display of haste.[198]

By September 16, Swain and company found themselves at the Eski-Shehir train station, arriving about 9:30 p.m. Securing seats on the train was an "unholy jam." Seats were impossible to find, and the group members had resigned themselves to sitting on their suitcases in the train's corridor. Through a bit of luck and perseverance—not to mention some *baksheesh*—they managed to sneak onto a car coupled at the last minute onto the first-class carriage and pass their baggage through an open window.

Eventually, Swain and his colleagues reached Constantinople, where they boarded a ship to Naples along with both vehicles. The voyage, which lasted from September 23 to 28, was described by Swain as a "dandy 6-day trip," spent indexing and writing. The steamer docked for one night in Smyrna, then plowed straight on to Naples. "I sent a cable home today," Swain writes to his family, "so you would know I was well out of Turkey, and back into the Roman alphabet again! Needless to say, I am glad to be back where I can read signs once more—I can guess at a good many things in Italian anyway" (figs. 84–85).[199]

Kelsey had given Swain various assignments—in particular, photographing select sites and artifacts in various Neapolitan museums. Swain found himself preoccupied with work as soon as he landed. On October 7, he left Naples for Rome, where he again had more assignments from Kelsey.

But it was not all work for Swain. While visiting the town of Arpino (home of the famous orator Cicero), he encountered a wealthy aristocrat who noticed the University of Michigan car and was interested in meeting its occupant (fig. 86). Once they met, the marquis escorted Swain and his colleague Woodbridge to his palazzo. As Swain writes, "He . . . showed us all around, furniture and pictures etc., and with the family (his mother speaks English) served us sandwiches, gateaux, grapes and Wine (one kind was 30 years old!), gave us cards to admit to various places, and was kindness itself."[200]

Swain had access to both vehicles, which were stored in Rome, and his comments about driving ring true to anyone who has ever driven in that city:

> An edict had gone forth here that beginning Oct. 14 all street traffic of all sorts shall pass to the right, instead of to the left as heretofore. I am not sure

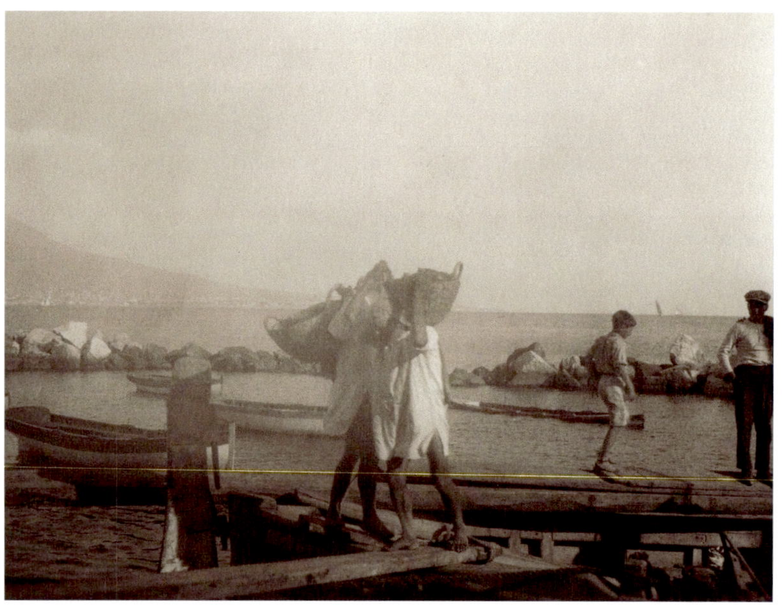

Fig. 84. Porters bringing baskets off a boat, Naples, Italy, September 30, 1924 (Kelsey Museum neg. no. KS 295.04).

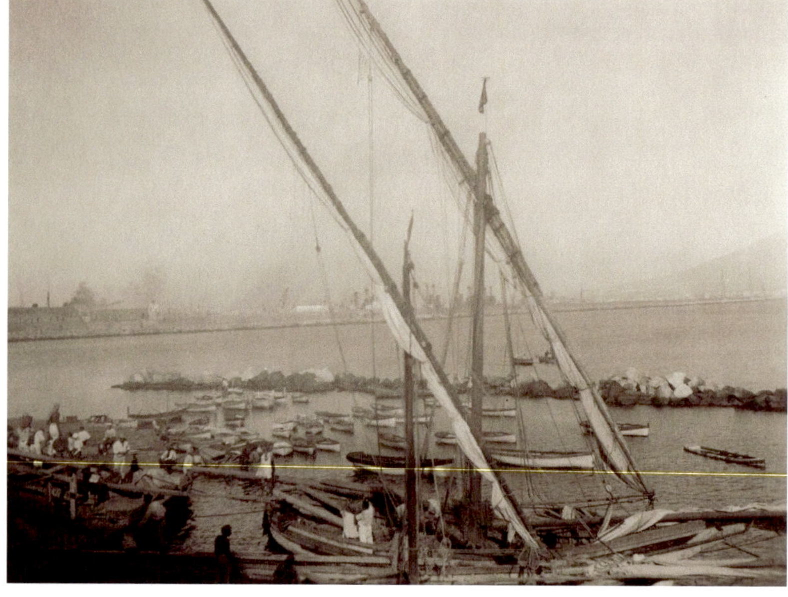

Fig. 85. Boats at the Naples waterfront, Italy, September 30, 1924 (Kelsey Museum neg. no. KS 295.02).

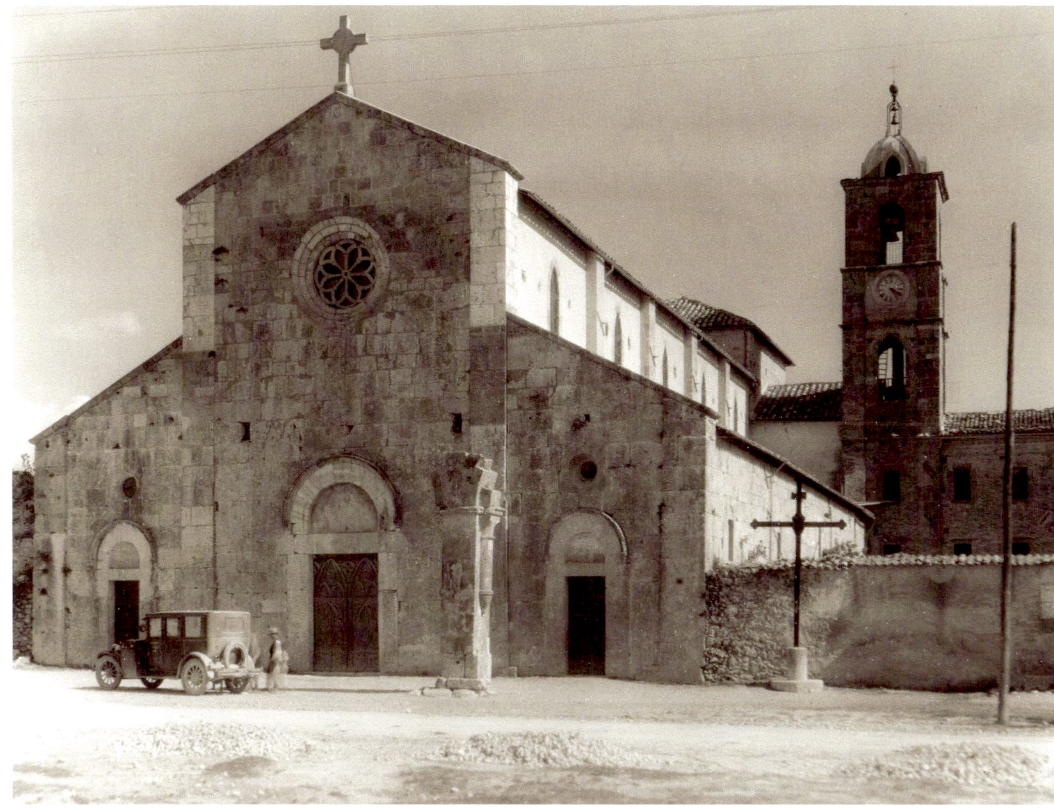

Fig. 86. Church near the birthplace of Cicero, with the Dodge sedan at left, Arpino, Italy, October 7–12, 1924 (Kelsey Museum neg. no. 7.1695).

> but that driving in Rome for a day or two after that goes into effect will need to be classed as an extra hazardous occupation! At present in the city, autos and street cars pass on the left, carriages any old way they please; in the country . . . all autos pass to the right, seven eighths of horse traffic to the left, rest any way—only when the driver is sound asleep . . . the horse usually turns to the left when you honk for the road.[201]

The perils of driving were nothing, however, compared to two incidents that marred his last days in Rome, both within 24 hours of each other:

> Now I may as well relate a sad tale. While the truck was in the custom house dock the week at Naples, someone, evidently with a lot of keys, skeleton and otherwise got into the truck and went through one of my grips and small trunk. No locks were forced, so it must have been keys. Aside from about $7.50 worth of souvenirs, I lost the following: 1 pr. Half-soled black shoes, 1 pr. Almost new black shoes, 6 prs. Socks, 7 shirts, 2 prs. B.V.D's, 1 night shirt, about 10 handkerchiefs, trousers to my dress suit, one pair of trousers from the last Gross suit I bought and the coat and both pairs of trousers of the grey Cairo suit. . . . This leaves me with the Gross suit. As my only presentable suit left, and with the pair of half worn oxford shoes. . . . It is of

> course exasperating in the highest degree, but there is nothing one can do. The Cairo suit had seen its best days—I wore it constantly from Feb 26 to May 15, and it was hard service too. But it was wonderful cloth. I wish I were going to be in London a week before coming home, could get a suit there more cheaply than anywhere else I think.[202]

> I shall have to chronicle another loss—while at Palestrina today, while we were looking up some mosaics, the door of the sedan was forced open, ruining the lock, and my field glasses stolen. I paid 425 francs for them in Paris. . . . I am certainly playing in hard luck.[203]

Finally, Swain left Rome on October 25 for Paris. By the 29th, he was on board the SS *Majestic* for the final leg of his trip, arriving in New York on Tuesday, November 4, at 2:30 p.m. His wife, Edith, was at the dock, eagerly awaiting his return. The two vehicles wintered in Rome and would not lay their headlights on Swain again for several months.

The 1924 expedition resulted in a highly productive and exciting season for the University of Michigan crew. Excavations had unearthed important new finds and architecture, sufficiently intriguing to warrant a return for another campaign. Swain had hundreds of photos from the site, as well as a larder full of local photographs that chronicled life in and around the town of Yalivadj. While a return visit to Antioch was never actualized, Swain and his valiant vehicles would reunite in February 1925 for a very different but equally intriguing adventure—this time in North Africa.

Chapter 8
TRAVELS OF 1925

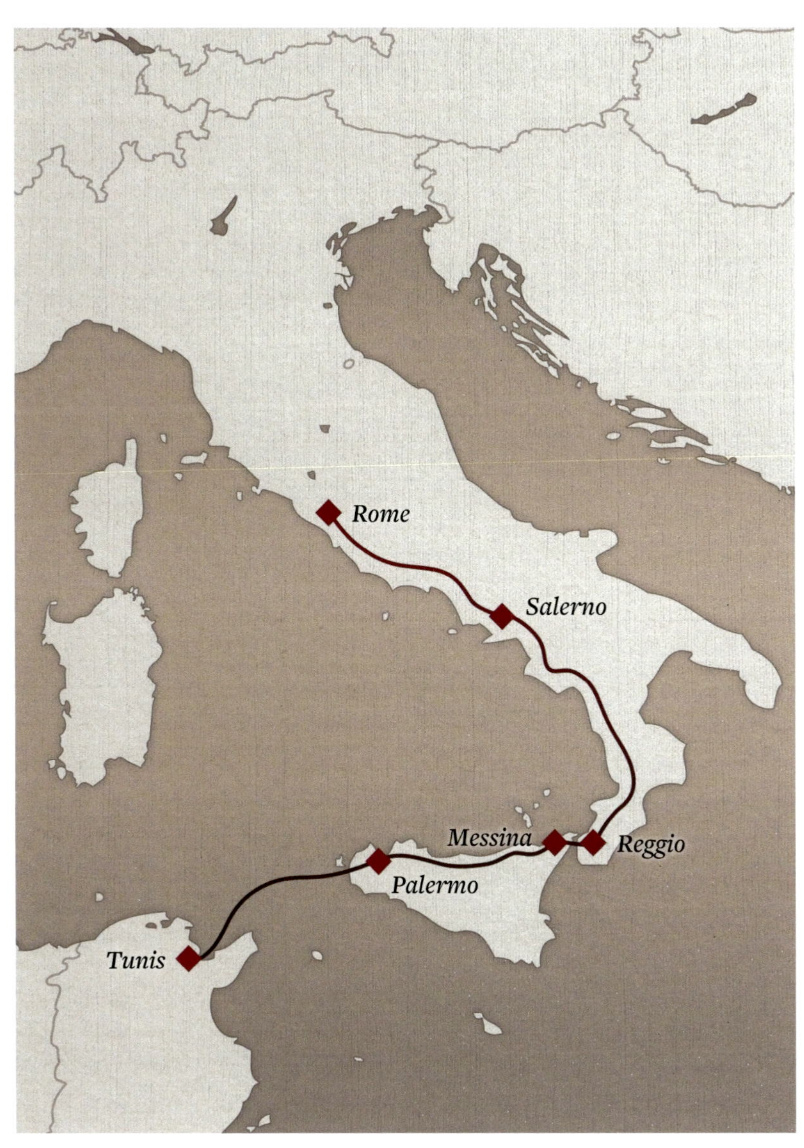

Approximate route of the university vehicles from Rome, Italy, to Tunis, Tunisia.

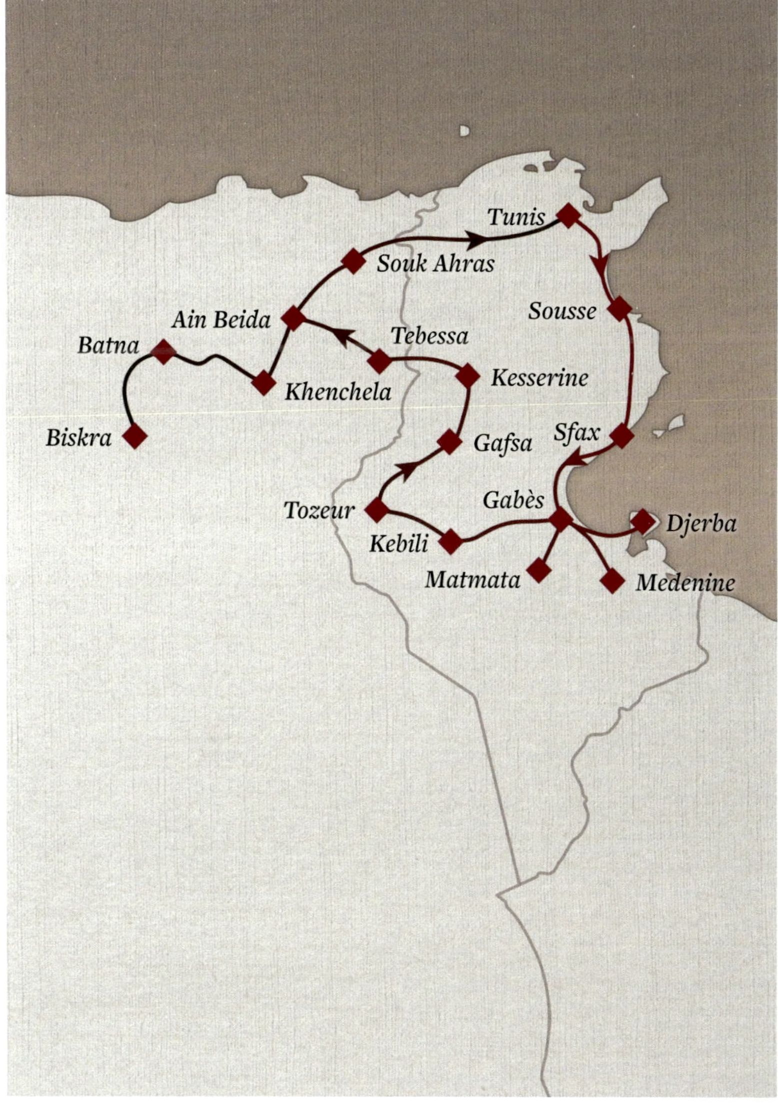

Approximate route of the truck and sedan in Tunisia and Algeria, starting at Tunis.

Date	Location	Notes
January 27	Swain and son Robert leave New York	SS *President Harding*
February 4	Swain and Robert arrive in Cherbourg, France	
February 7	Paris–Rome Express (train)	
February 9?	Vehicles picked up in Rome, Italy	
February 11–27	Vehicles driven around Campagna region, Italy, logging ca. 100 miles around Rome	Swain photographs ancient aqueducts around Rome
March 4–6	Vehicles driven from Salerno to Reggio, Italy	
March 6 or 7	Vehicles loaded on railway ferry to Messina, Sicily	
March 7–9	Vehicles driven from Messina to Palermo, Sicily	
March 11	Vehicles shipped from Palermo to Tunis, Tunisia	
Mid-March–early April	Vehicles in daily use at Carthage, Tunisia, excavations and for study of Roman ruins within a 100-mile radius of site	
April 7–29	Vehicles undertake a long road trip through Tunisia and Algeria, covering 1,975 miles in 23 days	
May 1–12	Vehicles driven in Carthage and vicinity	
May 15	Vehicles shipped to Palermo	
May 17–19	Vehicles driven several hundred miles through Sicily	
June 7–11?	Sicily to Rome	Swain delayed in Rome, awaiting shipment from Eastman Kodak (1,500 8-by-10 films)
June 16–August 22	Swain and Robert travel in Greece: Athens, Volos, Salonica, Piraeus, Sounion, Patmos, Corinth, Nauplia, Olympia, Delphi, Mycenae, and other sites	Sedan and truck left in Rome; rental cars used occasionally
August 29–September 16	Vehicles travel through Italy, Switzerland, France, and Belgium, covering 1,200 miles from Rome to Brussels	Route includes Rome, Siena, Florence, Milan, Bellinzona, St. Gotthard Pass, Basle, Belfort, Paris, and Brussels
Mid-September	Vehicles stored in Brussels	

Summary of the 1925 Expedition

George Swain returned to a still-troubled and economically depressed Europe in 1925, accompanied by his 19-year-old son Robert, who was eager to experience life overseas on an archaeological project. Father and son set sail from New York on January 27. The SS *President Harding* left in a "shrieking gale of wind," while Swain watched "the Woolworth Building and the rest of the sky scraper clan that home on lower Manhattan" fade under clouds of snow. After a little more than a week at sea, the ship docked at Cherbourg, France, having endured hurling water that poured through several portholes and smashed thick, plate-glass windows many feet above the water line.[204]

Safely on French soil, Swain and Robert traveled 36 hours on the Paris–Rome Express, reuniting in Rome with the well-rested Graham Brothers truck and Dodge sedan. Both vehicles had been in storage for four months and were now ready for new experiences, starting with one of Swain's first photographic assignments: several weeks of tracking down the fast-vanishing ancient aqueducts around Rome.

By the beginning of March, father and son drove south from Rome to the island of Sicily and then on to North Africa via ferry, where they would be firmly ensconced for several months. Their primary focus was the famed archaeological site of Carthage in Tunisia.

In addition to the 1925 excavations at Carthage—which exposed a cemetery containing the charred bones of children—the North African trip included a 23-day trek across northern and central Tunisia and eastern Algeria, partially in search of "lost civilizations" hidden in the Saharan desert. The project was organized by the intriguing Count de Prorok (see pp. 49–51, 85–86), who was head of a small French contingent.

By the time the group returned to Carthage in late April, the University of Michigan vehicles had clocked nearly 2,000 miles (fig. 87). Swain logged equally impressive numbers

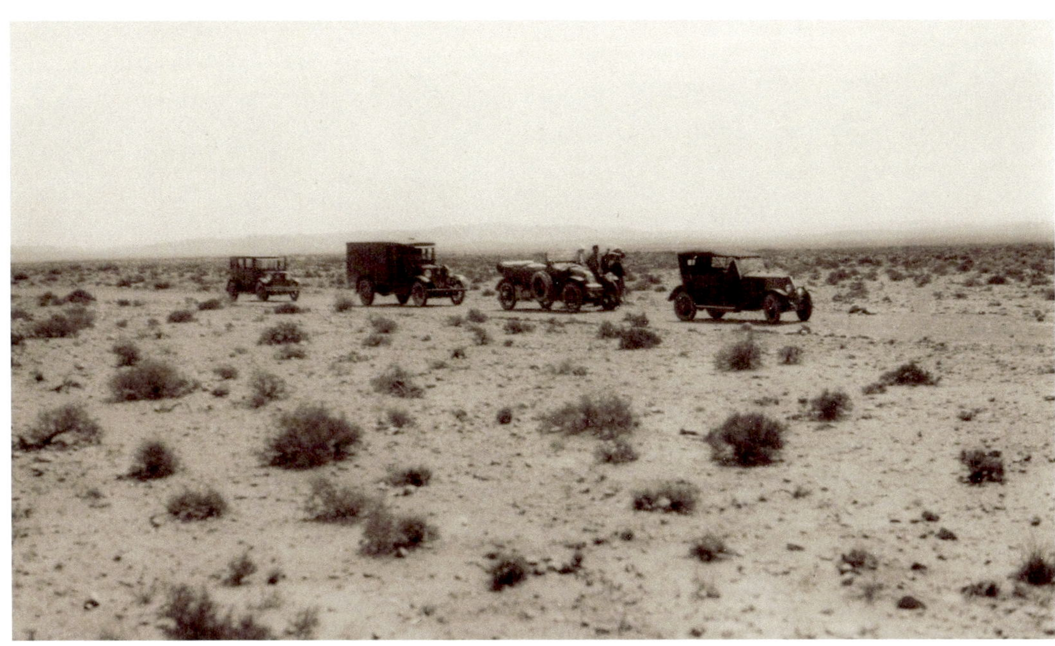

Fig. 87. The Dodge sedan, Graham Brothers truck, and two vehicles belonging to de Prorok's contingent on the road to Kebili, Tunisia, April 14, 1925 (Kelsey Museum neg. no. KS 326.09).

with his photographs, exposing 135 of his 7-by-11 films, countless Kodaks, and 18 Cirkut negatives measuring 10 by 36 inches. In a somewhat unusual move for the time, the French contingent had hired a filmmaker as well. Maurice Kellerman, a renowned cinematographer from Pathé News (fig. 88), was similarly productive, shooting approximately 10,000 feet of film, apparently now lost (Side Car 7).[205]

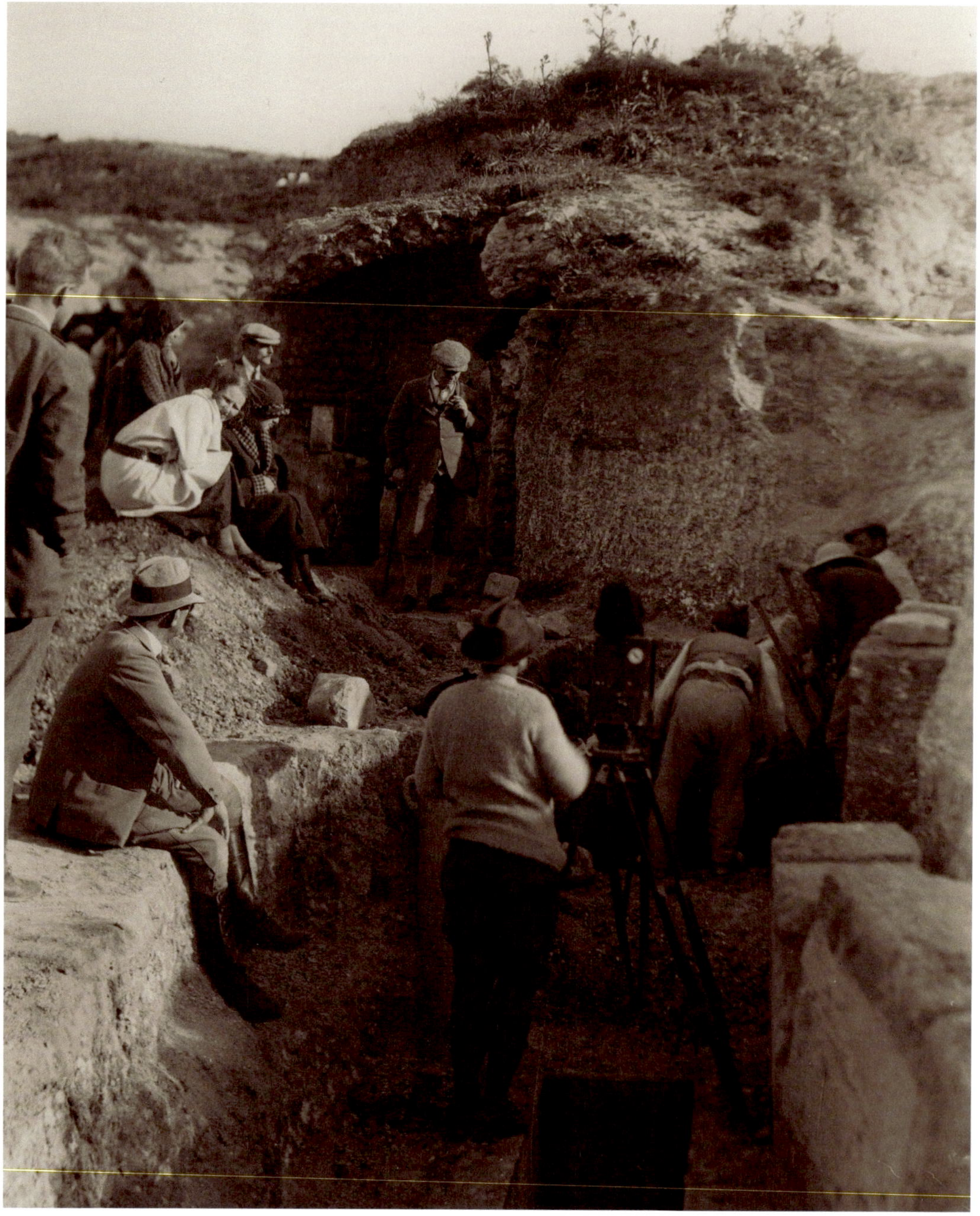

Side Car 7: Disaster at Sea

Maurice Kellerman was one of the most respected cinematographers of his time. He worked on the infamous 1931 film *The Viking*, which suffered one of the deadliest on-site accidents in the history of cinema. The movie centers on a seal-hunting expedition off the coast of Newfoundland, Canada, and was the first film to feature sound and dialogue recorded on location. Many of the scenes depict actual sealing ships and expeditions. After a private screening of the film, director and producer Varick Frissell decided additional footage was needed. In early March 1931, the director and his crew boarded the SS *Viking* to record its annual hunt off the coast of Labrador. The ship became trapped in ice and exploded when crates of dynamite (stored for ice breaking) accidentally ignited, killing Frissell, one of the photographers, and more than 25 crew members. Kellerman was not on location at the time. The 1931 film was considered lost until the 1960s, when it was discovered in a Newfoundland fish-storage plant.[206]

Fig. 88. Filmmaker Kellerman preparing to shoot footage at the site of Carthage, Tunisia, March 28, 1925 (Kelsey Museum neg. no. 7.1839).

Upon the completion of their North African campaigns in mid-May, the vehicles ultimately returned to Rome while Swain and Robert traveled to various sites in Greece via boat, train, and occasionally, rented car. By the end of August, the foursome was reunited, and the truck and sedan embarked on their last major trip of the season. Both were driven north to Florence via Siena, Italy, then through Milan to Bellinzona, Switzerland, and over the impressive St. Gotthard Pass in the Alps. The long journey ended in Brussels, Belgium, where the vehicles were turned over to a Dodge representative "to be put in trim for next year."[207] Swain ends his annual report with unalloyed praise: "It is a conservative statement to say that [the two vehicles] have been simply invaluable, and we feel that their usefulness, instead of being over, is now only fairly well begun."[208]

A Visit to Italy and God's Error

The brief trip to Sicily began with a drive from Rome—via Naples, Salerno, and Reggio—to the Sicilian town of Messina. Halfway between Rome and Naples, Swain and Robert stopped at an "almost" luxurious guesthouse on the flanks of a high mountain. Swain was pleased to report that the guesthouse still maintained an old custom: lodgers were never given a bill but donated whatever they could afford to the Abbey of Saint Benedict.[209] On the road again after a night at the guesthouse, they finally reached Reggio, where they loaded the truck and sedan onto a steamer, disembarking at Messina. Both Reggio and Messina were still recovering from the devastating earthquake of 1908, which had caused massive destruction in both cities and approximately 80,000 deaths.

As usual, misadventures dogged the truck and sedan; apparently, one wheel of the truck crashed through the dock at Reggio, with no damage . . . at least to the vehicle, according to Swain. The team of four—Swain, his son, the truck, and the sedan—spent only a few days driving around Sicily, an island that Swain deemed one of God's topographical errors. Swain was unsparing in his comments about the island:

> Sicily is a land of hills and mountains jumbled together without rhyme or reason. Were I to hazard a guess at its genesis, it would be that when the rest of Europe was made, the *Fabricator Mundi* made a few miscalculations in his specifications and came out with a plain or two, a lot of unmatched hills, and a few unwanted mountains and one huge volcano left over. Hoping to conceal his mistake, he hurled the whole lot of leftovers in a mass into the sea expecting them to sink in the Mediterranean, but they struck in shallow water—and later men called it Sicily.[210]

Swain was also leery of the country roads, crowded with an unrelenting assortment of animals (Side Car 8), and he deplored how sulfur mining had scarred the landscape. But Sicily partly redeemed itself with impressive archaeological sites, architecture (fig. 89), and vistas over valleys dotted with lemon trees that turned the landscape into a rapture of yellow.

Side Car 8: Sicilian Hazards, According to Swain

"Driving through small Sicilian towns is at times hardly a rest cure as the one main street is so infested with goats, donkeys, pigs, children, and chickens that you wonder whether you can get through without committing murder in some degree or other, but you dodge the donkeys, the goats scramble up somewhere, pigs squeal, chickens squawk and flutter, and adults snatch children to places of comparative safety—and we drive about half as fast as native chauffeurs at that."[211]

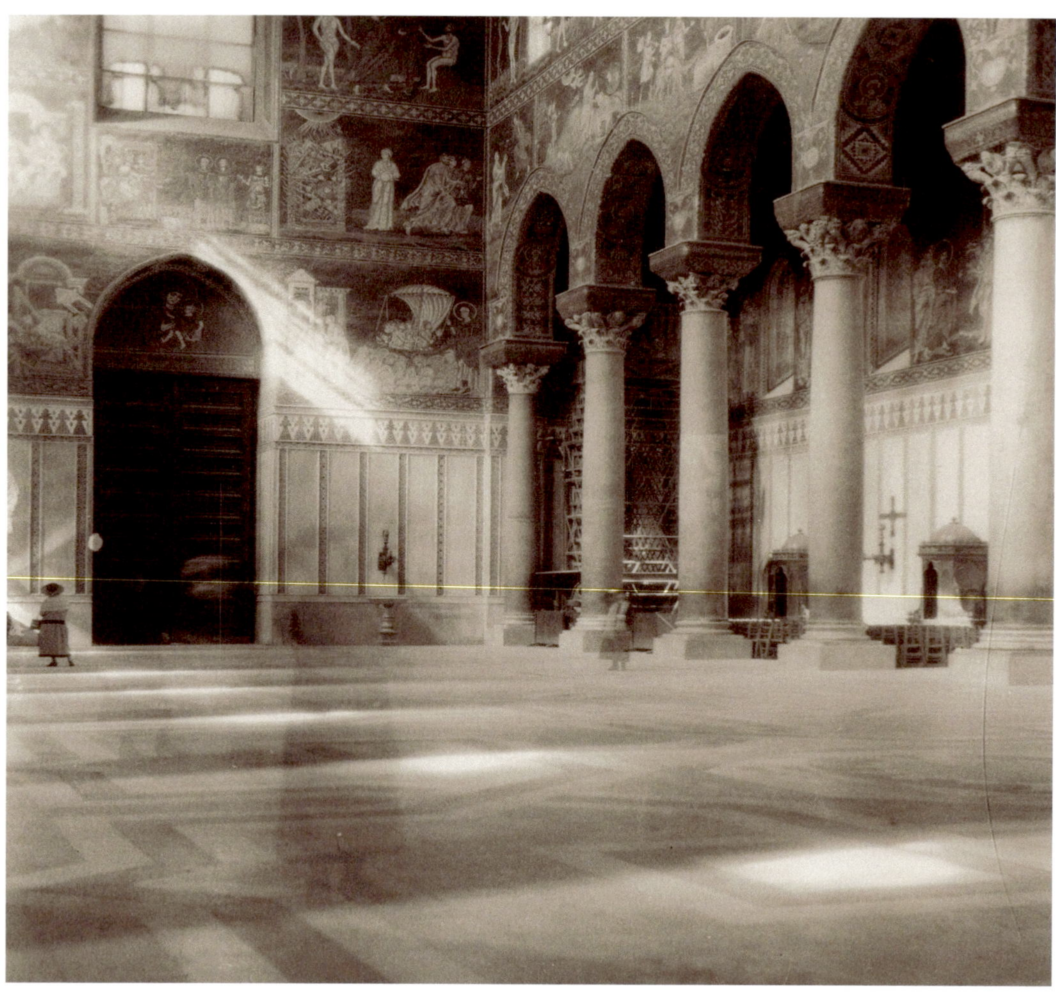

Fig. 89. Interior of Monreale Cathedral, Palermo, Sicily, March 9, 1925 (Kelsey Museum neg. no. KS 307.08).

Searching for Lost Worlds in Tunisia and Algeria

Swain, Robert, and the two vehicles had ample time to experience life in North Africa, residing there from mid-March to mid-May of 1925. The Graham Brothers truck and Dodge sedan served as the official dig cars for excavations at Carthage, Tunisia, as well as indispensable transport to Roman ruins within a 100-mile radius of the site. Excavations at Carthage revealed intriguing remains—most notably, the discovery of the Tophet, a sanctuary containing the burned bones of infants and young children placed in cinerary urns, sometimes mixed with the remains of goats, lambs, jewelry, and objects of gold, silver, and bronze. The charred bones became a source of debate, with some scholars supporting the notion that, as several ancient sources reported, the Carthaginians sacrificed infants to appease the main deities of the city. Kelsey was skeptical of such seemingly barbaric practices, but current research suggests that the sacrifice of living infants was, in fact, part of early Carthaginian history.[212]

Interesting archaeological discoveries notwithstanding, Swain was hardly a fan of Tunisian weather, observing that the capital city, Tunis, suffered from "the most disagreeable" climate he had ever met—raw, damp, chilly, windy, and rainy in March–April and dusty in May.[213] He was, however, enchanted by the array of colors, both in the Gulf of Tunis and the dazzling, chromatic fields that blanketed the hillsides in spring (see p. 45). While Swain may not have appreciated the inclement weather, the crew's "digs" were more than adequate. The Franco-American team headquartered at the Palais Hamilcar, a comfortable villa in the picturesque village of Sidi Bou Said, located near the site of Carthage (fig. 90). Even the food received good marks: Swain pronounced the meals prepared by a "first class French chef" to be far above the quality of dining room service at most hotels, unlike some of the culinary experiences from the year before in Yalivadj.[214] Given the comfort of his accommodations at the Palais, Swain may have been reluctant to embark on the long trek that lay ahead. But Swain was a voyager at heart, rarely shying away from exploration.

The 23-day journey through Tunisia and eastern Algeria engineered by de Prorok was inspired by a "strange tale" that piqued the count's curiosity. According to de Prorok, "an unmapped village [was] situated in a small oasis of the Northern Sahara, cut off from the world by gigantic sand dunes. . . . [The] inhabitants are believed to be the direct descendants of the Carthaginians, many of whose usages they still conserve."[215] Count de Prorok was no stranger to tall tales and sensational explorations. During his career, he launched a 15-year search for King Solomon's mines, which he believed lay in Ethiopia, and an equally intense hunt for the lost island of Atlantis, which he alleged was in North Africa. Sometimes likened to Indiana Jones, de Prorok recounts many of his fantastic journeys in several books, each replete with colorful, if not always believable, details (figs. 91a–b).[216]

Fig. 90. General view of the Carthage waterfront and Sidi Bou Said, Tunisia, May 1–12, 1925 (Kelsey Museum neg. no. 7.2039).

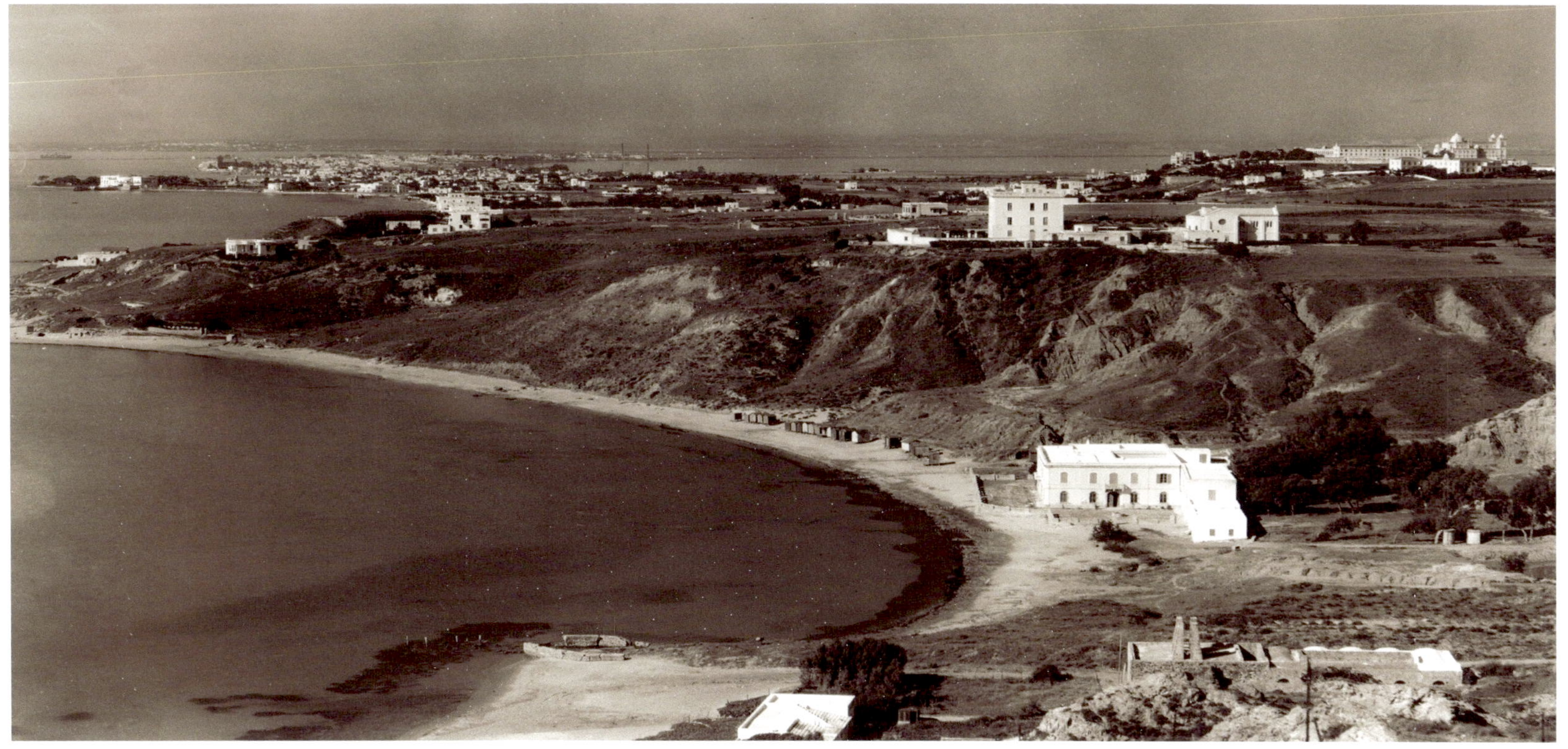

Fig. 91a. Byron de Prorok's signature (recreation by Eric Campbell).

Fig. 91b. The count and his wife, Alice Josephine Kenny, ca. 1925 (Library of Congress, Prints & Photographs Division, LC-B2-6492-1).

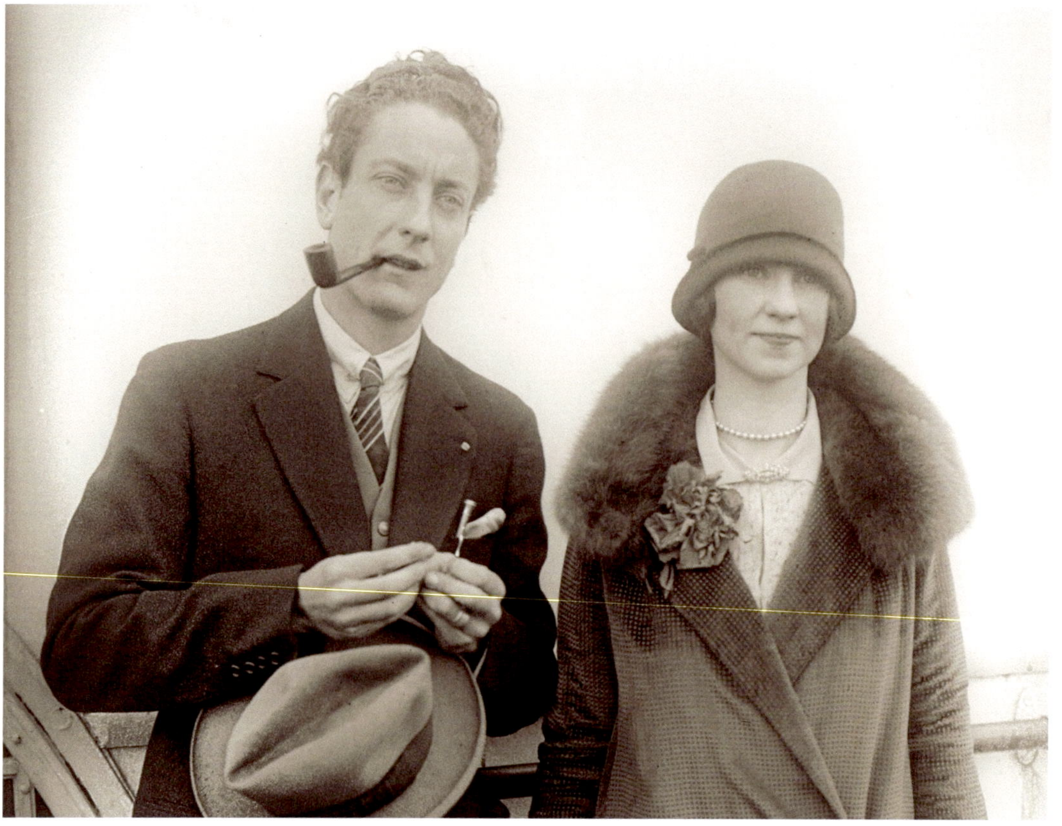

To wit, on one of his trips deep into so-called "darkest Africa," he reports coming upon "blood-drinkers, eaters of living flesh, lycanthropic ceremonies presided over by a witch doctor . . . and men and women . . . [who] howled like jackals."[217]

The University of Michigan's 1925 sojourn into the desert, however, was not just to search for de Prorok's purported lost race. It also involved other, more traditional goals—namely, exploring the prehistory of the region, as well as hunting for a possible submerged city off the island of Djerba.

Approximately a dozen individuals participated in the expedition, including de Prorok, the eminent filmmaker Maurice Kellerman (see Side Car 7, p. 82), Kellerman's wife, George and Robert Swain, a Mr. Streit from the *New York Times*, and a chauffeur. Most of the crew set out on April 7, 1925, from Sidi Bou Said. The French came with two cars, both Renaults, one of which was outfitted with six wheels. As Swain explains, the other Renault actually had *twelve* wheels, "two double wheels in front and two pairs of double wheels behind. . . . The two pairs of double wheels behind are all driving wheels so these cars can go up a very steep grade and over sand too soft to hold up an ordinary four-wheel car."[218] By all accounts, the American truck and sedan held their own against their fancy French relatives, with only a few mishaps.[219]

The vehicles transporting the American representatives were bulging with effects. Personal baggage, camping gear, and photographic equipment were stowed to the very top of the truck, weighing in, according to Swain, "at three-quarters of a tone [*sic*] at least."[220]

While Swain and his American colleagues traveled somewhat modestly, the French had a slightly different approach. "The party 'roughed it,'" remarks Swain with his usual wry humor, "with tents, cot beds, mattresses, blankets, pillows, a Transatlantique lunch (which this year always contained canned lobster), a mandolin, and phonograph."[221]

Swain's comments and photographs underscore life in the area, focusing on local markets, dockside activities, and the attention that the vehicles attracted (figs. 92–95). Several images depict the approaching harvest, when northern Tunisia was dotted with

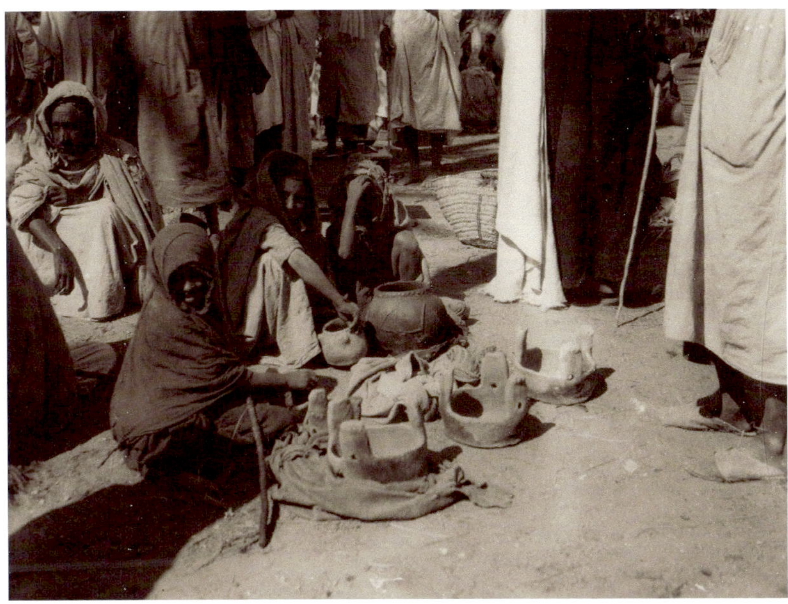

Fig. 92. Village market near Tozeur with cooking pots for sale, Tunisia, April 17, 1925 (Kelsey Museum neg. no. KS 330.04).

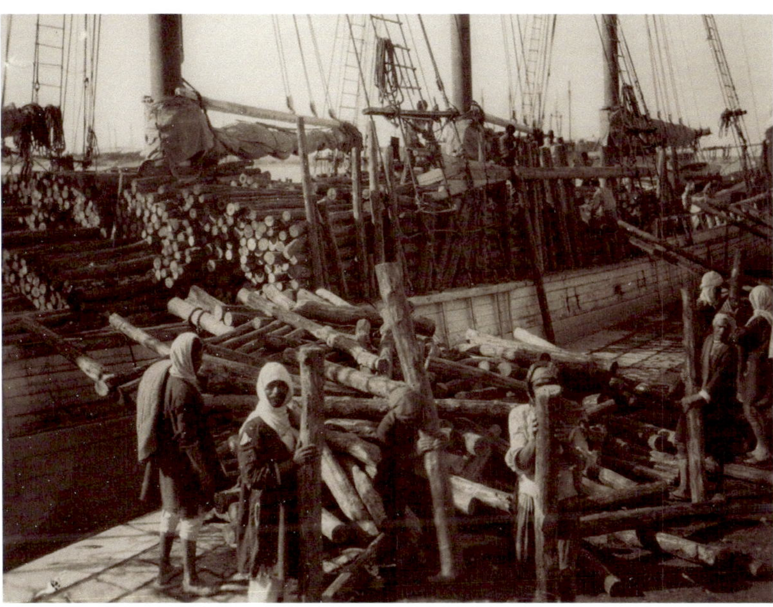

Fig. 93. Unloading wood from a docked ship, Sfax, Tunisia, April 9, 1925 (Kelsey Museum neg. no. KS 318.10).

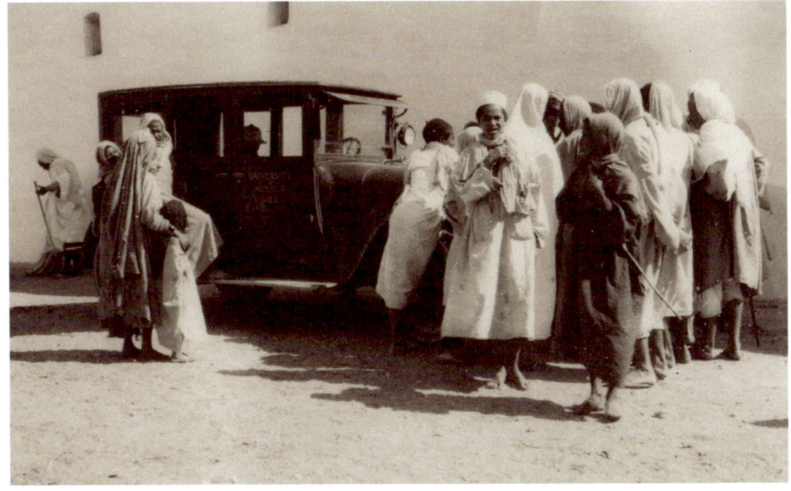

Fig. 94. "Natives" around the Dodge sedan, village near Tozeur, Tunisia, April 17, 1925 (Kelsey Museum neg. no. KS 330.07).

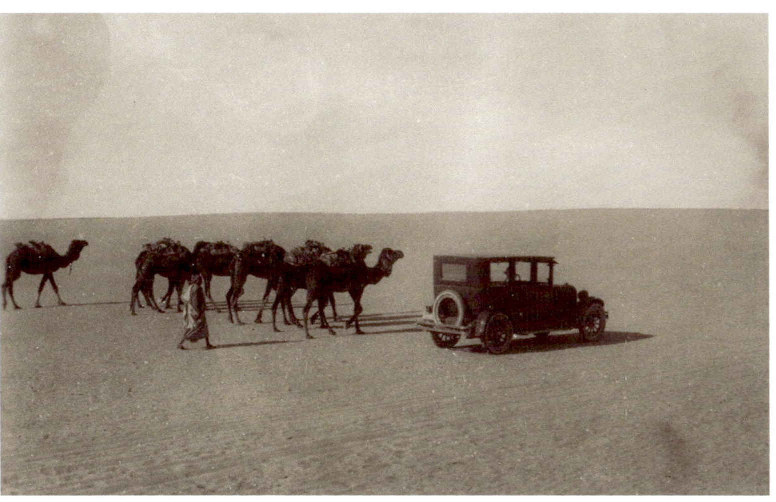

Fig. 95. The Dodge sedan accompanied by a group of camels in the desert near Nefta, Tunisia, April 17, 1925 (Kelsey Museum neg. no. KS 331.01).

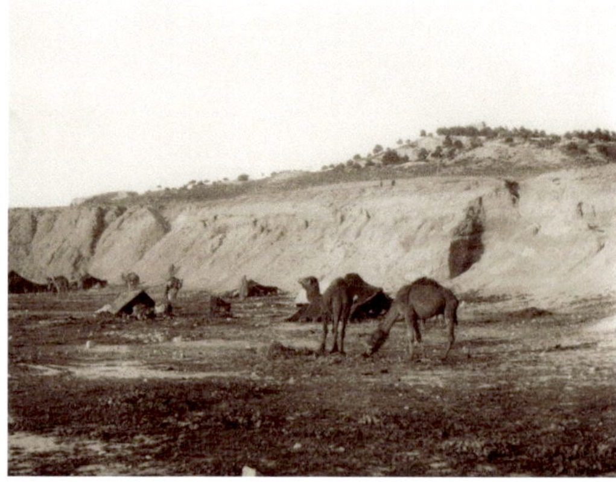

Fig. 96a. "Bedouin camp just outside the city, Zaghouan road. Several tents and numerous camels," Tunis, Tunisia, March 29, 1925 (Kelsey Museum neg. no. KS 316.09).

Fig. 96b. "Two children of the country, girls," Matmata, Tunisia, April 13, 1925 (Kelsey Museum neg. no. KS 326.05).

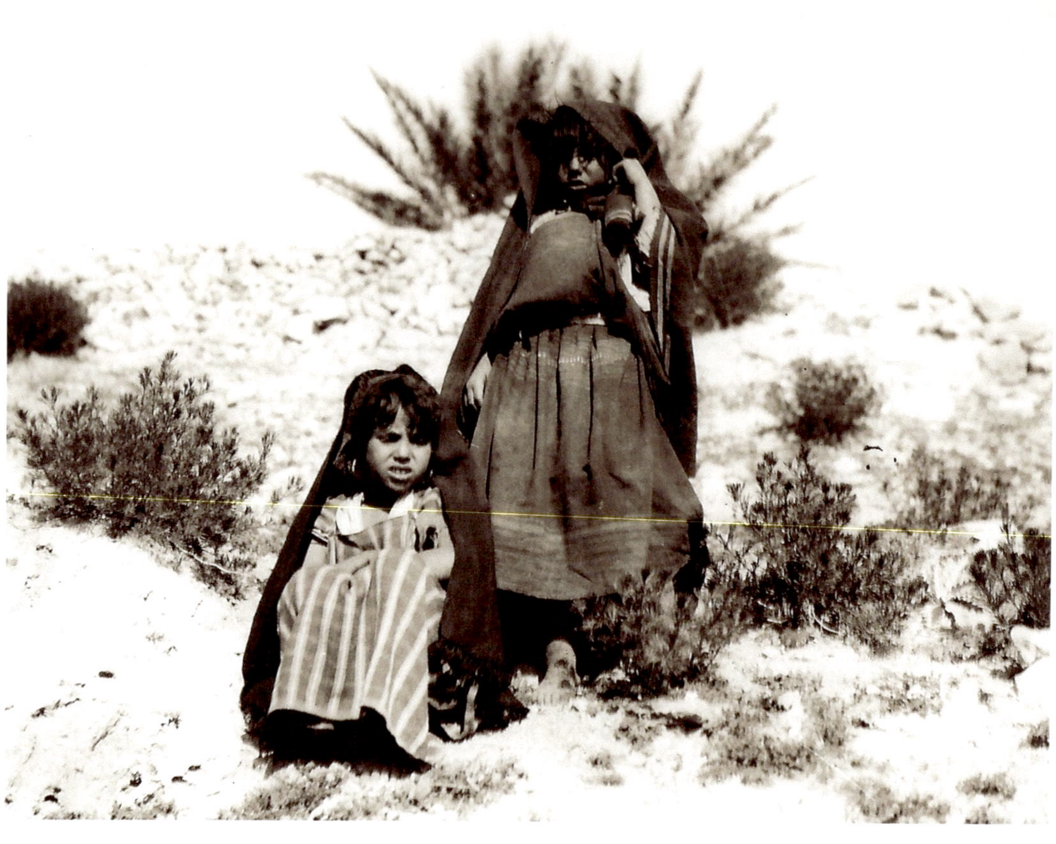

peripatetic Bedouins, who traveled with their tents, "camels, goats, donkeys, sheep, and swarms of children."[222] The rhythm of the Bedouins' year consisted of drifting north, when all family members worked the harvest, then traveling back south before the cold weather set in. Given his painterly eye, Swain notes, "Many of the women go unveiled, girls and their mothers wear great copper earrings, and with their love for glaring colors, their garments give a colorful note to the green landscape" (figs. 96a–b).[223]

The Bedouins formed only a small part of the region's population. This stark and remote landscape was also home to several settlements that had grown up around a number of oases. Living conditions were harsh, and some of the towns were known for their unusual architecture, designed to cope with an often unforgiving environment. Swain was particularly intrigued by the structures at the desert towns of Medenine and Matmata, both more than 300 miles south of Carthage. "In Medenine," he writes, "are the queerest houses any crazy architect ever dreamed of, even after a rarebit and mince pie late the evening before" (at the time, rarebit—essentially, toasted cheese—was thought to cause vivid, even hallucinatory, dreams). Swain continues to describe the houses as "made of mud, at least dried clay, up to five or six stories in height, with flimsy outside stairways up the front and almost no windows at all—they might be the homes of monstrous gregarious wasps!" (fig. 97).[224]

Matmata (which served as a setting for several *Star Wars* movies[225]) contained equally arresting dwellings, which Swain likens to "the homes of the Troglodytes of antiquity." Swain's descriptions are informative:

> To enter, you follow a low narrow descending tunnel and come out into a sort of rotunda with walls twenty or thirty feet high, quite open to the sky. . . . [These] rooms, or caves if you like, lead off into the ground in every direction, each room . . . lighted only by a door, and there are usually two tiers of rooms. One may be a bed room, one a storehouse for supplies, one a weaving room (in the looms we saw thread was put through by hand, no shuttle being used), and so on. . . . In one I examined, there was a total absence of disagreeable odors, the rooms were clean and neat, and there were attempts at wall decoration by the use of figured plates and cheap colored pictures. The clay is so tough and hard that it can be smoothed or worked into various shapes and then whitewashed. Outside, around the tops of the "rotundas" the soil is graded away so that surface water from winter showers will not run in, but of course rain falls directly into the opening. Up and down the sides of the valley I was overlooking I was told several thousand people lived, yet all that could be seen was an occasional door and the rings of dirt graded away from central openings. Judged by their habitations, their remote evolutionary ancestors were not arboreal apes but terrestrial woodchucks.[226]

Leaving the land of ancient woodchucks, the party journeyed west to Kebili, one of the oldest oases in Tunisia. The crew spent only one night there, but what caught Swain's

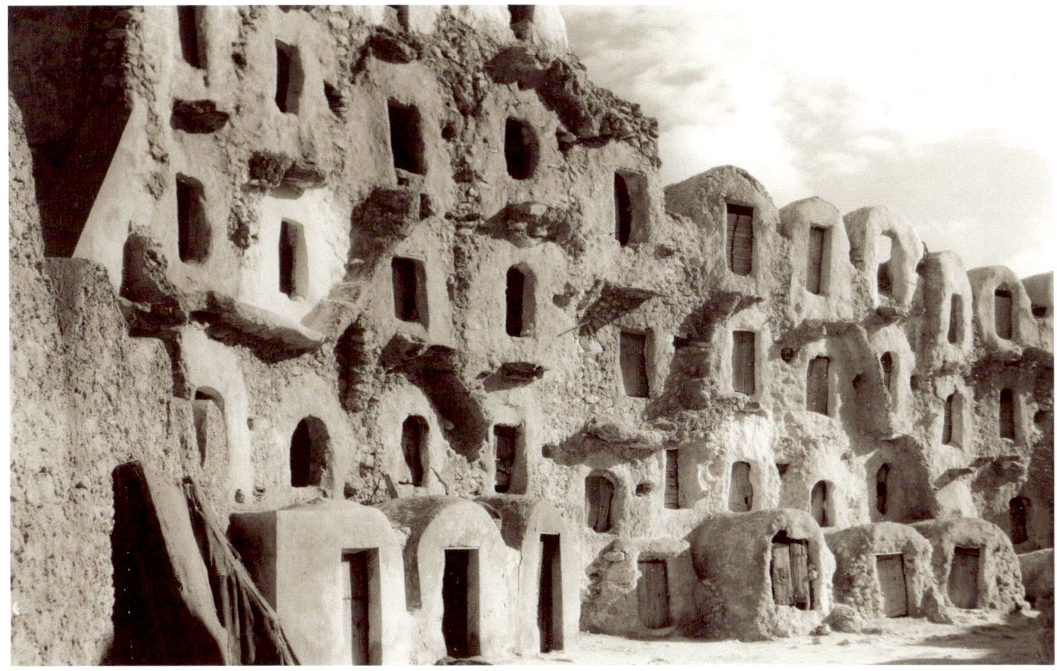

Fig. 97. "Some of the weird stone-plaster-mud constructions, up to five stories high, with outside stairways. Probably chiefly for storage of grain and other products, but part perhaps for dwellings. NOTE: Count de Prorok said these were dwellings. The guide book says storehouses and granaries. The absence of people along the streets bordered by the queer buildings, would seem to carry out the statement of the guide book." (On verso of one copy, in pencil in an unknown hand: "Strange mud houses at Medenine. Note the outside stairways. Article #3.") Medenine, Tunisia, April 12, 1925 (Kelsey Museum neg. no. 7.1923).

attention was the dinner, not because of the food but because they were able to request their meal long-distance—in the middle of the desert, no less. "Dinner [at Kebili] has been ordered in advance," Swain marvels. "Ordered, as you please, from Gabes [about 65 miles from Kebili] by wireless."[227]

After their night in Kebili, the team faced the arduous task of crossing Chott el Djerid, one of the largest endorheic salt lakes in North Africa, measuring roughly 150 miles in length.[228] During summer, this gigantic salt pan is almost entirely dry, while winter brings a tributary of water that floods the area. When the lake is wet, it can be crossed by boat; when dry, it can be cautiously traversed by car, but the salt crust is unstable.[229] Like Matmata, Chott el Djerid served as a location for *Star Wars* (the Lars homestead on Tatooine), not surprising given the eeriness of the environment.[230] Known for its rainbow-hued salt deposits and sitting at 30–80 feet below sea level, the Chott can reach summer temperatures of 122 degrees Fahrenheit, with the intense heat and vast, open horizons generating *fata morganas*—shimmering, colorful, and strange dancing mirages.[231] According to Swain, the oases scattered along the lake's periphery supported nearly 40,000 people, with approximately a million date palm trees. These rich palms allegedly produced, annually, "some 60,000,000 pounds of dates, only a small portion of which however is of high enough quality to export."[232]

Traveling in April, the cars had to cross the flat floor of the mostly dried-up salt lake, taking care to follow a fairly straight road that was marked by posts supported by rock piles (fig. 98). Attempts to deviate from the road were considered highly risky. "Legend has it," Swain cautions, "a small army with a thousand camels once dropped out of sight in crossing." For Swain and his crew, the last five miles of the crossing became especially challenging, with "dirt, alkali, and salt in a dense sticky slimy mud three to six inches

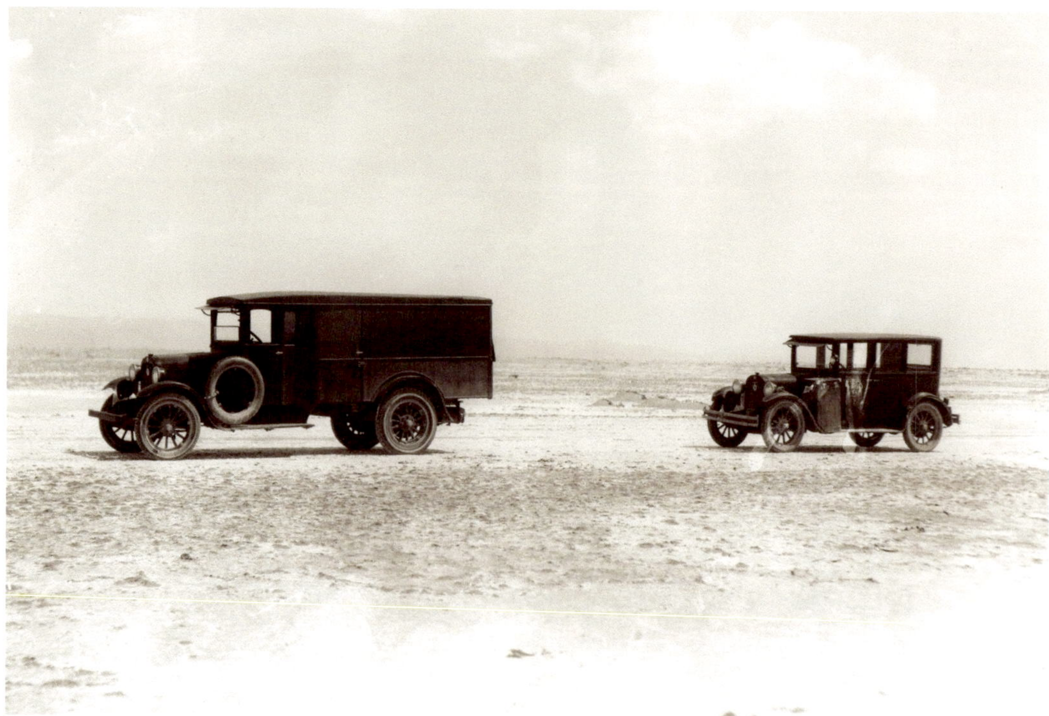

Fig. 98. "The two cars, truck and sedan, out on the Chott Djerid, where the surface was hard and nearly white with alkali and salt. This was on the earlier part of the Chott nearer Kebili." (On verso of one copy, in pencil: "On way to Kebyles. Cars in Chott al Djerid"; on verso of a second copy, in pencil in an unknown hand: "The two U. of M. cars on the Chott Djerid. Article #3.") Tunisia, April 15, 1925 (Kelsey Museum neg. no. 7.1938).

deep. We got through all right, but the stuff spattered all over the underpart of the car and rusted everything it hit."[233]

After surviving the Chott crossing, the party continued farther west to Tozeur and then Gafsa, a distance of approximately 65 miles. The rough roads stymied the valiant efforts of at least one of the vehicles. Swain records that three of the cars (the American truck and the two French cars) managed to get across a particularly deep gulch followed by a sandy climb, but the tracks they left "had so cut up the apology for a road that the Dodge Sedan gave up in despair. However, the truck was fortunately on hard ground, so we ran back a fifty-foot tow line and literally snaked the sedan up the ascent."[234]

The desert journey never seemed to lack for trials. Leaving Gafsa, Swain records "another new experience—a high hot wind behind us, so strong that the fans did not function—one radiator boiled dry before the driver knew anything was wrong. However, by giving them water frequently we kept going, although when we changed direction, it seemed at times as if the cars would literally be blown into the ditch."[235]

Forging on bravely, the four vehicles and passengers stopped briefly at a small town, where Swain was surprised to see a circling throng of people. Curious, he sauntered over "to find a snake charmer giving a fearsome entertainment with two or three cobras and some other snakes to me unknown. He did his usual 'stunt' of letting the serpents bite him of course. The crowd parted to let me use a Kodak, the snake charmer posed, I snapped the shutter, whereupon his helper promptly passed the hat for a contribution."[236] (See fig. 44, p. 40, for a Swain photograph of another snake charmer, who met a less happy fate.)

The Land of the Lotus Eaters

Perhaps the most remarkable vehicular challenge of the desert sojourn was the sedan and truck's trip to the island of Djerba (also a *Star Wars* location), three miles off the southeastern coast of Tunisia.[237] The outing was a three-day affair, carried out on April 10–12, 1925. Djerba had long been identified as Homer's "Land of the Lotus Eaters" (the *Lotophagi*). According to legend, anyone who ingested the flower or fruit of the tree would lapse into a blissful, almost coma-like state, with no desire to leave and return home.

The island sits just off the coast in fairly shallow water. Swain was fascinated by the machinations that went into ferrying the cars over to the island. His description, coupled with his photos, helps us envision what was surely a lively and at times heart-stopping event (fig. 99):

> Cars are ferried by lashing two fishing boats together, placing across them two pairs of heavy planks eight or ten inches wide and sixteen or eighteen feet long. These are carefully spaced to match the gauge of the car, the contraption placed with the boats parallel to the low stone dock, the ends of the planks resting on the dock. Then you gingerly drive on to the accompaniment of much shouting and gesticulation lest you should drive too fast or advance too far, either alternative fraught with disaster. When a proper trim is achieved, wheels are trigged with stones, and if there is any wind the sail is raised and

Fig. 99. The Graham Brothers truck being loaded onto the ferry at Djerba, Tunisia, preparing to return to the mainland, April 12, 1925 (Kelsey Museum neg. no. 7.1922).

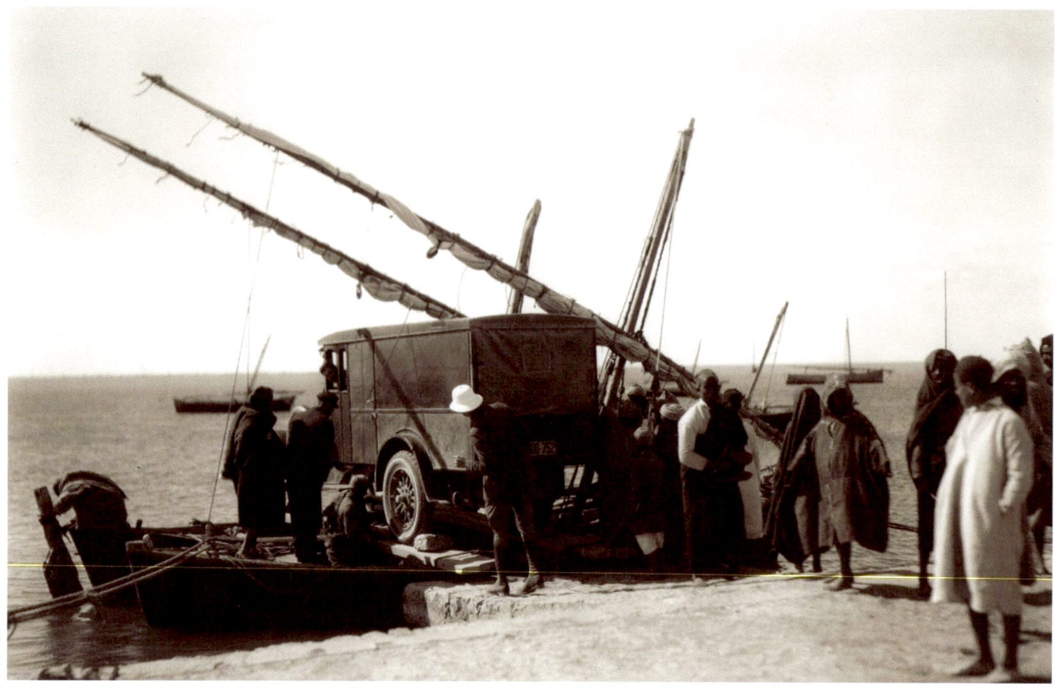

> you slowly move across while most of the crew goes to sleep. You may strike a sandbar, but what difference does an hour's delay make when you are bound for the *Lotophagi*? Failing wind the crew must pole the craft over. The whole performance is rather spectacular.[238]

Djerba itself is small, approximately 17 miles long and 16 miles wide. According to Swain, "the whole area is covered with grain fields, olive and palm trees, with here and there a village of white flat-roofed houses—roofs are always flat hereabouts in order to collect rainwater. The inhabitants are mostly Berbers and have been long noted for their industry. The exception is one town with a population of nearly three thousand Jews—and the streets of this town are clean" (fig. 100).[239] Today, Djerba is still home to a Jewish population, one of North Africa's largest, with occupation extending back several millennia.[240]

Once the vehicles were safely back on the mainland's terra firma, Swain seemed relieved, remarking that "as the cars had not partaken of the fruit of the lotus, we had no difficulty in persuading them to leave the island."[241]

Swain surely welcomed the inclusion of the filmmaker Maurice Kellerman during the 1925 expedition. Both Swain and Kelsey had enduring interests in moviemaking and often talked about shooting footage of excavations that were in progress. In fact, during Kelsey's last discussion with Swain, while Kelsey lay dying in the hospital, the two discussed the possibilities of developing "movie photography" for work in Egypt, agreeing that it had to be of the highest professional standard.[242]

Filming in North Africa was met with various responses from locals—mostly intense curiosity and crowds around Kellerman, effectively blocking views that he was endeavoring to capture. In an interview with a *New York Times* reporter, de Prorok offers humorous though less-than-kind words about the work ethic of the Tunisian laborers and the impact that filming had on their habits:

> The [Berber workmen at the site of Carthage] have never been so industrious and willing as they have since Maurice Kellerman began taking moving pictures of the archaeological operations going on here.
>
> In the drama of the uncovering of a buried civilization which he is filming the role of the workmen is, of course, to work. Though some of them had hitherto shown little aptitude for this part, they have all revealed for the movie camera a mastery of the pick and shovel.
>
> "Judging from our experience," says Count de Prorok, "it is a pity that the Carthagenians [*sic*] had no moving-picture cameras. If they had spurred on the slave labor they used with a strip of celluloid film instead of the whip they could have raised structures so enormous that we would not have to dig down for them today."[243]

The desert sojourn finally concluded on the evening of April 29, when the crew returned to its headquarters at Sidi Bou Said. In retrospect, the casualties had been minimal: "One sprained ankle, one wrecked truck tire, several flat ordinary tires, and one scored axle (in

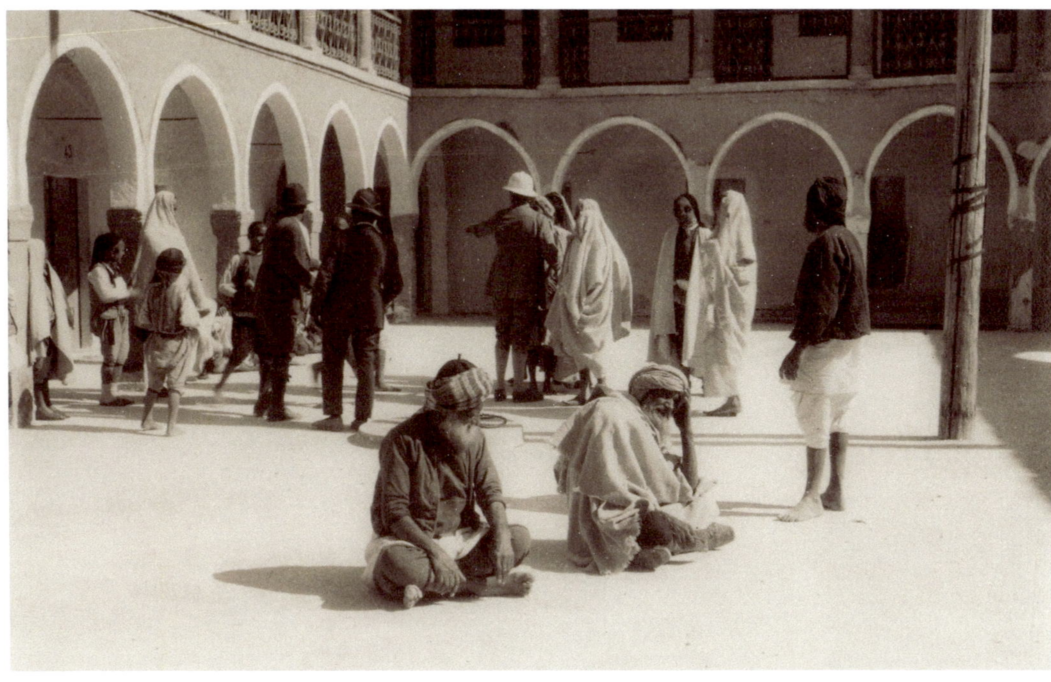

Fig. 100. "Some of the Jews in their cloister, Jewish town, not far from Houmt Souk," Djerba, Tunisia, April 11, 1925 (Kelsey Museum neg. no. KS 325.03).

one of the Renault cars) represented the total list of mishaps to man and car. In twenty three days, over the best and worst of roads, the Dodge Sedan had been driven nineteen hundred and seventy five miles, and the Graham Truck despite its load had cheerfully trundled along on good roads at thirty five miles an hour, nor had it, on bad roads, ever lain down on the job—when it could dig its toes in!"[244]

No Cars Permitted

After Swain's sojourns in North Africa, he turned his attention to photographing early Christian manuscripts at some of Greece's famous monasteries—the monastic complex on Mount Athos (figs. 101–102) and the Monastery of Saint John on the island of Patmos (fig. 103). The requests came from several biblical scholars, including Kirsopp Lake of Harvard Divinity School, who was well known for his study of New Testament manuscripts, Greek paleography, and church history.

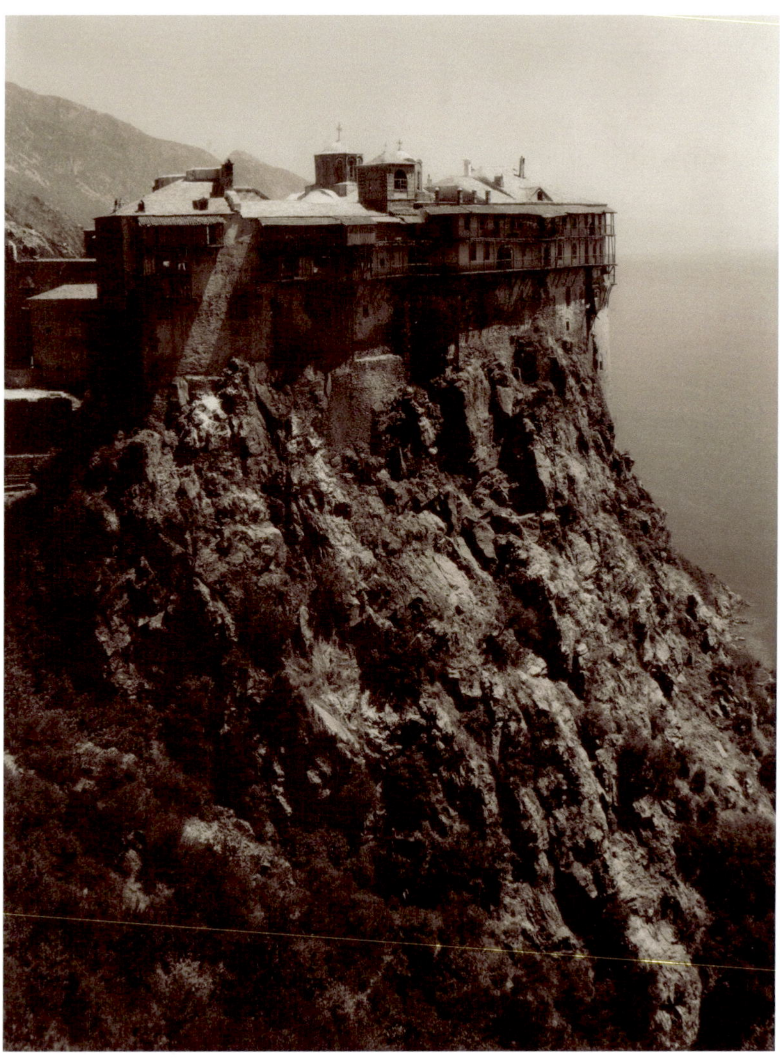

Fig. 101. "The monastery from the Daphne trail, from a point close by the cave where Simon is reputed to have lived. Shows how monastery is built up on a rocky cliff inaccessible from all but one side. The guest rooms open on the upper balcony at the right. From that point the views are unrivalled," Simonpetra, Mount Athos, Greece, July 11, 1925 (Kelsey Museum neg. no. 8.0246).

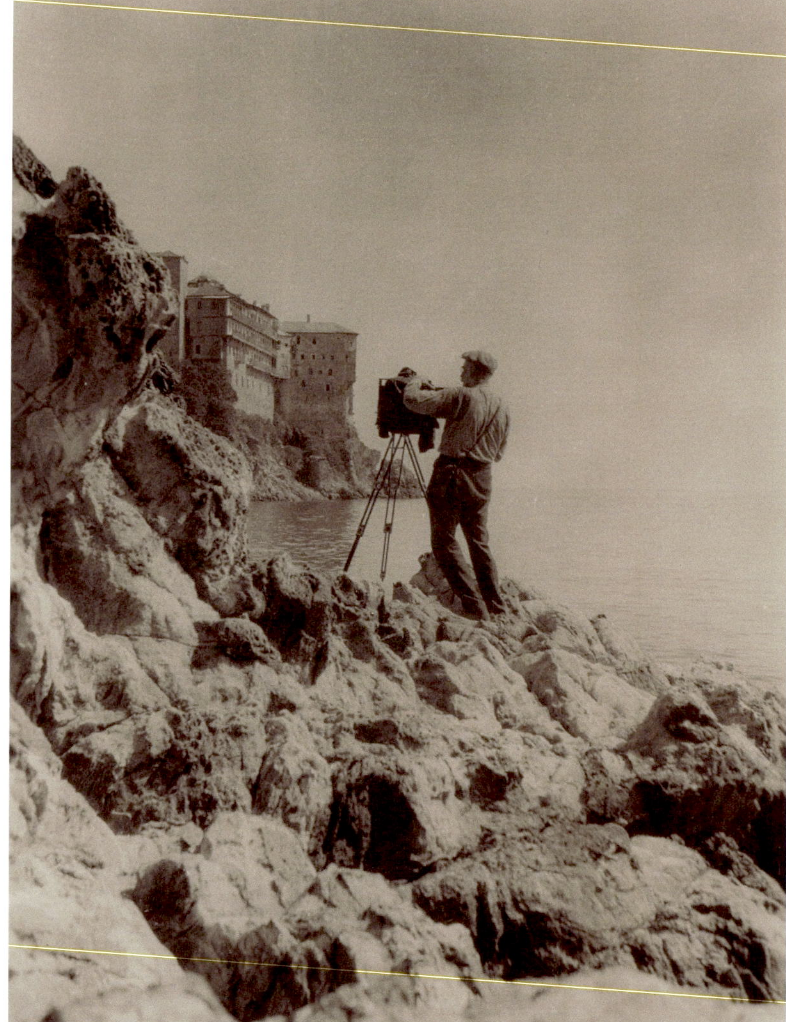

Fig. 102. George R. Swain photographing the Monastery of Gregoriou, Mount Athos, Greece, July 10, 1925 (Kelsey Museum neg. no. KS 351.03).

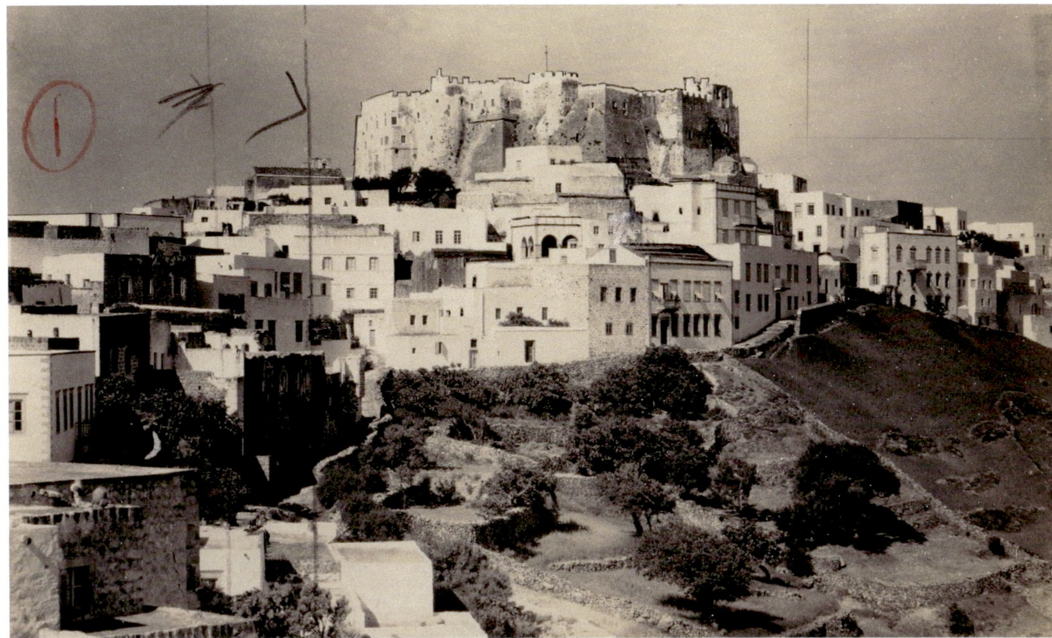

Fig. 103. "The monastery of St. John and the 'subjacent' buildings of the town of Patino. The guest rooms are on top of the monastery at the right," May 1920, Patmos, Greece. The pencil lines and number present here suggest that Swain or the *Detroit News* were planning to crop or enhance the image for publication (Kelsey Museum neg. no. 7.0396).

Swain and his son combined their visits to these sacred locations with stopovers at well-known Greek cities and archaeological sites. Altogether, they spent two months traveling to various parts of the country, but unlike the previous two trips, both the sedan and truck did not participate, instead relaxing in Rome. No explanations for leaving the cars behind are offered in any of the letters or reports, but educated guesses are possible. Part of the reason may have been that, at least on Mount Athos—where the Swains would spend more than three weeks—no outside cars were allowed. Swain was also well aware that traveling without the truck and sedan would obviate the inevitable and exasperating bureaucracy involved in obtaining transit visas for foreign cars. Finally, it seems that part of the Greek trip was for pleasure, with Swain delighted to show his son the "glory that was Greece," free from the constant care and feeding of an automobile.

When not at the monasteries, their itinerary, from the middle of June to the last week of August, reads like a fast-paced Tripadvisor blog, describing their time at locations such as Sounion, Olympia, Delphi, Eleusis, Corinth, Athens, Epidaurus, Mycenae, Tiryns, Nauplia, and Volos, among others. Swain pronounced the Temple of Poseidon at Sounion impressive from a distance but close up sadly defaced by the written and carved names of visitors and tourists (including the poet Lord Byron). Olympia's extensive remains were "so quiet [they seem] almost engulfed in an audible stillness."[245] Delphi was dramatic and picturesque, but father and son eschewed climbing nearby Mount Parnassus since the trail was "infested with robbers."[246] And at least one hillside village was gently berated for being "beautified (?) by advertisements (including one of the Singer Sewing Machine)" brandished in whitewashed stones.[247]

In contrast to Swain's travelogue-like commentary about classic stops in Greece, his visits to an orphanage in Corinth and the two monasteries elicit the thoughtful, ethnographic side of his nature that we often see in his letters and photographs.

Miss Cushman's Orphanage

Passing through Corinth, Swain and Robert called on Emma Cushman, known for her invaluable international service in Turkey during the Great War. In a show of his home-grown roots, Swain is extremely grateful to her for "American bread, strawberry jam, delicious cakes, iced melon, and water tinkling with ice served to two hot and tired Americans."[248] In a more serious vein, he writes admiringly about her success with children orphaned by the war (fig. 104):

> The orphans at Corinth are now housed in what were Greek barracks on high ground. The number of children has shrunk from over 6,000 to 1,800 at present—there are 600 more at Athens at the Zappeion. Of the 1,800, 500 are boys. These last look like Boy Scouts out camping, while the girls wear white middies, short blue skirts and go barefoot—this last is not a hardship, rather a luxury at this season. They are near a fine bathing beach of which they make much use. The object of the Near East Relief is now to place them in self-supporting positions as rapidly as possible. In response to a request, it is probable that 400 of the older girls will soon be sent to Marseilles to work in rug factories there.
>
> When the orphans were brought to Corinth two or three years ago—they had been on the island of Euboea—the place was infested with malaria

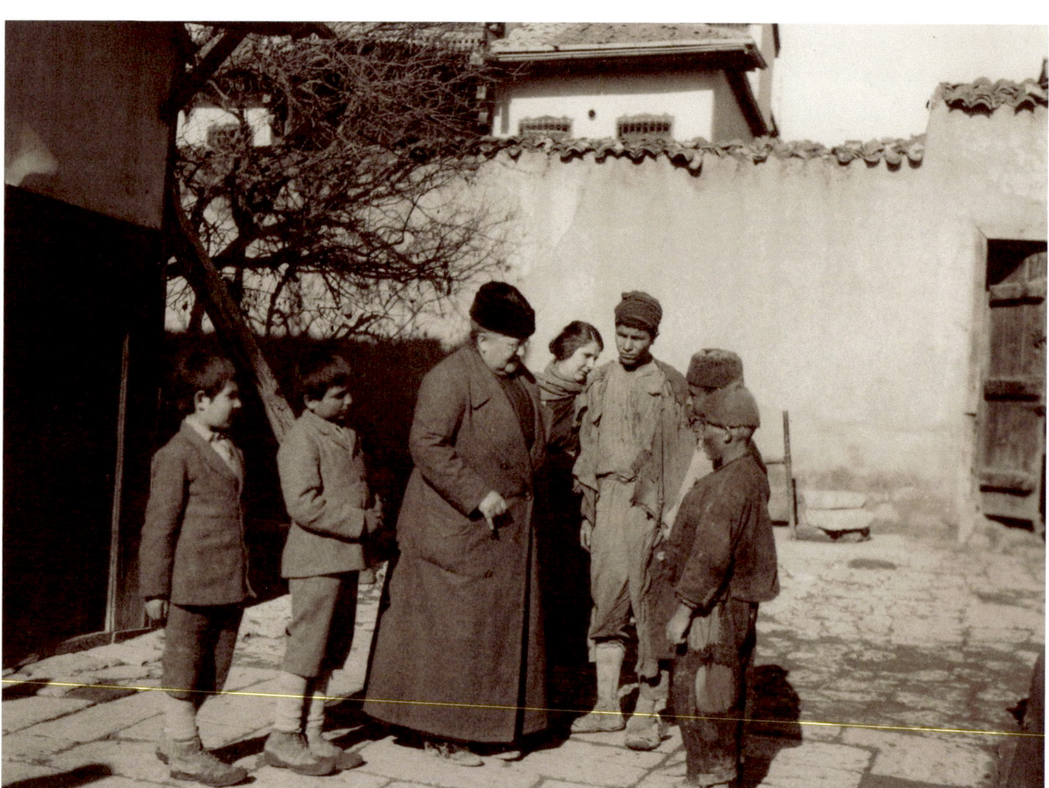

Fig. 104. "Miss Cushman talking to some boys," Turkey, December 29, 1919 (Kelsey Museum neg. no. KS057.12).

and Corinth was about dead as a town because of its evil reputation on the score of healthfulness. The first year the Near East Relief people had 2,000 cases of malaria to deal with. Then, under the immediate supervision of Miss Carr, things began to happen. In one year the boys dug a hundred miles of ditches for drains; wells were careened, pools oiled. A square mile of land was reclaimed for vineyards—and all this by sheer persuasion with no official backing. . . . [W]here the children now are there are no mosquitoes and of course no malaria. One unforeseen result has followed—a boom in New Corinth, a hundred new buildings are going up, two hotels, and a college is planned.

In Miss Cushman's opinion the incoming of the Greeks, deported from Asia Minor in the exchange of nationalities, while heavy enough a burden on impoverished Greece at first, may ultimately prove to have been a blessing in disguise, for it bids fair to lead to little less than a renaissance of energy and progress in Greece itself—here's hoping it does![249]

A Tale of Two Monasteries

Unlike the tourist-paced visits to various well-known Greek sites, the ensuing trips to several monasteries offer a different view of the country. Father and son spent 23 days on Mount Athos and 16 days on the island of Patmos. Swain had previously visited Patmos for a month in 1920 and would return in 1926 for a very brief stay, in addition to a longer visit to Mount Athos. The monastic institutions on Mount Athos and Patmos presented a study in contrasts for Swain—one was an isolated community that failed to meet his standards of religious commitment, while the other aligned with his religious sense of moral obligation.

The Kelsey Museum now houses approximately 800 photographs from Mount Athos and roughly 550 from Patmos. Although many of the images are of ancient manuscripts, well over 600 depict life in and around both monasteries, serving as testaments to Swain's curiosity about these unusual monastic worlds.[250]

Mount Athos

Mount Athos, dedicated to Eastern Orthodox monasticism, has a long, complex history. Monks and hermits probably inhabited the remote peninsula at least by the 4th century CE. Swain's comments about the institutions on the Athos peninsula are clearly unvarnished. Writing about Iveron (one of approximately 20 monasteries in the complex), for example, he observes that "there are no young monks or novitiates, few monks of middle age; but mostly gray old men, some with feeble steps. As an institution I have the feeling its day is done, that it is already in a state of coma preceding final dissolution."[251]

His perceptions were probably not helped by the food or accommodations. Swain and Robert arrived at Vatopedi (another of the Mount Athos monasteries) in the midst of a church fast, a "dietetic debacle" for the six-foot, three-inch Swain. Fortunately, the fast came to an end a day before they were scheduled to leave for the next monastery. Much to their horror, however, the two men discovered that the next monastic complex ran on a different calendar in which the cycle of fasting was just beginning. Swain admits, however, that he would not have died of starvation, for he was "given plenty of whole wheat bread and water."[252]

The accommodations fared no better in Swain's estimation:

> Of course, "the wicked flea [*sic*] when no man pursueth" is omnipresent and inescapable . . . and you may count gnats, flies, and almost everywhere mosquitoes owing to open tanks of stagnant water around courtyards, these often being fairly alive with the wriggling larvae. The initiated traveler takes a fine mosquito bar along with him everywhere. Then to end the enumeration with a climax, in one or two out of every three beds you can confidently expect to find bed bugs—all the way from the attenuated Davids to corpulent Goliaths, all equally hungry and all equally anxious to be entertained by the stranger within their gates."[253]

Adding to Swain's view of the "state of coma" at Mount Athos was the centuries-old rule that women were not allowed in any of the 20 monasteries, nor anywhere on the mountain itself. The restriction holds to this day, and in 1925, this ban became a point of reflection for Swain:

> Centuries ago, first by becoming a haunt for hermits, later by founding monasteries, the peninsula of Mt. Athos acquired in the eyes of the Greek church a peculiar sanctuary, being considered second only to Jerusalem and Constantinople. Also in order that the pious meditations of the holy monks might not be distracted by the carnal attraction of frivolous females, women were debarred from the whole area, and this prohibition was extended to the weaker sex of whatever ilk, no matter whether clad in feathers, fur, wool, or hair—at least as far as domestic animals and fowls were concerned.
>
> So, as even monastic wit could invent no substitute for the obstinate biological fact that even a monk must be born of woman, all novitiates had to be imported. As a minor dietetic consequence, milk could form no part of food supplies (until the condensed sexless tin cow invaded markets) and eggs, butter, and cheese had to be brought in. Of course, as elsewhere, olive oil acted as a substitute for butter in many ways, but imported eggs in a hot climate early lost their virginal modesty and speedily became archaeological museum specimens to be treated with distant respect "sed caveat emptor!"
>
> But—again the "world do move"—two or three years back the ban was lifted on domestic fowls, so that now the triumphant cackle of the gallinaceous female is heard in the land. And I have seen ducks, tame rabbits, and one lonely milch goat. One other exception to ostracized disturbing femininity was authorized centuries ago—cats. Thereby hangs a legend: One of the monasteries was pestered with a plague of mice and rats which the fat and

lazy tomcats were quite too indolent to pursue. The pious abbot earnestly besought heaven for relief. Shortly thereafter one of the tomcats gave birth to a litter of kittens of mixed sexes. The monks with reverent mien exclaimed "Behold, a miracle! Who are we to interfere with the plain will of heaven?" So they withheld their hands while the cats waxed and multiplied, and the pest of rodents ceased. If you don't believe the story, here's the proof—and there have long been dozens of felines in every monastery. First cats, then hens, rabbits, pigeons, and one goat—maybe roads, Fords, and bobbed flappers will yet invade the Eveless precincts of Mt. Athos.[254]

Patmos

Swain clearly related more to the monastic life at the monastery of Saint John on the island of Patmos. Monks could marry and live outside, reporting to the monastery only for required church duties. Moreover, the monastery maintained a free dispensary for the poor, paid a substantial portion of the municipal physician's salary, and distributed a large percentage of money to support local schools. Swains sums up his feelings by writing, "For the monks themselves here at Patmos I have a very cordial liking and sincere respect—their manner of life deserves it."[255]

Swain is also quick to note that the accommodations and food service on Patmos far outstrip those "in vogue on Mt. Athos. You are assigned comfortable rooms, and your meals are gratis for three days. . . . The meals . . . are excellent with a fair variety of dishes. . . . Certainly a striking contrast to the cucumbers and salt fish of certain monasteries we suffered and survived on Mt. Athos!"[256]

Despite Swain's kind words about monastic life on the small island of Patmos, he is not blind to numerous difficulties, including a shrinking population, both in the monastery and surrounding towns. Nor are his views always charitable: Although he finds the good deeds of the monastic members laudable, he also characterizes the island as a "backwater with an eddy where driftwood ceaselessly sailed around and around in a circle instead of moving on with the street."[257] There were no roads on the island, nor was there any kind of "newspaper, theater, 'movie,' gas or electric lights, telegraph or public telephone." There was, however, one official phone line running from the main town to a higher hill "whence messages are heliographed (flashed) to Leros, thence relayed to Rhodes, and there, I think, sent on by wireless."[258] Despite limited communication on Patmos, it seems to have fared better than one of the monasteries on Mount Athos: "When instant communication is called for, megaphones are used."[259]

What seemed to keep the Patmian communities afloat was the presence of returning emigrants from the United States or remittances from those who had stayed abroad. Swain hoped the monastery would continue to exist "through the organization of some theological or literary school . . . or in some other way with Uncle Sam as a Big Brother in the Background," the latter suggested by some of the inhabitants who had been to the United States.[260]

Swain also had the opportunity to observe an unusual burial ritual on Patmos that is still practiced throughout Greece today. In Greece (as in other countries), grave sites are considered impermanent. After the initial burial of an individual and (usually) when three, five, or seven years have passed, the bones of the deceased are exhumed. As Swain writes,

> One custom here—not limited to Patmos—as regards cemeteries is a bit different from our American practice, for here bodies are not buried "for keeps" but for several years, after which the bones are disinterred and heaped up with many others in a stone repository—this in order that space formerly occupied may be used for a new-comer. Two things at least are to be said for this system: it does not for a population of a given size, remove nearly so much real estate from productive use as is done in our American cemeteries, nor is nearly so much money buried in tombstones and monuments—in fact a wooden cross is quite permanent enough. I am not too sure it isn't the next best thing to cremation.[261]

Swain's reactions to Mount Athos and Patmos were clearly different. According to him, the former suffered from a "failure of morale" and "lifeless rituals"; it was "an utterly non-productive, abnormally organized, completely hedged off community." In contrast, he writes sympathetically about the supportive monastic life on Patmos. For Swain, Greek monasteries had long since ceased as centers of learning, and Patmos aligned with his ideals of how modern monastic institutions should behave: "Lapses of ages has changed the stress from going off in a corner and being good to going out in the [world] and doing good. . . . The social needs of today call imperatively not for potential goodness but for kinetic righteousness."[262]

In one of Swain's journalistic pieces, he offers his personal agenda for a viable future on Mount Athos. His comments underscore a strong entrepreneurial and growing American attitude. In particular, Swain suggests there are potential profits to be garnered by extracting marble from the large deposits in the area and increasing the output of olives and wine, although he recognizes the heavy labor costs in clearing or terracing the land. He further proposes that only two monastic institutions should survive, serving as the main repositories for all the books and manuscripts from the other 18 establishments. Finally, Swain wonders whether the "whole peninsula might be turned into a great national park or monument—its natural beauty in this land of bare brown hills would warrant it."[263]

Given Swain's divergent views of both monasteries, it is instructive to compare the kinds of photographs he produced from each location.[264] Although both institutions existed to some extent outside of time, Swain chose to treat Mount Athos as a kind of archaeological site rather than a living institution. It was as if he were a time traveler visiting the sacred mountain and observing life within compounds that no longer seemed viable. His mission, as an American photographer, was to visually document what was in imminent danger of vanishing. Indeed, he begins one of his reports quoting a famous poem and its relevance to life on Mount Athos: "If the author of 'Backward, turn backward, O Time, in thy flight' really wanted the wish gratified, all he had to do was come to the monasteries of Mt. Athos."[265]

His photographs of Mount Athos barely show any signs of local life, instead featuring buildings surveyed from a distance for their (admittedly dramatic) settings and construction. Swain's closer views of building exteriors and their interiors are even more obvious in their emptiness. His meticulous captions concentrate on mechanical, structural, or surface features of the buildings, with no mention of the monastic life that attended to them (figs. 105–106).

On the other hand, Swain measures the viability of life on Patmos in "the current of time" with more animated images.[266] His photographs of the island and locals offer greater spontaneity and a sense that, despite hardships, the island has some life and prosperity. One gets a sense of a town at work (fig. 107) and a monastery in action (figs. 108–109).

As an American abroad who held both colonial presumptions about salvaging the past as well as particular views of how monastic life should intersect with the world, Swain produced images that reflect his biases. Mount Athos suffered from a "monastic self-centeredness," brought out by the almost clinical images of the compounds, while Patmos had a charitable and righteous dimension that comes through in Swain's more varied and rich documentation.[267]

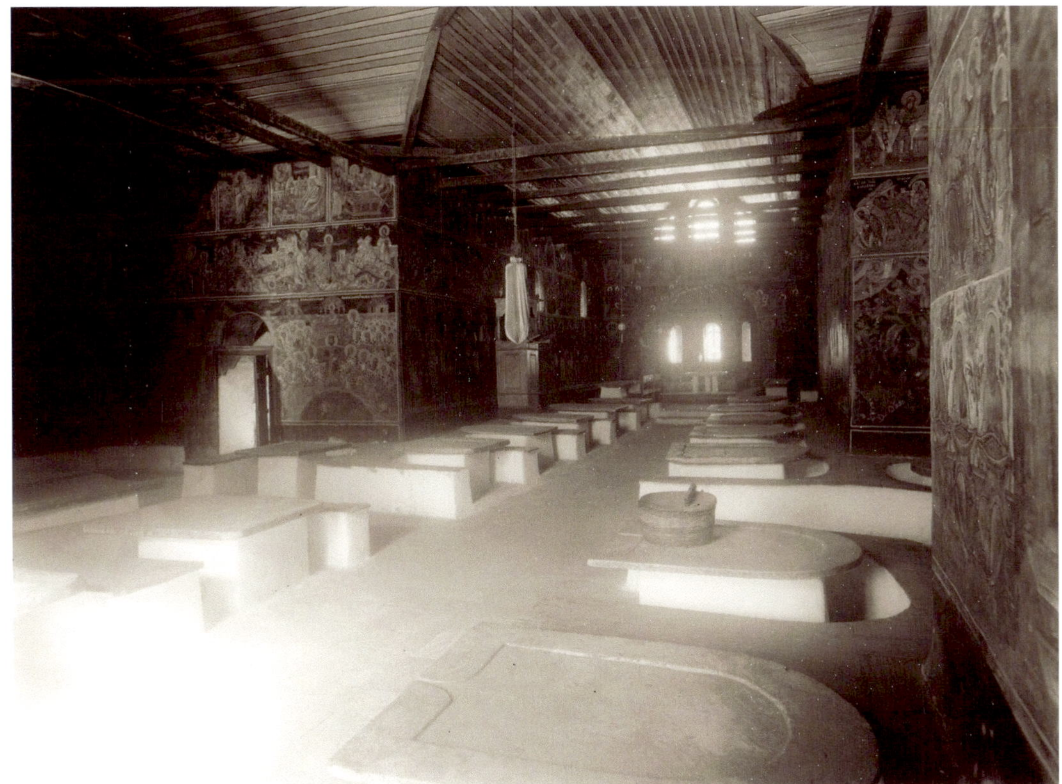

Fig. 105. View down the long axis of the refectory showing drainage arrangements and walls covered with mural paintings, Lavra Monastery, Mount Athos, Greece, July 4–6, 1925 (Kelsey Museum neg. no. 8.0211).

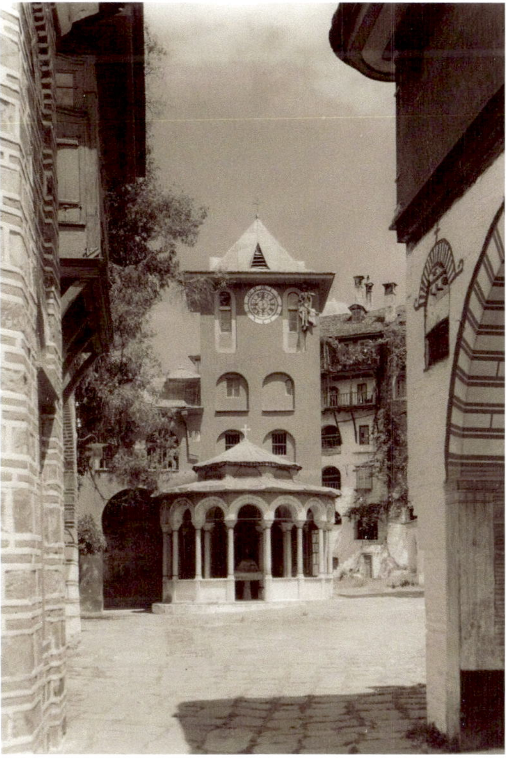

Fig. 106. Clock tower, fountain, and buildings, Vatopedi Monastery, Mount Athos, Greece, June 22–29, 1925 (Kelsey Museum neg. no. 8.0172).

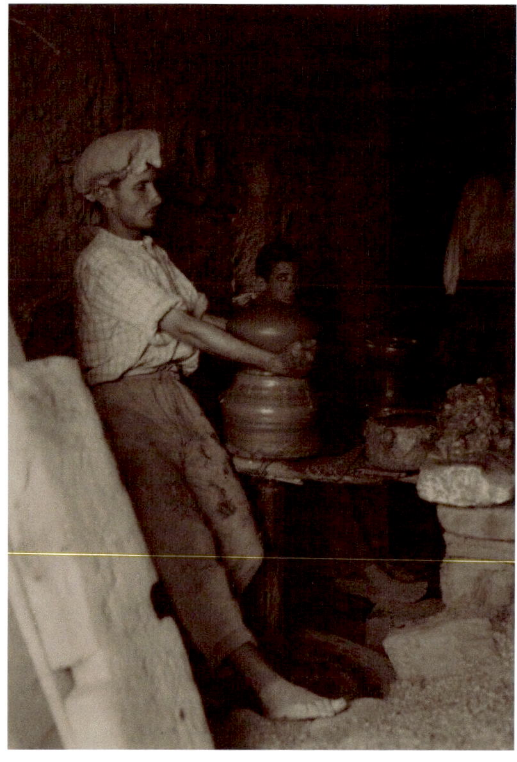

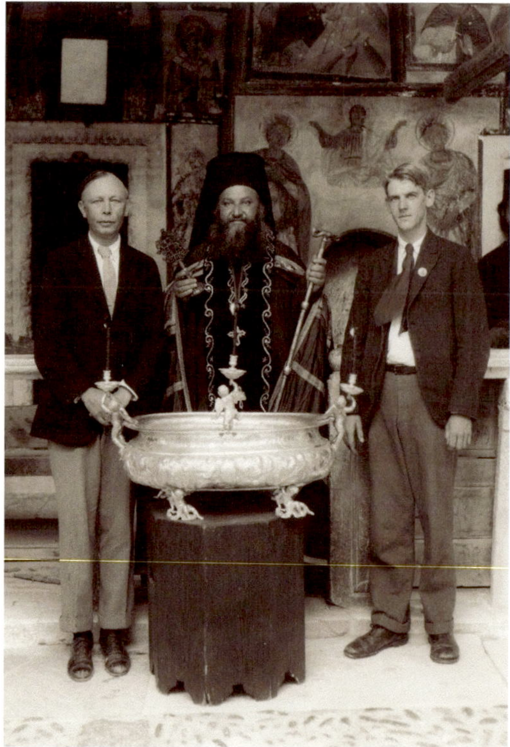

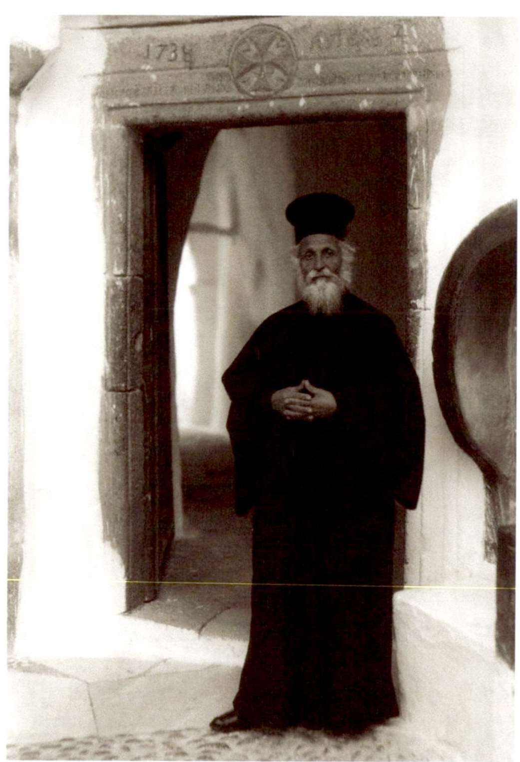

Fig. 107. A young potter at his wheel, Patmos, Greece, July 30, 1925 (Kelsey Museum neg. no. KS 359.11).

Fig. 108. From left to right: Professor Kirsopp Lake, the hegumen (monastery head), and Robert Casey in the monastery courtyard, Patmos, Greece, July 25–31, 1925 (Kelsey Museum neg. no. 8.0267).

Fig. 109. Father Gerassimos Smynakes at the Monastery of Saint John, Patmos, Greece, May 1920 (Kelsey Museum neg. no. 7.0421).

Swain and Robert's trip to Greece came to a close toward the end of August. They said "good bye to Athens on the forenoon of August 22" and boarded their Italy-bound steamer at 10:30 a.m. for an 11:00 departure.[268] True to form, the vessel left at 3:00 p.m. Swain refrained from commenting on the delay but instead mentions his experience at the passport office in Athens, where he was clearly impressed by a "lingual gymnast." The official "asked us questions in English, wrote the answers in Greek, and at the same time replied to an agitated Teutonic female in German, and sent a direction or two to someone else in French—all pretty near synchronously."[269]

Like the 1924 trip, the 1925 expedition had been filled with extraordinary experiences for Swain, his son, and the two vehicles. The Graham Brothers truck and Dodge sedan had, once again, been pressed into service, maneuvering over rugged mountain passes, finding their way on virtually nonexistent desert roads, and visiting strange architectural structures in a desolate Saharan landscape, to say nothing of attending faultlessly to their archaeological responsibilities. But even more, this year seemed to address a sense of moments paused—of de Prorok's obsession with civilizations lost, villages hidden in uncharted areas barely seen by the outside world, and monasteries where time stood still.

The unusual year ended with a two-week drive from Italy to Belgium. The vehicles were stored in Brussels, awaiting the adventures of 1926—unaware that it would likely be their last.

Chapter 9

TRAVELS OF 1926

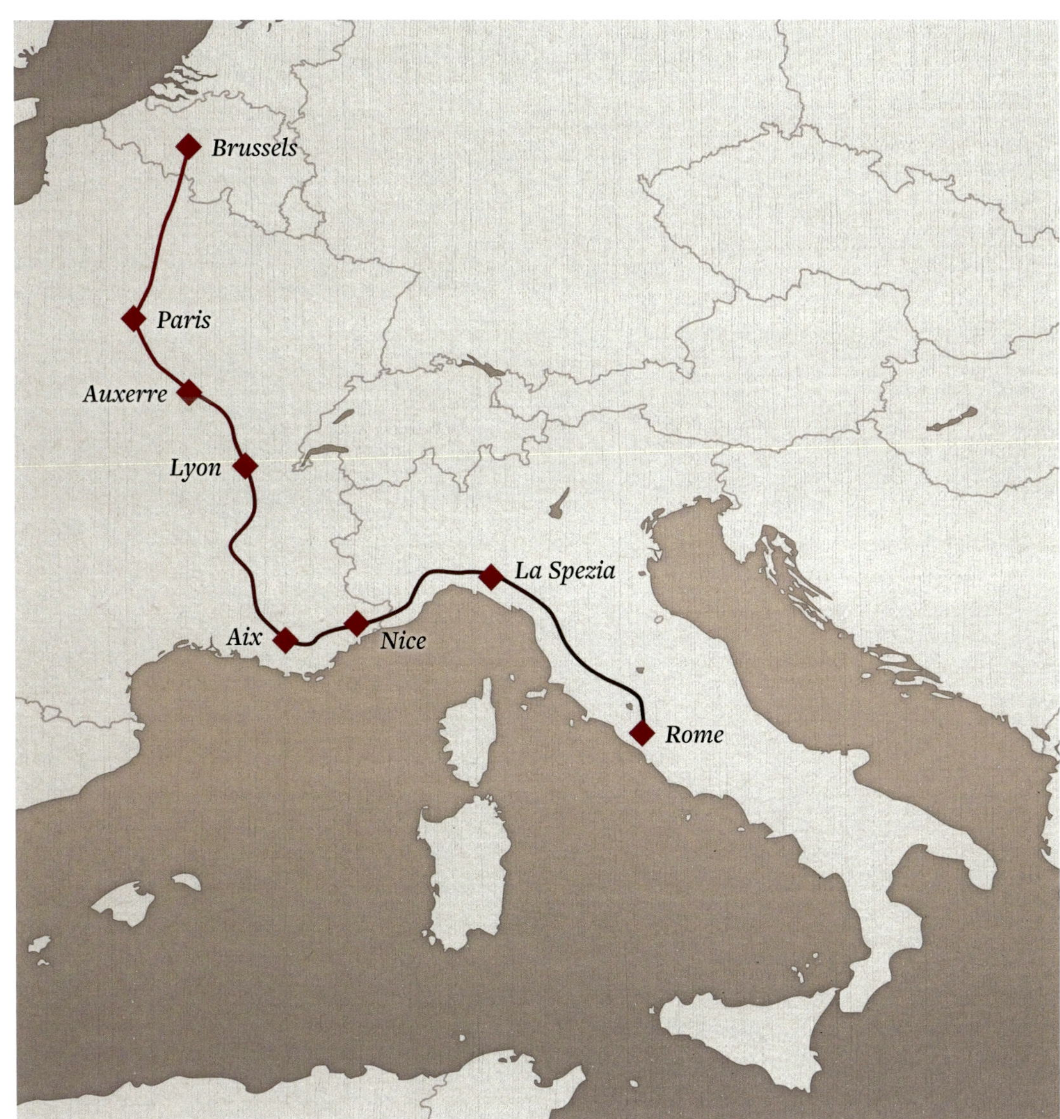

Approximate route of the Graham Brothers truck and Dodge sedan from Brussels, Belgium, to Rome, Italy.

Date	Location	Notes
March 6	Swain and son Edwin (Ned) leave New York	SS *Berengaria*
March 12	Swain and Ned arrive in Cherbourg, France	
March 13–17	Swain and Ned are forced to remain in Paris, awaiting permits for the two vehicles	
March 18	Permits finally arrive. Train to Brussels, Belgium, to pick up the truck and sedan	The vehicles had been in storage since September 1925
March 20	Back in Paris with both vehicles	
March 21–31	The Swains leave Paris on March 21, starting the long trip to Rome, Italy	Drive via Auxerre, Lyon, Aix, Brignoles, and Nice, France, then to La Spezia, Italy
April 2–June 24	Swain and Ned arrive in Rome on April 2 and spend the next three months based mostly in Rome and Pompeii, with visits to Vesuvius, Paestum, Sorrento, Capri, Cumae, Naples, and other locations	
June 25	Swain and Ned sail from Brindisi, Italy, to Salonica, Greece	SS *Goriza*
June 26	Corinth Canal	
June 29–30	Salonica	
July 2	Swain, Ned, and Dr. Lake sail from Salonica to Mount Athos	Cars prohibited
July 2–16	Mount Athos	
July 18–19	Salonica	
July 20–26	Athens	
July 28–30	Patmos	
August 3–6	Andros	
August 7–15	Athens	
August 13	Side trips to Eleusis and Corinth	
August 17	Corinth Canal	
August 24	Genoa, Italy	
August 25?	Swain and Ned leave for New York	SS *President Harrison*

Summary of the 1926 Expedition

Unable to find letters or reports of Swain's 1926 expeditions, I resigned myself to cobbling together photographs and accompanying captions to build a basic outline for the year's travels. Little did I suspect that a search in the Kelsey Museum archives by Sebastián Encina, the museum's registrar at the time, would unearth a long-buried bound journal containing letters that Swain had sent home to his family from early March to mid-August 1926 (figs. 110a–b).[270] What the correspondence tells us is that well-laid plans for Swain and Edwin (Ned), his 19-year-old son, did not go smoothly. Their long-awaited trip to an archaeological project in Egypt was unexpectedly canceled after they arrived in Europe, leaving them spinning their wheels in Italy for what turned out to be much of April, May, and June. Fortunately, fate intervened, and for most of July and part of August, they had an assignment in Greece, which entailed visiting several monasteries and photographing ancient manuscripts, as Swain had done in 1925.

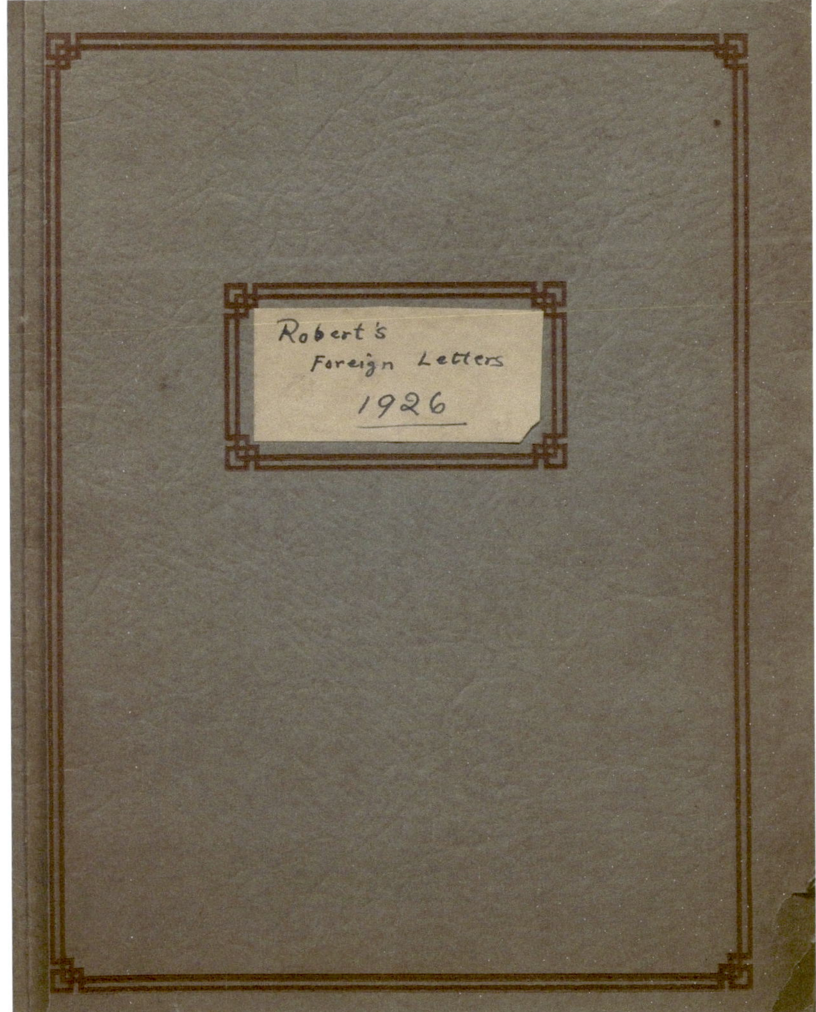

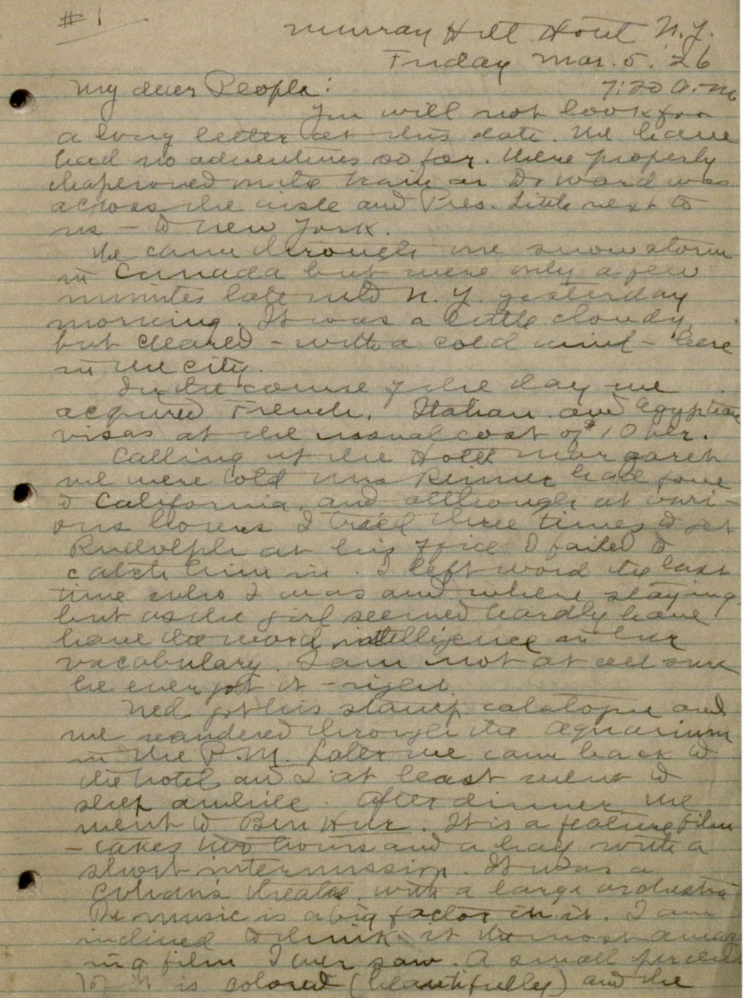

#1

Murray Hill Hotel N.Y.
Friday Mar. 5. '26
7:20 a.m.

My dear People:

You will not look for a long letter at this date. We have had no adventures so far. Were properly chaperoned into train as Dr Ward was across the aisle and Pres. Little next to us – to New York.

We came through one snow storm in Canada but were only a few minutes late into N.Y. yesterday morning. It was a little cloudy but cleared – with a cold wind – here in the city.

In the course of the day we acquired French, Italian and Egyptian visas at the usual cost of $10 per.

Calling up the Hotel Margaret we were told Mrs Renner had gone to California, and although at various hours I tried three times to get Rudolph at his office I failed to catch him in. I left word the last time who I was and where staying but as the girl seemed hardly to have the word intelligence in her vocabulary I am not at all sure he ever got it – right.

Ned got his stamp catalogue and we wandered through the Aquarium in the P.M. Later we came back to the hotel and I at least went to sleep awhile. After dinner we went to Ben Hur. It is a featured film – takes two hours and a half with a short intermission. It was a Cohan's theatre, with a large orchestra. The music is a big factor in it. I am inclined to think it the most amazing film I ever saw. A small per cent of it is colored (beautifully) and the

Figs. 110a–b. The cover of Robert Swain's bound collection of his father's letters home from 1926 and a letter that George Swain sent to his family from New York on March 5 (scans courtesy of the Harlan Hatcher Graduate Library, University of Michigan).

Although the 1926 expedition doesn't boast the same archaeological and cultural excitement of the previous two years, the Graham Brothers truck and Dodge sedan provide ample drama, with a passel of troubles on their journeys. And there was plenty of local color, as Swain's letters home attest. If 1924 was the year of important finds at an archaeological site and lives lived in a remote postwar Turkish village, and 1925 was the year of time seemingly halted, as well as unusual, sometimes perilous travels through Tunisia and Algeria, then 1926 was the year of car troubles and permit predicaments—interspersed with observations on the ordinary and extraordinary in the daily life of 1920s Italy and Greece.

Reviving a Dead Truck

Swain and Ned (fig. 111) left Ann Arbor in early March on a much-anticipated trip overseas to Karanis, Egypt, the site of a University of Michigan excavation, to be followed by a brief stint in Italy for photographic assignments requested by Kelsey. Before boarding a transatlantic steamer in New York, they spent a few days in the city, attending to business, which included the purchase of visas for Italy, France, and Egypt at $10 each (around $155 in today's dollars). Ned was pleased to find a special stamp catalog, and father and

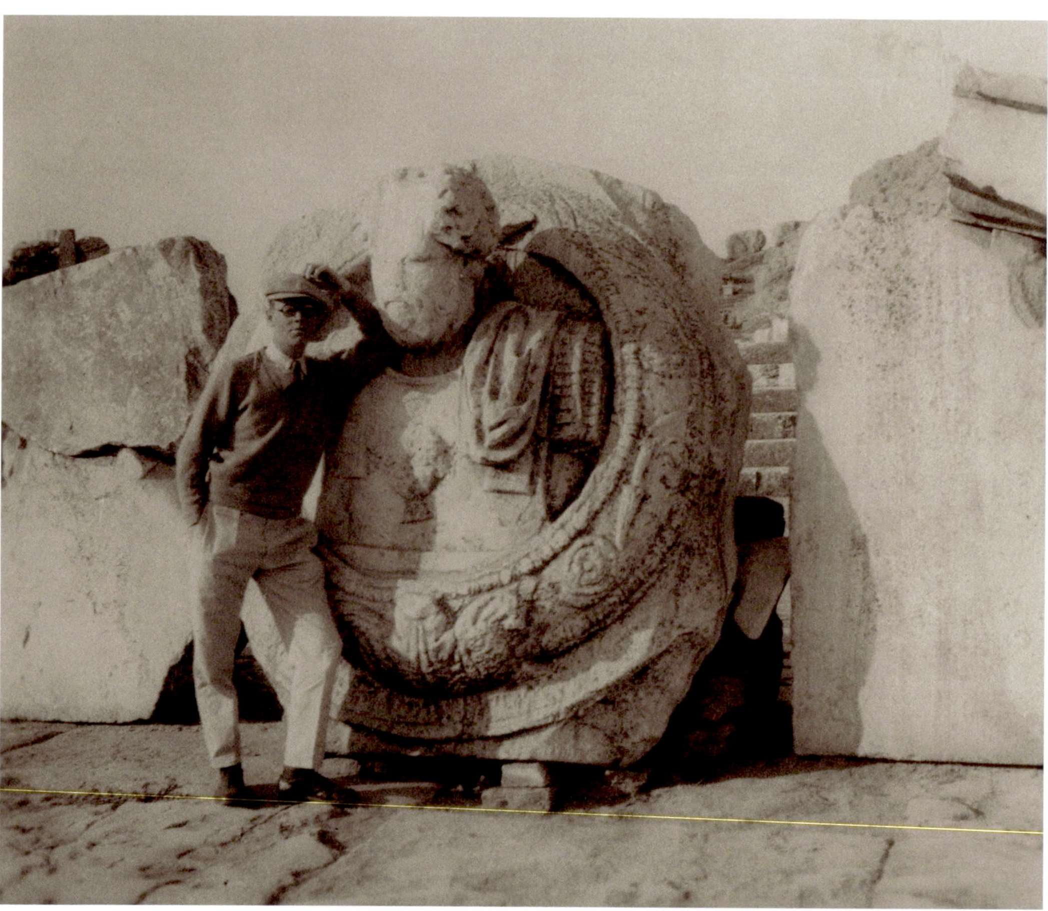

Fig. 111. Edwin (Ned) Swain at Eleusis, Greece, August 13, 1926 (Kelsey Museum neg. no. KS 388.06).

son filled one evening watching the silent, two-and-a-half-hour epic film *Ben-Hur: A Tale of the Christ* (1925), starring Ramon Novarro (whose tragic life and brutal murder in 1968 would later become the subject of harsh Hollywood gossip). Plagued by accidents and disagreements, MGM studios had spent $3.9 million (the equivalent of approximately $65 million today) on production costs, awarding *Ben-Hur* the dubious claim of the most expensive movie of the silent era (fig. 112).[271] The film was shown in the cavernous George M. Cohan Theatre on Broadway and accompanied by a full orchestra. Much to Swain's delight, *Ben-Hur* contained several two-color Technicolor sections. This cinematic blockbuster enthralled Swain—it was a perfect match for his photographic interests and his long-standing fascination with the classical world. Indeed, he proclaimed *Ben-Hur* "the best film I have ever seen."[272]

On the morning of March 6, Swain and Ned boarded the SS *Berengaria*, the largest of the Cunard fleet.[273] They enjoyed a restful week on the relatively smooth but chilly crossing to Cherbourg, France. Swain wrote home almost daily, describing their small berth, the ship's large and attractive lounge and smoking room, the five-piece orchestra on board, and the food, which Swain dubbed "quite beyond criticism."[274] Once they arrived in Paris (March 13) and settled into a hotel—with the luxury of hot and cold running water—the inevitable business of obtaining permits for the sedan and truck began. Both vehicles were in Brussels, ready to emerge from a well-deserved rest of six months. The plan was to retrieve the truck and sedan from Brussels, drive back to Paris to pick up their supplies and stored luggage, and then start the long trek through France and Italy, with a final stop in Egypt. Not surprisingly, but surely annoyingly, Swain discovered that the permits required for driving the two vehicles across the Belgian-French border had not been issued. Although Swain doesn't explain the details, he notes that some kind of political "upset" had occurred in France. As his contact at the American Embassy grumbled, "When this happens, the officials stand around halls and corridors talking instead of doing anything."[275]

Stuck in Paris waiting for permits, father and son immersed themselves in French culture, catching a musical revue that Swain quips was characterized by some very pretty "costuming," as well as "some chiefly conspicuous by its absence." Days were filled with visits to Notre Dame, Sainte-Chapelle, the Luxembourg Gardens, the Louvre, Sacré-Coeur, and Versailles, among other notable French sights. Despite the charms of Paris, Swain was anxious to get to work; finally, on March 18, they were cleared to leave for Brussels.[276]

After an uneventful train ride, Swain was pleased to find that both vehicles had been given new coverings and finishes, looking "much better than they did when [we] turned them over last September."[277] The truck and sedan appeared, both inside and out, fully serviced for the drive to Paris and beyond.

Assured by the presence of nine spare tires and ready for a smooth journey, the vehicles began their travels, Ned driving the truck and Swain the sedan. When they reached the French border, however, Swain was informed that the vehicles' permits were nowhere to be found (presumably, the paperwork had not been given to Swain but was stalled in Paris). Ever the problem solver, Swain (and Ned) headed back to the nearest small town and sent a telegram to the US Embassy in Paris, describing the issue and letting officials there know they were waiting at a local hotel. Several hours later, Swain's contact at the

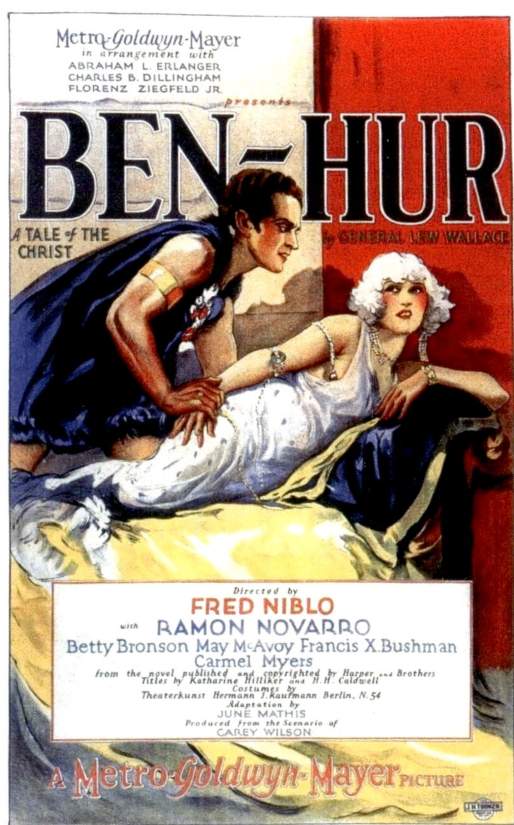

Fig. 112. Poster for the 1925 movie *Ben-Hur: A Tale of the Christ* (Metro-Goldwyn-Mayer).

embassy telephoned to say that an express telegram was on its way and that all would be fine. Feeling much better, father and son spent a night at the Grand Hotel (more third-class than grand, according to Swain), "endured" an additional hour and a half of border formalities the next morning, and finally "hit er up" for Paris. In the interim, they had obtained two new passengers: one of the customs officials had asked if Swain might take his wife and three-year-old son to Paris. Swain obliged, noting that the wife was "small, so there was plenty of room on the front seat." According to Swain, the vehicles were "full of pep," no doubt excited to be back on the road after such a long rest.[278] Little did they know what lay ahead.

After a night in Paris, Swain and Ned were set to leave the City of Light early on the morning of Sunday, March 21. But they encountered another unexpected snag: the baggage and photographic equipment they had stored at the hotel were missing. It took some time for the hotel staff to remember that the suitcases and equipment had been moved to a fifth-floor storage room. All was quickly resolved, however, and they headed to Auxerre, approximately 160 kilometers (100 miles) south of Paris, which, Swain noted in his letter home, "doesn't sound much in Michigan, but try it in N.E. France and Belgium!"[279]

The first day of traveling was filled with small troubles, slow roads, and the truck leaking half of its water due to a loose connection. By day two (March 22), things got considerably worse. Driving in tandem to Lyon, Swain lost sight of Ned, who was behind the wheel of the truck and keeping close track of the sedan's lead. When Swain doubled back, he found his unhappy son standing by a dead vehicle. The lifeless truck was unceremoniously towed by the sedan to a local garage, where the mechanics delivered bad news: the vehicle required a new distributor. Swain had no choice but to catch a train back to Paris to purchase the piece of equipment. Ned would remain behind in the village of Arnay-le-Duc. Given train schedules, it was a race against time for Swain; he barely boarded the train at a flag station—arriving in Paris at midnight—and purchased a new mechanism the next day at the Service Department of the Dodge dealership. Back to Arnay-le-Duc with the replacement in hand, Swain reported that it took the mechanics three attempts to get the truck running.[280]

Finally, the worst was behind them, and the Swains were back on the road by March 24 for the last, long stretch to Rome. But once again, the car gods conspired against them. They experienced a flat in one of the older tires (the rim had worn clear through the valve stem), were delayed by a delivery truck that jackknifed across the road, ran into hail "the size of small peas," endured a second flat, and encountered endless muddy, curving roads, with Swain wishing he had a dollar for every curve they negotiated.[281]

Disappointments and Predicaments

It was with much relief that Swain and Ned finally arrived in Rome on April 2, almost two weeks after leaving Paris. They had logged in a little over 1,300 miles on their trip from Brussels. A telegram from Kelsey awaited them, reading, "Cable me if long delayed before going on with Egyptian trip." Swain cabled back that they couldn't reach Alexandria (Egypt) until April 12, given steamer schedules.[282] Despite the delay and all the setbacks of the previous weeks, Ned maintained his youthful exuberance, excited by the imminent prospect of visiting Egypt and working on an excavation.

While waiting in Rome for the steamer, Swain and Ned took advantage of Italy's many wonders, visiting various sites and cities (fig. 113). Swain's letter home on April 6, however, reports surprising and disheartening news. "As usual, the unexpected," he writes. "Kelsey has cabled to cancel the Egypt trip. . . . I am extremely disappointed for Ned as this was in his eyes the big thing of the trip."[283] The cable added, somewhat cryptically, "Confidential Trouble Egypt."

The cancellation of work at Karanis appears to have been rooted in personnel problems at the site (Swain was not privy to the details at the time). As early as January, Kelsey—

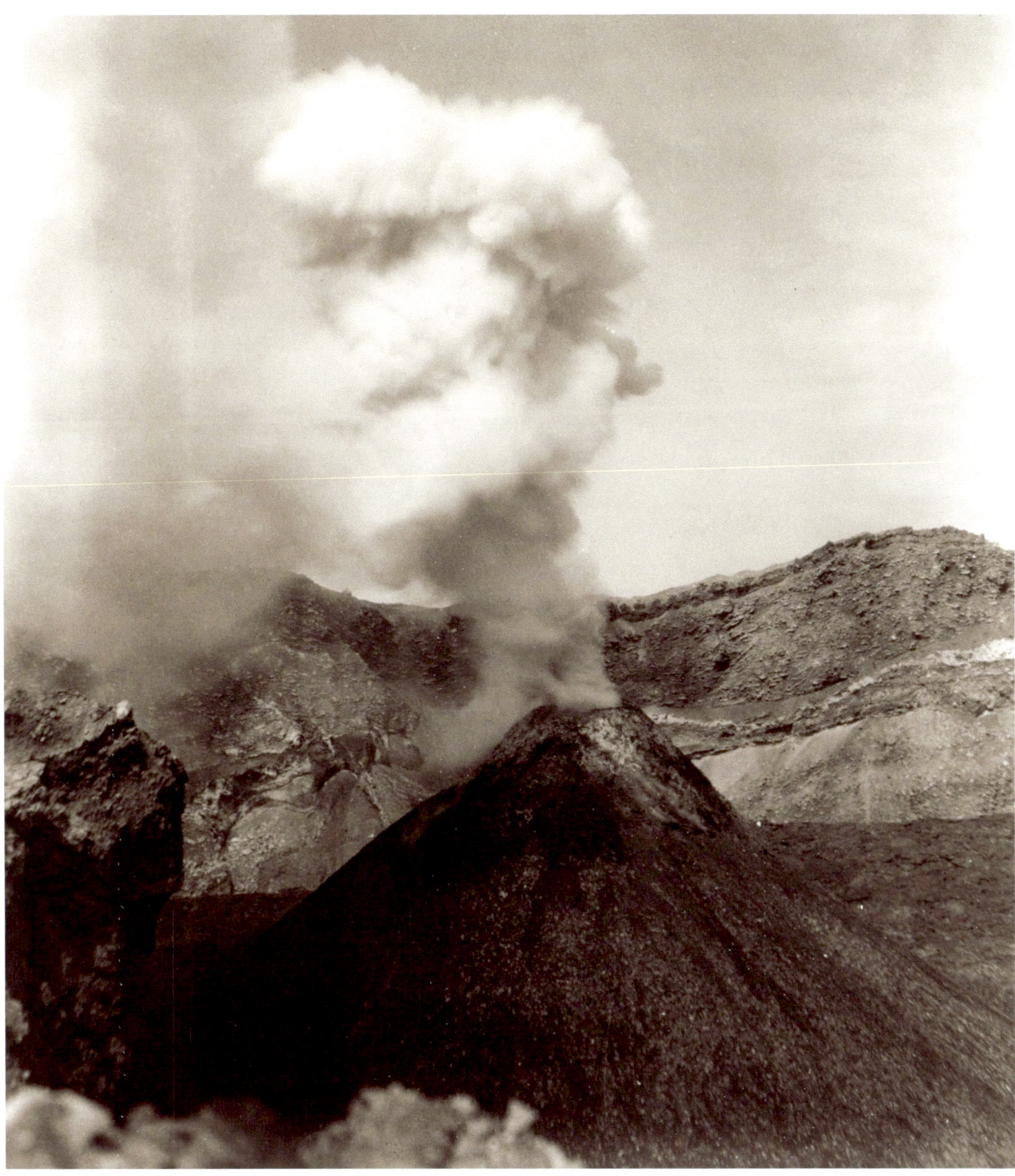

Fig. 113. Mount Vesuvius's inner cone aperture, Italy, May 12, 1926 (Kelsey Museum neg. no. 8.1605).

who was still in the United States—was made aware of tensions among several members of the project through letters and cables from Egypt. One member of the group, J. L. Starkey, was accused of overspending by $4,000 dollars (a princely sum in those days), hostilities were burgeoning, and a seeming lack of leadership roiled operations.[284] Starkey was also singled out for "tardiness, colonial attitudes toward the servants, selfishness with the whiskey supplies, and bad behavior toward his wife."[285] (He was murdered many years later in Palestine for reasons that are still a matter of debate.)[286]

Regardless of the messy situation at Karanis, Swain had his own problems to solve. Among the cables he received from Kelsey was a request to secure permits for taking photographs in the ancient city of Pompeii. The cables further warned Swain that obtaining permits for this renowned site would require "much tact" and that his photographs should include "whatever you Consider Profitable."[287] Although Swain was fully apprised of Kelsey's long and highly respected work at Pompeii, he was perplexed by his colleague's directive: "I am rather in the dark about what we are supposed to do in Pompeii as I supposed F. W. K. [Francis W. Kelsey] would be here by the time we got back from Egypt and we would be working under his direction."[288] Kelsey had planned to visit Karanis and Italy earlier that year, overlapping with Swain, but periodic bouts of ill health, as well as other illnesses within his family, delayed his trip. In fact, Kelsey didn't arrive in Europe until mid-July.

Until Kelsey arrived, Swain needed to interpret what his colleague meant by photographing "whatever you Consider Profitable" and, more importantly, determine how to expedite permits for work at Pompeii without the presence of his mentor, who had years of experience negotiating with the sometimes uncooperative ministry. According to Swain, Professor Maiuri, the person in charge of issuing the relevant permits, "'has it in' for F. W. K. and is in a position practically to block any photographing K. wants done till . . . things are oiled over."[289] Ultimately, Maiuri seems to have had a change of heart and, on April 20, granted a token permit, which allowed "up to 50 views around streets etc." of Pompeii.

Impatient to start work, Swain vents his exasperation in a letter of May 2, with uncharacteristic criticism of Kelsey: "The outlook for any working permits, Pompeii or elsewhere, is extremely poor, except the one permit for 50 views in Pompeii which we have—and this covers only streets and monuments all of which were photographed a generation ago. It seems we are wasting time and money through F. W. K.'s failure to be here to engineer things in person—if he can. . . . Ned . . . gets tired of doing nothing . . . So I feel frequently like saying biblical words *staccato fortissimo*."[290]

Meanwhile, Swain received a letter from Kelsey alerting him to the prospect of meeting Dr. Kirsopp Lake (the eminent scholar at Harvard Divinity School; see p. 94) in mid-June to photograph some important ancient manuscripts housed in Greek libraries and monasteries. Soon after, however, a cable arrived noting that Lake had been detained and that Swain should "work according to your best judgement [in] Pompeii or elsewhere." A frustrated Swain wrote home: "We have been away from home almost two months, and aside from getting the cars to Rome—and the sedan here [in Pompeii], getting an adequate darkroom ready, and learning more about Pompeii and some of the country hereabouts, I don't see we have done anything."[291]

With work at a virtual standstill, Swain and Ned used the sedan to visit sights and local areas of interest (the truck remained in Rome). They also kept up to date on world news. At one point, Swain reports that a "crazy English woman" attempted to assassinate Mussolini, and then a few days later, "another crank—woman—was caught with a gun looking for him." Swain wonders "if this goes to prove that the female of the species is more deadly than the male!"[292] Swain's offhanded comment notwithstanding, the first attempted assassination caused an international stir. The woman was identified as the daughter of the lord chancellor of Ireland and was later certified as mentally ill, spending the rest of her life in a British asylum.[293]

Swain fills his letters home with news about life in Pompeii, both the mundane and uncommon. One day, Swain and Ned witnessed a ferocious gasoline fire off a main square—flames reached 20 to 30 feet high, and billows of black smoke choked the air. Mild pandemonium broke out, with police and firefighters struggling to extinguish the main fire, control the stream of blazing gasoline running down streets, and keep hundreds of gawking bystanders at bay.[294] It must have felt historic: Vesuvius may not have erupted, but Pompeii was burning once again.

In another letter, Swain writes with delight about the system of delivering milk to local residents. Goats and cows (with their calves) were herded through the town's streets, ambling door to door. The quadrupeds were milked in front of each house—with the liquid coming from what Swain once referred to as its "original packaging"—filling pails provided by each resident.[295]

The weather—a perennial topic of conversation in Swain's letters—was becoming increasingly hot, and Swain was amused to note a change in children's dress: "Kids are reducing clothes to lowest terms—in some cases clothing equals a fraction with no denominator—i.e., one abbreviated garment." On a more distressing note, Swain writes about the difficulties confronting Mr. Cimmino, the proprietor of their hotel. "Il Padrone," as Swain calls him, had a troubled family life, with a son who had been afflicted with infant paralysis and recently expelled from a special school that he "was attending for disobedience." Mr. Cimmino's brother was another cause of distress. One day, Swain and Ned found masses of broken glass around the hotel. Apparently, Il Padrone's "worthless younger brother"—who had been jailed for various offenses—smashed some windows because he had been refused a loan of 1,000 lire. Adding to Cimmino's struggles was his wife: she had been thrown from a carriage and suffered shoulder pain that was misdiagnosed, causing a significant delay in her healing. Swain may have been frustrated by Italian bureaucracy, but he fully realized that Mr. Cimmino faced more significant hardships.[296]

Fortunately, plans for the trip to Greece to join Dr. Lake were moving forward, although steamer scheduling was problematic, given the infrequency of ships to his next port of call, Salonica. Swain and Ned booked passage aboard the SS *Goriza* from Brindisi, Italy, on June 25. They were scheduled to arrive in Salonica on June 28 and meet with Lake on June 30. With still more time to spare in Italy, they continued to travel with the sedan to various archaeological sites and local towns. Swain took advantage of his seemingly never-ending stint in Italy to experiment with a telephoto lens that he rarely used, finding himself pleased with the results.

Bugs, Rugs, and the Bible

As always, once aboard a ship, Swain became intrigued by the seaworthy behemoth—in this case, a 3,000-ton steamer designed for both passengers and freight. He and Ned shared a three-berth room, with two portholes and an electric fan; the food was pronounced "varied and excellent"; and the seas were quiet as a "mill pond." Swain informed his wife that she need not take pity on them. The only problem was the discovery that one of Swain's suitcases had been "tampered with" and some things stolen, including four or five unexposed rolls of Kodak film, four blue work shirts, and all of his white collars.[297]

Swain was particularly fascinated by the ship's cargo. The SS *Goriza*, one of the larger Mediterranean steamers, was loaded with goods heading to and hailing from far-flung ports. The deck was piled "high with boxes, casks, threshing machine, and boxed at least 27 Ford cars and tractors for Constantinople and Black Sea points . . . and sugar sacks from Brazil."[298] At a stop in Piraeus, Greece, bales of dried zebra hides, probably from South Africa, were picked up.[299] At one point, they passed through the famous Corinth Canal, taking 45 minutes to traverse its four miles. Swain briefly describes the passage: "A tug partly pulls the steamer with a tow line to either side of the bow. I say 'partly' for the steamer uses its own power in part."[300]

The Ford cars and tractors onboard—which Swain later counts closer to 50 in number—were not accompanied by the Michigan vehicles. The Graham Brothers truck and Dodge sedan remained in Italy for the duration of the trip to Greece. Given some of the alternate modes of transportation they were soon to encounter, there were times when Swain and Ned must have sorely missed the Detroit-made wonders.

By June 29, Swain and Ned were once again on terra firma, waiting for the arrival of Dr. Lake in Salonica. Lake finally arrived, but his luggage—which included rolls of film that were vital to Swain's work—were lost in transit (fortunately, they were later recovered). The weather proved no more propitious, with the night characterized as "Jupiter Pluvius [tipping] over barrels of water . . . [and] a deluge interspersed with big hail."[301]

Swain's letters continue to comment on matters more consequential than the weather, periodically providing asides about news in his part of the world. His stay in the Mediterranean overlapped with an uprising in Syria (1925–1927), which had been under French control since the end of World War I. Various ethnic and religious groups were attempting to liberate themselves from the yoke of French rule. According to Swain, the French papers dismissed the unrest, with France's civilian high commissioner "asserting that everything there now was (apparently) little less than a love feast." To the contrary, Swain met an American who had just returned from Syria and reported that, soon after the alleged peace, the "French cut loose with artillery and shelled the native quarter much of the night."[302]

Although mentioned only in passing, Swain also provides an interesting comment about Greek currency. In the wake of the war, Greece faced ongoing financial troubles. The drachma was highly devalued in 1922—worth 50 percent of its face value (fig. 114)—and somewhat more favorable in 1926, at 75 percent. As Swain writes, the currency presented "a problem in high finance," with the bills having one-quarter of one end cut off to signify its diminished value.[303]

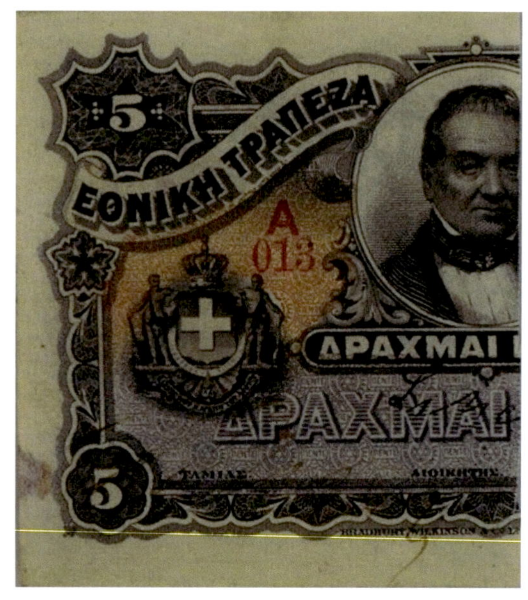

Fig. 114. A cut drachma from the 1920s (courtesy of Wikimedia Commons/Amscheip).

Finally, on July 2, Swain, Ned, and Lake set sail from Salonica to Mount Athos, weighing anchor at 3 a.m. For part of their journey, they were aboard the USS *Scorpion*, a former private yacht commandeered by the US government during the Spanish-American War and later attached to the US Embassy in Constantinople. The former yacht had arrived in Greece to transport the US consul general to Mount Athos; Swain was delighted to be invited aboard the boat with his colleagues for the initial leg of travel to this isolated region in northern Greece. Apparently, Swain had not forgotten the disastrous food from his visit the previous year. Forewarned was forearmed: among his nine pieces of luggage was one devoted solely to food—crackers, teas, biscuits, lots of chocolate bars, and "the best" Norwegian sardines, "all to be used as antidotes for a fast diet on Mt. Athos!"[304]

On July 3, Swain and the others were joined by one "Deacon" Cyril Johnson, an American who was ordained as a Greek priest (fig. 115). Swain gives few details about their companion, although the deacon was apparently an "essential cog in the machine."[305] Perhaps his priestly status served as entrée to some of the monasteries, enabling access to valuable manuscripts. What crumbs Swain offers about the deacon are tantalizing. Swain notes, for example, that at some point, Johnson had been thrown in prison by Turkish authorities. The circumstances are puzzling, but according to information garnered by Dr. Lake from the US State Department, the deacon was arrested for talking to an American tourist "in the street." Hardly a punishable offense in Swain's estimation, especially given that the

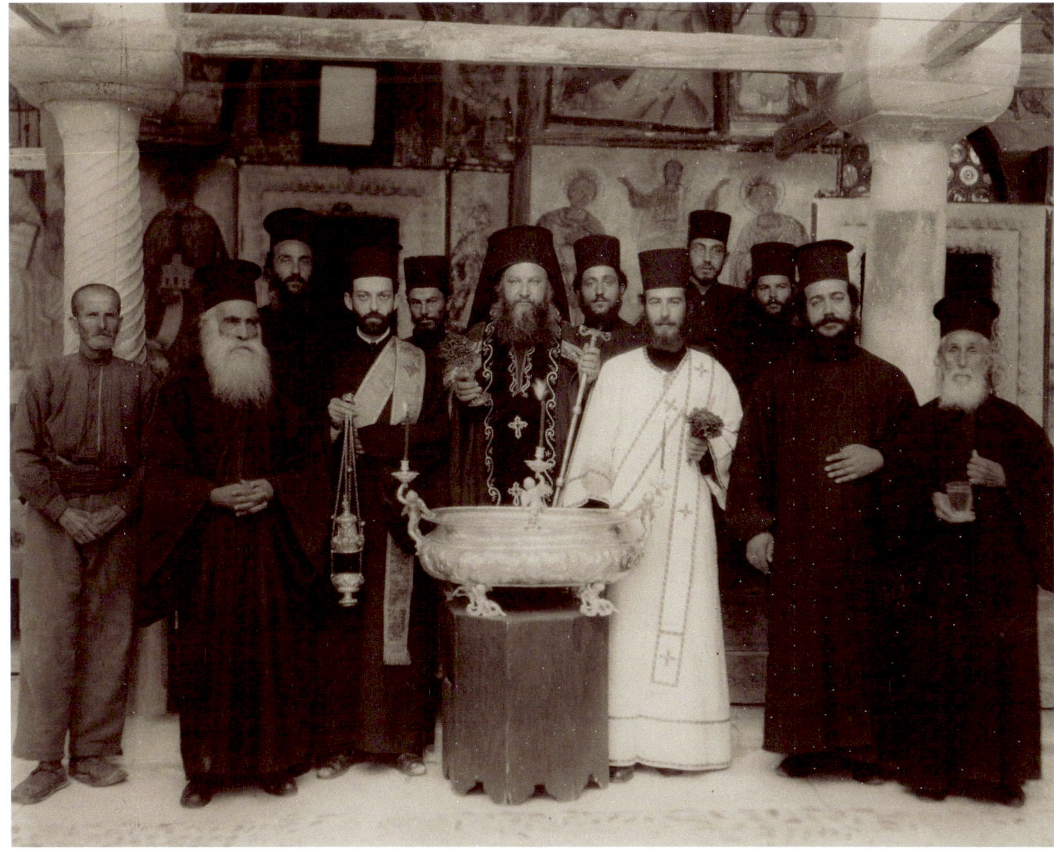

Fig. 115. The "deacon" can be seen on the left, holding a censer, Patmos, Greece, July 25–31, 1925 (Kelsey Museum neg. no. 8.0265).

deacon was an American citizen by birth. As Swain speculates, it was possible—in light of strained relations between Greece and Turkey—that "the Turks [were] hunting for excuses to abuse Greek priests."[306] Toward the end of the trip, for reasons that are again mysterious, the deacon removed all his clerical garb, shaved his beard, and became, at least "externally, an ordinary American."[307]

The roughly two-week stay on Mount Athos would take Swain, Ned, Lake, and the deacon to several monasteries, including Daphne, Vatopedi, Iveron, Lavra, Karyes, and the Russian monastery Russiko. Travel between the institutions was either by small boat or mule—a far cry from the journeys with the sedan and truck—with overland routes often traversing steep terrain, sometimes for hours. According to Swain, walking, rather than straddling the trusted mule, was often the better part of valor. As he notes, "We came via mules from Iveron to Daphne by the 'direct' trail which is a fright—goes up some 2200 feet then down. I walked the last part of the 'down' as the mule had lost one shoe, and was so afraid of the rocks I really didn't dare ride down the crazy trail."[308]

As usual, the Greek sense of time and persistent bureaucratic roadblocks created complications for thc travelers. One morning, after a 9 a.m. breakfast, Swain and Ned found that the librarian who was to facilitate access to designated manuscripts "had gone to sleep and would be awake again—sometime. This sometime proved to be about 3:15, so we wasted two-thirds of the day—which is not unusual here."[309] On another day, they arrived in the evening at a small port near one of the monasteries, left their baggage below, and walked up a 500-foot hill only to find the monastery closed for the night. "Knocking at the front door was of no avail. A native took us round to a back door, where neither he nor an 'outside' monk could do anything with the porter. . . . So the upshot was Ned and I slept (?) at first on [the] floor or benches of a summer house by the gate, and at 1:00 a.m. in the brilliant starlight I discovered some hay in a field across the trail, and we spent the rest of the night there."[310] Fortunately, the next day, they were able to photograph at least some of the requested manuscripts.

In addition to such wasted time, and despite battling ants, mosquitoes, bedbugs, and gnat bites that itched "villainously," there was one highlight of the trip—namely, access to an invaluable Georgian Bible that Lake had been attempting to photograph for 26 years. According to Swain, the manuscript had been written in 978 CE and contained over 850 large pages. It allegedly came from "an earlier lost Armenian version, which in turn came from a lost [and earlier] Syriac text."[311] After several days of intense work, Swain and Ned produced 856 images in their attempt to document this exceptional manuscript.

Following a productive, sometimes frustrating, and no doubt cracker- and chocolate-filled few weeks in the wilds of Mount Athos, Swain and Ned boarded a boat back to Salonica, arriving on July 18. They spent two days there, continuing with their remit of photographing manuscripts, shooting nearly 145 exposures. The next stop consisted of a few days in Athens to photograph yet another manuscript, part of the collection at the National Library of Greece. An unexpected delay arose, however, because the man with the key to the library was out of town and had apparently taken it with him.[312] Eventually, all was settled, and the Swains found life in Athens more than satisfactory: "We are enjoying good food, good beds, and absence of flies, gnats, bedbugs and mosquitoes."[313] When not working, they entertained themselves with nights out in the warm Athenian air. One

Sunday evening, they ventured to a seaside restaurant, dining at a hotel terrace lit up by "an almost full yellow moon hanging over the gleaming water of the bay." The shorefront was filled with locals, dressed in their Sunday best, promenading back and forth for much of the night.[314] In an assuring gesture to his wife, Swain notes, "I found only two women I would call attractive for looks—one a blonde (peroxide?), [the] other a bobbed brunette of say 23. So I have not been tempted to elope."[315]

Swain and Ned left for the island of Patmos on July 28. Waiting in the port of Piraeus, Swain offers an unusual description of transporting sheep off a steamer that is anchored nearby. Hundreds of sheep, which had been crowded onto the deck and into the hold, were "hoisted . . . in bunches of six, each one held only by a rope around one hind leg down close to the foot. It didn't look pleasant but they didn't seem to mind it. By the way there were some 200 sheep in the forward deck of the *Ierex* when we came from Salonica—and we were told they were [almost] all sea sick when we struck rough water."[316]

Patmos, which Swain had visited in the past and enjoyed, was home to an important manuscript that needed photographing, this one of the Apocalypse. It must have been of substantial size since Swain notes that it required 108 films, "all we had with us—by 'splitting' two—exposing in halves."[317]

Once the Patmian manuscript was finished, Swain and Ned continued to the island of Andros aboard a steamer that made brief stops at Syros and Tenos (fig. 116). Andros was far off the beaten path (figs. 117–119), and they stayed at a "native hotel" in a tiny town approximately 50 stairsteps uphill from the port. Despite their less-than-stellar accommodations, Swain reports that they had "an entirely satisfactory meal—chicken soup which was almost a stew, veal chops, fried eggs, bread, water, wine, coffee (a la Turque of course) pears and grapes."[318]

The manuscript that awaited them on the island of Andros was housed at the Panachrantou Monastery (fig. 120). Travel to the monastery entailed an hour's trek by mule, a mode of transport that Swain never quite seemed to trust. His letter does not mince words:

> At first the trail was along a narrow level fertile green valley with fruit trees, cypresses, and a few grass fields. Then it hit off up the mountain side and the only adjective that occurs to me in the least adequate is "gosh awful," which is not very descriptive. It varied from normal steepness of a mountain trail (if there be such a quality) to long crazy flights of zig-zag stone steps—natural slabs of stone-shale—of varying width and height, un-repaired for three generations, and often half washed out by winter torrents. To say it is the worst trail I ever rode is merely to hint at its cussedness.[319]

The remote monastery sat "on a wild mountainside with ragged cliffs." Swain estimated that it could accommodate 75 to 100 monks, although only 6 or 8 lived there at the time—a sign of its tenuous state. Sadly, the library and its contents were in deplorable condition; whatever holdings the monastery once held had "shrunk to less than two dozen books, mostly mss., but on paper and not parchment." As Swain laments, "Most of . . . the books are in an utterly ruinous condition, rotting to pieces, both paper and parchment.

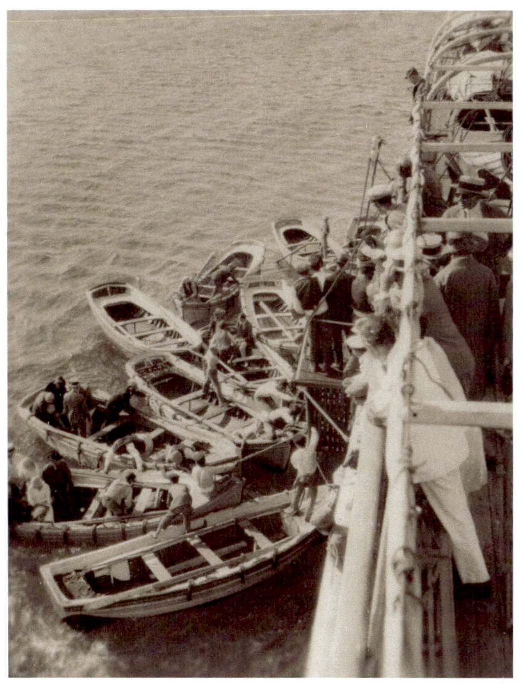

Fig. 116. Stop at the island of Tenos, Greece, August 3, 1926 (Kelsey Museum neg. no. KS 385.03).

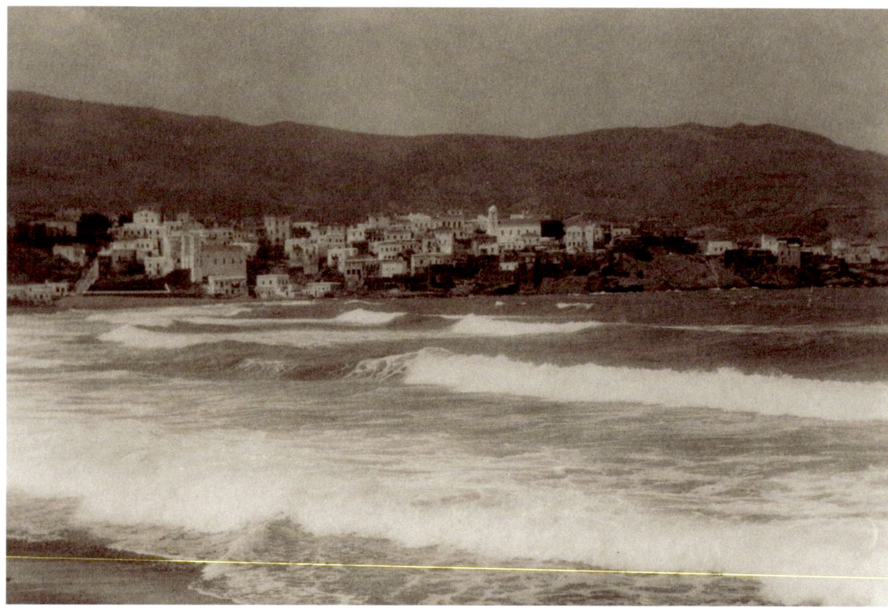

Fig. 117. "A look along the beach toward the town of Andros, when there was a strong wind. We went in surf bathing here," Greece, August 5, 1926 (Kelsey Museum neg. no. KS 387.10).

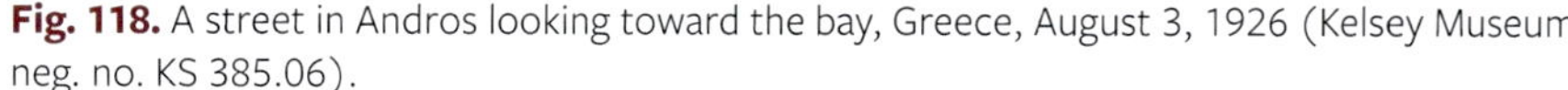

Fig. 118. A street in Andros looking toward the bay, Greece, August 3, 1926 (Kelsey Museum neg. no. KS 385.06).

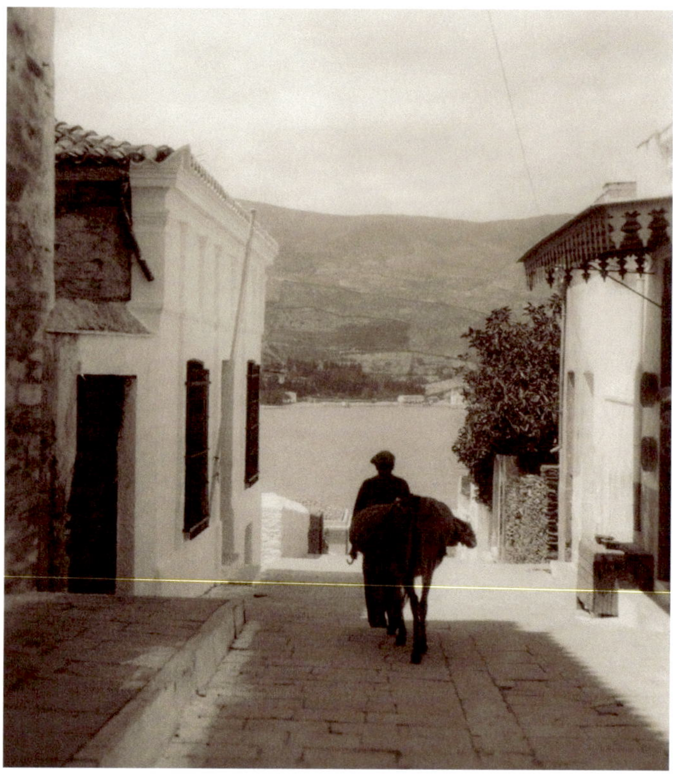

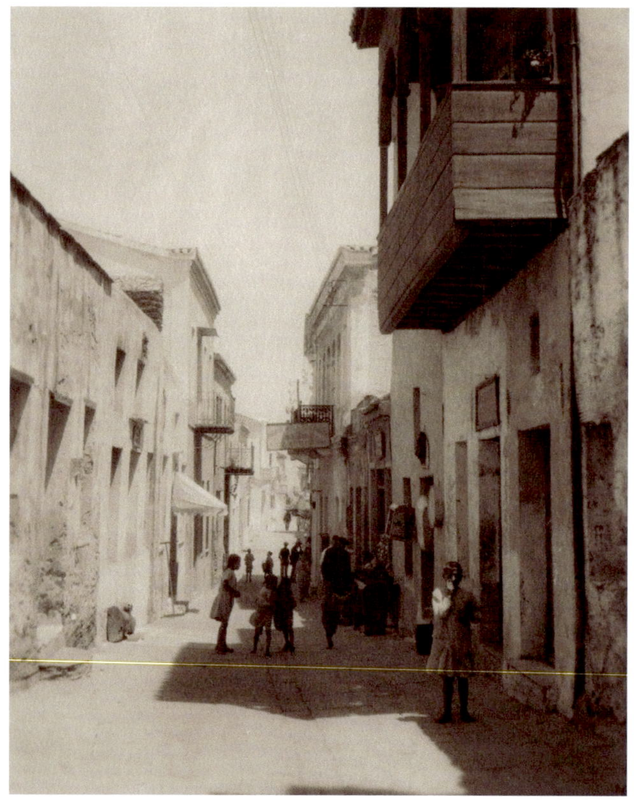

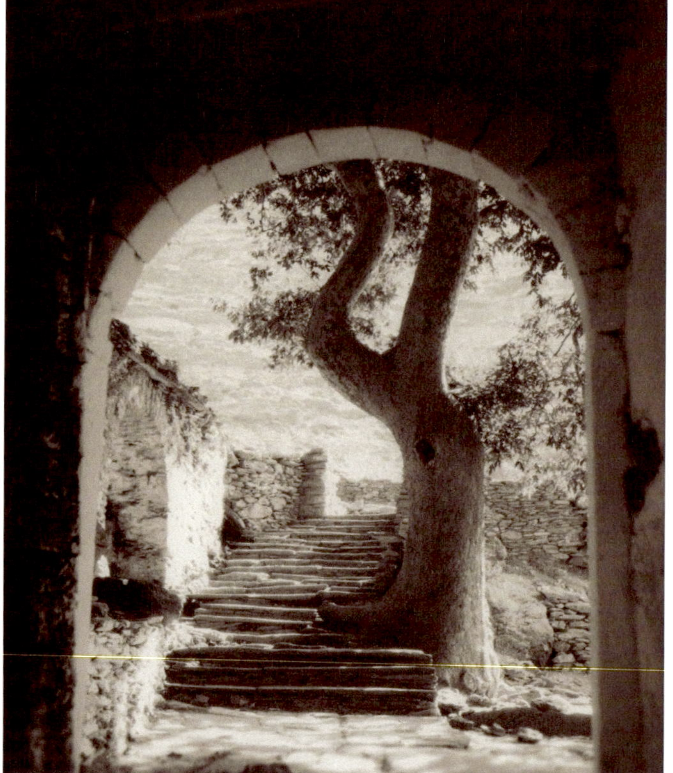

Fig. 119. Main street in the old part of Andros, Greece, August 5, 1926 (Kelsey Museum neg. no. KS 387.09).

Fig. 120. Monastery of Panachrantou, looking out from the entrance to the monastery, Greece, August 3, 1926 (Kelsey Museum neg. no. KS 385.09).

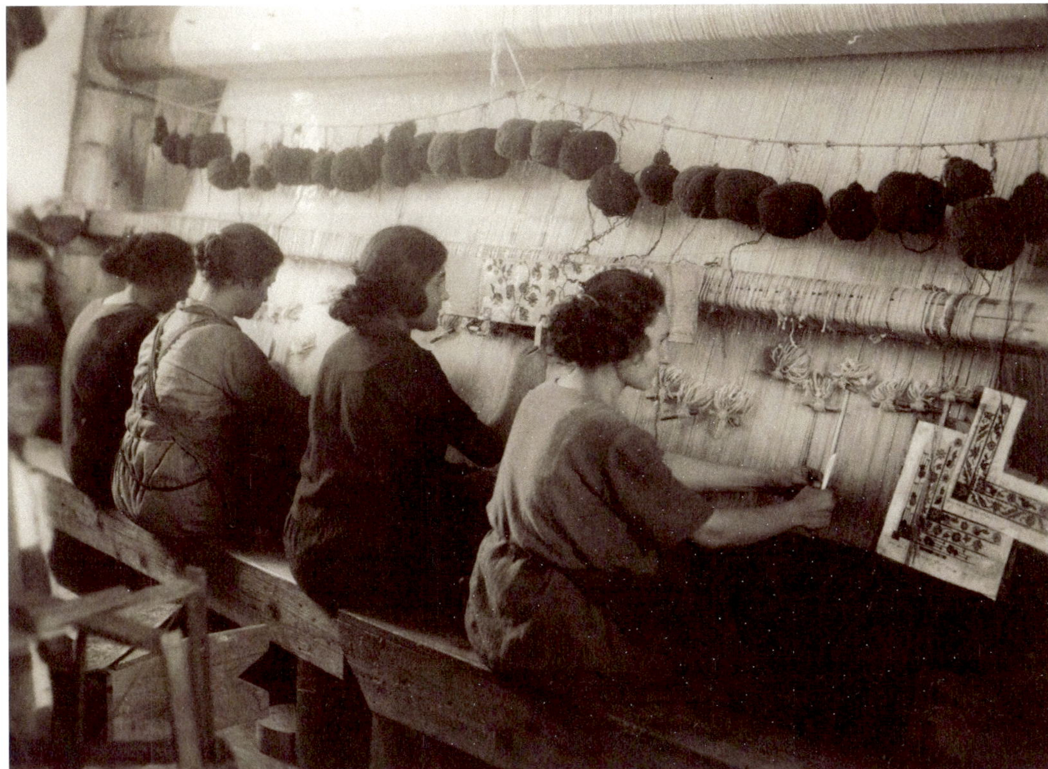

Fig. 121. Women weaving at a loom in a suburb near Athens, Greece, August 12, 1926 (Kelsey Museum neg. no. KS 387.11).

Most of them got utterly soaked in a big storm a year or two back, and have never 'recovered.' In some the leaves are badly stuck together from the soaking and of the paper ones, some are literally rotting to powder." The Apocalypse manuscript that Swain had been charged with photographing was luckily in good condition, "well written on parchment."[320]

As the trip of 1926 neared its close, father and son revisited Athens and scheduled a trip to Naples on August 17. During their stay in Athens, they frequented several local rug production factories, which captured Swain's interest. He offers a detailed description and assessment of the business, once again displaying his curiosity about local economies (fig. 121):

> The rug industry is rapidly becoming a major industry. We saw three quite large factories (one story) the other day, and there are lots of looms in private houses—or shacks. There are some 200,000 refugees in and around Athens. I should guess that at least three quarters of them are in fairly comfortable houses, according to standards here. They are planning to supplant the work of the East—and may well do it. It takes about nine workers a month to make a 9 x 12 rug. It is piece work—you know they are made by tying on the yarn in knots. They are paid 3 drachmas a thousand knots, and experts tie from 10,000 to 12,000 knots a day of 10 hours or less—or something like 30 per minute. The working conditions seem good. Dyes are supposed to be fast vegetable colors. I imagine that most of the product artistically is of but fair average quality. Some of the wool used there comes from Australia.[321]

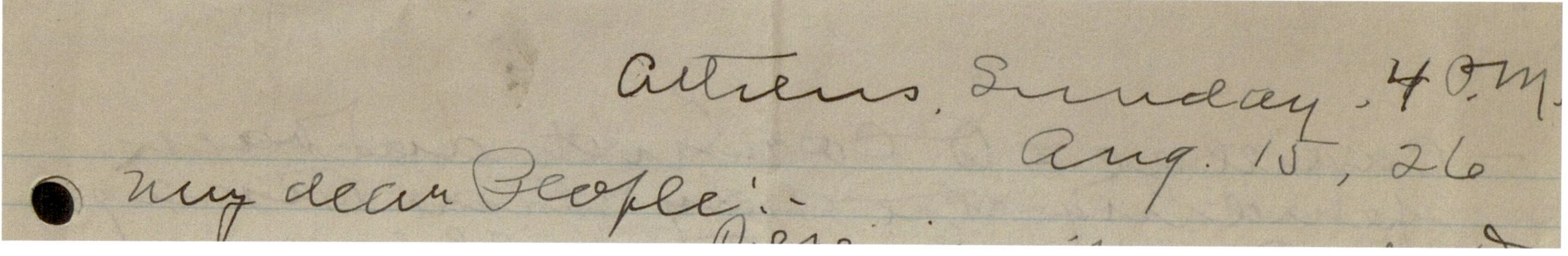
Athens, Sunday, 4 P.M.
Aug. 15, 26
My dear People:–

Fig. 122. Detail, last letter home from George R. Swain to his family, 1926 (Kelsey Museum Archives).

Swain's very last letter is marked "Athens. Sunday, 4 p.m. Aug. 15, 26" and reads, in part, that he and Ned planned to sail from Naples to America on September 5, arriving in New York on September 23 (fig. 122). What transpired between August 15 and September 5 is mostly unknown, although there are 14 photographs of Genoa (dated August 24) that include shots of the dock, the railroad station, and several monuments. There are also some images taken from the SS *President Harrison* on August 25 and 28, indicating that Swain and his son left earlier than initially planned on their last, homeward voyage across the Atlantic.

What remains an even greater mystery is the fate of the ever-reliable, Detroit-made vehicles at the end of the 1926 trip. Did the Graham Brothers truck and Dodge sedan remain in Italy or were they stored elsewhere? When last seen at the end of June, the truck was temporarily stored in Rome and the sedan "working" in Pompeii. There is no indication that one or both were part of excavations during the following year at Karanis, Egypt. Photos of cars at Karanis do exist from 1927, but they are, alas, not of our intrepid heroes. Knowing how much the sedan and truck had experienced over their three-year sojourn, I wouldn't be surprised if they decided to rest and sun themselves somewhere in Italy, far from mudslides, impassable roads, and frustrating delays.

While Carthage and Antioch may not have matched the fame of other roughly contemporaneous projects, such as King Tut's tomb or the Royal Cemetery at Ur, the truck and sedan had been vital members of significant campaigns in remote parts of the world during the 1920s. The University of Michigan was a premier institution in archaeological discoveries during the early decades of the last century, and the two vehicles were an indispensable part of those endeavors. Hopefully, after a much-deserved break, they embarked on new adventures, no doubt delighting in whatever challenges arose (fig. 123).

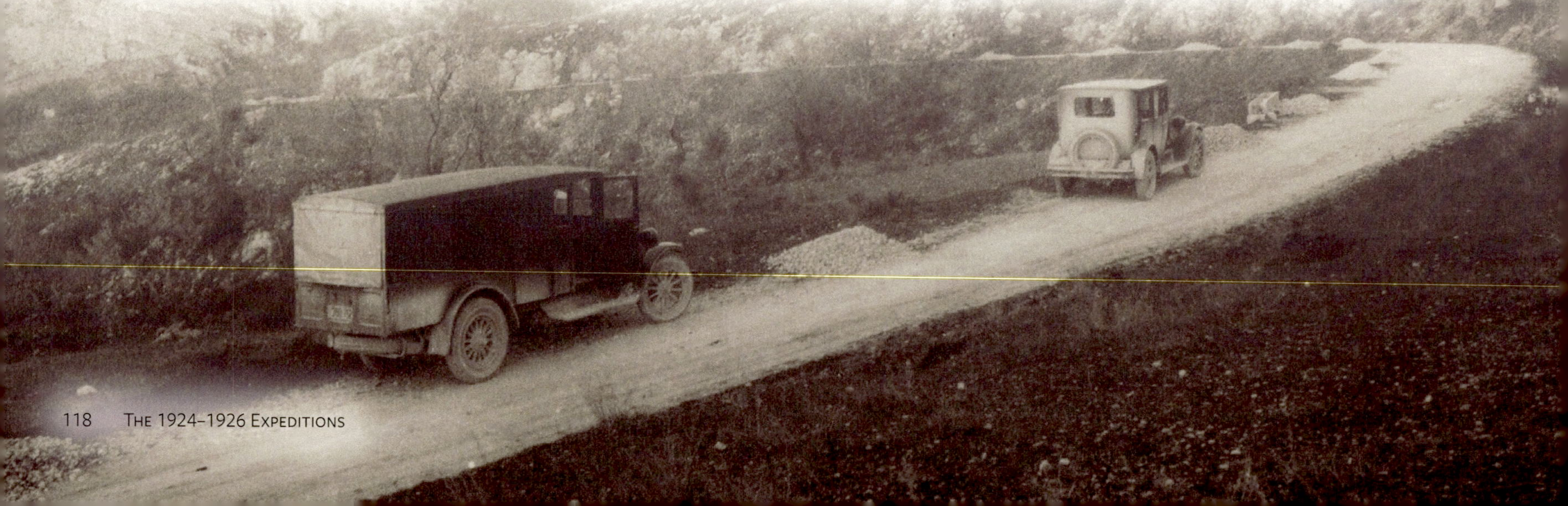

Fig. 123. The Dodge sedan and Graham Brothers truck traveling from Salerno to Reggio, Italy, March 4, 1925 (Kelsey Museum neg. no. KS 305.08).

Part IV.

OBSERVATIONS A CENTURY LATER

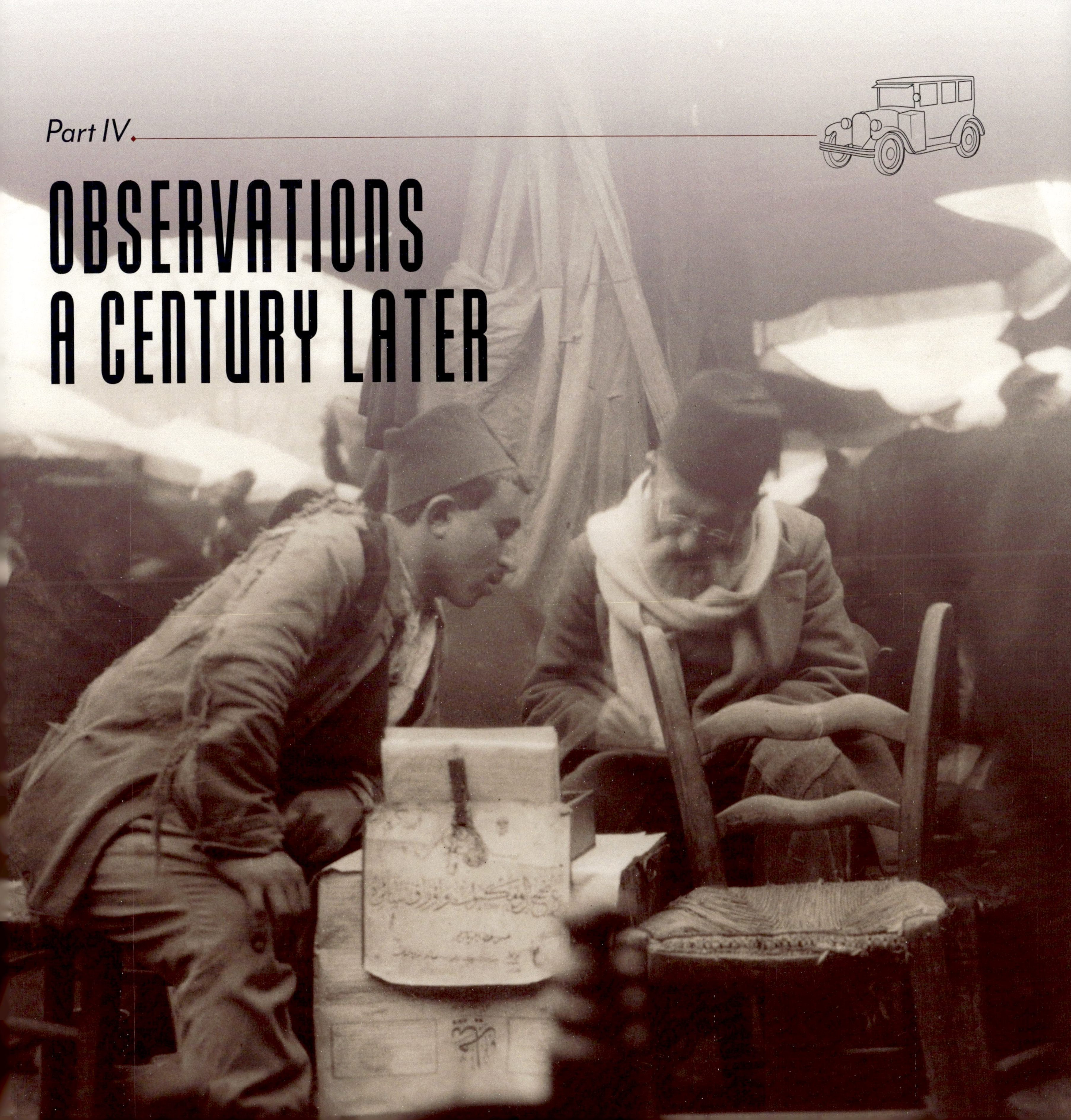

Chapter 10
REFOCUSING THE LENS

Nearly a century has elapsed since George Swain, the Dodge sedan, and the Graham Brothers truck embarked on their Mediterranean adventures. This distance offers us not only retrospective sight lines but also an opportunity to reflect on Swain's work through the filters of recent scholarship. In this last section of the book, I focus on three overarching questions: 1) what motivated Swain to create a portfolio of ethnographic images during his trips; 2) how did his understanding of photography as a highly selective medium guide his choice of subjects; and 3) how did the politics and social conversations of the 1920s shape his work?

Although the sedan and truck take a back seat in these discussions, it is important to remember that these two remarkable vehicles did not just facilitate Swain's travels; they also served as mobile storage units for his enormous volume of photographic equipment. In turn, the final collection of non-archaeological photographs are themselves vehicles, transporting us back to the early years of the last century. It is these images that help us envision—in ways that the written word cannot—what life was like in the often remote regions of Swain's expeditions.

The Lure of the Present

Swain was well aware of the remit given to him by the University of Michigan: he was hired to create a complete and accurate photographic inventory of archaeological finds and architecture unearthed during the projects of 1924–1926, as well as a number of ancient manuscripts housed in various libraries and monasteries. As the principal photographer, he provided vital documentation and irreplaceable records that would be studied by an array of international scholars. His photographs were, for their time, exemplary in detail, clarity, and organization—an impressive feat in light of the often hurried, sometimes chaotic, and less-than-ideal circumstances under which he worked. Equally important, Swain's photographs brought home each country's history without pilfering its antiquities.

Conscious of time's inexorable march, Swain assumed a different role with his ethnographic images, though they, too, reveal a keen eye for detail, clarity, and composition. Where his archaeological images documented the distant past, his more anthropological ones detailed the fleeting present, trapping and stilling the flow of time.[322] He captured stories of life as conveyed by local inhabitants—such vivid events could not be retrieved in archaeological photographs. But Swain had been commissioned to record time *past*, not to focus on time *present*. What, then, compelled Swain to turn his lens toward modernity? What enticed him to cross these temporal boundaries? And whom did he envision as his audience?

At least initially, some of Swain's earliest documentary photographs were likely requested by Professor Kelsey, particularly ones that focused on relief efforts during and after World War I. Kelsey was deeply committed to humanitarian causes, working tirelessly on behalf of refugee children.[323] In the years following the war, Kelsey supported the American Committee for Relief in the Near East (ACRNE), and a small number of Swain's images depict children cared for by these American missions (fig. 124). Other images, also ordered by Kelsey, record the devastations of the Great War. Still other photographs were requested by the Smithsonian Institution during Kelsey and Swain's trip of 1919–1920; they include approximately 50 portraits of "ethnic types" from Asia Minor and Syria, as well as shots of contemporary culture.[324]

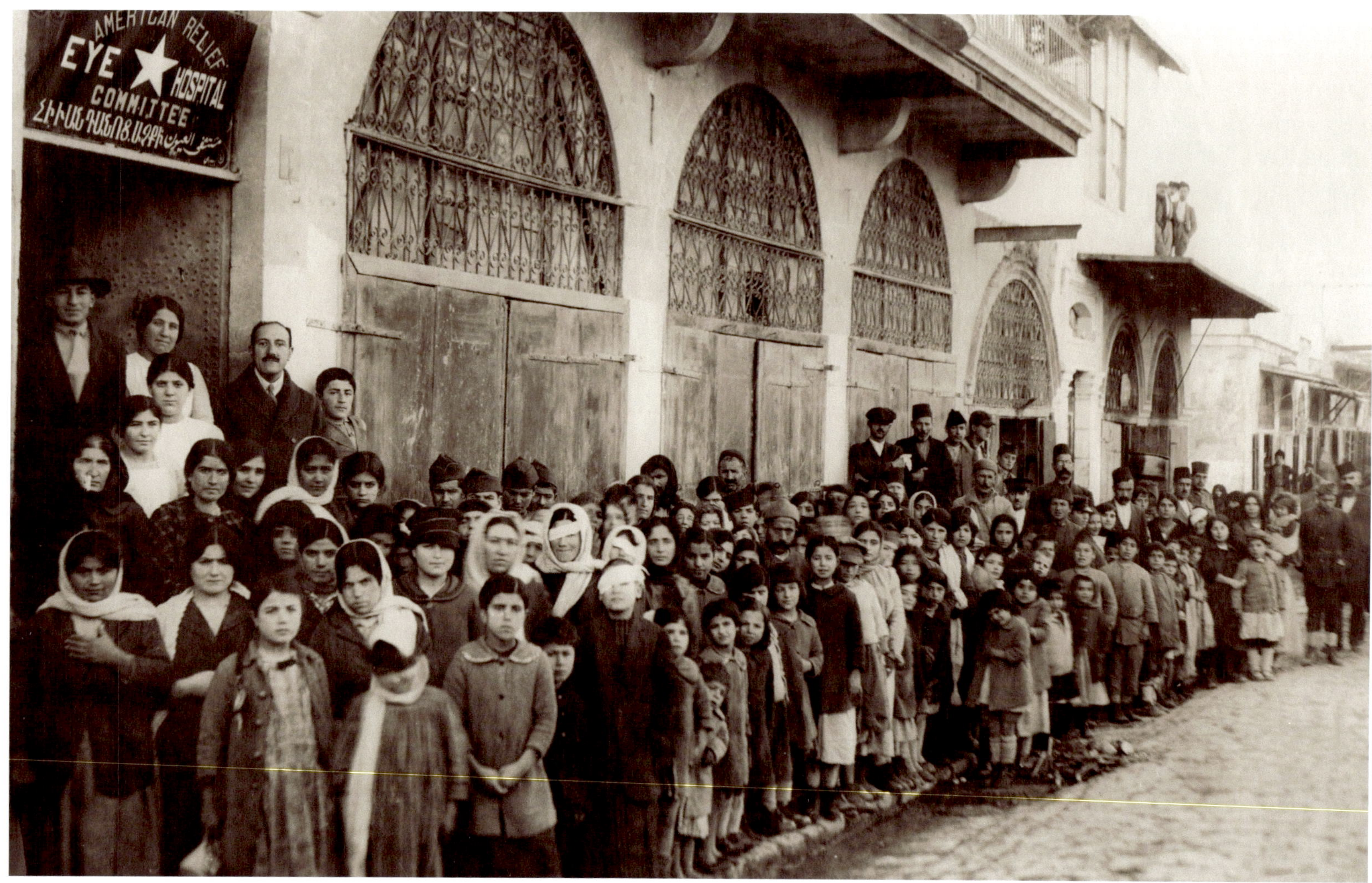

Fig. 124. The American Committee for Relief in the Near East (ACRNE) eye hospital in Aleppo, Syria, January 7, 1920 (Kelsey Museum neg. no. 7.0193).

Swain's early trips overseas, therefore, set the stage for his later venture into visual anthropology. He clearly enjoyed taking photographs of contemporary society, from the newsworthy and exotic to the ordinary and mundane. Part of that impulse surely lies in his personal history. As we have seen, since his young 20s, Swain was accustomed to viewing both his social and physical environment through the photographic lens. Whether as a commercial or university photographer, he saw potential compositions everywhere, mediating the world around him with his images. It is therefore not surprising that Swain pivoted his lens toward the modern world during his archaeological expeditions; he was simply continuing what he often did on his home turf—this time, however, in mostly non-Western and unfamiliar settings.

While Swain's history and innate curiosity may have sustained his interest in documenting the poverty and poetics of daily life overseas, there were probably other factors at play—modest ambitions as a photographic journalist and travel writer, an enduring engagement in learning and teaching, the prospect of some small financial remuneration, and fund-raising for the university.

Swain appears to have harbored aspirations of becoming an occasional photojournalist; he published at least seven articles in the *Detroit News* of 1924—"Notes and Comment of a Wolverine Abroad"—each illustrated with his photographs. It is unclear how the partnership was forged, but Swain's letters home often mentioned that he was working on a story, busy selecting relevant images to send back to the paper.[325] Swain took pride in his work for the *Detroit News*, and a letter to his family notes how delighted he was to discover that one of his articles was featured in "the photograph section."[326] As noted elsewhere (see p. 135, endnote 12), Swain also entertained hopes that he might transform his observations and photographs into a book.

Although we don't know what Swain assumed about the readership of the *Detroit News*, he no doubt knew that the paper focused on an audience from southeastern Michigan. In 1918, several years before his articles appeared, the paper had a weekday circulation of around 225,000.[327] We can imagine that Swain saw himself as an agent who shaped the public's perception of life in remote parts of the Mediterranean, the Near East, and North Africa. His photographs and texts were carefully selected to feed the appetite of his readers, many of whom probably knew little about life in the emerging nations and contested lands of post–World War I.

Swain reached a smaller audience through a lecture series offered in America at some point in the 1920s. A small brochure—*Travel with Mr. Swain from the Danube to the Nile!*—notes that this "keen observer with a Yankee knack for picking out the things that count . . . [possesses] a live[ly] interest in things and especially people" (see figs. 41a–b, p. 38).[328] His well-honed skills as a teacher and his ethnographic photographs, along with his archaeological images, surely generated engaging presentations—and provided a small income stream as well.

In addition, Swain seems to have been adept at what one scholar has labeled "scripting spadework."[329] Western archaeologists working in the Near East from the late 19th to the early 20th century often brought their work to the public—in vivid detail—through newspapers, lectures, and publications, creating a carefully constructed picture of life in "exotic" settings. One of the prime motives for educating the public and underscoring the allure and mystery of archaeology was to attract financial support for overseas expeditions.[330] The University of Michigan's campaigns were expensive undertakings, and Kelsey constantly struggled to raise money. Swain probably did his share of fund-raising as well; his photographs—both archaeological and ethnographic—helped entice potential donors. Indeed, in a letter home, Swain writes that one of the reasons for publicizing the work at Antioch in the *Detroit News* was to "make public what U of M funds have done [and] partly to satisfy men who have put up money."[331]

While Swain's interest in capturing life in the Mediterranean and Near East was partially compelled by financial concerns, as noted earlier, the driving force for photographing the lives he encountered abroad was his fascination with other worlds. In some ways, Swain was a natural ethnographer. He was curious about patterns of daily life and individual behaviors: How did people ply their trades? What did they wear? What did they seem to be thinking? How did they spend their days? Artisans, businessmen, herders, soldiers, snake charmers, sailors, café denizens, migrants, children, orphans, and monks alike intrigued him, as did the local architecture, the "land of little shops," and the often wild countryside. The camera allowed him to construct pictorial texts that helped him make sense of foreign cultures, archaic technologies, unusual landscapes, and unexpected social narratives.

Acutely aware of the contrasts between East and West, Swain periodically compared the two in his letters and articles. At one point, he became intrigued by the traffic on a typical main street in the interior of Turkey, contrasting it to one in Michigan. With his usual attention to detail, Swain writes, "From sheer curiosity I analyzed traffic both ways for eight minutes just now in front of the 'hotel.' Here is the tabulation: Sixty-four men, 12 women, 13 children, 23 donkeys, and two horses. Of the men, a few had European clothes and a fez; most had baggy trousers . . . and polychrome belts. Some, of course, were in rags. Most of the women were peasants . . . and [were] ragged, tanned, and barefoot. . . . In Michigan, a person in rags is an exception on the street, here they are the rule."[332]

Comparisons between ancient and modern worlds were also never far from his mind. Approaching the Trojan plain on a boat, Swain imagines Hector and Achilles valiantly fighting on the now-legendary battlefield. But he doesn't linger in the past; instead, he notes that the waters near the plain are a "grim reminder of the just past present—on the beach at the entrance to the Dardanelles you see the rusty wreckage of English warships."[333]

Regardless of how well we understand Swain's motives for composing an impressive album of ethnographic images, we are now the inheritors of his often carefully constructed photographs that a slice of the American public consumed in the 1920s. As we will see in the next section, Swain's intimate knowledge of the camera's power to build visual texts helped guide what he chose to show and where to pivot his lens.

Narrative as Image

Photographs are complex.[334] From yesterday's glass plate to today's infinitely reproducible digital image, photos converse in a silent language that has the capacity to narrate, document, question, elicit sensory experiences, and recast reality. Even the most seemingly insignificant photographic image is born from a visual vocabulary that has extensive and unique powers. As various scholars have argued, photographs capture the "here-now" and give us a sense of "having been there."[335]

Photos are also shapeshifters. As the Greek photographer and writer John Stathatos observes, the photographic medium is "changeable, treacherous, and even protean in its nature. What was functional one day is artistic the next, what was truth yesterday is falsehood tomorrow. What a photographer intends, what a photographer thinks he sees is not necessarily what others will see in his photographs."[336] Stathatos's observations ring especially true today, in the age of Photoshop, faked images, and AI.

In the case of Swain's ethnographic images, we are both distant observers and part of an ongoing conversation with his work, seduced by their narrative powers.[337] Swain's momentary encounters hold seeds to a story. The viewer is enticed, wondering who the individuals are, what events led to the scene, and what perhaps ensued after the shutter snapped (figs. 125–126). It is important to remember that Swain had a long history as an adept spinner of tales. He had written for a literary magazine as an undergraduate at

Fig. 125. "A poverty stricken woman in the street," Turkey, December 29, 1919 (Kelsey Museum neg. no. KS 057.09).

Fig. 126. "Mustapha (orphan) just outside the door to our 'hotel,'" Yalivadj, Turkey, August 17, 1924 (Kelsey Museum neg. no. KS 288.01).

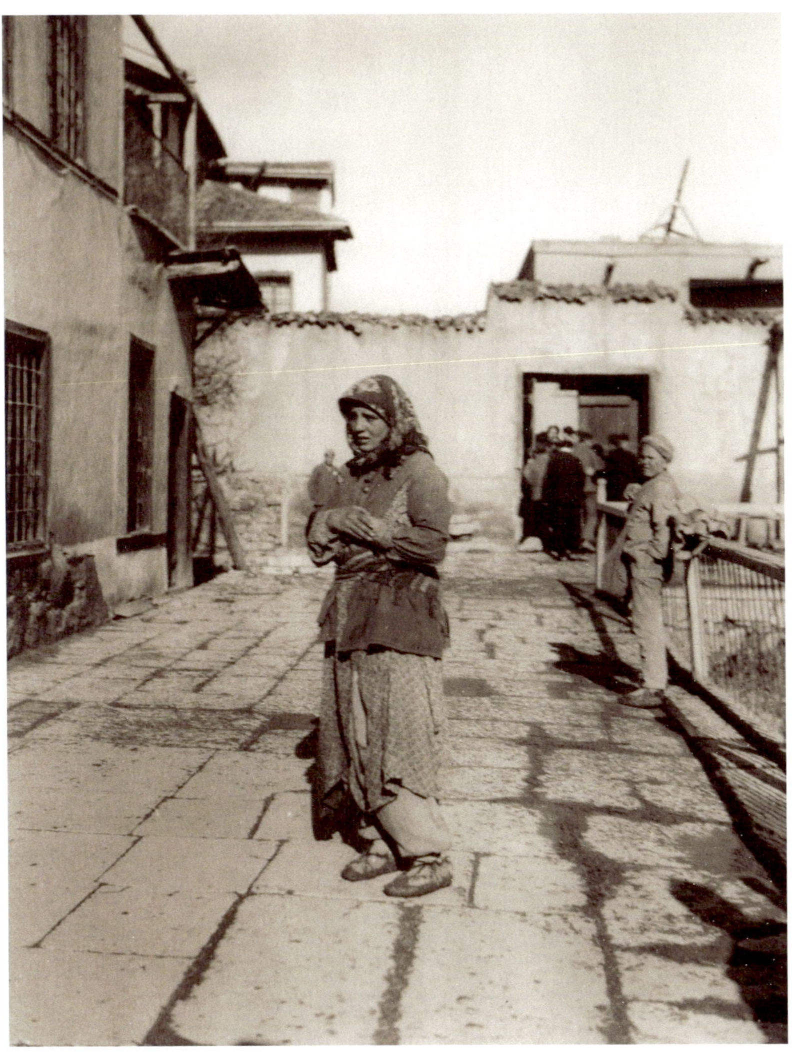

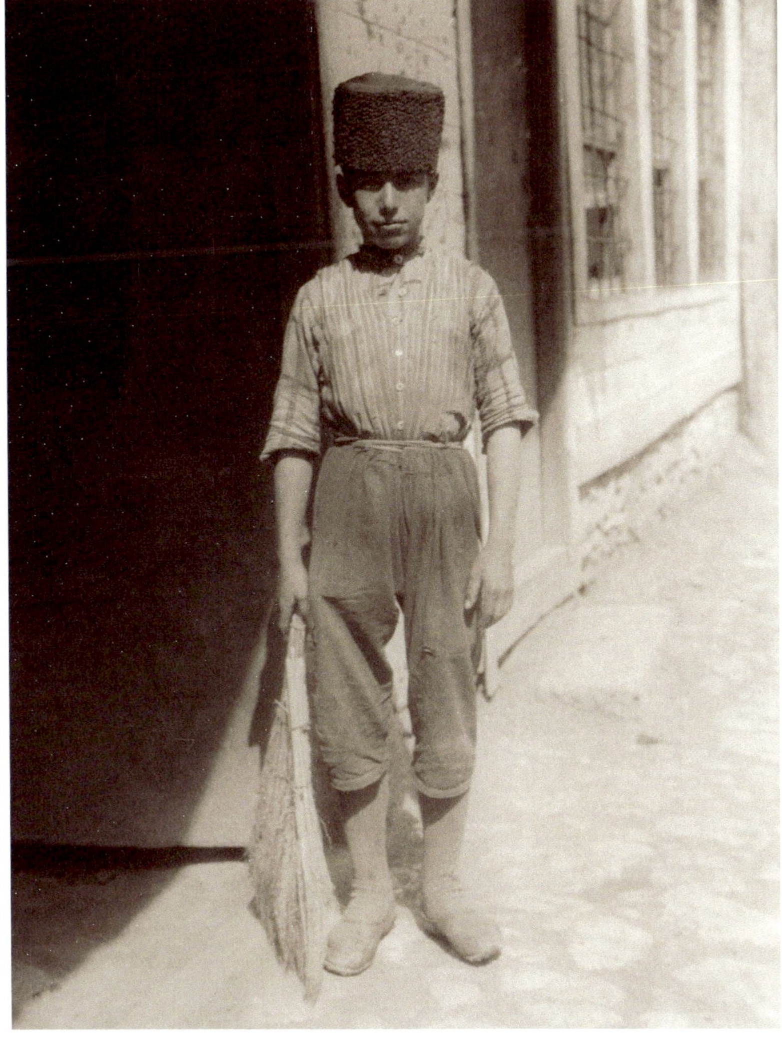

the University of Michigan, penned articles for the *Detroit News*, was an inveterate letter writer, and gave lectures to the public. Each one of those endeavors tapped into his skills as a storyteller. That fluency translated seamlessly into his photographic work.

Swain's "image-stories" can be parsed into at least three categories: single shots that are best read within the changing tides of contemporaneous politics, single images accompanied by either extended captions or keyed to lengthier descriptions in his letters or articles, and multiple shots of a single event or subject captured over the course of several days or even years.

Swain's 1919 photograph taken near the Spice Bazaar, or "Egyptian Bazaar," in Constantinople is an example of a narrative summarized by a single image that is best understood in the context of contemporary politics (see fig. 8, p. 5). In that photo, a young man leans forward to dictate a letter to an older man, a letter writer who turns the youth's words into Ottoman script. Both men don fezzes and are completely absorbed in the moment, as if time were standing still. We might imagine that they are so focused on the exchange that they are momentarily unaware of the life-altering revolution that is beginning to churn around them.[338] Major political forces are agitating in Turkey—in a few years, the nationalist revolution will abolish not only the fez (officially outlawed in 1925) but also the empire that gave the letter writer his script (the Ottoman Empire was dismantled by treaty in 1922). With this singular photograph, Swain narrates an evanescent moment in history.[339]

For most of Swain's images, a short, informative, or pithy caption sufficed for his records: "The snake charmer at Kom Aushim. The charmer later died from a cobra bite" (see fig. 44, p. 40). Some captions are slightly longer: "Monastery of St. John. Interior of Library with the Keeper seated at a table. . . . It possesses many old manuscripts of great interest and value. The manuscripts were of course written by hand on parchment." There are also captions that reflect Swain's passion for time and measurement: "Under the huge plane tree in the center of Yalivadj. Tree is 21 feet in circumference five feet above the ground, spreads 81 by 88 feet. Perhaps 100 feet high. Said to be 200 years old. Numerous men seated at benches. . ." (see fig. 71, p. 66). At times, however, he provides extended captions that enhance the narrative quality of the photograph. An arresting photograph from his visit to the monastery on Patmos in May 1920 provides a good example (see fig. 54, p. 46). The image depicts a *semandron* played by attendant monks. Swain beautifully captures several features: the rhythmic placement of robed monks; the echo between the black, pillar-like monastic dress and the smooth, white columns; the delicate shadows behind the monks; and the subtle, decorative quality of the pebbled floor. Its masterly composition aside, an immediate and simple question comes to mind: "What, indeed, are these men doing?" Swain's caption is not only instructive but also reflects his characteristic curiosity about the stories that inform his photographs. His caption goes beyond the descriptive: "Monastery of St. John. Four monks playing with mallets on the rear 'semandron' in the court. A fifth monk beyond with a small semandron in his hand. The use of these wooden bars is said to have originated in a time when the use of bells was forbidden to monasteries. The great semandron is a bar of oak (25′ 9″ long, 2′ 6.5″ section). One wonders if it is some old ship timber."

Greater storytelling powers emerge from Swain's photographs that were keyed to his articles in the *Detroit News* or letters home. One dynamic example (reported in both a letter and an article) tells the story of an unusual trip to the island of Djerba, off the coast of Tunisia (see p. 91). Swain shot approximately 20 images in his attempt to portray the ingenuity involved in transporting both the University of Michigan vehicles and the French team's automobiles over the short distance from the mainland to the "Land of the Lotus Eaters." His photographs of the improvised ferry—two small fishing boats lashed together and straddled by precarious wooden planks—are filled with details that compel us to look closely at the unfolding event. If we couple the images with Swain's descriptions of the shouting and maneuvering (see pp. 91–92), we can easily conjure a cinematic scene—full of color, debate, potential disaster, and ultimate relief.

Finally, Swain's collection of work includes a series of photos, taken over the course of days or even years, that have the force of a picture album (without its tactility) or a sequence of digital photos that one can quickly flip through, allowing a story to unfold. Two examples stand out. One sequence depicts Monday market days in Yalivadj. Swain's images draw from two separate Mondays—July 28 and August 17, 1924—when the market was densely packed with sellers and buyers. His captions signal which section of the market we are viewing: the yogurt seller, the cloth maker, the vegetable producer, the water jar potter, and the basket seller. Women and men sort through the merchandise, and donkeys stand quietly by, burdened with stacks of wood. Immersing ourselves in the sequence of images, we are transported back to the Monday market, wandering through the quarters piled high with goods, almost hearing the cacophony of bartering voices. The photographs take on motion, as if stepping through a sequential narrative.[340]

Equally album-like is the series of images that portray both vehicles over their three years of service in the Mediterranean. If we compiled a narrative of the Graham Brothers truck and Dodge sedan during that time, the chronicle would move from their maiden voyage through France in 1924, to the long, arduous drive to Yalivadj that same year (replete with near disasters), to the realities of life on the excavation, followed by trips through the wild landscapes of Algeria and Tunisia in 1925, and finally to the vehicles' travels in the comparatively tame countryside of Italy. Even if we don't know the details of the truck and sedan's travels, the photographs provide us with an "auto-biography," inspiring us to conjure up stories about their adventures in these often remote locations.

As many writers have noted, travel often entails encounters between the "self" and the "other." A traveler's particular values, preoccupations, assumptions, and personal histories bring into high relief the similarities and differences between his or her own culture and the places visited.[341] Swain's ethnographic photographs (and attendant commentaries) of modest lives unfolding in a politically shifting landscape provide us with a personal record of how he saw the other, as well as how he saw himself. While Swain seems to have viewed himself as sympathetic to the ongoing trials of life in these foreign areas, his belief in the superiority of "American know-how" is equally on display.[342] Swain is clearly aware of his impatience and biases toward different and at times incomprehensible worlds. But he tries his best to work through ongoing frustrations, often saved by his sense of humor, which rarely fails him. Most of Swain's introspection comes through in the handful of poems that survive; there, he delves into questions about life, love, nature's beauty, and what is right and wrong in a just society. An astute and thoughtful individual, he surely learned about himself during his photographic journeys in the early 1920s with the Michigan vehicles.

The Colonial Gaze

It is impossible to interrogate Swain's letters and photographs from the 1924–1926 expeditions without briefly discussing the issue of Western colonialism. Swain's perceptions of modern life in the places he traveled were certainly shaped by attitudes that typified most encounters between Western and non-Western cultures in the early 20th century. A complicated and much-discussed topic, Western colonialism sought—and still seeks—to control or dominate foreign nations and states and to impose Western ideals on those societies. While the binary division between the West and the "rest" is susceptible to simplistic overstatement, colonized subjects were traditionally portrayed as fixed in the past, lacking initiative, and in need of outside control or guidance. Travelogues, reports, and popular publications in the early 1900s were filled with photographs and commentaries that effectively dehumanized native people, underscoring their different, exotic, and "primitive" nature. Cultural pluralism was rarely celebrated.

Arguments to the contrary notwithstanding, archaeology was hardly a disinterested party. It played a critical role in legitimizing and perpetuating the colonial gaze, even if those entanglements sometimes seemed less apparent. Archaeologists either tacitly or explicitly argued that Western countries were in a better (and clearly more powerful) position to excavate, analyze, publish, and own the antiquities of often impoverished, colonized nations. Imperial powers saw themselves as saviors, rescuing the world's heritage from neglect and destruction. More often than not, Western archaeologists ended up controlling the narrative of the past in the East and elsewhere.

Museums present one of the more visible and tangible expressions of these attitudes and behaviors, often cast as privileged sites for displaying purloined or purchased booty. Indeed, Western museums in the 18th through 20th centuries had an almost insatiable appetite for expropriating the cultural history of subjugated countries.

These perspectives have come under close scrutiny in the past few decades, and requests for the repatriation of objects and works of art from host countries are an ever-increasing reality for museums. The problem of repatriation and postcolonial attitudes, however, is no longer the exclusive purview of scholars and curators. The blockbuster film *Black Panther* (2018), for example, has a telling scene in which the revolutionary Erik Killmonger confronts a white curator at a Western museum about the provenance of an ax on display. Killmonger contests the label, saying, "It was taken by British soldiers in Benin, but it's from Wakanda. . . . And it's made out of Vibranium [a valuable metal]. . . . I'm gonna take it off your hands for you." The director of the museum tries to stop him, telling him it isn't for sale. Killmonger argues, "How do you think your ancestors got these? Do you think they paid a fair price? Or did they take it . . . like they took everything else?" While only a short scene in the movie, it has helped seed ideas in popular culture about archaeology and colonialism.

When Swain arrived in the Mediterranean, colonialism was thriving. At the same time, momentous changes were afoot. Nationalist movements were beginning to become well established in Turkey, Egypt, Greece, and some countries of the Near East. As part of these nation-building efforts, local governments were seizing control of their antiquities, writing laws to protect the export of objects, and confronting foreign archaeologists, whom they viewed as agents of Western imperialism.[343] Not surprisingly, host governments and Western excavators often clashed.

Despite Swain's progressive views about education for women and the separation of church and state in places like Turkey (see p. 6), he harbored decided colonial views about the "natives" of the countries in which he worked. As noted earlier, Swain was known to comment about workmen at Antioch wantonly destroying priceless finds and wrote that the Turks "took delight in destroying whatever may partake of Christianity." He even went so far as to write that the local Yalivadjians are "imbued by a spirit of pure cussedness which moves them to destroy whatever they cannot put to immediate use in their own building operations" (see pp. 72–73).

Swain's attitudes were in step with many of his contemporaries working in the Near East. Their "writings overflowed with disparaging references to the 'natives,'" whom they viewed as "incapable of respecting the ancient sites and monuments."[344] At least some of the photographs that Swain published in the *Detroit News* buttressed those colonial objectifications and discourses by showing the "primitive" dress, poverty, and on occasion, somewhat empty stares of the locals.

In the final analysis, Swain held both colonial attitudes and progressive ideas, producing a complex and layered perspective on the worlds he encountered. His letters and images narrate in concert how he—an outsider, an American, a classical scholar, a storyteller, and to some extent, an innocent abroad—tried to make sense of the Byzantine legacies and ways of life that he paradoxically desired to both save and modernize.[345]

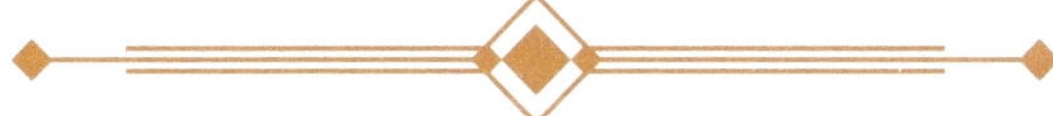

Curatorial "excavation" in museums and archives can offer surprising rewards: the discovery of an overlooked but telling artifact, the unearthing of a significant letter that has languished in obscurity, the study of evidence that challenges long-cherished concepts, or the assignment of a forgotten work of art to an artist's canon. What is noteworthy about Swain's ethnographic collection is that we have not only his photographs—"the seeable"—but also his commentaries—"the sayable." By melding the seeable and the sayable, we are able to gain some understanding of what motivated Swain to amass his album of anthropological images, what kinds of subjects he chose to capture, and how contemporary politics as well as his own biases shaped his views of local populations.

I never suspected that the unassuming photographs of two 1920s vehicles, which kept intruding into my archival research at the Kelsey Museum, would lead me to a treasure trove of letters, newspaper articles, and photographs, all providing insight into one man's resonant experience throughout the Mediterranean at a pivotal time in history. Although Swain's commentaries and photographs are a small, personal, and fragmented record, they loom large, allowing us to capture moments from the past that might have been forever lost.

ACKNOWLEDGMENTS

I love reading acknowledgments—and humorous unacknowledgments, where select individuals receive ignominious blame. Well-crafted acknowledgments, however, are an unrecognized art. Tired phrases such as "first and foremost" and "last but not least," as well as thanking everyone, including the family cat, are standard fare. Probably for good reason, but they are hardly inspired writing. That said, I have an orchestra full of people that I want to thank—all of them, first and foremost, last but not least, as well as my loyal imaginary dog, Sneakers. For any errors in the previous pages, I have no one to blame except the authors of bad mystery novels who kept me up well past my bedtime.

Much of this book was researched and written during the COVID era, which imposed new ways of working. Valuable archives, museum collections, and libraries were often closed or afforded only restricted access. These frustrating disruptions notwithstanding, I was fortunate to encounter many individuals who helped me navigate the intricacies of off-site research.

The Kelsey Museum staff consistently offered their time and expertise. I am grateful to Sebastián Encina, who shares my interest in Swain; he answered my endless queries quickly and never failed to track down even the most obscure images and correspondence in the Kelsey archives. Michelle Fontenot was equally helpful, particularly when I sent her long lists of potential photographs to unearth and scan so that I could examine them online. Eric Campbell, the museum's graphic designer, provided invaluable assistance during the final stages of this book. I am indebted to him for creating the maps, skillfully editing the images, and designing the cover of *From the Motor City to the Mediterranean*. Thanks also to illustrator Bruce Worden, who created the charming drawing of the sedan that accompanies each part opener. Other members of the "Kelsey Family" deserve recognition: Over the years, I benefited enormously from the support, friendship, and advice of Janet Richards, Margaret Root, Elaine Gazda, and Sharon Herbert. I also offer heartfelt thanks to the late Peg Lourie for her incredible talents and friendship.

Working at the Bentley Historical Library was a joy. It's an extraordinary archive, with an exceptional staff. I am particularly grateful to Diana Bachman, Madeleine Bradford, Abigale Mumby, Sarah McLusky, and Karen Wright.

One of the hurdles I faced when I first started my research was transcribing Swain's handwriting—akin to breaking a cryptographic code. I am forever grateful to Todd Gerring, who spent many months transcribing Swain's letters and became an expert in "Swainscrawl." Todd was a perceptive transcriber and often asked interesting questions that led me down valuable research paths.

As I moved forward with my research, I serendipitously encountered three people who lent invaluable help and knowledge. Michael Keller, the author of an award-winning book on the Graham brothers, was amazing. He is the world's authority on the brothers, their history, and "all things Graham." Michael was easily accessible via email and always willing to answer questions, read sections of my book, and clarify the many car queries of an auto-illiterate. I am also indebted to the generosity of John Porter, whose assiduous research discovered a cache of approximately 2,600 lantern slides created by Swain (the Kelsey Museum is currently exploring which ones are not already included in its collections). In addition, John is the most knowledgeable scholar on the history of Kamp Kairphree, an innovative summer camp in Michigan that Swain and his wife started and then managed for many years. It was through John that I met the wonderful Liz Babcock, Swain's granddaughter. What a special discovery that was! Although Liz was only eight or nine when her grandfather died, she had many memories that she graciously shared with me. Until that point, I had only a sketchy idea about Swain's personal history. She filled in many gaps and gave contours to the man behind the lens.

Other individuals helped in a myriad of ways, both large and small: Geoff Emberling, Jack Bernard, and Alyson Grigsby—all from the University of Michigan—Carla Reczek from the Detroit Public Library, and Rochelle Collins from the Alice and Jack Wirt Public Library in Bay City, Michigan. I also greatly appreciate comments from two outside reviewers who asked insightful questions and offered thoughtful advice.

Emily Allison-Siep and Terry Wilfong deserve particular recognition. Emily Allison-Siep, communications editor at the Kelsey Museum, was nothing less than extraordinary. She spent countless hours editing my text, catching mistakes, suggesting alternate wording, streamlining the endnotes, and proposing several excellent ideas for enriching the narrative. Emily also faced the daunting task of laying out a book that included approximately 130 images. I thank her for producing a lovely design that beautifully highlights the quality of Swain's photographs. Terry Wilfong, curator of Graeco-Roman Egyptian collections and head of Kelsey publications, was a source of invaluable support and encouragement, as well as an astute reader. In addition, both Emily and Terry were a pleasure to work with (yes, Emily, even your kitties know I shouldn't end a sentence with a preposition).

One doesn't usually thank one's cars, but they deserve a shout-out for their many years of faithful service: Sophie, Brownie, The Yellow Bug, Cammie, Hondy, Silver Streak, Dusty, and Beautie.

I count myself lucky to have special friends who encouraged me to write this book and who were generous enough to read portions of my drafts and ask about the book's progress: Howard (aka Bob) and Sharon Harrison, Dudley and Barbara Brown, Jim Bowers, and Deborah Sandberg. I am particularly grateful to Jim, a car aficionado and erstwhile race-car driver who became my personal "Wicarpedia," patiently explaining the meaning of pump and splash feed, worm and wheel steering, and updraft carburetors. I am also endlessly thankful to Becky Loomis, Despina Margomenou, Sue Langdon, and Shelby

Brown, as well as to my remarkable friend Artemis Leontis, who conceived of casting the two vehicles as protagonists in a Mediterranean adventure. Tracey Cullen, friend extraordinaire, deserves special note—we have worked together for nearly five decades on overseas projects, books, and articles, and we have survived life's challenges with humor and cherished mutual support.

Finally, to my quirky family, a constant source of laughter and love. Many thanks for the unfailing support of Bobbi, (the amazing) Charles, Eric, Stacy, Rachel, and Josh. This book could not have been written without the encouragement of my extraordinary sister, Nina; my twin, Kathy; and my husband, Steve. Kathy and Steve, whom I asked to read too many drafts, did so graciously (or so they let me think) and offered constructive suggestions, even if I occasionally resisted them.

Profound thanks to all of you for taking this journey with me.

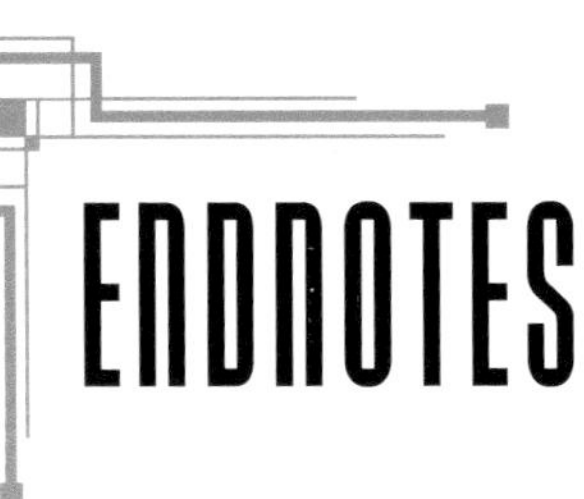

ENDNOTES

NOTES TO CHAPTER 1

1 Swain 1925b, *IV: An Archaeological Reconnaissance, Concluded*, 6–7.

2 I am grateful to Donald Keller, director of the Southern Euboea Exploration Project (SEEP), for his humorous accounts of life with the YAK-Mobile.

3 Swain's work included photographing ancient manuscripts housed in two Greek monasteries, one at the monastic complex on Mount Athos and the other on the island of Patmos.

4 Although I have tried to be faithful to Swain's original wording when quoting his letters, I have taken the liberty of making limited silent edits, especially when Swain's sentences seem to have missing words or were otherwise unclear.

5 Many of Swain's photographs are unpublished, and most of his notes and letters (which run to several hundred pages) are not transcribed. They are currently housed in two locations at the University of Michigan: the Bentley Historical Library and the Kelsey Museum of Archaeology.

6 It is difficult to determine how many photographs Swain exposed and printed during his early years on university-sponsored expeditions (1919–1926). He apparently jettisoned those he deemed not up to his standards.

7 For a masterful biography of Francis W. Kelsey, see Pedley 2012.

8 Goodnow 1924, 1. Swain rarely alludes to feeling threatened by the volatile political situation during his 1924–1926 journeys. That perspective contrasts with comments made by James Henry Breasted, founder of the Institute for the Study of Ancient Cultures, West Asia & North Africa (formerly the Oriental Institute) at the University of Chicago and an eminent archaeologist working in the Near East. During Breasted's travels to the Near East from 1919 to 1920, he frequently mentions politically charged and menacing circumstances. Breasted's travels, however, immediately followed the end of World War I and were focused on areas farther east, which were suffering radical upheavals, riots, tribal warfare, and European interventions. Swain's visits to Turkey, Greece, Tunisia, and Egypt occurred later, and the political circumstances in those countries, though highly troubled, were slightly different. See Emberling 2010.

9 Swain seemed dismissive of the need for a gun, but he carried an automatic pistol when alone in the countryside to protect himself against hostile dogs. In one of his letters home, he writes that the landlord of their residence in Yalivadj had a military carbine "and his extensive [?] was encircled with a belt of cartridges, but I judge this a matter of jewellery and show rather than a matter of business." Swain letter to family, July 5, 1924.

10 Swain 1925b, *IV: An Archaeological Reconnaissance, Concluded*, 1.

11 Goodnow 1924, 1.

12 The seven essays published in the *Detroit News* appeared on July 13, July 27, August 24, August 31, September 14, October 26, and November 9, 1924. University archives also contain a rejection letter from a New York publishing house (Brandt & Kirkpatrick, July 1, 1924) where Swain had apparently submitted a book manuscript. The manuscript has yet to be unearthed, but the publisher's letter suggests that it may have been based on his *Detroit News* articles. Additional essays in the series exist but were never published in the newspaper. Some are housed in the Kelsey Museum, others at the Bentley Historical Library. Swain entitled those essays *Notes and Comments of a Wolverine Abroad*. The *Detroit News* altered the title slightly, labeling his essays "Notes and Comment of a Wolverine Abroad."

13 I have recounted some of Swain's illuminating captions word for word in this book. These verbatim descriptions are set apart by quotation marks in the image captions.

14 Swain wrote a number of poems, including romantic poetry to his wife, and verses inspired by his travels throughout the Mediterranean and the Near East. I am extremely grateful to Elizabeth Babcock for sending me her transcriptions of several of Swain's

poems from 1919 and 1920, all of which are part of the Swain Family Collection.

15 Swain 1924b, July 27, 30.

16 Swain 1924b, September 14, 35.

17 In 1919, following the end of World War I, the King-Crane Commission was tasked by US President Woodrow Wilson to gather information from people residing in various countries of the Middle East. The goal was to ascertain the range of opinions regarding self-determination. While many individuals in places like Syria, Palestine, and Lebanon clearly favored independence from outside rule, the commission determined that the region was not yet ready and would be better served by colonial oversight. After various negotiations, France and Britain were mandated control of much of the region.

18 Barthes 1977, 44.

19 Hamilakis, Anagnostopoulos, and Ifantidis 2009, 285.

20 Coles 1998, 17.

Notes to Chapter 2

21 Lorenzi 2004, http://abc.net.au/science/news/stories/s1094767.htm; Universal Leonardo, n.d., http://universalleonardo.org/work.php?id=512.

22 Bellis 2019, https://thoughtco.com/who-invented-the-car-4059932.

23 She did, in fact, drive to see her mother, but her main goal was getting publicity for her husband's car.

24 For a concise history of Bertha Benz and her exploits, see Tweney 2010, https://wired.com/2010/08/0812berta-benz-first-road-trip. In 2018 and 2019, Mercedes Benz also produced a series of short videos chronicling Bertha's journey.

25 Neil 2006, https://latimes.com/news/la-hy-125mbz21jun21-story.html.

26 German History in Documents and Images, n.d., https://ghdi.ghi-dc.org/sub_document.cfm?document_id=1746.

27 Schlenoff 2017, https://scientificamerican.com/article/the-motor-vehicle-1917-slide-show.

28 Williams 2015, https://money.usnews.com/money/personal-finance/articles/2015/01/02/a-glimpse-at-your-expenses-100-years-ago.

29 For statistics on Model T ownership, see Stewart 2021, https://popularmechanics.com/cars/g23320934/car-history. For statistics on vehicle registration in the United States, 1900–1947, see Federal Highway Administration 1997, https://www.fhwa.dot.gov/ohim/summary95/mv200.pdf.

30 Rosenberg 2019, https://thoughtco.com/nickname-tin-lizzie-3976121.

31 Wik 1983, 43.

32 Berger 2001, 8.

33 White 1936.

34 Wik 1983, 39.

35 Wik 1983, 37.

36 Swain 1924b, July 13, 20.

37 The burning of Smyrna in 1922 remains a highly charged and emotional event, with competing and polarizing narratives. Smyrna (modern Izmir, Turkey) was a prosperous port city on the western coast of Anatolia, with a mixed population of mostly Greeks, Turks, and Armenians, along with some Jews. The city became contested ground during the Greco-Turkish War (1919–1922), which erupted in the aftermath of World War I. Following the Allied victory, Greece had been promised new territory, which included Smyrna. Greek forces (allegedly with 20,000 soldiers) occupied the town on May 15, 1919, and soon proceeded to push further into Anatolia, seeking to take control of western and northwestern Anatolia. The Turkish army halted the Greek advance in 1921. Ultimately, Greece was defeated and Smyrna retaken by Turkish forces, effectively ending the Greco-Turkish War in August 1922. The fire started soon after the Turkish military entered the city. According to eyewitness reports, the conflagration began in the Armenian quarter, late on the afternoon of September 13, 1922. The fire spread quickly, reinforced by strong winds and a losing battle to quell the conflagration. The fire raged for 10 days, with thousands of newly homeless people fleeing to the sea and many dying in their attempts to escape. The fire destroyed most of the port, with estimated deaths ranging from 10,000 to 100,000. Accounts differ as to who was responsible, but most eyewitness reports attribute the devastation to Turkish soldiers setting fire to Greek and Armenian homes and businesses. The burning of Smyrna and its political implications have been detailed in a number of books and articles; see, for example, Milton 2008, Dobkin 1998, and Halley 2022.

38 Swain letters to family, June 4 and 5, 1924.

39 Swain 1925b, *V: En Route to the Sacred Mountain—Mt. Athos*, 2.

40 Swain 1925b, *V: En Route to the Sacred Mountain—Mt. Athos*, 2.

41 Swain 1925a, unpaginated p. 2.

42 Swain letter to family, July 16, 1924.

43 By 1924, Graham Brothers had been bought out by Dodge, so Swain's title is technically correct.

44 Pedley 2012, 312. Although I have not attempted to situate Swain's images in the early history of archaeological and

commercial photography, there are a number of excellent publications on the topic. For recent discussions, see McFadyen and Hicks 2020, Lyons, Papadopoulos, Stewart, and Szegedy-Maszak 2005, and Riggs 2018.

45 All quotes come from Kelsey letter to Swain, August 24, 1923.

46 Swain letter to Kelsey, July 3, 1923.

47 According to the University of Michigan Board of Regents Proceedings (December 1925, pp. 160 and 788), the cost of shipping both vehicles to Bordeaux, France, and subsequent repair and overseas storage of the machines was to be covered by the Dodge and Graham Brothers companies. Bentley Historical Library, University of Michigan.

48 For the base price of the Graham Brothers truck, see Graham Brothers Trucks 1924. For the base price of the 1924 Dodge sedan, see Classic Car Database, n.d., http://classiccardatabase.com/specs.php?series=1849&year=1924&model=6066. Today's dollar amounts were determined using DollarTimes' inflation calendar at https://dollartimes.com/inflation.

49 Swain 1925c, 1.

Notes to Chapter 3

50 Keller 1998, 10–12. The best source for the early history of the Graham brothers is Michael E. Keller's award-winning 1998 book, *The Graham Legacy: Graham-Paige to 1932*. Meticulously researched and engagingly written, it covers not only various aspects of Graham cars and trucks but also family and personal history and relevant historical contexts.

51 For a detailed history of the Graham brothers' venture into the glass bottle business, see Keller 1998, 21–29.

52 Keller 1998, 17.

53 Godshall 1975, https://grahamownersclub.com/history.html.

54 Keller 1998, 15.

55 Keller 1998, 15.

56 Keller 1998, 16.

57 Keller 1998, 16.

58 Godshall 1975.

59 Klingler, n.d., http://evansvilleboneyard.org/graham_brothers.htm. According to Michael Keller, "Most Graham historians consider this account to be apocryphal. Published decades after the Graham brothers had become successful and well-known manufacturers, this supposedly prescient exchange has no verifiable documentation. Nor did Joseph Graham, or his brothers, ever describe his first foray into the world of horseless carriages. The construction and details of this experimental motor car were never documented. It was not uncommon for the era's paid-by-the-word journalists to invent stories out of whole cloth to embellish their 'reporting.' This fanciful scenario's hagiographic conversation is undoubtedly journalistic invention."

60 Klingler, n.d.

61 Hyde 2005, 170.

62 Keller 1998, 47.

63 McNessor 2018, https://hemmings.com/stories/article/last-graham-standing-1929-model-be.

64 Hyde 2005, 173.

65 The cause of the fracture between the Dodge and Graham brothers is a matter of speculation. See Keller 1998, 54; Hyde 2005, 182–183; and Godshall 1975.

66 Keller 1998, 116–117.

67 Keller 1998, 123–124.

68 Keller 1998, 130–131.

69 Keller 1998, 128.

70 Keller 1998, 128.

71 Keller 1998, 177. The Graham brothers never forgot how much they owed the people of Evansville, Indiana, where their business began.

72 The Dodge brothers invented one of the first all-steel cars in America, as well as an oven that could bake enamel onto steel auto bodies.

73 Hyde 2005, 133.

74 Hyde 2005, 125.

75 Zatz 2017, https://allpar.com/d3/corporate/bios/dodge-brothers.html.

76 Zatz 2017.

77 Zatz 2017.

78 Zatz 2017.

79 *Columbus Dispatch* 2014, https://dispatch.com/story/business/2014/12/18/dodge-celebrates-century-automobiles/23527504007.

80 Adolphus 2017, https://hagerty.com/media/archived/dodge-brothers.

81 Zatz 2017.

82 The request was denied, based on a calculation that it would take the full complement of workers more than 12 hours to view the body. Hyde 2005, 118.

83 Hyde 2005, 122.

84 Adolphus 2017.

85 Swain letter to Dodge Brothers, Inc., November 4, 1925.

86 Classic Car Database, n.d., http://classiccardatabase.com/specs.php?series=1849&year=1924&model=6066.

87 Courtesy of Michael E. Keller.

Notes to Chapter 4

88 Crafting even a short biography of George Swain presents challenges. Until recently, I had only the sketchiest details of his early life. Most of what I could glean about his adult years was extracted from letters written to various family members and colleagues. As noted in my acknowledgments, in 2021, I had a fortunate and unexpected encounter. John Porter, who was writing a book on a summer camp managed by Swain and his wife, had been in communication with Swain's granddaughter, Elizabeth Babcock. Although Mrs. Babcock was only eight or nine years old when her grandfather died, she had a substantial collection of family memorabilia and was able to fill in vital gaps and provide intriguing information that helped shape a more nuanced picture of "the man behind the lens." I am extremely grateful to her for her generosity. In addition to the Swain Family Collection, I have relied on University of Michigan records, including a brief summary of his life that serves as an introduction to the George Robert Swain Photographs and Papers housed at the Bentley Historical Library. The Bentley's collection also contains a selection of essays from Swain's undergraduate classes, which provided additional insight. The classes were Paragraph Writing, Theme Writing, Science of Rhetoric, and Essays. His essays are all bound in a small book entitled *Written Work in English Courses 1, 1a, 2, and 2a* (Swain, n.d.).

89 Swain, n.d, essay no. 106–G–1.

90 *Ann Arbor News* 1947, https://aadl.org/aa_news_19470408_p3-george_r_swain_u_photographer_dies_at_80_years.

91 New Hampton School, n.d., https://newhampton.org/bicentennial/history.

92 Swain, n.d., essay no. 106–I–2.

93 Elizabeth Babcock, interview by Gary Babcock, January 28, 2012, Swain Family Collection.

94 Elizabeth Babcock interview.

95 Elizabeth Babcock interview.

96 Elizabeth Babcock interview.

97 Elizabeth Babcock interview.

98 Elizabeth Babcock interview.

99 Elizabeth Babcock interview.

100 Swain letter to Edith Swain, March 10, 1920.

101 Swain letter to Edith Swain, March 10, 1920.

102 Swain, n.d., essay no. XVI–I–1.

103 Swain, n.d., essay no. 106–VI–1.

104 Swain, n.d., "The Possum Hunt" (no essay number; second entry in book).

105 Swain 1896–1897.

106 Clarke 2014, https://gilmantonnhhistory.org/ckfinder/userfiles/files/Demographics/2014AfricanAmericans.pdf.

107 I thank Madeleine Bradford from the Bentley Historical Library for tracking down information on African American student enrollment at the University of Michigan during the years that Swain attended.

108 Swain's mentor, Professor Kelsey, was also thinking about race and education at this time. Kelsey was directly, if only briefly, connected with William Sanders Scarborough (b. 1852), the first Black person to hold a professorial position in classics in the United States. The son of an enslaved woman and a freedman, Scarborough—who had to learn to read in secret—overcame countless obstacles to become a well-respected scholar and president of Wilberforce University in Ohio. In 1898, just a year after Swain's short story was published, Scarborough was invited to become a member of the prestigious Archaeological Institute of America—one of the first Black people to receive such a singular honor. That same year, Kelsey invited Scarborough to a gathering at his home in Ann Arbor, where Scarborough could meet many of his peers. These invitations did not go unrecognized. As Scarborough wrote in his autobiography, "Such invitations may seem too small to mention, but their worth was incalculable to me and should be to the race struggling upward" (Scarborough 2005, 154). We have no way of knowing if Swain knew about, or approved of, these invitations. Given his close association with Kelsey and his interest in classics, however, it is possible that Swain at least had heard about the invitations and was aware of their importance in the racist world of academia. For a fascinating monograph on the life of Scarborough, see his autobiography (Scarborough 2005). I am indebted to Terry Wilfong for alerting me to the story of Scarborough's life.

109 Swain letter to Kelsey, August 31, 1897.

110 Swain letter to Kelsey, April 28, 1898.

111 Kelsey letter to Swain, May 20, 1913.

112 Swain letter to Kelsey, June 10, 1900.

113 Ventura letter of reference, January 11, 1895.

114 It is challenging to piece together the details of Edith's early history with Swain. The available information from family interviews is scanty and somewhat contradictory. We know that Edith met Swain when she was a student at Ventura High School and he was teaching there. After graduating, Edith may have attended

college for two years in California and then expressed interest in going to the University of Michigan to complete her degree. In the intervening years between high school and University of Michigan, the two seem to have kept in touch. According to family interviews provided by Elizabeth Babcock, Edith's parents "didn't want this sheltered girl to go all the way to Michigan, but she said, 'Well, it's all right because Mr. Swain is there teaching school.'" The family knew full well that if they sent her to Michigan, she was probably going to marry Swain. The interview notes also provide the following story: "[Swain] and his wife had a very warm relationship . . . when they got married . . . Edith had a beau in California, and they used to write back and forth." Apparently, the beau asked Swain if he could continue to write to Edith. Swain responded, "Yes, I give you permission to write to her as long as it's on a postcard." And so they continued to correspond for the rest of her life. Elizabeth Babcock, interview by Gary Babcock, January–February 2012, Swain Family Collection.

115 Swain letter to Frances, December 15 or 19, 1919.

116 Elizabeth Babcock interview.

117 Swain 1911. In one case, the superintendent of Swain's high school ordered that the students spend fewer hours studying than had been previously agreed. In response to the superintendent's demand, Swain conducted an assessment of the students' hourly work habits. Much to his surprise, he discovered that they spent approximately half the time required. Swain was not willing to agree to the superintendent's ultimatum, apparently with good reason.

118 Swain letter to Kelsey, May 17, 1913.

119 Kelsey letter to Swain, May 20, 1913.

120 Elizabeth Babcock interview.

121 The *Directory of Early Michigan Photographers* (Tinder 2013, 2443) cites part of an advertisement for Swain's commercial business in Ann Arbor. It reads, in part, "DO YOU WANT an especially fine Photograph of your family, your children, your house, or your horses, cows or other fine stock? Then call on or phone Swain."

122 Kimball and Porter 2015, 9.

123 Pedley 2012, 398.

Notes to Chapter 5

124 Swain, n.d., Individual Report, I–4.

125 Swain letter to family, October 26, 1924.

126 Swain letter to Ned, 1926.

127 Swain letter to family, July 2, 1924.

128 Weisberger 1972.

129 Kelsey mentions in a letter that in 1920, Swain and Easton (Kelsey's son and an assistant to Swain) were allowed, on occasion, to use the darkroom at Robert College in Constantinople (Pedley 2012, 279, n. 103). In 1924, Swain set up a darkroom in Yalivadj for printing his large glass plates, but the Kodak images had to be sent out for printing. Some of Swain's photographic projects were substantial. In July 1920, for example, Kelsey sent Swain and Easton to London to photograph the famous Beatus manuscripts, which contain more than 400 often lavishly illustrated pages. The work took three weeks and involved a large number of 11-by-14 photographic plates (Pedley 2012, 282).

130 Brown 2013, https://record.umich.edu/articles/a4689-first-u-m-photographer.

131 Swain letter to family, June 2, 1924.

132 Swain 1925b, *II: Tunis and the University of Michigan at Carthage*, 1–2. Given Swain's attentiveness to color, it is possible that he may have occasionally hand-colored some of his images. The hand-coloring of glass-plate prints was common during his time and, at least in professional contexts, was often carried out by women. One example of a hand-tinted Swain print (from the Karanis excavations) exists in the Kelsey Museum archives (neg. no. 5.3130). I am grateful to Terry Wilfong for this information.

Notes to Chapter 6

133 Mustafa Kemal Atatürk is considered the founding father of the modern Turkish Republic. He served as the country's first president from October 29, 1923, until his death on November 10, 1938, at the age of 57. Atatürk rose to power at the end of World War I, after the collapse of the Ottoman Empire—a largely Muslim-governed entity that granted limited rights to non-Islamic minorities under Ottoman rule. Western powers were eager to gain control of Turkey after its defeat in the war, jockeying to carve up the country for their own agendas. Atatürk held those powers at bay, hoping to industrialize his economically impoverished and underdeveloped country and create a modern, self-ruling, secular nation-state. He fostered a new national ethos, ushering in sweeping changes and progressive reforms, including progress in education and literacy, rights for women (such as voting), a ban on polygamy, the replacement of the Arabic script with a modified Latin alphabet, the adoption of secular law, a concomitant reduction in the power of religious leaders, and many more modernizing reforms. His changes, however, were not universally supported, especially by those who believed he was maligning and undercutting the role of religion. He was quick to silence opposition, often resorting to violence against the pro-Islamic elements of Turkish society, as well as religious and ethnic minorities. Today, Atatürk remains a controversial figure—his legacy a source of fierce debate between his supporters and

detractors. Scores of books have been written about his life and work, some with almost hagiographic overtones, others critical of his reforms and what his detractors view as a dictatorial and repressive regime. For a few of the better-known biographies of Atatürk and the founding of modern Turkey, see Landau 1984, Mango 1999, Hanioğlu 2011, and Gingeras 2019.

134 The tragic life of Dido, the mythical queen of Carthage, has inspired writers, composers, painters, astronomers, and even the creators of modern strategy games. According to several ancient writers—most notably Virgil—Dido escaped from Tyre (a city in ancient Phoenicia) following the murder of her husband. She eventually landed in North Africa and, after some clever bargaining with locals, founded the city of Carthage. The Trojan prince Aeneas encountered Dido on his voyage from Troy and fell in love with her. Struck by Cupid's arrow (or in some versions, by the machinations of Juno and Venus), Dido fell hopelessly in love with the prince. He had to leave, however, to fulfill his destiny. Bereft, she committed suicide, reportedly by a sword or by throwing herself on a funeral pyre. In some accounts, as she was consumed by flames, she cursed Aeneas and his Trojan descendants, foreshadowing the Punic Wars.

135 Pedley 2012, 352.

Notes to Chapter 7

136 Goodnow 1924, 1.

137 For discussions of archaeologists as spies during World War I, see Harris and Sadler 2003 and Browman 2011.

138 Gjenvick-Gjønvik Archives, n.d., https://ggarchives.com/OceanTravel/Brochures/USL-1924-TheAmericanWayToEurope.html.

139 Swain 1925c, 1.

140 Swain 1925c, 1.

141 The original *Res Gestae* was a bronze inscription, located in Rome in front of the mausoleum of Augustus. That inscription is lost, but much of its contents is known from a copy, also found in Turkey. The Antioch version, which consisted of 200 marble fragments, filled in several lacunae.

142 Gazda, Ng, and Demirer 2011.

143 Swain letter to family, June 15, 1924.

144 Swain letter to family, June 8, 1924. Swain's comment came after he was notified by officials supervising the loading of the two vehicles onto a steamer that they were going to raise "the price of taking the cars 10 £.T. when the sedan was on and the truck half way."

145 Swain letter to family, June 19, 1924.

146 Swain letter to family, August 28 or 30, 1924.

147 Swain 1925b, *IX: Patmos to Naples via Greece and Malta*, 1–2.

148 Swain 1924b "Homeward Bound," November 9, 40.

149 Swain letter to family, June 25, 1924.

150 Swain 1924b, "Homeward Bound," November 9, 40.

151 For a good discussion of the Sardis Affair, see Goode 2007, Chapter Two.

152 Goode 2007, 31.

153 Goode 2007, 31. Croesus was the king of ancient Lydia, a powerful kingdom in what is now western Turkey. He ruled during the 6th century BCE and was renowned for his extraordinary wealth—hence the expression "rich as Croesus"—his brilliant military campaigns, and his outsize sense of pride. His hubris is on ample display in a story later recounted by the Greek historian Herodotus. Allegedly, the famous Greek sage Solon visited Croesus at his palace in Sardis. During that visit, Croesus wasted no time displaying his wealth, although the sage seemed less than impressed. Annoyed, Croesus asked Solon two questions: Have you ever seen anyone as fortunate as I, and who do you think is the happiest person in the world? Croesus clearly expected Solon to single out the great king of Lydia. Solon responded without flattery: He did not name the king but instead told Croesus about three common people who were neither rich nor powerful but led happy lives filled with devotion, simple pleasures, and loving children. They all died surrounded by caring families and friends. Solon explained that no man could be counted as happy until he dies; one never knows what the gods have in store. Croesus decided the great sage was a fool and that his wisdom was overrated. But the sage's words proved prophetic: the king's once-powerful empire was defeated by the Persians, his son died a tragic death, and his wife allegedly committed suicide. Croesus's legendary wealth and hubris are well-known themes in popular culture, referenced, for example, in *The Simpsons*, *The Sopranos*, and Steinbeck's *East of Eden*, among other works.

154 Goode 2007, 33.

155 At the time, Greece occupied part of the western region of Anatolia, including the area of the Sardis excavations. The material was removed under a Greek permit of export.

156 Interestingly, this comment came from an American numismatist working at Sardis in regard to his feelings about the board at the Metropolitan Museum. Another eminent American labeled the board "a stiff-necked and stupid crowd." Pedley 2012, 315–316.

157 Goode 2007, 41.

158 Kelsey letter to De Forest, April 9, 1924, 5.

159 Goode 2007, 39.

160 Pedley 2012, 318.

161 Swain letter to family, June 15, 1924.

162 Swain letter to family, June 16, 1924.

163 The Greek-Turkish compulsory population exchange enacted in 1923 was linked to a complex set of procedures, treaties, and tangled histories that continue to have far-reaching effects. Following the dissolution of the Ottoman Empire, the end of World War I, and the ensuing Greco-Turkish War of 1919–1922, new boundaries and rising nation-states emerged in the Mediterranean and Near East. Notable was the birth of the Republic of Turkey, which arose from the smoldering ashes of the Ottoman Empire (see endnote 133). Radical displacements, massacres, and expulsions of select populations followed the creation of Turkey in an attempt to "cleanse" the composition of people who lived in both Turkey and Greece. Greek Orthodox Turkish nationals living in Turkey were forced to migrate to Greece, while Muslim Greek nationals living in Greece were likewise moved to Turkey. Although the precise numbers are debated, it is estimated that 1.5 to 2 million people were involved in the exchange. Before the official exchange of 1923 went into effect, however, hundreds of thousands of individuals, who were facing dire circumstances, had already fled. The exchange created a humanitarian crisis of epic proportion, countless deaths, and deep animosities that continue to shape the current relationship between Greece and Turkey. Among books on the subject, see Hirschon 2003 and Iğsiz 2018.

164 Swain letter to family, June 16, 1924.

165 Swain letter to family, June 15, 1924.

166 Swain letter to family, June 15, 1924.

167 Swain 1925c, 2.

168 Swain letter to family, June 30, 1924.

169 E. Kelsey 1925b, 8.

170 E. Kelsey 1925a, 17.

171 Swain 1924b, July 27, 30.

172 Swain letter to family, June 6, 1924.

173 Swain 1924b, August 31, 21.

174 Swain letter to family, August 10, 1924.

175 Swain letter to family, June 4, 1924.

176 Thomas 1992, https://exhibitions.kelsey.lsa.umich.edu/galleries/Exhibits/DangerousArchaeology/MainDangerous.html. See "From Caravan to Railroad."

177 Swain letter to family, June 30, 1924.

178 Swain 1925c, 3.

179 Swain letter to family, June 30, 1924.

180 Swain letter to family, June 30, 1924.

181 Swain 1924a.

182 Swain 1925c, 3.

183 E. Kelsey 1925b, 8–9.

184 Swain 1924b, August 31, 21.

185 Swain letter to family, July 7, 1924.

186 Swain letter to family, July 13, 1924.

187 Swain letter to family, June 4, 1924.

188 Swain 1924b, September 14, 35.

189 With apologies to Annie Dillard, whose precise quote is: "How we spend our days is, of course, how we spend our lives" (Dillard 1989, 32).

190 Swain 1924b, "Homeward Bound," November 9, 40.

191 Swain letter to family, July 25, 1924.

192 Swain letter to family, July 18, 1924.

193 Robinson and Peterson 1924.

194 Swain letter to family, August 24, 1924.

195 Shoenfield 1924.

196 Swain letter to family, July 21, 1924.

197 Swain letter to family, July 31, 1924.

198 Swain letter to family, September 12, 1924.

199 Swain letter to family, September 25, 1924.

200 Swain letter to family, October 10, 1924.

201 Swain letter to family, October 11, 1924.

202 Swain letter to family, October 10, 1924.

203 Swain letter to family, October 11, 1924.

Notes to Chapter 8

204 Swain 1925b, *Second Series, I: Italy and Sicily*, 1.

205 Swain 1925a, unpaginated p. 2.

206 Valjak 2018, https://thevintagenews.com/2018/02/22/the-viking-1931/?A1c=1; AFI Catalog, n.d., https://catalog.afi.com/Catalog/MovieDetails/54309.

207 Swain 1925c, 5.

208 Swain 1925c, 3.

209 Swain 1925b, *Second Series, I: Italy and Sicily*, 4.

210 Swain 1925b, *Second Series, I: Italy and Sicily*, 6–7.

211 Swain 1925b, *Second Series, I: Italy and Sicily*, 7–8.

212 Talalay and Alcock 2006, 22; F. Kelsey 1926, 47–49; and Harden 1927, 297–298. For arguments supporting the theory that Carthaginians indeed practiced infant sacrifice, see Smith et al. 2011.

213 Swain 1925b, *II: Tunis and the University of Michigan in Carthage*, 2.

214 Swain 1925b, *II: Tunis and the University of Michigan in Carthage*, 5.

215 De Prorok 1925, 25.

216 De Prorok's books include, among others, *Mysterious Sahara: The Land of Gold, of Sand, and of Ruin* (1929); *Dead Men Do Tell Tales: A 1933 Archaeological Expedition into Abyssinia* (1942); and *In Quest of Lost Worlds* (1935).

217 Field 1936, 9.

218 Swain 1925b, *IV: An Archaeological Reconnaissance, Concluded*, 1.

219 Swain 1925a, unpaginated p. 2.

220 Swain 1925b, *III: An Archaeological Reconnaissance*, 1.

221 Swain 1925b, *III: An Archaeological Reconnaissance*, 8.

222 Swain 1925b, *III: An Archaeological Reconnaissance*, 2.

223 Swain 1925b, *III: An Archaeological Reconnaissance*, 2.

224 Swain 1925b, *III: An Archaeological Reconnaissance*, 5.

225 *Smithsonian* 2016, https://smithsonianmag.com/sponsored/star-wars-tunisia-film-locations-180960144.

226 Swain 1925b, *III: An Archaeological Reconnaissance*, 6.

227 Swain 1925b, *III: An Archaeological Reconnaissance*, 6.

228 Endorheic lakes are closed drainage systems that allow no outflows to other external bodies of water.

229 *Carthage Mag* 2021, https://carthagemagazine.com/chott-el-jerid-tunisia.

230 *Smithsonian* 2016.

231 Tunisia Travel Guide 2023, https://tunisia-travel-guide.com/things-to-do-in-tozeur.

232 Swain 1925b, *III: An Archaeological Reconnaissance*, 7.

233 Swain 1925b, *III: An Archaeological Reconnaissance*, 7.

234 Swain 1925b, *IV: An Archaeological Reconnaissance, Concluded*, 1.

235 Swain 1925b, *IV: An Archaeological Reconnaissance, Concluded*, 3.

236 Swain 1925b, *IV: An Archaeological Reconnaissance, Concluded*, 4.

237 *Smithsonian* 2016.

238 Swain 1925b, *III: An Archaeological Reconnaissance*, 4–5.

239 Swain 1925b, *III: An Archaeological Reconnaissance*, 5.

240 For a brief history of the Jewish population on Djerba, see Jewish Virtual Library, n.d., https://jewishvirtuallibrary.org/djerba.

241 Swain 1925c, 4.

242 Pedley 2012, 398. Between 1928 and 1930 (and possibly later), Swain filmed roughly four hours of footage documenting excavations at Karanis, Egypt, and 15 minutes at Terenouthis, also in Egypt (see Wilfong 2014, 26).

243 *New York Times* 1925, 21.

244 Swain 1925b, *IV: An Archaeological Reconnaissance, Concluded*, 1.

245 Swain 1925b, *IX: Patmos to Naples via Greece and Malta*, 7.

246 Swain 1925b, *IX: Patmos to Naples via Greece and Malta*, 5.

247 Swain 1925b, *V: En Route to the Sacred Mountain—Mt. Athos*, 2–3.

248 Swain 1925b, *X: Patmos to Naples via Greece and Malta, Concluded*, 4.

249 Swain 1925b, *X: Patmos to Naples via Greece and Malta, Concluded*, 4–5.

250 Part of the following is taken from a paper delivered at the conference *Greek (Hi)stories Through the Lens: Photographs, Photographers, and Their Testimonies*, held in June 2011 at the Centre for Hellenic Studies, King's College London. The paper was cowritten with Professor Artemis Leontis (Talalay and Leontis 2011). I am extremely grateful to her for her many insights and fruitful discussions about Swain's contrasting views of Patmos and Mount Athos (see endnote 264).

251 Swain 1925b, *VI: Where To-Day Is Yesterday—Some Monasteries of Mt. Athos*, 8.

252 Swain 1925b, *VI: Where To-Day Is Yesterday—Some Monasteries of Mt. Athos*, 8.

253 Swain 1925b, *VI: Where To-Day Is Yesterday—Some Monasteries of Mt. Athos*, 2.

254 Swain 1925b, *V: En Route to the Sacred Mountain—Mt. Athos*, 6–7.

255 Swain 1925b, *VII: More Monasteries I Have Met*, 9.

256 Swain 1925b, *VIII: A Chronological Backwater—Patmos*, 6–7.

257 Swain 1925b, *VIII: A Chronological Backwater—Patmos*, 6.

258 Swain 1925b, *VIII: A Chronological Backwater—Patmos*, 6.

259 Swain 1925b, *VII: More Monasteries I Have Met*, 7.

260 Swain 1925b, *VIII: A Chronological Backwater—Patmos*, 8.

261 Swain 1925b, *VIII: A Chronological Backwater—Patmos*, 8. The anthropologist Margaret Kenna provides a few more details after witnessing and photographing one of these ceremonies on the small island of Anafi, Greece. In the Anafiote village, after a grave is broken open and the coffin lifted out, the bones are "sprinkled with wine, wrapped in white linen, together with a sprig of basil." Later, the bones are taken to a chapel on family land and placed in an ossuary (Kenna 2016, 282). For a detailed study of Greek burial practices, see Danforth 1982.

262 Swain 1925b, *VII: More Monasteries I Have Met*, 9.

263 Swain 1925b, *VIII: A Chronological Backwater—Patmos*, 4.

264 The discussion in this section on Swain's visits to the monasteries is based on a coauthored conference paper, "Observing the Observer: Comments on George R. Swain's Records of Greek Monasteries, 1920–1926" (Talalay and Leontis 2011; see endnote 250).

265 Swain 1925b, *V: En Route to the Sacred Mountain—Mt. Athos*, 1. Written by Florence Percy (the pen name for Elizabeth Akers Allen), the poem "Rock Me to Sleep" was first published in the *Saturday Evening Post* in 1859, though controversy arose when a man named Alexander M. W. Ball claimed authorship. In 1860, the composer Ernest Leslie set the poem to music, which became a popular song. See Poets.org, n.d., https://poets.org/poet/elizabeth-akers-allen.

266 Swain 1925b, *VIII: A Chronological Backwater—Patmos*, 8.

267 Swain 1925b, *VII: More Monasteries I Have Met*, 9.

268 Swain 1925b, *X: Patmos to Naples via Greece and Malta, Concluded*, 6.

269 Swain 1925b, *X: Patmos to Naples via Greece and Malta, Concluded*, 5–6.

Notes to Chapter 9

270 The bound journal was created by Robert, one of Swain's sons, and was labeled *Robert's Foreign Letters, 1926.*

271 General Lew Wallace Study & Museum 2011, https://ben-hur.com/ben-hur-1925-the-most-expensive-silent-film-ever-made.

272 Swain letter to family, March 5, 1926.

273 The SS *Berengaria* was built as a German ocean liner, used for the transportation of American troops from Europe at the end of World War I, and finally turned over to the British as part of war reparations. Great Ocean Liners, n.d., https://greatoceanliners.com/ss-imperator-rms-berengaria.

274 Swain letter to family, March 6, 1926. In his letter of March 12, 1926, Swain indicates that this is his ninth transatlantic crossing.

275 Swain letter to family, March 14, 1926.

276 The days in Paris are described in Swain's letters of March 14–17, 1926, to his family.

277 Swain letter to family, March 18, 1926.

278 Swain letter to family, March 18, 1926.

279 Swain letter to family, March 21, 1926.

280 Swain letter to family, March 24, 1926.

281 Swain letter to family, March 31, 1926.

282 Swain letter to family, April 2, 1926.

283 Swain letter to family, April 6, 1926.

284 Pedley 2012, 364.

285 Pedley 2012, 361.

286 Pedley 2012, 317, n. 80. See also, Garfinkel 2016.

287 For full details about the telegrams, see Pedley 2012, 364.

288 Swain letter to family, April 6, 1926.

289 Swain letter to family, April 13, 1926.

290 Swain letter to family, May 2, 1926.

291 Swain letter to family, April 30, 1926.

292 Swain letter to family, April 13, 1926.

293 For the sad but fascinating life of Violet Gibson, see Saunders 2010.

294 Swain letter to family, May 3, 1926.

295 Swain letter to family, June 22, 1926.

296 Swain letter to family, May 3, 1926.

297 Swain letter to family, June 25, 1926. Stiff white collars of the early 1900s were separable from shirts. This allowed men of modest means to look well-dressed when the occasion warranted, even if they couldn't afford to launder their shirts. For an interesting discussion on the white collar as a sartorial hallmark of occupational status, see Friedel 2018, https://americanhistory.si.edu/blog/white-collar-message.

298 Swain letter to family, June 25, 1926.

299 Swain letter to family, June 28, 1926.

300 Swain letter to family, June 25, 1926.

301 Swain letter to family, June 30, 1926.

302 Swain letter to family, June 30, 1926.

303 Swain letter to family, July 1, 1926.

304 Swain letter to family, July 2, 1926.

305 Swain letter to family, July 2, 1926.

306 Swain letter to family, June 3, 1926.

307 Swain letter to family, August 7, 1926.

308 Swain letter to family, July 15, 1926.

309 Swain letter to family, July 6, 1926.

310 Swain letter to family, July 14, 1926.

311 Swain letter to family, July 18, 1926.

312 Swain letter to family, July 21, 1926.

313 Swain letter to family, July 25, 1926.

314 Swain is likely referring to the Greek tradition of the Sunday evening *volta*, where locals dress in their finest clothes and stroll throughout the evening.

315 Swain letter to family, July 26, 1926.

316 Swain letter to family, July 28, 1926.

317 Swain letter to family, July 30, 1926.

318 Swain letter to family, August 4, 1926.

319 Swain letter to family, August 4, 1926.

320 Swain letter to family, August 4, 1926.

321 Swain letter to family, August 15, 1926.

Notes to Chapter 10

322 Chiotis 2016, 187.

323 As testament to his extraordinary accomplishments, Kelsey was awarded a medal by the king of Belgium. Pedley 2012, 3.

324 Pedley 2012, 255. The request for photographs of "ethnic types" was not unusual at the time. Both archaeologists and anthropologists had been collecting data on race, facial construction, and skull shape for decades. Unfortunately, much of the information was used to fuel racist discourses, as well as to support discussions of selective breeding and eugenics. See Sheppard 2010; Riggs 2018, 126; and Challis 2013.

325 According to Swain's letters home, he had an arrangement with a Mr. G. E. Miller of the *Detroit News*. A letter dated Sunday, August 17, 1924, reads, "There is no definite arrangement with Miller except the following letter date March 24. 'The arrangement you made with Maj. Pickering is entirely satisfactory to me, and I trust is to you. In case of pictures or ms. which he finds unavailable for national and international circulation, I shall certainly be grateful of the opportunity to examine the same and if I can possibly find them available on account of the local interest, I surely will use them. In case we do use some of the material sent on to us from Major Pickering under this arrangement you and I can agree upon a fair compensation upon your return. Very truly yours—G. E. Miller.' So this is all the information I can give you on this point. I think the most important thing is it has put me in personal touch with a large city daily." Swain letter to family, August 17, 1924.

326 Swain letter to family, July 2, 1924.

327 I thank Abigale Mumby at the Bentley Historical Library for tracking down these details.

328 Swain 1921.

329 Thornton 2018, 1.

330 Thornton 2018, 21.

331 Swain letter to family, August 10, 1924.

332 Swain 1924b, September 14, 35.

333 Swain 1924b, July 27, 30.

334 The literature on the nature of photography is vast, and the topic has been a source of discussion ever since the invention of photography. Classic theoretical works include Barthes 1977, Barthes 1981, Sontag 1978, and Edwards 1992, among many others. See also, Carabott et al. 2016, 7–12, for a concise discussion on the "ontologies of the photographic field." For relatively recent works focusing on anthropology and photography, see El Guindi 2004, Banks and Vokes 2010, and Pinney 2011.

335 Kenna 2016, 285.

336 Stathatos 2016, 50.

337 Banks and Vokes 2010, 347.

338 Leontis and Talalay 2006, 91.

339 Talalay and Leontis 2011.

340 Batchen 2004, 49.

341 Thompson 2011, 9–10.

342 Swain 1924b, September 14, 35.

343 Goode 2007, 2.

344 Goode 2007, 9.

345 Talalay and Leontis 2011.

REFERENCES

Books, Published Articles, & Other Sources

Adolphus, David T. 2017. "The Inseparable, Irascible Dodge Boys." *Hagerty*, May 26, 2017. Accessed March 17, 2020. https://hagerty.com/media/archived/dodge-brothers.

AFI Catalog. n.d. "The Viking (1931)." Accessed April 17, 2023. https://catalog.afi.com/Catalog/MovieDetails/54309.

Ann Arbor News. 1947. "George R. Swain, 'U' Photographer, Dies at 80 Years." April 8, 1947. Accessed February 20, 2020. https://aadl.org/aa_news_19470408_p3-george_r_swain_u_photographer_dies_at_80_years.

Banks, Marcus, and Richard Vokes. 2010. "Introduction: Anthropology, Photography and the Archive." *History and Anthropology* 21 (4): 337–349. https://doi.org/10.1080/02757206.2010.522375.

Barthes, Roland. 1977. *Image-Music-Text*. Translated by Stephen Heath. New York: Hill and Wang.

———. 1981 [1980]. *Camera Lucida: Reflections on Photography*. New York: Hill and Wang.

Batchen, Geoffrey. 2004. *Forget Me Not: Photography and Remembrance*. New York and Amsterdam: Princeton Architectural Press and Van Gogh Museum.

Bellis, Mary. 2019. "A History of the Automobile." ThoughtCo., July 6, 2019. Accessed April 22, 2021. https://thoughtco.com/who-invented-the-car-4059932.

Berger, Michael L. 2001. *The Automobile in American History and Culture: A Reference Guide*. Westport, CT: Greenwood.

Browman, David L. 2011. "Spying by American Archaeologists in World War I." *Bulletin of the History of Archaeology* 21 (2): 10–17. https://doi.org/10.5334/bha.2123.

Brown, Kevin. 2013. "First U-M Photographer Swain Hired 100 Years Ago." *University Record* (University of Michigan), June 24, 2013. Accessed November 19, 2020. https://record.umich.edu/articles/a4689-first-u-m-photographer.

Carabott, Philip, Yannis Hamilakis, and Eleni Papargyriou, eds. 2016. *Camera Graeca: Photographs, Narratives, Materialities*. London and New York: Routledge. https://doi.org/10.4324/9781315570761.

Carthage Mag. 2021. "Chott El Jerid: An Unforgettable Journey to a Different Planet." August 9, 2021. Accessed August 4, 2023. https://carthagemagazine.com/chott-el-jerid-tunisia.

Challis, Debbie. 2013. *The Archaeology of Race: The Eugenic Ideas of Francis Galton and Flinders Petrie*. London: Bloomsbury Academic.

Chiotis, Theodoros. 2016. "Archaeology of Refraction: Temporality and Subject in George Seferis's Photographs." In Carabott et al. 2016, 169–192.

Clarke, Warren E. 2014. "An Invisible Presence: African Americans in a Rural New Hampshire Town, 1860 to 1940." Gilmanton NH History. Accessed November 22, 2023. https://gilmantonnhhistory.org/ckfinder/userfiles/files/Demographics/2014AfricanAmericans.pdf.

Classic Car Database. n.d. "Dodge 1924 Series Sedan B: Standard Specifications." Accessed March 17, 2020. http://classiccardatabase.com/specs.php?series=1849&year=1924&model=6066.

Coles, Robert. 1998. *Doing Documentary Work*. Oxford: Oxford University Press.

Columbus Dispatch. 2014. "Dodge Celebrates Century of Automobiles." December 17, 2014. Accessed February 18, 2020. https://dispatch.com/story/business/2014/12/18/dodge-celebrates-century-automobiles/23527504007.

Danforth, Loring M. 1982. *The Death Rituals of Rural Greece*. Princeton: Princeton University Press.

de Prorok, Byron Khun. 1925. "Hunts Lost Towns in Sands of Sahara." *New York Times*, April 9, 1925.

———. 2001 [1929]. *Mysterious Sahara: The Land of Gold, of Sand, and of Ruin*. Santa Barbara: Narrative Press.

———. 2001 [1935]. *In Quest of Lost Worlds*. Santa Barbara: Narrative Press.

———. 2001 [1942]. *Dead Men Do Tell Tales: A 1933 Archaeological Expedition into Abyssinia*. Santa Barbara: Narrative Press.

Dillard, Annie. 1989. *The Writing Life*. New York: Harper & Row.

Dobkin, Marjorie Housepian. 1998. *Smyrna 1922: The Destruction of a City*. New York: Newmark Press.

Edwards, Elizabeth, ed. 1992. *Anthropology and Photography, 1860–1920*. New Haven, CT, and London: Yale University Press in association with the Royal Anthropological Institute.

El Guindi, Fadwa. 2004. *Visual Anthropology: Essential Method and Theory*. New York: AltaMira.

Emberling, Geoff, ed. 2010. *Pioneers to the Past: American Archaeologists in the Middle East, 1919–1920*. Chicago: Oriental Institute Museum. https://isac.uchicago.edu/sites/default/files/uploads/shared/docs/oimp30.pdf.

Field, Louise M. 1936. "The Strange Discoveries of Count de Prorok." *New York Times*, January 19, 1936, 9.

Federal Highway Administration. 1997. "State Motor Vehicle Registrations, by Years, 1900–1995." Accessed December 15, 2019. https://www.fhwa.dot.gov/ohim/summary95/mv200.pdf.

Friedel, Robert. 2018. "A White Collar with a Message." *O Say Can You See? Stories from the Museum* (blog), October 4, 2018. https://americanhistory.si.edu/blog/white-collar-message.

Garfinkel, Yosef. 2016. "The Murder of James Leslie Starkey near Lachish." *Palestine Exploration Quarterly* 148 (2): 84–109. https://doi.org/10.1080/00310328.2016.1138217.

Gazda, Elaine K., Diana Y. Ng, and Ünal Demirer, eds. 2011. *Building a New Rome: The Imperial Colony of Pisidian Antioch (25 BC–AD 700)*. Ann Arbor: Kelsey Museum of Archaeology, University of Michigan.

General Lew Wallace Study & Museum. 2011. "Ben-Hur 1925: The Most Expensive Silent Film Ever Made." April 30, 2011. Accessed July 6, 2023. https://ben-hur.com/ben-hur-1925-the-most-expensive-silent-film-ever-made.

German History in Documents and Images. n.d. "Nominal Wages, Cost of Living, and Real Wages in Industry, Trade, and Transportation (1871–1913)." Accessed April 20, 2023. https://ghdi.ghi-dc.org/sub_document.cfm?document_id=1746.

Gingeras, Ryan. 2019. *Eternal Dawn: Turkey in the Age of Atatürk*. Oxford: Oxford University Press. https://doi.org/10.1093/oso/9780198791218.001.0001.

Gjenvik-Gjønvik Archives. n.d. "The American Way to Europe—United States Lines—1924." Accessed August 14, 2020. https://ggarchives.com/OceanTravel/Brochures/USL-1924-TheAmericanWayToEurope.html.

Godshall, Jeffery I. 1975. "What Is a Graham? The Graham Brothers and Their Car." *Automobile Quarterly* 13 (1). Accessed at https://grahamownersclub.com/history.html.

Goode, James F. 2007. *Negotiating for the Past: Archaeology, Nationalism, and Diplomacy in the Middle East, 1919–1941*. Austin: University of Texas Press.

Goodnow, Louis L. 1924. "Trains Camera on Asia Minor." *Detroit News*, February 13, 1924.

Graham Brothers Trucks. 1924. "Food for 30,000,000." Advertisement. *Saturday Evening Post*.

Great Ocean Liners. n.d. "SS Imperator/RMS Berengaria." Accessed February 24, 2022. https://greatoceanliners.com/ss-imperator-rms-berengaria.

Hamilakis, Yannis, Aris Anagnostopoulos, and Fotis Ifantidis. 2009. "Postcards from the Edge of Time: Archaeology, Photography, Archaeological Ethnography (A Photo-Essay)." *Public Archaeology* 8 (2–3): 283–309. https://doi.org/10.1179/175355309X457295.

Halley, Catherine. 2022. "September 1922: The Great Fire of Smyrna." JSTOR Daily, September 22, 2022. Accessed June 23, 2023. https://daily.jstor.org/september-1922-the-great-fire-of-smyrna.

Hanioğlu, M. Şükrü. 2011. *Atatürk: An Intellectual Biography*. Princeton: Princeton University Press.

Harden, Donald B. 1927. "Punic Urns from the Precinct of Tanit at Carthage." *American Journal of Archaeology* 31 (3): 297–310. https://doi.org/10.2307/497821.

Harris III, Charles H., and Louis R. Sadler. 2003. *The Archaeologist Was a Spy: Sylvanus G. Morley and the Office of Naval Intelligence*. Albuquerque: University of New Mexico Press.

Hirschon, Renée, ed. 2003. *Crossing the Aegean: An Appraisal of the 1923 Compulsory Population Exchange between Greece and Turkey*. New York and Oxford: Berghahn Books. https://doi.org/10.3167/9781571817679.

Hyde, Charles K. 2005. *The Dodge Brothers: The Men, the Motor Cars, and the Legacy*. Detroit: Wayne State University Press.

Iğsız, Aslı. 2018. *Humanism in Ruins: Entangled Legacies of the Greek-Turkish Population Exchange*. Stanford: Stanford University Press.

Jewish Virtual Library. n.d. "Virtual Jewish World: Djerba, Tunisia." Accessed July 5, 2023. https://jewishvirtuallibrary.org/djerba.

Keller, Michael E. 1998. *The Graham Legacy: Graham-Paige to 1932*. Paducah, KY: Turner.

Kelsey, Easton T. 1925a. "Digging for Ruins Centuries Old." *Michigan Chimes* (University of Michigan) 6, no. 4 (January): 15–17, 41, 45–46.

———. 1925b. "The Romance of Excavating." *The Scholastic*, May 16, 1925, 8, 9, 29. Bentley Historical Library, University of Michigan.

Kelsey, Francis W. 1926. *Excavations at Carthage 1925: A Preliminary Report*. New York: Macmillan.

Kenna, Margaret E. 2016. "From 'Here and Now' to 'Then and There': Reflections on Fieldwork Photography in the 1960s." In Carabott et al. 2016, 277–293.

Kimball, Judith, and John Porter. 2015. *Grand Lake and Presque Isle (Postcard History Series)*. Charleston, SC: Arcadia Publishing.

Klingler, Ed. n.d. "The Graham Brothers: 'Evansville was the Capital of the Universe.'" *Evansville Boneyard*. Accessed April 20, 2023. http://evansvilleboneyard.org/graham_brothers.htm.

Landau, Jacob M., ed. 1984. *Atatürk and the Modernization of Turkey*. Boulder, CO: Westview.

Leontis, Artemis, and Lauren E. Talalay. 2006. "A Day's Journey: Constantinople, December 9, 1919." *Michigan Quarterly Review* 45, no. 1 (Winter 2006): 73–98. http://hdl.handle.net/2027/spo.act2080.0045.111.

Lewis, Davis L., and Laurence Goldstein, eds. 1983. *The Automobile and American Culture*. Ann Arbor: University of Michigan Press. https://doi.org/10.3998/mpub.7219.

Lorenzi, Rossella. 2004. "Da Vinci Sketched an Early Car." *Discovery News*, April 26, 2004. Accessed January 3, 2020. https://abc.net.au/science/news/stories/s1094767.htm.

Lyons, Claire L., John K. Papadopoulos, Lindsey S. Stewart, and Andrew Szegedy-Maszak. 2005. *Antiquity & Photography: Early Views of Ancient Mediterranean Sites*. Los Angeles: J. Paul Getty Museum.

Mango, Andrew. 1999. *Atatürk: The Biography of the Founder of Modern Turkey*. London: John Murray.

McFadyen, Lesley, and Dan Hicks, eds. 2020. *Archaeology and Photography: Time, Objectivity, and Archive*. London: Bloomsbury. https://dx.doi.org/10.5040/9781350029712.

McNessor, Mike. 2018. "Last Graham Standing—1929 Model BE." *Hemmings*, September 23, 2018. Accessed August 18, 2023. https://hemmings.com/stories/article/last-graham-standing-1929-model-be.

Milton, Giles. 2008. *Paradise Lost: Smyrna 1922: The Destruction of a Christian City in the Islamic World*. New York: Basic Books.

Neil, Dan. 2006. "Before the Rumble Seat." *Los Angeles Times*, June 21, 2006. Accessed August 18, 2023. https://latimes.com/news/la-hy-125mbz21jun21-story.html.

New Hampton School. n.d. "Re-Learning Our History." Accessed July 5, 2023. https://newhampton.org/bicentennial/history.

New York Times. 1925. "Movies Speed Work in Carthage Ruins." April 6, 1925, 21.

Pedley, John G. 2012. *The Life and Work of Francis Willey Kelsey: Archaeology, Antiquity, and the Arts*. Ann Arbor: University of Michigan Press. https://doi.org/10.3998/mpub.1266159.

Pinney, Christopher. 2011. *Photography and Anthropology*. London: Reaktion Books.

Poets.org. n.d. "Elizabeth Akers Allen: 1832–1911." Accessed August 29, 2023. https://poets.org/poet/elizabeth-akers-allen.

Riggs, Christina. 2018. *Photographing Tutankhamun: Archaeology, Ancient Egypt, and the Archive*. London and New York: Routledge.

Robinson, David M., and Enoch E. Peterson. 1924. *Journal of Antioch Excavations, Prepared by David M. Robinson and Enoch E. Peterson*, Box 73, Francis W. Kelsey Papers, 1891–1953, Bentley Historical Library, University of Michigan.

Rosenberg, Jennifer. 2019. "Why the Model T Is Called the Tin Lizzie." ThoughtCo., January 3, 2019. Accessed August 3, 2020. https://thoughtco.com/nickname-tin-lizzie-3976121.

Saunders, Frances Stonor. 2010. *The Woman Who Shot Mussolini*. New York: Henry Holt.

Scarborough, William Sanders. 2005. *The Autobiography of William Sanders Scarborough: An American Journey from Slavery to Scholarship*. Edited by Michele Valerie Ronnick. Detroit: Wayne State University Press.

Schlenoff, Daniel C. 2017. "The Motor Vehicle, 1917 [Slide Show]." *Scientific American*, January 1, 2017. Accessed December 20, 2019. https://scientificamerican.com/article/the-motor-vehicle-1917-slide-show.

Sheppard, Kathleen L. 2010. "Flinders Petrie and Eugenics at UCL." *Bulletin of the History of Archaeology* 20 (1): 16–29. https://doi.org/10.5334/bha.20103.

Shoenfield, Allen. 1924. "Paul's Antioch Yields Relics." *Detroit News*, November 12, 1924, 1.

Smith, Patricia, Gal Avishai, Joseph A. Greene, and Lawrence E. Stager. 2011. "Aging Cremated Infants: The Problem of Sacrifice at the Tophet of Carthage." *Antiquity* 85, no. 329 (September): 859–874. https://doi.org/10.1017/S0003598X00068368.

Smithsonian. 2016. "Discover the Real and Imagined Cities of Luke Skywalker's Tatooine." September 15, 2016. Accessed August 5, 2023. https://smithsonianmag.com/sponsored/star-wars-tunisia-film-locations-180960144.

Sontag, Susan. 1978 [1977]. *On Photography*. New York: Farrar, Straus and Giroux.

Stathatos, John. 2016. "The Three-Way Mirror: Photography as Record, Mirror and Model of Greek National Identity." In Carabott et al. 2016, 25–52.

Stewart, Ben. 2021. "From Model T to Model 3: How Driving Changed Over a Century." *Popular Mechanics*, December 23, 2021. Accessed December 20, 2022. https://popularmechanics.com/cars/g23320934/car-history.

Swain, George R. 1896–1897. "Because of a Kodak." *The Inlander* VII (June): 399–402.

———. 1911. "Open Letter to Bay City People." *Bay City Times*, March 28, 1911.

———. 1921. *Travel with Mr. Swain from the Danube to the Nile!* Folder, Swain, George, 1921–1924, 1926, Box 32, Kelsey Museum of Archaeology Papers, Bentley Historical Library, University of Michigan.

———. 1924a. *Archaeological Results of First Importance Attained by the Near East Research of the University of Michigan during Its First Campaign*. Near East, Antioch of Pisidia, Swain Reports, Box 73, Francis W. Kelsey Papers, Kelsey Museum of Archaeology Records, Bentley Historical Library, University of Michigan.

———. 1924b. "Notes and Comment of a Wolverine Abroad." *Detroit News*.
- July 13.
- July 27.

– August 31.
– September 14.
– "Homeward Bound," November 9.

———. 1925a. *An Archaeological Reconnaissance*. Box 1, George Robert Swain Photographs and Papers, Bentley Historical Library, University of Michigan.

———. 1925b. *Notes and Comments of a Wolverine Abroad*. Box 1, George Robert Swain Photographs and Papers, Bentley Historical Library, University of Michigan.
– *Second Series, I: Italy and Sicily*.
– *II: Tunis and the University of Michigan in Carthage*.
– *III: An Archaeological Reconnaissance*.
– *IV: An Archaeological Reconnaissance, Concluded*.
– *V: En Route to the Sacred Mountain—Mt. Athos*.
– *VI: Where To-Day Is Yesterday—Some Monasteries of Mt. Athos*.
– *VII: More Monasteries I Have Met*.
– *VIII: A Chronological Backwater—Patmos*.
– *IX: Patmos to Naples via Greece and Malta*.
– *X: Patmos to Naples via Greece and Malta, Concluded*.

———. 1925c. "Travels of Two Dodge Motors." November 5, 1925. Swain, Manuscript Materials, Box 1, George Robert Swain Photographs and Papers, Bentley Historical Library, University of Michigan.

———. n.d. *Written Work in English Courses 1, 1a, 2, and 2a*. Manuscripts, Materials Writings, Swain, Box 1, George Robert Swain Photographs and Papers, Bentley Historical Library, University of Michigan.

Talalay, Lauren E., and Susan E. Alcock. 2006. *In the Field: The Archaeological Expeditions of the Kelsey Museum*. Ann Arbor: Kelsey Museum of Archaeology, University of Michigan.

Talalay, Lauren E., and Artemis Leontis. 2011. "Observing the Observer: Comments on George R. Swain's Records of Greek Monasteries, 1920–1926." Paper presented at *Greek (Hi)stories Through the Lens: Photographs, Photographers, and Their Testimonies*, London, June 2011.

Thompson, Carl. 2011. *Travel Writing*. London and New York: Routledge.

Thornton, Amara. 2018. *Archaeologists in Print: Publishing for the People*. London: University College London Press. https://discovery.ucl.ac.uk/id/eprint/10050677/1/Archaeologists-in-Print.pdf.

Thomas, Thelma K. 1992. *Dangerous Archaeology: Francis Willey Kelsey and Armenia (1919–1920)*. Kelsey Museum of Archaeology, University of Michigan. Accessed November 27, 2020. https://exhibitions.kelsey.lsa.umich.edu/galleries/Exhibits/DangerousArchaeology/MainDangerous.html.

Tinder, David V. 2013. *Directory of Early Michigan Photographers*. Edited by Clayton A. Lewis. Ann Arbor: William L. Clements Library, University of Michigan. https://clements.umich.edu/files/tinder_directory.pdf.

Tunisia Travel Guide. 2023. "Discovering Tozeur: An Oasis of Experiences." September 19, 2023. Accessed August 4, 2024. https://tunisia-travel-guide.com/things-to-do-in-tozeur.

Tweney, Dylan. 2010. "Aug. 12, 1888: Road Trip! Berta Takes the Benz." *Wired*, August 12, 2010. Accessed August 18, 2023. https://wired.com/2010/08/0812berta-benz-first-road-trip.

Universal Leonardo. n.d. "Self-Propelled Cart—Codex Atlanticus Fol 812r." Accessed January 3, 2020. http://universalleonardo.org/work.php?id=512&fb_source.

Valjak, Domagoj. 2018. "The Most Dangerous Set in Cinema History." *Vintage News*, February 22, 2018. Accessed April 17, 2023. https://thevintagenews.com/2018/02/22/the-viking-1931/?A1c=1.

Weisberger, Bernard A. 1972. "You Press the Button, We Do the Rest." *American Heritage* 23, no. 6 (October 1972). https://americanheritage.com/you-press-button-we-do-rest.

White, Elwyn B. 1936. "Farewell, My Lovely!" *New Yorker*, May 16, 1936.

Wik, Reynold M. 1983. "The Early Automobile and the American Farmer." In Lewis and Goldstein 1983, 37–47.

Wilfong, Terry W. 2014. *Karanis Revealed: Discovering the Past and Present of a Michigan Excavation in Egypt*. Ann Arbor: Kelsey Museum of Archaeology, University of Michigan.

Williams, Geoff. 2015. "A Glimpse at Your Expenses 100 Years Ago." *U.S. News*, January 2, 2015. Accessed November 24, 2020. https://money.usnews.com/money/personal-finance/articles/2015/01/02/a-glimpse-at-your-expenses-100-years-ago.

Zatz, David. 2017. "John and Horace Dodge: From Building Fords to Dodge Brothers." Allpar. Accessed March 17, 2020. https://allpar.com/d3/corporate/bios/dodge-brothers.html.

Letters

Kelsey, Francis W. Letter to George R. Swain. May 20, 1913. Box 152, Francis W. Kelsey Papers, 1891–1953, Bentley Historical Library, University of Michigan.

———. Letter to George R. Swain. August 24, 1923. Box 152, Francis W. Kelsey Papers, 1891–1953, Bentley Historical Library, University of Michigan.

———. Letter to Robert De Forest. April 9, 1924. Near East and Asia Minor, Misc. Material, Box 1, Bentley Historical Library, University of Michigan.

Swain, George R. Letter to Francis W. Kelsey. August 31, 1897. Box 152, Francis W. Kelsey Papers, 1891–1953, Bentley Historical Library, University of Michigan.

———. Letter to Francis W. Kelsey. April 28, 1898. Box 152, Francis W. Kelsey Papers, 1891–1953, Bentley Historical Library, University of Michigan.

———. Letter to Francis W. Kelsey. June 10, 1900. Box 1, George Robert Swain Photographs and Papers, Bentley Historical Library, University of Michigan.

———. Letter to Francis W. Kelsey. May 17, 1913. Box 32, Francis W. Kelsey Papers, 1891–1953, Bentley Historical Library, University of Michigan.

———. Letter to Frances Swain. December 15 or 19, 1919. Swain Family Collection.

———. Letter to Edith Swain. March 10, 1920. Swain Family Collection.

———. Letter to Francis W. Kelsey. July 3, 1923. Box 152, Francis W. Kelsey Papers, 1891–1953, Bentley Historical Library, University of Michigan.

———. Letters to family. 1924. Box 1, George Robert Swain Photographs and Papers, Bentley Historical Library, University of Michigan.

- June 2, June 4, June 5, June 6, June 8, June 15, June 16, June 19, June 25, June 30, July 2, July 5, July 7, July 13, July 16, July 18, July 21, July 25, July 31, August 10, August 17, August 24, August 28 or 30, September 12, September 25, October 10, October 11, and October 26.

———. Letter to Dodge Brothers, Inc. November 4, 1925. Box 1, George Robert Swain Photographs and Papers, Bentley Historical Library, University of Michigan.

———. Letters to family. 1926. *Robert's Foreign Letters, 1926*. Kelsey Museum of Archaeology, University of Michigan.

- March 5, March 6, March 12, March 14, March 15, March 16, March 17, March 18, March 21, March 24, March 31, April 2, April 6, April 13, April 30, May 2, May 3, June 3, June 22, June 25, June 28, June 30, July 1, July 2, July 6, July 14, July 15, July 18, July 21, July 25, July 26, July 28, July 30, August 4, August 7, and August 15.

———. Letter to Ned Swain. 1926. Folder 1, 1924–1926, Asia Minor, Box 1, Enoch Earnest Peterson Papers, 1924–1962, Bentley Historical Library, University of Michigan.

Ventura Union High School. Letter of reference for George R. Swain. January 11, 1895. Teachers, Swain, George, 1890–1899, Box 152, Francis W. Kelsey Papers, 1891–1953, Bentley Historical Library, University of Michigan.

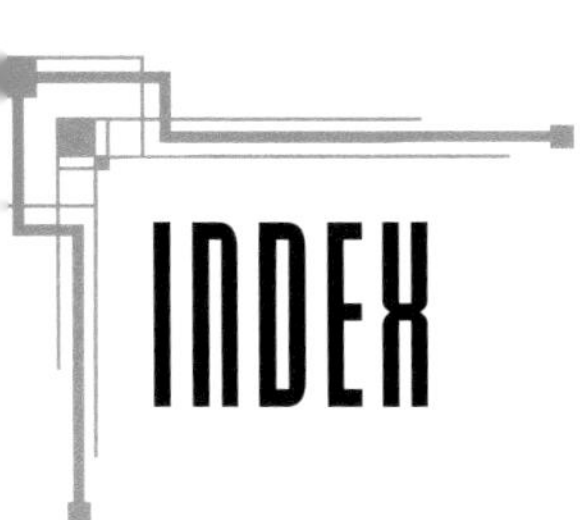

INDEX

Abbey of Saint Benedict, 83
Aeneid, 140 (n. 134)
Algeria, 49–50, 79, 80, 81, 84–85
America, 1920s, 8, 14–15, 24
American Committee for Relief in the Near East (ACRNE), 122; fig. 124
Armenia, 6, 61–62, 63, 114, 136 (n. 37); fig. 14. *See also* refugees: Armenian camps
Atatürk, Kemal Mustafa, 8, 49, 68, 139–140 (n. 133)
Augustus, Emperor, 56–57, 140 (n. 141)
auto shows
  Grand Palais, fig. 47
  New York, 22, 24

Babcock, Elizabeth, 36, 132, 135–136 (n. 14), 138 (n. 88), 138–139 (n. 114)
Bay City Times, 36, 139 (n. 117). *See also* Michigan: Bay City
bazaar, 61, 65, 68, 126; figs. 9, 74–80
Bedouins, 87–88; figs. 96a–b
Belgium, 25, 34, 53, 54, 56, 80, 83, 102, 103, 104, 108, 144 (n. 323)
Ben-Hur (movie), 107; fig. 112
Bentley Historical Library, ix, 32, 131, 135 (nn. 5, 12), 137 (n. 47), 138 (nn. 88, 107), 144 (n. 327); figs. 16, 31–35, 37–38, 40–41, 62
Benz, Bertha, 13–14, 136 (nn. 23–24); fig. 18. *See also* Motorwagen III; European Route of Industrial Heritage
Benz, Karl, 13. *See also* Motorwagen III
Black Panther (movie), 128
Bloomer, Howard R., 17–18, 25
Breasted, James Henry, 135 (n. 8)
Butler, Howard Crosley, 60

California, 29–31, 33, 138–139 (n. 114)
  Borden, 30, 33
  Fresno, 30
  Paso Robles, 31
  Petrolia, 30
  San Francisco, 30, 32
  Ventura, 30–32, 35, 138–139 (n. 114); fig. 33
Canada
  Newfoundland, 82
  Windsor, Ontario, 23
cameras, 2, 10, 17, 30, 39, 42–43, 49, 73, 82, 93, 124; figs. 5, 42, 48–49, 102
  Cirkut, 39, 43, 82; figs. 50a–b
  large format, 2, 39, 42–43, 82
  Kodak, 2, 32–33, 39, 42–44, 72, 75, 80, 82, 91, 112, 139 (n. 129); fig. 48
cars brands, x, 14–16, 17, 22, 24. *See also* Model T; Motorwagen III; sedan and truck
  Cadillac, 15–16, 17; fig. 20
  Dodge. *See* Dodge Brothers (company); *see also* sedan and truck
  Ford, x, 6, 14–16, 23, 112; fig. 19. *See also* Ford, Henry; Model T
  Graham Brothers. *See* Graham Brothers (company); *see also* sedan and truck
  Oldsmobile, x, 15, 23
  Renault, 86, 93–94; fig. 87
Century Magazine, 34
child sacrifice, 84, 142 (n. 212)
Christian Brothers College, 19
Chrysler Corporation, 25
colonialism, 6, 9, 33, 60–61, 72–73, 101, 110, 128–129, 136 (n. 17). *See also* Swain, George R.: views of non-Western nations
Cornell University, 30–31
Cushman, Emma, 96–97; fig. 104

Daimler, Gottlieb, 13
darkrooms, 33, 44, 110, 139 (n. 129)
da Vinci, Leonardo, 13
de Prorok, Byron Kuhn, 49–50, 81, 85–87, 93, 102, 142 (n. 216); figs. 57–58, 87, 91a–b, 97
Detroit News, 4–6, 55, 72–73, 123–124, 126–127, 135 (n. 12), 144 (n. 325); fig. 103
Detroit Public Library, 132; figs. 19, 24, 28
Detroit Symphony Orchestra, 24
Dido, Queen, 49, 140 (n. 134)
Dodge, John and Horace, 9, 17, 19, 21, 23–25, 137 (nn. 65, 72, 82); fig. 28
Dodge Brothers (company), 17–18, 21–22, 23–25, 136 (n. 43), 137 (n. 47); figs. 29–30

East Side High School. *See* Michigan: Bay City
Egypt, ix, 4, 50, 55, 92, 93, 105, 106–107, 108–110, 126, 128, 135 (n. 8), 142 (n. 242); figs. 5, 9. *See also* Nile River
  Cairo, figs. 39, 45
  Giza, 6; figs. 5, 9, 15
  Karanis, 106, 108–110, 118, 139 (n. 132), 142 (n. 242); figs. 6, 44
"ethnic" photos, 122, 144 (n. 324)
European Route of Industrial Heritage, 13. *See also* Benz, Bertha
Evansville Press, 20, 137 (n. 59). *See also* Indiana: Evansville
Evans and Dodge Bicycle Company, 23

Feizy, Hussein Shefik, 70–72

fez, 124, 126; figs. 8, 12
Ford, Henry, 14–15, 23; fig. 19. *See also* car brands: Ford; Model T
Fordham University, 19
France, 6, 15–16, 34, 41, 53, 54, 56, 60, 61, 80, 81, 103, 104, 106–108, 112, 127, 136 (n. 17), 137 (n. 47); fig. 63
  Arnay-le-Duc, 108
  Auxerre, 103, 104, 108
  Cannes, fig. 64
  Cherbourg, 80, 81, 104, 107
  Forest of Fontainebleau, fig. 65
  Lyon, 103, 104, 108
  Paris, 41, 53, 54, 61, 78, 80, 81, 103, 104, 107–108, 143 (n. 276); figs. 43, 63–64. *See also* auto shows: Grand Palais
  Reims, fig. 20
Frissell, Varick, 82

George M. Cohan Theatre, 107
Germany, 13–14, 34, 62, 143 (n. 273); fig. 18
Gibson, Violet, 111, 143 (n. 293). *See also* Mussolini, Benito
Graham Brothers (company), 17–18, 21–22, 137 (n. 47); figs. 23–26. *See also* Graham, Joseph, Robert, and Ray; Graham-Paige Motors Corporation
Graham, Joseph, Robert, and Ray, 9, 19–23, 132, 136 (n. 43), 137 (nn. 50–51, 59, 65, 71); figs. 22, 27
Graham, Ziba F., 19, 21
Graham-Paige Motors Corporation, 22–23, 137 (n. 50); fig. 27
Great Falls High School. *See* Montana
Greco-Turkish War, 63, 136 (n. 37), 141 (n. 163)
Greece, 1, 6, 8, 49–50, 53, 54, 60, 80, 94–102, 104, 105–106, 110–118, 128, 135 (nn. 3, 8), 136 (n. 37), 140 (n. 155), 141 (n. 163), 142 (n. 261)
  Andros, 104, 115; figs. 117–120. *See also* monasteries
  Athens, 16, 80, 95, 96, 102, 104, 114, 117–118; figs. 121–122
  Corinth, 80, 95–97, 104, 112
  Delphi, 80, 95
  Eleusis, 95, 104; fig. 111
  Mount Athos, 94–95, 97–101, 104, 113–114, 135 (n. 3), 142 (n. 250), 143 (n. 264); figs. 59, 101–102, 105–106. *See also* monasteries
  Mycenae, 80, 95
Greece (*cont.*)
  Mytilene, 63
  Nauplia, 80, 95; fig. 46
  Patmos, 80, 94, 97, 99–101, 104, 115, 126, 135 (n. 3), 142 (n. 250), 143 (n. 264); figs. 7, 54, 60, 103, 107–109, 115. *See also* monasteries
  Piraeus, 16, 44–45, 80, 112, 115
  Salonica, 80, 104, 112–113, 114–115
  Sounion, 80, 95
  Syros, 115
  Tenos, 115; fig. 116
  Volos, 80, 95
Greek currency, 112; fig. 114
Greek funerary traditions, 100, 142 (n. 261)

Harlem Renaissance. *See* America, 1920s

Indiana, 19–21
  Evansville, 21–22, 137 (n. 71)
  Washington, 19–21
Inlander, The (magazine), 32–33
inscriptions, 57, 72–73, 140 (n. 141); fig. 83. See also *Res Gestae*
Italy, 8, 41, 49–50, 53, 54, 56, 59, 60, 76–78, 79, 80, 83, 102, 103, 104, 105–112, 118, 127; fig. 123. *See also* Mount Vesuvius
  Arpino, 76; fig. 86
  Bellinzona, 80, 83
  Florence, 80, 83
  Messina, 53, 79, 80, 83
  Milan, 80, 83
  Naples, 53, 54, 56, 61, 75–76, 77, 83, 104, 117–118; figs. 66, 84–85
  Palermo, 79, 80; fig. 89
  Pompeii, 54, 104, 110–111, 118
  Reggio, 79, 80, 83; fig. 123
  Rome, 41, 49, 53, 54, 56, 75–78, 79, 80, 81, 83, 95, 103, 104, 108–111, 118, 140 (n. 141)
  Salerno, 79, 80, 83; fig. 123
  Sicily, 54, 80, 81, 83; fig. 89

Jewish population (Tunisia), 92, 142 (n. 240); fig. 100
Jim Crow, 33. See also *Plessy v. Ferguson*; racism
Johnson, Cyril (the “deacon”), 113–114; fig. 115

Kamp Kairphree, 37, 132, 138 (n. 88); fig. 40
Keller, Michael, 22, 132, 137 (nn. 50, 59), 138 (n. 87); figs. 19, 22, 26
Kellerman, Maurice, 82, 86, 92–93; fig. 88
Kelsey, Easton, 17, 38, 54, 55–57, 59, 61–66, 70–72, 139 (n. 129); figs. 2, 60
Kelsey, Francis Willey, 4–5, 17–18, 32, 34, 36–38, 41, 49–50, 54, 55, 60–61, 76, 84, 92–93, 106, 108–110, 122, 124, 135 (n. 7), 138 (n. 108), 139 (n. 129), 144 (n. 323); figs. 10, 17, 21, 37
Kelsey Museum of Archaeology, ix, 17, 43, 97, 105, 129, 131–132, 135 (nn. 5, 12), 139 (n. 132); figs. 110a–b
King-Crane Commission, 6, 136 (n. 17)
King Croesus, 60, 140 (n. 153)
Ku Klux Klan. *See* America, 1920s

Lake, Kirsopp, 94, 104, 110–114; fig. 108
Land of the Lotus Eaters, 91–92
Lockport Township High School, 37
looting, 72–73

manuscripts, 2, 4, 42, 50, 94, 97, 100, 105, 110, 113–115, 117, 121, 126, 135 (n. 3), 139 (n. 129); fig. 7
Metropolitan Museum of Art, 60–61, 140 (n. 156)
Michigan, 5, 23–24, 31–32, 35–37, 123–124, 138–139 (n. 114), 139 (n. 121)
  Ann Arbor, x, 17, 36–37, 44, 106, 138 (n. 108), 139 (n. 121); figs. 21, 42
  Bay City, 36, 132. See also *Bay City Times*
  Detroit, 17, 22, 23–24. See also *Detroit News*; Detroit Public Library; Detroit Symphony Orchestra
  Niles, 23
MGM Studios, 107; fig. 112
Model T, 14–15; fig. 19. *See also* car brands: Ford; Ford, Henry
monasteries, 4, 50, 94–95, 97–102, 105, 110, 113–116, 121, 126, 135 (n. 3), 142 (n. 250), 143 (n. 264); figs. 7, 108. *See also* Greece: Andros, Mount Athos, Patmos
  Daphne, 114; fig. 101
  Gregoriou, figs. 59, 102
  Iveron, 97, 114
  Karyes, 114
  Lavra, 114; fig. 105
  Panachrantou, 115; fig. 120
  Russiko, 114
  Simonpetra, fig. 101
  Saint John, 94, 99–101, 126; figs. 54, 103, 108–109

monasteries (*cont.*)
  Vatopedi, 97–99, 114; fig. 106
Montana, 34
Mosque of Ali, fig. 45
Motorwagen III, 13–14, 136 (n. 23); fig. 18. *See also* Benz, Bertha; Benz, Karl
Mount Vesuvius, 104, 111; fig. 113
Mussolini, Benito, 8, 111. *See also* Gibson, Violet

Near East Relief Committee, 96–97
Near East research (University of Michigan), xi, 1–2, 4–5, 17–18, 37–38, 49, 54, 56–59, 60–61, 65, 72–73, 75, 78, 118, 121, 123–124, 128–129
New Hampshire, 29–30, 33, 36–37. *See also* New Hampton School
New Hampton School, 29; fig. 32
New York City, 22, 24, 54, 55–56, 60–61, 78, 80, 81, 104, 106–107, 118, 135 (n. 12); figs. 61, 110a–b. *See also* auto shows: New York
New York Times, 86, 93
Nile River, 6, 123; figs. 15, 41a–b
Notre Dame University, 22
Novarro, Ramon, 107

Oberlin College, 30–31
Odysseus, 59, 91
Ohio, 20, 30, 34, 138 (n. 108)
  Cleveland, 34–35
Olds, Ransom E., 23. *See also* car brands: Oldsmobile
Oriental Institute (University of Chicago), 135 (n. 8)
Ottoman Empire, 49, 60–61, 126, 139–140 (n. 133), 141 (n. 163)

Paige-Detroit Motor Car Company. *See* Graham-Paige Motors Corporation
Peterson, Enoch Earnest, 70–71; fig. 67
Pathé News, 50, 82
Pedley, John Griffiths, 135 (n. 7)
Plessy v. Ferguson, 33. *See also* Jim Crow; racism
Porter, John, 132, 138 (n. 88)
pyramids. *See* Egypt: Giza

racism, 8, 32–33, 138 (n. 108), 144 (n. 324)
refugees, 6, 63, 117
  Armenian camps, 6; fig. 14
  children, 112
  Russians, 61–62

Res Gestae, 57, 140 (n. 141). *See also* inscriptions
Robinson, David M., 57, 65, 70–71; figs. 81–82
"Rock Me to Sleep" (poem), 100–101, 143 (n. 265)
Romania, fig. 46

Sacco and Vanzetti. *See* America, 1920s
Sahara Desert, 81, 85–91, 142 (n. 216)
Sardis Affair, 60–61, 140 (nn. 151, 155–156)
Saturday Evening Post, 143 (n. 265); figs. 23, 29
Scarborough, William Sanders, 138 (n. 108)
Scopes trial. *See* America, 1920s
sedan and truck. *See also* Dodge Brothers (company); Graham Brothers (company)
  as dig cars, xi, 2, 5, 17–18, 23, 25, 50–51, 54, 75, 80, 81, 84–85, 102, 118
  acquisition of, 17–18
  maintenance of, 2, 17–18, 25, 83, 108, 137 (n. 47)
  mishaps, 1–2, 23, 63–65, 71, 83, 90–91, 93–94, 107–108; figs. 3–4, 81
  photography of, ix, 1–2, 127; figs. 1–4, 21, 50a, 65–66, 68, 81, 86–87, 94–95, 98–99, 123
  specs for, 26
  transport of, 17–18, 54, 56–59, 75, 80, 83, 91–92, 126–127, 137 (n. 47), 140 (n. 144); figs. 66, 68, 99
Smithsonian Institution, 122; figs. 27, 30
snake charmers, 91, 126; fig. 44
spies, 55, 140 (n. 137)
Starkey, James L., 109–110
Star Wars, 89–91
ships, 2, 16, 44, 54, 55–56, 59, 76, 82, 83, 102, 106, 108–109, 111–112, 115, 140 (n. 144); fig. 68. *See also* sedan and truck: transport of
  SS *Albania*, 54
  SS *Berengaria*, 104, 107, 143 (n. 273)
  SS *Costantinopoli*, 54; fig. 66
  SS *Goriza*, 104, 111–112
  SS *Majestic*, 54, 78
  SS *President Harding*, 54, 55, 80, 81; figs. 61–62
  SS *President Harrison*, 104, 118
  SS *Viking*, 82
  USS *Scorpion*, 113
St. Gotthard Pass, 80, 83
Swain, Edith Louise (née Rice), 32, 34–36, 78, 138–139 (n. 114); figs. 36–37

Swain, Edwin (Ned), 35–36, 50, 104, 105–115, 117–118; figs. 38, 111
Swain, Frances, 35–36; figs. 37–39
Swain, George R., fig. 31
  as a teacher, 30, 34–37, 123; figs. 33, 34a–b, 41a–b
  as a photographer, 2, 5–6, 8–10, 17, 30, 37–38, 39–45, 49–51, 65, 68, 75–76, 82, 87, 94, 97, 100–101, 110, 111, 114–115, 117, 121–127, 129, 135 (nn. 5–6, 13), 139 (nn. 121, 129, 132); figs. 5, 7, 34a–b, 35, 42
  biography of, 29–38, 39, 138 (n. 88), 138–139 (n. 114)
  education of, 29–32; fig. 32
  views of non-Western nations, 5–6, 8–9, 33, 58–59, 61–63, 68, 70, 72–73, 75, 88–89, 97–101, 114, 124, 127–129. *See also* colonialism
  writings of, 5–6, 8–10, 25, 32–33, 36, 41, 44–45, 61–62, 63, 65–68, 70, 73, 75–78, 83, 86–89, 91–92, 96–101, 105, 110–115, 117; 123–129, 135 (nn. 5, 12–13), 135–136 (n. 14), 138 (n. 88), 143 (n. 270), 144 (n. 325); figs. 11, 16, 39, 110a–b, 122
Swain, Robert, 35–36, 80, 81, 83–86, 90–91, 95–98, 102, 143 (n. 270); figs. 38, 110a–b
Switzerland, 34, 80, 83
Syria, 4, 112, 122, 136 (n. 17)
  Aleppo, figs. 53, 124
  Baalbek, fig. 10

Tanit, 49; fig. 56
Tophet, 84; fig. 56
trains, 20–21, 41, 54, 64, 75–76, 80, 81, 104, 107–108; fig. 70
truck and sedan. See *sedan and truck*
Tunisia, 1, 4, 49–50, 79, 80, 81, 84–93, 126–127, 135 (n. 8); figs. 57, 92
  Carthage, 49–50, 80, 81, 84–85, 93, 118, 140 (n. 134); figs. 56, 58, 88, 90. *See also* Tophet; child sacrifice
  Chott Djerid, 90–91, 142 (n. 228); fig. 98
  Djerba, 79, 86, 91–92, 126–127, 142 (n. 240); figs. 99–100
  Gabès, 79, 90
  Gafsa, 16, 79, 91
  Gulf of Tunis, 45, 85
  Kebili, 79, 89–90; figs. 87, 98
  Matmata, 79, 88–90; fig. 96b

Tunisia (*cont.*)
Medenine, 79, 88; fig. 97
Nefta, fig. 95
Sfax, 79; fig. 93
Sidi Bou Said, 85–86, 93; fig. 90
Tozeur, 79, 91; figs. 50a–b, 92, 94
Tunis, 50, 79, 80, 84–85; fig. 96a
Turkey, 4–9, 16–17, 49, 53, 54, 57–76, 96, 114, 124, 126–129, 135 (n. 8), 136 (n. 37), 139–140 (n. 133), 140 (nn. 141, 153), 141 (n. 163); figs. 104, 125
Adana, figs. 14, 70
Ak-Shehir, 53, 54, 64, 67, 75; figs. 2–3
Ankara, 70–71; figs. 81–82
Antioch of Pisidia, 49, 53, 54, 56–57, 60–61, 65, 71–75, 78, 118, 124, 129, 140 (n. 141); figs. 1, 49, 55, 67
Broussa (Brusa), 54, 57, 62–64
Constantinople, 16, 53, 54, 56–59, 61–63, 75–76, 98, 112–113, 126, 139 (n. 129); figs. 8, 12–13, 17, 51, 63–64, 66, 69
Eski-Shehir, 75–76
Konya, 71, 75
Moudania, 53, 54, 57, 59; fig. 68
Smyrna, 6, 15, 53, 63, 75–76, 136 (n. 37)
Yalivadj, 49, 53, 54, 56–57, 62–70, 72–75, 78, 85, 126–127, 129, 135 (n. 9), 139 (n. 129); figs. 4, 71–80, 83, 126

University of Illinois, 19
University of Michigan, ix–x, 1–5, 17–18, 23, 31–38, 51, 56–57, 60–61, 70–71, 76, 78, 86, 106, 118, 121–122, 124, 127, 132, 135 (n. 5), 137 (n. 47), 138 (nn. 88, 107), 138–139 (n. 114); figs. 4, 21. *See also* Bentley Historical Library; Kelsey, Francis W.; Kelsey Museum of Archaeology; Swain, George R.
University School, 34

volta, 114–115, 143 (n. 314)
Viking, The (movie), 82

Western colonialism. *See* colonialism
white collar, 112, 143 (n. 297)
White, E. B., 15
Wilson, Woodrow, 136 (n. 17)
Wolverine, 5, 123, 135 (n. 12)
Woodbridge (project architect), 67, 70–72, 76
World War I (the Great War), 5–6, 8–10, 24, 49, 54, 55, 57, 60, 64, 96–97, 112,

World War I (*cont.*)
122–123, 135 (n. 8), 136 (nn. 17, 37), 139–140 (n. 133), 140 (n. 137), 141 (n. 163), 143 (n. 273)
World War II, 22, 24

ABOUT THE AUTHOR

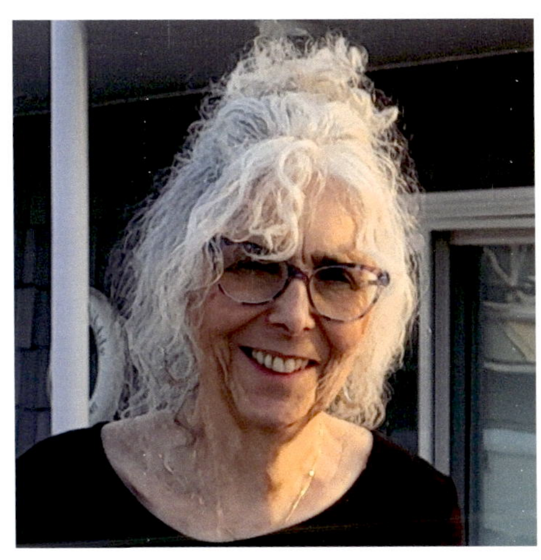

Lauren E. Talalay is curator emerita and former associate director and acting director of the Kelsey Museum of Archaeology at the University of Michigan. She has written, coauthored, or coedited seven books, as well as numerous articles and book chapters. Her research, fieldwork, and conference presentations have taken her to the Mediterranean, Europe, and the Balkans, with a focus on figurines, gender, and the human body as a symbol in the Neolithic period. Lauren has also published articles on contemporary issues, including the use of archaeological images in political cartoons and modern advertising. Her coedited book on the Greek poet Constantine Cavafy was voted one of the best books of 2002 by the *Times Literary Supplement*. She is the recipient of several external grants, including from the Michigan Humanities Council, the Chrysler Foundation, and the American Council of Learned Societies. Lauren is currently coauthoring two chapters on prehistoric material from the site of Plakari on the island of Euboea, Greece.